LITTLE GER

Little Germany

Exile and Asylum in Victorian England

ROSEMARY ASHTON

Oxford New York

OXFORD UNIVERSITY PRESS

1986

Oxford University Press, Walton Street, Oxford OX2 6DP

Oxford New York Toronto
Delhi Bombay Calcutta Madras Karachi
Kuala Lumpur Singapore Hong Kong Tokyo
Nairobi Dar es Salaam Cape Town
Melbourne Auckland

and associated companies in
Beirut Berlin Ibadan Nicosia

Oxford is a trade mark of Oxford University Press

British Library Cataloguing in Publication Data

Ashton, Rosemary
Little Germany : exile and asylum in Victorian England.
1. Germans—Great Britain—History—19th century 2. Germany—Exiles—History
I. Title
941'.00431 DA125.G4
ISBN 0-19-212239-8

Library of Congress Cataloging in Publication Data

Ashton, Rosemary, 1947–
Little Germany
Bibliography: p.
Includes index.
1. Germans—England—History—19th century.
2. Refugees, Political—England—History—19th century.
3. England—Foreign population. I. Title.
DA125.G4A84 1986 942.'00431 85-28529
ISBN 0-19-212239-8

Set by Rowland Phototypesetting Ltd.
Printed in Great Britain by
Billing & Sons Ltd., Worcester

For Ben and Kate

Preface

Influxes of refugees from one country into another may be viewed by the indigenous population either as a nuisance, even a threat, or as an asset, an enrichment of the existing society and culture. Examples of the former kind would include, in British history, the large numbers of Irish immigrants used to break strikes in the 1840s and 1850s, European tailors brought over for the same purpose in the 1860s, and the group of poor Jews fleeing from East European pogroms in the 1890s and early 1900s. Such groups of workers pressed on the already suffering poor of the cities; they took employment which the native population needed, or accepted the lowest-paid jobs at salaries and under conditions which their British peers refused, thus making it difficult for the combinations of workers (trade unions) to fight for better wages and conditions all round. They were, understandably, both miserable and resented.

The other kind of refugee was one who had a special skill which complemented, rather than competed with, the existing labour force, or who arrived at a time when unemployment was not a pressing problem. Such were the Huguenots who fled from religious persecution in France at the end of the seventeenth century. Among them were skilled silk-weavers who settled down to their traditional work, many of them in the Spitalfields area of London, and who seemed to add to, rather than drain, the resources of the host society. More recently, many of the Germans and other Europeans, mostly Jewish, fleeing from Hitler's Germany in the 1930s, have enriched the scientific and cultural life of Britain to a quite remarkable degree. Other 'exiles' who were clearly assets were those who came, not because of religious or political persecution, nor because they were starving for lack of work in their native countries, but because Britain offered them a wider field for their activities. Thus the Hanoverian Georges brought with them, or in their wake, talented artists and musicians of whom the most famous was Handel, a number of learned men including the astronomer Sir William Herschel, and a community of businessmen and financiers who set up international banking-houses in London. Among these latter were the Rothschilds, the Goldsmids, the Barings, and the Grotes, some of whose descendants were to play a part in the story of the German refugees in Britain after the 1848 revolutions which this book sets out to tell.

To which of the above-mentioned groups do the refugees of 1848 belong? The answer is to neither, specifically, and to both, in certain cases. As a group, they were heterogeneous in their politics, religion, and profession or trade. Though all suffered under repressive German governments—many had been imprisoned for anti-state activities—and all of them were forced into exile, their political views varied widely, from the communism of Marx and Engels to the international republicanism of Karl Blind and the intermittent constitutionalism of Gottfried Kinkel. In some cases, as with the tailors and carpenters among them, they competed with their poor British brethren for jobs at low wages and under appalling conditions. No doubt they were often resented, though a few of them, chiefly Marx's friends Lessner, Eccarius, and Lochner, became leading members of English trade unions in the 1860s and after, and one, Friedrich Lessner, was a founder-member of the Independent Labour Party in 1893. The artists and musicians among them had a hard time getting commissions in the face of competition, resentment, and their being at a disadvantage in the matter of references and contacts. Those who taught, either in schools and colleges or as resident tutors and governesses, faced poor conditions and an unwonted lowly status. Jobs were hard to find, but the German exiles often struck lucky because the existing German communities in cities like London, Manchester, and Bradford—financial families such as the Rothschilds, the Huths, and the Schwabes of Manchester—took on exiles as tutors and governesses to their children. Moreover, education in England was expanding in the 1850s. The founding of Queen's College, Bedford College, the North London Collegiate School, and many other educational institutions for women and girls created openings of which some German refugees, notably Gottfried Kinkel and Friedrich Althaus, were able to take advantage on their arrival in England.

The group contained people not only of a wide variety of political opinions, talents, and occupations, but also of varying attitudes to exile, to Britain, and to one another. A high proportion of them were educated men and women, who had been teachers and professors at home. Two of them, Friedrich Althaus and Engels's friend Carl Schorlemmer, became professors, at University College London and Owens College, Manchester, respectively. Others, like Freiligrath and Kinkel, tried for chairs and failed, though Kinkel almost succeeded. Many attempted to publish socialist or radical German journals in London, in order to continue their political agitation against German repression. This was the way Marx and Engels chose, but, like many British oppositional papers, their journals failed for lack of finance. Marx made some money from writing articles, largely for American papers, but at no time did he earn enough to live on. Engels had to spend twenty years in the Manchester office of the family firm, Ermen and Engels, to keep himself and the Marx family more or less solvent.

Almost all the exiles were greatly preoccupied by their economic situation. Only a very few of them were wealthy. One such exile was Count Oskar von Reichenbach, who helped his fellows by taking them on as tutors to his children. Another, Baroness Marie von Bruiningk, also hired German tutors and kept open house for that group among the exiles, led by August Willich, which disdained to look for gainful employment, preferring to plot the military overthrow of Prussia in the Baroness's drawing-room or in the lounge of a German pub in Soho, in the mistaken belief that a new revolution could be sparked off in a matter of months. Apart from the few rich refugees, the rest were more or less destitute on arrival in Britain. They tended, naturally, to approach one another for help. Thus, as so often happens, certain areas became the focus of refugee groups. Soho, particularly Leicester Square, with its cheap housing and its model lodging-houses set up to new specifications of hygiene to offer bare accommodation to the very poor, was one such area. St John's Wood, not then so smart as it is today, though airier and more spacious than noxious Soho, was another. The richer Germans, mostly merchants established in London for a generation or more, also had their favoured parts of London, Hackney and Camberwell being popular for their fresh air and large, comfortable houses. Many a political exile travelled to Camberwell to lecture to his non-political fellow countrymen.

The story of the German refugees in England is one which has not been told before, though much has been written, of course, on the life of Marx in Dean Street and Engels in Manchester. The rest of the exiles—made up of colourful army captains like Willich, professors of art history and literature like Kinkel and Althaus, poets like Freiligrath, journalists like Karl Blind and Arnold Ruge, a host of teachers, a few brave governesses such as Malwida von Meysenbug, some tradesmen (mainly tailors and cabinet-makers), artists, and a proportion of cheats, beggars, thieves, and madmen—these have been rather ignored, except inasmuch as they are mentioned in the voluminous letters and acrimonious pamphlets of Marx and Engels. The Italian refugees, with Mazzini at their head, have received more attention, partly because, of all the national groups, they appealed most to English sympathies. The chief Hungarian, French, and Polish refugees have also had their biographers. The Germans, one supposes because of the existence in their midst of the most famous (and daunting) of all political refugees, Karl Marx, and possibly also because of the heterogeneity of their aims and interests, have not had their chronicler. The present book is an attempt to go some way towards filling this gap.

The aim is twofold. Firstly, it is to tell the life story of a number of interesting people, all of them German and all opposers of German reactionary politics, who made their way to Britain after 1848. Secondly, it is to add to the cultural history of Victorian England by viewing it through the eyes of these Germans. Why did they choose England (if it *was* a matter of choice)? What did they expect? What did they find? Many of them knew English literature and history and were excited by the prospect of finding themselves in the most civilized and advanced country in Europe. They reached for their pens and wrote articles, pamphlets, letters, autobiographies, memoirs, and novels in which 'England' is a major character. Dickens, Carlyle, and Shakespeare (as well as Dante for the scenes of urban misery) were plundered for their descriptive passages; Marx is only the most notable of the many exiles who quoted richly from English literature to convey, usually to a German reader or correspondent, a sense of English life in the mid nineteenth century. The German exiles, more than any other national group, have left records of their responses to all aspects of British life: social, political, religious, and cultural. They add to our stock, already rich, of descriptions and assessments by their British contemporaries John Stuart Mill, George Eliot, Dickens, Carlyle, Disraeli, and others in works of history, fiction, and criticism.

The German refugees in England were divided, as the Russian exile Alexander Herzen said, into forty times forty schisms. But they may be studied in interlocking groups, the grouping being on partly chronological, partly political, and partly professional grounds. Thus Engels and his fellow 'communist businessmen', Weerth and Freiligrath, will be discussed together, both because they all first came to England before 1848, and because they came first for professional reasons, though two of them, Engels and Weerth, seized the opportunity to analyse English capitalist society from the communist point of view. Marx and his 'party', consisting chiefly of Liebknecht, Wilhelm Wolff, Ernst Dronke, Wilhelm Pieper, and Peter Imandt, come under the next heading of 'communist intellectuals', though most of them, as Marx himself noted in despair, lacked incisive intellects and did little to further the Marxist cause. Many of them made their living from teaching and journalism, so that their views of English life (and Scottish life in the case of Imandt, who settled in Dundee) are of largely domestic and social interest. Ruge, Blind, and Kinkel, not themselves much in agreement, are close enough in their political positions, their egotism and desire to lead, and their literary and journalistic careers, to be treated together. They are the chief among the 'Great Men of the Exile' whom Marx pilloried in pamphlets and letters. They are also the exiles who, with Friedrich Althaus and Karl Tausenau, settled down most comfortably and fully in English society. All of them except Kinkel remained in England to the end of their lives; all of them, whether they espoused democratic, republican, or socialist political views, lived quiet 'bourgeois' lives.

The women of the exile merit a chapter to themselves. Johanna Kinkel and Malwida von Meysenbug, with Amely Bölte, Frau von Bruiningk, and Therese Pulszky (German wife of a Hungarian exile), made their livings mainly from teaching and governessing, so that they were well placed to observe English home life and English attitudes to education. They wrote fiction and memoirs which are of the greatest interest. Then there are the workers and the sad figures of the unemployed, the idlers, the beggars, the cheats, and the insane—in other words, the equivalent among the refugees of the great mass of the English proletariat and beneath it the lumpenproletariat. While most of these did not leave memoirs, they appear regularly in the letters and autobiographies of the better-off Germans on whom they often depended. We can therefore catch a glimpse of their situation in exile. Lessner and Eccarius, both tailors and disciples of Marx, wrote pamphlets and articles the grammar and spelling of which Marx and Engels, as often as not, had to correct for publication. The modest Lessner was asked to write his memoirs after the death of Engels in 1895. These were published in 1898, the same year in which Lessner, as the last survivor of Marx's original group in England, took Eleanor Marx's ashes to the premises of the Social Democratic Federation.

In their relations with one another, the exiles formed a colourful microcosm of the larger society to which they came as uninvited guests. They taught one another's children, gave one another lodgings, lent and borrowed a pound here and a coat there, and used one another's skills, whether tailoring, cabinet-making, doctoring, or lecturing on the future dictatorship of the proletariat. Their interaction with the host society was partial and varied. Marx, at least, left his mark on English political thought late in the century, and Marx, Blind, and Althaus (who became Professor of German at University College London in 1874) left a personal legacy which was fruitful. Their children all contributed to the education and literature of England. It was one of the exiles, Johannes Ronge, the leader of the liberal religious community 'the Friends of Light', who founded the first kindergarten in England in 1851. The story of the exiles' lives and their responses to England illustrates both the phrase coined by one, 'Flüchtlingsleben/Dornig leben' ('A refugee's life is a thorny life'), and the remark made by Johanna Kinkel in a letter of 1854:

> We are the last to deny or defend the dark side of English life. But if we are to make a comparison, England is without question superior . . . The Englishman does not like to quarrel; he is altogether the most peaceful, well-meaning, human type you can find, and that is certainly the result of long years of political freedom. The police hinder no one in the development of his talents. Thus people here are not bitter and angry.
>
> But—one must work terribly hard here . . . No wonder this island is overpopulated, since it is the only free spot in Europe. It has become a narrow stable, it is true, and the impatient sheep find the space very restricted.

As Engels conceded in an essay analysing English 'liberties' in 1844, 'England is undeniably the freest, in other words, the least unfree, country in the world'. The German refugees experienced the freedoms and the limitations, the advantages and drawbacks of English life the more intensely for belonging to the identifiable but heterogeneous category of political exile.

What follows will be an account of the debts on both sides, the successes and the failures, the positive and negative effects which German exiles exercised on Britain and Britain on them. I have chosen to examine in detail the lives and responses of men and women who seem to be representative of their class, their profession, their sex, or of a particular political point of view, while I have been guided also by the amount of material, published and unpublished, which is available on them. Thus the work concentrates on the lives of twenty or so refugees whose letters, books, pamphlets, and articles are a rich source of comment on themselves and their adopted country. Where an English translation of key works exists—as in the case of many of Marx's and Engels's works—I have used it, in the expectation that many readers will have no knowledge of German. Otherwise, I have used German editions, referring to them in the notes and bibliography, and have myself translated passages for quoting in the text. I have had recourse to many libraries for unpublished manuscript sources. A list of libraries and also of individuals to whom I am indebted follows.

It will perhaps be noted that among those acknowledged are several scholars connected with University College London, where I teach. I cannot forbear pointing out that University College plays a noble part in the story of the exiles. From Althaus, who was appointed to a chair, to Kinkel, who almost was; from the working-class friends of Marx who attended Professor Huxley's lectures on physiology in the 1860s, and the eminent Germans, like the engineer Siemens, whose literary and scientific clubs met there, to the children of so many German exiles who were pupils at University College School (founded on the same liberal, non-denominational principles as the College itself), exiles found in University College a natural place of resort. An earlier generation of 'exiles', foreign and national, had founded and benefited from the institution: the prominent Jewish rights agitator Isaac Goldsmid gave his time and money to help found the College and endow several chairs. Alexander Baring and George Grote, descendants of German immigrants, were also among the founders and first members of the College Council. The first Professors of Italian and German, Panizzi and Mühlenfels, were political refugees in the late 1820s; the Professor of Sanskrit was Theodor Goldstücker, not strictly an exile but a liberal unwanted in Berlin. I, too, owe a debt to the College for the use of its excellent library, including many of its collections of manuscripts, and for conference and research grants which have helped in the preparation of this work.

My greatest debt is to Professor Chimen Abramsky of University College London, who lent me books unavailable in libraries, shared his wide knowledge of Marx literature with me, and referred me to several works in the Rare Books Room of the British Library of Political and Economic Science. I am indebted also to Professor E. M. Wilkinson, Mr Dan Jacobson, and Mr René Quinault, all of University College. Others who have helped me in various ways are Dr Bernard Porter of the University of Hull, Miss Christine Lattek of the University of Cologne, Dr Gregory Claeys and Dr Thomas Fock of the University of Hanover, Miss Christiane Eisenberg of the University of Bielefeld, Lord Walston, Sir Isaiah Berlin, Professor Karl Miller, Professor Clyde Ryals of Duke University, and Professor G. Ziegengeist of the Akademie der Wissenschaften der DDR. Special thanks go to Mr Nigel Althaus, Mr Karl Ruge, Herr Wolfgang Ruge, Herr Arnold Ruge, and Pastor Albrecht

Plag. I am grateful to Professor Karl Miller of University College London for granting me leave of absence, to the German Academic Exchange Service for a travel grant, and to the British Academy for awarding me a Thank-Offering to Britain Research Fellowship which enabled me to finance my leave of absence in order to write this book. I would also like to thank Judith Luna and George Tulloch of OUP for their help and encouragement.

I wish to thank the librarians and archivists of the following libraries for help and for permission to quote from their manuscript holdings: the British Library, University College London Library and Record Office, the British Library of Political and Economic Science, the Public Record Office, the Institute of Germanic Studies, University College School, the North London Collegiate School, the German Hospital, the German Evangelical Church at Sydenham, and the House of Lords Library, all in London. My thanks go also to the Trustees of the National Library of Scotland in Edinburgh, and the librarians of the Co-operative Union in Manchester, Newnham College, Cambridge, the Hon. David Lytton-Cobbold, and the Hertford County Records Office. I have consulted, though not quoted from, papers in the Rothschild Archives in London. Libraries abroad whose material I have consulted are: the Henry W. and Albert A. Berg Collection, New York Public Library, the International Institute for Social History, Amsterdam, the Jagiellonian Library, Cracow, the Deutsche Staatsbibliothek, Berlin, the Universitätsbibliothek and the Stadtarchiv, Bonn, the Bundesarchiv, Aussenstelle Frankfurt-am-Main, the Cotta Archiv in the Schiller-Nationalmuseum, Marbach-am-Neckar, the Sächsische Landesbibliothek, Dresden, the Staatsbibliothek Preussischer Kulturbesitz, Berlin, the Generallandesarchiv, Karlsruhe, the Universitätsbibliothek, Heidelberg, the Lippische Landesbibliothek, Detmold, and the Stadtarchiv und Landesgeschichtliche Bibliothek, Bielefeld.

Contents

Introduction

In April 1867 Friedrich Engels wrote from Manchester to his friend Karl Marx, who had gone to Hanover to deliver the manuscript of *Das Kapital*, vol. i, to his publisher:

> I have always felt that this damned book, over which you have gestated such a long time, was the basic core of all your misfortunes and that you would and could never get out of them until you had shaken it off. This eternally unfinished thing weighed you down physically, mentally, and financially, and I can very well understand that, having shaken off this nightmare, you now feel an entirely different person, especially as the world, once you enter it again, no longer looks as gloomy as before.[1]

Though Engels was right to stress the mental and physical burden of nearly twenty years of study on Marx, he showed, as he always did, some delicacy in referring to the financial sacrifice involved in Marx's having spent so many hours in the British Museum, for that sacrifice had been chiefly Engels's. In November 1850 he had reluctantly returned to the family cotton mill in Manchester in order to earn a regular income sufficient to keep Marx and his family in London while the great work of political economy was in progress. Now Engels was near to being able to retire from 'this filthy commerce' with a pension large enough to keep them all, and he rejoiced in the same 1867 letter at the prospect of treating himself to 'a huge frolic' on his 'release' and to writing 'an entertaining book: *Woes and Joys of the English Bourgeoisie*'.[2]

Had such a book been written, it would doubtless have been a colourful and critical sequel to Engels's first book on England, *Die Lage der arbeitenden Klasse in England* (*The Condition of the Working Class in England*, 1845). For Engels was better placed, by experience and temperament, than any of his fellow political exiles in England to write a critique of the English middle class to which he himself, by 1867, amusedly belonged, having combined years of communist journalism with belonging to the wine-drinking, club-frequenting, fox-hunting community of prosperous Manchester businessmen.[3] Engels was, in fact, a benevolent godfather to scores of his fellow German exiles in England. He had the advantage over most of them of having spent long periods in England on his father's business since 1842, speaking good idiomatic English, and having a seemingly bottomless purse into which he was astonishingly willing to dip again and again to help less fortunate and less prudent friends who began to arrive from mainland Europe in the wake of the 1848 revolutions and the 1849 expulsions.[4]

Engels's two titles for his books—one completed, the other merely jokingly projected—suggest one of the main themes of this book: the responses to England of the large and interesting group of German refugees of 1848. What light may be thrown on Victorian institutions, attitudes, and customs by a group of intelligent, literate Germans who had reason to be grateful for the right of asylum but who might yet, by virtue of their political views, their temperament, and the very condition of being stateless and uprooted, be highly critical of the land of industrial progress, a liberal constitution, *laissez-faire*, individual liberty, and appalling urban distress? What interaction with England, intellectual and social, did such Germans have, such Germans as Marx and Engels, the poet Ferdinand Freiligrath, the journalist Karl Blind, the philosopher Arnold Ruge, and the art history professor Gottfried Kinkel, who spent at least fifteen and in some cases more than fifty years in England, and whose children were brought up here and educated in English schools?

The two dates, 1845 and 1867, are significant for the study of German political exiles in England. Refugees of other nationalities, particularly Italians such as Mazzini and a large group of Polish nationalists, had made England their home in the late 1830s and early 1840s. And although the largest influx of escapees from repressive European states—Hungarian nationalists like Kossuth and Pulszky, and French radical and socialist exiles led by Ledru-Rollin and Louis Blanc—came in the years immediately after the failed revolutions of 1848, there was already an established colony of German communists and workers in England before 1848. Some were non-political: sugar-bakers, furriers, tanners, and tailors who simply came looking for work. Others, like Karl Schapper, the watchmaker Joseph Moll, and the shoemaker Heinrich Bauer had fled to England around 1840, victims of press censorship, the repression of workers' associations, and the clamp-down on student societies (Burschenschaften). These men were the leaders of the London section of the international League of the Just, which became, in September 1847, the Communist League, and they dominated the closely associated German Workers' Education Association.

Thus when Engels first visited England in 1842, he found an established community which he could join, to which he could introduce his friend Marx on a visit from Brussels in November 1847, and, finally, in which he would stage in 1850 a takeover bid for the leadership of the German communists in London.[5]

The pivotal date is, of course, 1848. A kind of pattern of pre-revolutionary repression in Europe can be traced from the travels of Marx and others during the years up to 1848. The capital cities of the Continent had been alternately receiving and ejecting foreign liberals and radicals throughout the 1840s; by 1849 most of them ended up in England—the only country never to expel foreigners—though not before they had tried other centres first. Thus until 1845 or so, Paris, home of the 1798 and 1830 revolutions, was the favourite place of refuge for German, Polish, and Russian *émigrés*. Marx himself was there until he was expelled in 1845 at the behest of the Prussian authorities; and the Russian anarchist Mikhail Bakunin remembered arriving in Paris in July 1844, hoping for both 'safe refuge' and 'inspiration'.[6] He was expelled for a radical speech in 1847 and, like Marx two years before, made his way to Brussels, where police and government were generally less repressive. However, when the Paris revolution broke out in February 1848, sparked off by the government's banning of a political banquet planned by opposition leaders and reformers, Brussels in turn became unwelcoming to its political exiles. Most of them, including Marx and Bakunin, were anyway inclined to return to Paris to observe and further the activities of the (short-lived) revolutionary government.[7]

Then in March, when middle-class radicals and poor workers joined forces in Berlin, Vienna, and other cities in emulation of their French counterparts, most German radicals hurried from Paris to participate in events in their home towns. By the summer of 1849 uprisings all over Europe had been put down, and reactionary governments and monarchs who had been temporarily unseated had returned to power and were pursuing their repressive policies as before. From Paris, Brussels, Cologne, even Geneva and Zurich, which had been alternative refuges for some exiles before 1848, liberals and radicals were now systematically expelled. They came to England.

By a quirk of history, the major radical force in England, Chartism, was in decline by 1848, when one Continental revolution after another was being kindled at the French torch. As Palmerston complacently put it in a debate on refugees in the House of Commons in 1852:

> A single spark will explode a powder magazine, and a blazing torch will burn out harmless on a turnpike road. If a country be in a state of suppressed internal

discontent, a very slight indication may augment that discontent and produce an explosion; but if the country be well governed, and the people be contented, then letters and proclamations from unhappy refugees will be as harmless as the torch upon the turnpike road.[8]

Arguments still abound among historians about the reasons for the decline of Chartism and the failure of the Chartist demonstration on Kennington Common on 10 April 1848. Lack of unified Chartist leadership, a backward-looking programme of land reform intended to reassert artisan independence in a neo-feudal framework, England's monopoly of world trade and economic prosperity, and the improvement of police organization may all have been contributory factors to the fizzling out of Chartism.[9] (Palmerston's splendid political rhetoric about a contented and well-governed people ought to be taken, of course, with a pinch of salt.) Thus while most European refugee groups arrived in England too late to have much to do with Chartism at its zenith, the Germans, through Schapper and Engels, had contacts with the Chartist leaders Ernest Jones and George Julian Harney in their important years before the 1848 loss of credibility and influence.

Still pondering the date of Engels's *Condition of the Working Class in England*, we might note that, though Engels candidly described it to Marx in November 1844 as a 'compilation' from English newspapers and books, his work predated Henry Mayhew's celebrated and much-quoted *Morning Chronicle* articles on London labour and the London poor (1849–50), Kingsley's novel in response to Mayhew, *Alton Locke* (1850), and Dickens's novel of industrial relations, *Hard Times* (1854).[10] However, the idea for his book came partly from a British writer, Carlyle, whose *Past and Present* (1843) Engels reviewed in an article for the *Deutsch-Französische Jahrbücher* (a short-lived periodical edited by Marx and Ruge from Paris in 1844) under the title 'The Condition of England'. In *Past and Present* Carlyle, the admirer of Goethe and proselytizer of German spiritual pantheism,[11] diagnosed with celebrated passion and rhetorical fury the ills of industrial England. Marx and Engels found in Carlyle's writing both a recognizable 'Anglo-Germanism' and a model of indignant rhetoric to describe the misery of the English urban poor. Though Engels dissented from Carlyle's anti-democratic conclusions and his proposal of a neo-feudal, 'true aristocratic' cure for the modern English disease, he quoted copiously and admiringly from the descriptive passages of *Past and Present.* For example, when Engels quotes from the first chapter, entitled 'Midas', he says, 'I cannot resist the temptation to translate the finest of the book's often marvellously fine passages. Criticism will no doubt take care of itself.' Then follows Carlyle:

> The condition of England . . . is justly regarded as one of the most ominous, and withal one of the strangest, ever seen in this world. England is full of wealth . . . in every kind; yet England is dying of inanition. With unabated bounty the land of England blooms and grows; waving with yellow harvests; thick-studded with workshops, industrial implements, with fifteen millions of workers, understood to be the strongest, the cunningest and the willingest our Earth ever had; these men are here; the work they have done, the fruit they have realised is here, abundant, exuberant on every hand of us: and behold, some baleful fiat as of Enchantment has gone forth, saying, 'Touch it not, ye workers, ye master-workers, ye master-idlers; none of you can touch it, no man of you shall be the better for it; this is enchanted fruit!'[12]

When Engels came to build on his review of *Past and Present* for his book on the English workers, the main sources of his descriptions were his own firsthand experience of Manchester, 'the classic type of a modern manufacturing town', the English factory commissioners' reports for 1843, and Carlyle's 'Chartism' (1839) and *Past and Present.* Following Carlyle, he links the industrial misery of the nineteenth century historically to the French Revolution of 1789. Unlike Carlyle, his prophetic tone is gleeful and confident as he welcomes

> the deep wrath of the whole working-class, from Glasgow to London, against the rich, by whom they are systematically plundered and mercilessly left to their fate, a wrath which before too long a time goes by, a time almost within the power of man to predict, must break out into a revolution in comparison with which the French Revolution, and the year 1794, will prove to have been child's play.[13]

Though Engels could rival Carlyle in Dantesque descriptions of the living hell of the poor (his most celebrated vignette is that of an old man living in a cow-stable in a working-class district of Manchester, scraping a bare existence from the dung-heaps at his door[14]), his analysis of the problem was markedly different from Carlyle's. As the passage just quoted shows, Engels was not to be beguiled into talking of mysterious 'fiats as of Enchantment' as the cause of the worker's being alienated from the fruits of his labour. The cause lay squarely in the exploitation of the poor by the rich.

In short, *The Condition of the Working Class in England*, much read by, and influential upon, German radicals who had no personal knowledge of modern industrial life in 1845, was the first public assessment by a philosophically trained communist German observer of nineteenth-century capitalist English conditions.[15] That the work was published in German, and found no English outlet until an unsatisfactory American version of 1887 and an Engels-approved English translation in 1892, constitutes, with the similar history of the publication of *Capital*, a lost opportunity for closer mutual relations between English and German political thinking in the nineteenth century. Engels intended his work for a German audience, and indeed wrote much of it from his prim family's home in Barmen between visits to England. Marx, on the other hand, writing from a long and fixed residence in Britain, hoped to get *Capital* published in England as well as Germany. But as late as 1883 the publishers Macmillan & Co. wrote to Marx's friend Carl Schorlemmer, Professor of Chemistry at Owens College, Manchester, regretting that they were 'not disposed to entertain the publication of "Das Kapital" by the late Dr. Karl Marx'.[16]

The first volume of *Capital*, published in German in 1867, completed the historical picture of the rise of capitalism in England for which Engels's work might have been a preparatory sketch. Indeed, Marx quotes frequently from his friend's youthful work, and Marx, too, makes full and gratefully acknowledged use of the reports of English factory-inspectors, commissioners of inquiry into the exploitation of women and children, and medical reporters on public health. These are men celebrated by Marx as 'competent' and 'free from partisanship and respect of persons', to whose honest reports disgracefully little attention has been paid: 'Perseus wore a magic cap that the monsters he hunted down might not see him. We draw the magic cap down over our eyes and ears as a make-believe that there are no monsters' (Preface to the first German edition of *Capital*).[17] That Marx knew at first hand of the neglect of such reports is testified by his disciple and son-in-law Paul Lafargue, who tells how Marx picked up the reports and parliamentary blue books cheaply from a waste-paper dealer in Long Acre, members of the House of Commons being in the habit of disposing of the books either in that way or by using them for shooting practice. The ever-observant *Punch* noted too, in 1853, the public disregard of the blue books, which 'have hitherto been looked upon as so many blue pills by the public, . . . and have been to be found chiefly on the shelves of the second hand book-stalls'.[18]

Marx's work is a remarkable fulfilment of Engels's early boastful claim in his prefatory addresses to *The Condition of the Working Class in England*: namely, that the English, having ignored the reports and blue books which they alone in Europe are privileged to have available to them, have 'left it to a foreigner to inform the civilised world of the degrading situation you [i.e. the working classes of Great Britain] have to live in'.[19] Marx uniquely brings together his German philosophical training with his long study of the predominantly British literature of political economy (Adam Smith, David Ricardo, John Macculloch, James and John Stuart Mill, Nassau Senior) and the factual reports in order to 'examine the capitalist mode of production, and the conditions of production and exchange corresponding to that mode', the 'classic ground' of those conditions being England. Drawing painstakingly on material assembled by empirical British observers, Marx applies his powerfully theoretical mind to the discovery and description of the laws he sees underlying the observed conditions. The result is a wonderfully rich mixture. What would the British economists have said (always supposing they could have read *Capital* in German in 1867) to being plundered and quoted and browbeaten for their provincialism and naïvety? Marx's wit is nowhere more evident than when he opens his discussion of Nassau Senior's work in the field:

> One fine morning, in the year 1836, Nassau W. Senior, who may be called the bel-esprit of English economists, well known, alike for his economic 'science' and for his beautiful style, was summoned from Oxford to Manchester, to learn in the latter place, the Political Economy that he taught in the former.

And in one of his many trenchant footnotes, Marx robustly tells Senior and John Stuart Mill, those 'vulgar economists', to 'ponder, once in a way, over Spinoza's "Determinatio est Negatio"'.[20]

Capital, then, is the supreme document to emerge from among the German political exiles in England in the mid nineteenth century, and its peculiar qualities are traceable in part to its German author's peculiar translation to England at a particular historical moment.[21] Its date, 1867, also marks for some of the exiles the end of their time in Britain, though others stayed until their deaths in the 1880s or later. (In the Epilogue I will trace my German subjects, often through their children, on towards the end of the century and beyond.) Several of the German exiles had, by 1867, changed their views of the Germany they had fled. Many had accepted amnesties offered by German governments in the 1860s and returned to professorships, or retirement, or even political office, in their homeland. Though Marx, Engels, Eccarius, and Lessner, and their old comrade (now long estranged) Karl Blind, remained in Britain, implacably opposed to Germany, Bismarck, and the rise of Prussia in the 1860s, others saw in Bismarck's Prussia the possibility

—presaged in the Austro-Prussian War of 1866 and fulfilled in 1870–1 during the Franco-Prussian War, which was part-engineered by Bismarck for this very purpose—of the creation of a united, strong, independent Germany. Many had by now dropped their idealist demands for a democratic or socialist republic and welcomed unity as a possible, even necessary, prelude to the forming of the kind of state they desired. Freiligrath, once the 'red poet' of the 1848 revolution, returned to Germany on a public subscription, hailed as a national hero, in 1867, and sang of Prussia's 1870 victories in a patriotic poem called 'Hurra, Germania!' (Marx wrote of his erstwhile friend's effusion in words borrowed from Hotspur in *1 Henry IV*: 'I had rather be a kitten and cry mew / Than one of these same metre ballad-mongers.'[22])

Of the German exiles who remained in Britain, aloof from, or at least sceptical of, the course of politics in Germany in the 1860s, Marx and Engels, with their loyal disciples Eccarius and Lessner, the carpenter Lochner, and the painter Pfänder, had found by 1867 a genuinely international field for their activities. The founding of the International Working Men's Association in September 1864, with Marx as its undisputed leader until its decline and dissipation in 1872, brought the German communists in England into close working contact with English trade unionism and with international workers' associations for the first time.[23] Marx came out of the study (and the British Museum Reading Room) and into public meetings in St Martin's Hall, where he shared platforms with British workers' leaders and prominent political intellectuals like Edward Beesly, leading positivist and Professor of History at University College London. As a result, Marx began to be generally known in Britain. With his controversial International Address of June 1871 supporting the Paris Commune, he gained enemies among the press and public but admirers in the persons of John Stuart Mill, Beesly and his fellows Comtists Frederic Harrison, Richard Congreve, and J. H. Bridges.[24] When Marx applied for British citizenship in 1874—he did so in order to be able to travel to German health spas without fear of arrest—his request was turned down. Scotland Yard's Metropolitan Police Office report noted that Marx was 'the notorious German agitator, the head of the International Society, and an advocate of Communistic principles', adding naïvely (or disingenuously), 'This man has not been loyal to his own King and Country'.[25] Marx took a risk and travelled anyway, under the old pen-name of 'Charles Williams, gentleman'.

While Marx now became the most famous of the exiles still living in

England, Freiligrath deserted from exile in 1867, as did Gottfried Kinkel, once the greatest name among the German refugees, who succumbed in 1866 to the lure of a permanent and prestigious position. He had been the young and handsome Professor of Art History at Bonn University when the events of 1848 swept him suddenly into the political arena. For briefly and unsuccessfully taking up arms in 1849 in a rebel army unit, of which Engels was also a member, Kinkel was sentenced to life imprisonment at Spandau but managed a spectacular escape with the help of an admiring student. He came to London in January 1851, preceded by reports in the English press spreading the romantic story of his adventures far and wide. But in 1866 he accepted a chair of art history at Zurich, reasoning that, though not in Germany, it was a place close to his homeland, and that he had spent long enough in England doing bits and pieces of teaching but never finding a proper 'berth'.[26] Kinkel, too, became a supporter of the unification of Germany under Prussian hegemony.

It was not only such 'enemies' of Marx and Engels as 'the fat rhymesmith' (Freiligrath) and Kinkel, whom they despised for his political trimming and his 'Jesus-Christ' political histrionics,[27] who now left their English exile. By 1867 Marx's disciple Liebknecht had also returned to Germany to work with the infant German trade union movement and to found the German Social Democratic Party in opposition to Bismarck. Liebknecht, somewhat undervalued by Marx and Engels, who called him an 'oaf' and a 'donkey',[28] but whom he served faithfully and as usefully as his Panglossian temperament and his experiences of Prussian harassment and the insides of Prussian prisons allowed, reminisced in 1895 about his political education. He had, as he said, 'gone to school' to Marx to learn political theory. But he had also been a pupil of

> John Bull, the great practical man, who alone understands how to perform the feat of sweeping the cobwebs of philosophy and ideology out of our German skulls, and who, moreover, from his great worldly standpoint, lets us see into the bustle of the world market he dominates, thereby showing us in his present state the state that will be ours in the future.[29]

Liebknecht's words sound a theme of great importance for the study of German exiles in England. Among the heterogeneous group of Germans who arrived in England around 1850, many were intellectuals and most had studied philosophy. For good or ill, they brought to their English experience minds trained in the complexities of recent German philosophy from Kant to Hegel. Thanks to Carlyle's enthusiastic, if unfocused, essays endorsing Germany as the land of idealism as against the prevailing materialism of British philosophy since Locke and Hume, and thanks to the widespread view, expressed most famously by John Stuart Mill in his *Westminster Review* essays on Bentham (1838) and Coleridge (1840), that there existed a 'Germano-Coleridgean' influence on English thinking in opposition to Bentham's native English utilitarianism, the British view of Germany in the 1840s was of a country of philosophy, of idealism, even of mysticism.[30] When comparing the cultures of England and Germany, English writers invariably contrasted, with varying degrees of approval, the German tendency to speculation with the English habit of practical observation. Mill, who had himself briefly come under the 'German' spell of Carlyle in the early 1830s, wrote to his Austrian friend Theodor Gomperz that the main aim of *Logic*, the work of his which Gomperz was translating, was to place

> metaphysical and moral science on a basis of analysed experience, in opposition to the theory of innate principles, so unfortunately patronized by the philosophers of your country, and which through their influence has become the prevailing philosophy throughout Europe. I consider that school of philosophy as the greatest speculative hindrance to the regeneration so urgently required, of man and society; which can never be effected under the influence of a philosophy which makes opinions their own proof, and feelings their own justification. It is, besides, painful to see such a mass of cultivated intellect, and so great an educational apparatus, as exist in your country, wasted in manufacturing a false appearance of science out of purely subjective impressions.[31]

Mill's friend G. H. Lewes, biographer of Goethe and an early enthusiast of the Hegelian philosophy, soon climbed down from the dizzy heights of the Hegelian dialectic, which he called 'clouds of mysticism' and 'bogs of absurdity' in his *Biographical History of Philosophy* (1845–6).[32] His correspondence with Arnold Ruge, the self-styled philosophical successor to Hegel (Marx punningly called him the 'Confusius' of the German emigration, and the international 'doorkeeper to German philosophy', amongst other, yet more insulting, appellations[33]), is rather comic in this respect. Against his better judgement, Ruge translated Lewes's militantly anti-idealist, anti-Hegelian *History of Philosophy* into German in 1871. While Ruge confessed to his son that he had only translated Lewes's 'idiotic stuff' to please his publisher, his more tactfully worded expression of criticism to Lewes himself elicited the candid reply from the latter that 'what appears to you as plain as a pikestaff appears to me moonshine!'[34]

Yet Lewes and Mill could fully appreciate the contribution of recent German philosophy to the intellectual history of Europe, and they were quick to denounce British insularity and, borrowing a German word, 'philistinism'. So were Matthew Arnold, whose *Culture and Anarchy* (1867) contained a sustained attack on the philistine aspect of English culture, and Dickens, who in his periodical *Household Words* wrote ironically, in the person of the pugnacious 'Mr Bendigo Buster':

> What I say is, the Germans are a speculative people . . . The Germans are nice men! Nice un-English men! Why it's painful—as my prize-fighting friend the Chicken says, it's mean—to see how they sophisticate their children, willy-nilly. They have got a word like a Brazil nut, Schulpflichtigkeit, which means the duty of instructing children as a sort of moral law over a state and all its subjects.

This is folly, says Mr Buster. Look at England:

> England is acting, in regard to schools, as becomes her practical good sense . . . England, as a nation, don't trouble herself much about the education of the masses; something like forty-five out of a hundred of 'em can't read and write. That's what I call being practical.[35]

Germans and Englishmen alike noticed the difference. Kingsley brings the scholarly Prussian ambassador Chevalier Bunsen into a fictional circle in *Alton Locke* to rebuke the eponymous philosophical tailor for not knowing German:

> Well, you must learn it. We have much to teach you in the sphere of abstract thought, as you have much to teach us in those of the practical reason and the knowledge of mankind. I should be glad to see you some day in a German university.[36]

Richard Monckton Milnes, who *had* been to a German university, who prided himself on his knowledge of German affairs, and who offered financial aid and professional advice to several of the German exiles in London, assessed the political state of Germany in 1849 in the framework of its philosophy and education:

> Revolution has come upon the most instructed, the most literate, the most thoughtful people of the world . . . The old analogy of learning to swim without going into the water, remains accurately correct: for the whole art and mystery of constitutional government is to teach men to govern themselves, and this is to be learned by experience alone.[37]

The paradoxical link between politics, philosophy, and education had been noticed, too, by the Quaker author William Howitt, a shrewd observer of German affairs. In *The Rural and Domestic Life of Germany* (1842) he pointed out that while the British government neglected to educate its working class, that class was nevertheless educated in the political sense, by virtue of belonging to a country with a parliamentary system (though not yet a representative one), a relatively free press, and access to cheap books. In Germany, by contrast, there was universal education, but no parliamentary system and a muzzled press:

> Their minds are not quickened by politics, for that is a dead region to them . . . The world of politics, with all its mind-stirring schemes, is shut to them; and if they venture into it, they soon knock their heads against so many posts-and-rails of government prohibition that they are glad to walk out again.[38]

In fact, one of several curious facts about the state of society in the many loosely federated German states in the mid nineteenth century was that philosophy—even political philosophy—should thrive in the universities while actual political life was confined to the antics of a small number of feudal-minded noble families. Looking at the phenomenon in another way we may say that philosophy necessarily became political during the 1830s and 1840s, that the intelligentsia discussed politics in philosophical terms in the debating societies and lecture halls of the universities because they had no opportunity to do so in press or parliament. This tendency was intensified by the fact that Hegel's philosophy, preached from most university chairs at the time, lent itself beautifully to a debate between left and right. The very dialectical method—the notion of thesis opposed by antithesis and resolved into synthesis (the German term for this resolution, 'Aufhebung', means equally 'dissolution', 'destruction') which in turn becomes the new thesis, and so on—breathes paradox and ambiguity. In terms of human society, one may interpret this progressive but endlessly self-repeating process in either of two ways. Hegel himself, in the years before his death in 1831, viewed the reactionary Prussian state of the post-Napoleonic era as the embodiment of enlightened but strong government. Allowing his love of systematic patterning to dictate his presentation of historical facts, he drew a picture, in his *Philosophy of History* (1822–31), of oriental history dominated by despotism, Greek history by democracy, and modern European history by the progress from aristocracy to constitutional monarchy. The king—by whom he meant the unconstitutional Prussian king, whose servant Hegel was by virtue of holding a chair in Berlin—figures as 'the dot on the constitutional i'.[39] Many of the young men who studied Hegel, among them Marx and

Ruge, interpreted his drift in a quite different way. Reactionary Prussia was in a state of flux, and its antithesis—revolution, or at least the clamour for reform—would cause it to dissolve and become progressive.[40]

Ruge took the Hegelian ingredients of dialectic, paradox, repetition, and progress and preached a peculiar doctrine which, though it tended towards 'democratic republicanism', was most notable for its plethora of pleasing contradictions. He wrote a pamphlet, published in London in 1854 by the radical atheist publisher George Jacob Holyoake, and based on lectures given to what must have been a very bewildered English audience (an audience which, according to Alexander Herzen, rapidly dwindled to two: himself and the Polish refugee Worcell[41]). Ruge expressed himself on the 'dialectics' of religious atheism and voluntary repression:

> It will now be our task *to create, in the midst of tyranny, the Lodge of Humanism, the invisible church of humanity, voluntary freemasonry for our principles, an open conspiracy for the safety of all the achievements of the German genius; and to foster the belief in the unity and liberty of our nation, the saviour of all the rest.*[42]

Marx laughed at Ruge's propensity to cling to intellectual confusion and call it dialectic, and he and Engels were as wary as any commonsensical Englishman could be of the metaphysical excesses of Hegel and his more impressionable followers. In *The German Ideology*, written in 1845–7 but, like many of their polemical works, unpublished in any language in their lifetimes, they wrote a stinging attack on the 'young Hegelians' among whom they had only a few years previously counted themselves. The aim of the book was

> to ridicule and discredit the philosophic struggle with the shadows of reality, which appeals to the dreamy and muddled German nation.
>
> Once upon a time a valiant fellow had the idea that men were drowned in water only because they were possessed with the *idea of gravity*. If they were to get this notion out of their heads, say by avowing it to be a superstitious, a religious concept, they would be sublimely proof against any danger from water. His whole life long he fought against the illusion of gravity, of whose harmful consequences all statistics brought him new and manifold evidence. This valiant fellow was the type of the new revolutionary philosophers in Germany.[43]

But it takes a Hegelian to criticize Hegelianism, and Marx and Engels, naturally enough, wielded their inherited metaphysical weapons defensively as well as aggressively. Engels in his Preface to *The Condition of the Working Class in England* might criticize the lack of practical experience among German thinkers:

> German Socialism and Communism have proceeded, more than any other, from theoretical premises; we German theoreticians still knew too little of the real world . . . At any rate almost none of the avowed champions of such reform arrived at Communism otherwise than by way of the Feuerbachian dissolution of Hegelian speculation.[44]

(Engels was so alert to the different routes by which German and English socialists reached their positions as to omit this preface from the English editions of his work, though he kept it in all the German editions during his life.) But at the same time, as we have seen, he criticized the English for omitting to draw conclusions from the economic facts they observed. Marx, too, was frequently witty at German philosophy's expense, but his very wit was characterized by the delighted philosophical embracing of contradiction. In an early unpublished work, *Contribution to the Critique of Hegel's Philosophy of Law* (1843), he cut his teeth for later intellectual assaults on the factitious element in Hegelianism. Employing the master's use of analogy and verbal parallelism, he wittily 'proved' what so many of his contemporaries bemoaned: the non-existence, except as an 'idea', of Germany itself:

> As the ancient peoples went through their pre-history in imagination, in *mythology*, so we Germans have gone through our post-history in thought, in *philosophy*. We are *philosophical* contemporaries of the present without being its *historical* contemporaries. German philosophy is the *ideal prolongation* of German history. If therefore, instead of the *œuvres incomplètes* of our real history, we criticise the *œuvres posthumes* of our ideal history, *philosophy*, our criticism is among the questions of which the present says: *That is the question.*[45]

The italics proclaim the parody in this instance. As we shall see, however, Marx's wit most often manifested itself in the philosophical, see-sawing, punning manner of the Hegelian method. And his chief complaint about British thinkers, from Adam Smith to Charles Darwin, was always the German philosophical scholar's disapproval of the 'coarse' empirical development of their thought. As he coolly pointed out in a footnote about factory abuse in *Capital*, vol. i, 'the English . . . have a tendency to look upon the earliest form of appearance of a thing as the cause of its existence'.[46]

Of course, an exile is just the person to preserve, and get away with, the double view of the respective merits of his loathed (and beloved) fatherland and his admired (but resented) adopted country. Heinrich

Heine, whom Marx both respected and resembled, abused everything German to the French but also, while insulting the Germans to their faces in his books written and published in Germany, aimed some cunning side-thrusts at the country in which he had found refuge. It was he who coined perhaps the most famous phrase to describe the homelessness of the refugee, 'the sleepless night of exile'. But he did so in an ironic context. The work was the dream-poem *Germany: A Winter's Tale*, published by Marx himself in his short-lived Parisian periodical *Vorwärts!* in 1844. Heine's main target is Germany represented as the great sleeper among European countries during the years of struggles and revolution among its neighbours. The immediate reference is to the Paris revolution of 1830. The poet returns to his slumbering homeland. How often he had longed for the feather beds of home during the sleepless night of exile on the hard mattresses of France! How softly and sweetly one sleeps on German pillows . . . Innocent nostalgia, pathos, and simple pleasure at the familiar comforts of home are deftly and insultingly employed to criticize German inaction in stirring times:

> Ich ging nach Haus und schlief, als ob
> Die Engel gewiegt mich hatten.
> Man ruht in deutschen Betten so weich,
> Denn das sind Federbetten.
>
> Wie sehnt ich mich oft nach der Süssigkeit
> Des vaterländischen Pfühles,
> Wenn ich auf harten Matrazen lag,
> In der schlaflosen Nacht des Exiles!

[I went home and slept as if rocked by angels. One sleeps so softly in German beds, for they are feather beds, you know. How often I had longed for the sweetness of the pillows of my fatherland as I lay on hard mattresses in the sleepless night of exile.][47]

And yet, as Heine confessed, he needed to visit Germany (though only briefly) to 'breathe German air', in order to be able to write the verses so wittily critical of Germany.[48]

So, also, might the many refugees who made their way to England have contradictory feelings towards her. Some, like the poet Moritz Hartmann, who knew no English and was not lionized in London, or Amalie Struve, whose husband could not make a living and was, like many others, forced to move on to America and try his luck there, merely sneered at English coldness, which they invariably related to the English climate of cold, rain, and fog. They hugged their sense of German warmth and sentiment—also felt, and mistrusted, by Heine—as a precious possession in a time of deprivation. Most were emotionally more robust, including Marx who, as Ruge rightly observed, was the very type of the man who ought to have felt deracinated. Ruge described Marx, with whom he collaborated on the ill-fated *Deutsch-Französische Jahrbücher* in Paris, in a letter to Feuerbach in 1844. 'By virtue of his learned disposition', wrote Ruge, 'he belongs entirely to the German world. By virtue of his revolutionary thinking he is excluded from that world.'[49] Marx is, in fact, the most striking example—Ruge himself is another—of the type of the German 'professor *raté*' in the nineteenth century. The products of a particular educational and cultural tradition, such men found themselves unacceptable in the very state which had nurtured but now would not tolerate them.[50]

At its best, the condition of being an exile resulted in such a work as *Capital* (though the cost of the accompanying sacrifice for Marx's family was high). At its worst, it produced paranoia and whining, though not often in the form of published work. The most notable exception to this was the ill-informed and ill-tempered book dashed off by the French exile Ledru-Rollin, *De la décadence de l'Angleterre* (1850). The book won him no friends, either among the English or in refugee circles. Dickens replied in *Household Words* in the person of the outraged 'Christopher Shrimble' of 'Paradise Row, Tooting', who noted that Ledru-Rollin had 'been amongst us at least three months' and had viewed the state of England 'through a flaming pair of Red Spectacles'. Liebknecht echoed Dickens in one of his 'English sketches' for the German publisher Cotta. He criticized Ledru-Rollin for having shamelessly 'cobbled together a two-volume book' foretelling the imminent decline of England, having merely brought his ready-made ideas of England across the Channel with him.[51] Among the Germans, Lothar Bucher wrote a book critical of the English political system, *Der Parlamentarismus wie er ist* (*The Parliamentary System as it is*, 1855), which was disapproved of by most of his countrymen in England.

The systematic denigration of one's host country—even if that country was, as in many cases, a last rather than the first resort—was frowned on equally by Marx, whose path in exile was not a particularly smooth one, and by Kinkel, who had the easiest introduction of all. Marx understood well the causes of such ingratitude. Thus he added, in 1875, a mellow postscript to his earlier denunciation of his fellow communist August Willich. He now made allowances for Willich's excessively furtive and conspiratorial activities in the early 1850s.

These, too, he saw as consequences of the psychological stresses of exile:

> The violent suppression of a revolution leaves a powerful imprint upon the minds of those involved, especially if they are turned away from their homes and cast into exile. So that even people with steady personalities may lose their heads for a longer or shorter period. They can no longer keep pace with the march of events. They refuse to admit that history has changed direction. Hence that playing around with conspiracies and revolutions which compromises the cause they are serving no less than themselves; hence, too, the errors of Willich and Schapper.[52]

Kinkel, whose arrival in England was heralded by sensational accounts, in German and English newspapers, of his trials, imprisonment, and escape, found himself the centre of several exile factions, each hoping to get his name on their manifestos, money-raising letters, projected newspapers, and club lists. Having battled wearily for six months to keep the peace and offend no one, he might well complain to a female friend in Germany in July 1851 of the 'petty and vain' elements among the German refugees. 'Exile existence', he added, more charitably, 'makes most of them awkward, angry, and some even malicious.'[53] And his wife, Johanna, was impatient with the superior, carping tone adopted by several exiles towards England. 'You know', she wrote to the German authoress Fanny Lewald in 1852, 'it is the done thing among the refugees to find London and the English awful.' Moreover, she went on, every Tom, Dick, and Harry ('Hinz and Kunz') seemed to think all they had to do was to introduce themselves in English society as refugees, and the rest would follow. In her view, they were merely 'exiled tailors, shoemakers, scholars, artists, etc.' whose job it should be to try to make a decent living.[54]

There, of course, was the rub. Whereas earlier influxes of Europeans into England—the Huguenots, for example, and the German musicians, scientists, and financiers who came over with the Hanoverian Georges in the eighteenth century—often had special skills which enriched British society without threatening too much the employment prospects of the native population, the large numbers of exiles streaming into England around 1850 were less easy to assimilate.[55] The workers among them, tailors, cabinet-makers, jewellers, and shoemakers, for the most part, had to compete with an underpaid army of near-starving British proletarians who were overworked and out of work by turns. Thus Marx's friend Johann Georg Eccarius eked out a wretched tailor's existence in the 'tailor's hell' of the sweat-shop system. The evils of the tailoring trade were, of course, well publicized. Thomas Hood's 'Song of the Shirt' (1843), Carlyle's outcry in *Past and Present* about the wicked 'law' of over-production which brought about the 'novelty' of 'too many shirts' in 'this intemperate Earth, with its nine-hundred millions of bare backs!', and Mayhew's detailed descriptions of the 'honourable' and 'the cheap slop, or dishonourable trade',[56] educated the public by stirring its imagination. Mayhew may have been politically naïve (indeed, Eccarius was pressed by Marx to write an account of the system that would correct Mayhew's sentimental one[57]), but his work abounds in descriptions of situations ripe for dialectical analysis. Much of the power of Mayhew's articles lies in his innocent method of alternately quoting workmen and giving his own shocked middle-class response:

> 'Look here', cried one of his friends, dragging a coat from off the sick man's bed. 'See here; the man has no covering, and so he throws this garment over him as a shelter.' (It was a new pilot coat that was to be taken in that evening for the shop.) I expressed my surprise that the bed of the sick man should be covered with the new garment, and was informed that such in the winter time was a common practice among the workpeople. When the weather was very cold, and their blankets had gone to the pawnshop, the slop-workers often went to bed, I was told, with the sleeves of the coat they were making drawn over their arms, or else they would cover themselves with the trousers or paletots, according to the description of the garment they had in hand. The ladies' riding habits in particular, I was assured, were used as counterpanes to the poor people's beds, on account of the quantity of cloth in the skirts.[58]

Mayhew never makes the conscious political judgements on such scenes that Engels had done in *The Condition of the Working Class in England*, though the last sentence quoted here has something of Defoe's naïve yet somehow knowing reporting tone.

No wonder Mayhew was plundered by observers of the British working class; hardly a report from London appeared in the French, German, or American press around 1850 but it drew on Mayhew's accounts. Ledru-Rollin's diatribe on England borrowed wholesale from them. Liebknecht had to defend himself to his German editor against the (just) charge of sending reports 'from our London correspondent' which were entirely cobbled together from *Morning Chronicle* and other English newspaper reports.[59] And Lothar Bucher, one of those embittered exiles whom Johanna Kinkel criticized to Fanny Lewald for their anti-English attitude, used long quotations from Mayhew in his opportunist work on the Great Exhibition, *Kulturhistorische Skizzen aus der*

Industrieherstellung aller Völker (*Cultural-historical Sketches from the Industrial Manufacture of all Nations*), published in 1851.[60]

Reporting 'from our London correspondent' for foreign newspapers was, along with tutoring in the German language and literature, the most common activity of the middle-class members of the German exile community. Those, like Bucher, Liebknecht, and 'Bohemian' Strauss, who contributed to papers published in Germany, had to do so anonymously and cautiously as there was no permitted radical press. Cotta's periodicals, the *Morgenblatt* and the *Augsburger Allgemeine Zeitung*, were liberal-conservative, and some of Liebknecht's more Marxist phrases proved unacceptable to Cotta.[61] Strauss, in his late, rambling memoirs written in English for an English readership, *Reminiscences of an Old Bohemian* (1882), wrote with perverse glee:

> In the course of my long career I have been employed on journals of every shade of opinion—from republican to absolutist. But in the case of any except republican and liberal papers, it has always been simply in the capacity of a translator, excerptor, or summarist. It was wholly and solely in this capacity that, at the instance of my friend Hippolyte Baillière, I consented to work on the *Observateur de Londres*, a reactionary weekly, started in London in 1848, by Herr von Klindworth, one of the most active and most capable political agents of the period, then a refugee from France, where he had been Councillor of State and one of Guizot's right-hand men.[62]

Strauss goes on to say that the Austrian Chancellor, Metternich, the most reactionary European statesmen of the post-Napoleonic era, put up £2,000 to start the newspaper.

Marx and Engels, of course, had no access to the German press. Like other exiles, they tried more than once to set up a German-language paper in London, but capital was lacking, as was a willing, paying readership. Thus their continuation of the Cologne radical paper, the *Neue Rheinische Zeitung*, lasted only six months in London in 1850, as did their later venture, *Das Volk* (1859). Their problems in this respect mirrored those of many radical English publicists. Jones and Harney started Chartist newspaper after Chartist newspaper, all of which failed for lack of finances. The readership they aimed at, the working class, could not afford to buy even the cheapest newspaper. Of all the new papers launched in the 1850s, only the middle-class, gently radical *Leader*, set up by Thornton Hunt, G. H. Lewes, and others in 1850, achieved a steady paying public. It was through the *Leader*, even more than through Harney's *Red Republican* (in which an English translation of the *Communist Manifesto* was published in November 1850) or through Jones's *Notes to the People*, in which Jones himself translated Freiligrath's famous 'red' poem from the *Neue Rheinische Zeitung* in April 1852, that the activities of some of the European refugees reached a wider British public. Mazzini's European Central Democratic Committee, founded in 1850 with Ruge as the German representative, was given a great deal of attention during 1850 and 1851. Kinkel's sorry plight in prison was feelingly described (by Fanny Lewald) in November 1850, and even Marx and Engels, who mistrusted the 'bourgeois' press and who would be loath to appear in print in the same columns as 'the Pomeranian thinker' (Ruge) or 'the wily enthusiast' (Mazzini), wrote letters to the editor of the *Leader* when they wished to publicize political events in Germany.[63]

Not many of the exiles could make more than a partial and precarious living from journalism. The English radical editors opened their columns, but often had no editorial purse to open from which to pay their contributors. Marx wrote several articles for Ernest Jones's papers in the early 1850s for no remuneration.[64] The German press was either hostile or nervous with regard to its exiled countrymen. America offered the most openings, as there was both an English-language public eager to hear of events in Europe and a large German-speaking community, among which newspapers of every political hue appeared. The only proper 'earnings' Marx ever received came from the widely circulated *New York Daily Tribune*, to which he contributed excellent current affairs articles, some of them written or translated into English by Engels, from 1851 to 1862,[65] and he had contacts with several radical German-American papers. But these, too, like Marx's friend Joseph Weydemeyer's *Die Revolution*, for which Marx, Freiligrath, and other London exiles wrote articles in 1852, often lasted for only one or two numbers.

Teaching was the other chief resource of the educated exiles. Kinkel's fame and contacts with English public figures sympathetic to his plight, if not to his politics, brought him several teaching posts, mainly in the ladies' colleges which were being founded in London in the 1850s and 1860s.[66] Karl Tausenau, an Austrian democrat who came to London after six weeks in a Paris prison in 1849, followed the advice of an English lawyer, to whom he had a letter of introduction, by getting himself a good suit, joining the Whittington Club, and settling into smart lodgings in which he could respectably receive his hourly pupils.[67] Both Kinkel and Tausenau had the all-important letters of introduction and enough cash to get started. Others, including Marx's friends Liebknecht, Wilhelm Pieper, and Wilhelm Wolff, arrived in England nearly destitute, and had to borrow suits from one another, or redeem their coats from the pawnshop, in order to look presentable to the parents of prospective pupils.[68] Tutoring was an undervalued and underpaid occupation, as well as being dispensable in times of economic crisis. The American financial crisis of 1857 resulted not only in Marx's salary from the *New York Daily Tribune* being reduced summarily, but also in a loss of earnings among the German teachers and governesses in England. When the middle-class employers of language tutors felt the pinch, they naturally dispensed with the least essential elements of their children's education. This hit the exile community hard, for it seems that those who were not language teachers were invariably teachers of music or art and therefore most vulnerable to the belt-tightening of their employers. The unpolitical Charles Hallé had found this in Paris in 1848, when the 'damnable Revolution' deprived him of his livelihood and drove him to England to swell the numbers of musical refugees there.[69] Johanna Kinkel, also a music teacher, found during the years of increased taxation due to the Crimean War that people chose to keep up their standard of living at the expense of 'Bildung' ('education', 'culture'), so she lost pupils.[70] In an article on London's musical scene she remarked that the Hungarian exile community was almost entirely made up of pianists. And in one of her many lively letters to German friends commenting on exile life in London she summed it up succinctly: 'We are now a whole colony of teachers in search of pupils' (September 1851).[71]

Johanna, who, more even than Marx and certainly as much as Engels, was a keen, shrewd, and witty observer of English life and the German colony's part in it, provided in the same letter an image for the group to which she belonged. 'We are', she wrote, 'in a condition like that after a great shipwreck; each one of us grabs a plank and entrusts himself to the waves.'[72] Despite the establishment by sympathetic English groups and some wealthy Germans of refuges for the poor exiles in the East End, there were those who sank: the letters of the better-known (and better-off) exiles mention from time to time the fates of the unluckier amongst them. There were a couple of Germans known to Marx and his wife who ended up in lunatic asylums; Kinkel regularly received desperate begging letters from fellow countrymen; Carl Göhringer, who ran one of the German pubs in London, was in debtors' prison in 1854; 'poor Klose', a member of the Communist League, had no money for his wife's funeral in July 1852; and Marx, himself living in intermittent squalor (relieved by regular gifts of money and wine from Engels) in Soho, provides a perspective on the degrees of poverty and distress that existed in London. He reported to Engels in May 1854 the death of a Polish refugee Miskowsky:

> The poor devil had long been in the most wretched circumstances . . . and had thus sunk to being a lumpenproletarian in Whitechapel to whom we in the West End from time to time sent some small aid. A few days ago the *pauvre diable*, together with six other refugees, was *burned alive* in the wooden shack he occupied with them in Whitechapel.[73]

Marx wrote this from his three rooms in Dean Street, themselves described as follows by a Prussian government spy in 1852:

> In the whole apartment there is not one clean and solid piece of furniture. Everything is broken, tattered and torn, with half an inch of dust over everything and the greatest disorder everywhere. In the middle of the salon there is a large, old-fashioned table covered with an oilcloth, and on it there lie manuscripts, books, and newspapers, as well as the children's toys, the rags and tatters of his wife's sewing basket, several cups with broken rims, knives, forks, lamps, an inkpot, tumblers, Dutch clay pipes, tobacco ash—in a word, everything topsy-turvy, and all on the same table. A seller of second-hand goods would be ashamed to give away such a remarkable collection of odds and ends.[74]

Still, in spite of some very low periods, with the deaths of three of his children, the constant illness of his wife, the depositing of all his goods in pawn, and his creditors threatening to sue, Marx—baled out again and again by Engels—was among those who stayed afloat. But surviving in exile inevitably brought psychological problems. For the middle-class refugees, in particular, there was a loss of status, of occupation, of profession. The case of the former army generals who had deserted in 1848–9 to lead rebel units was perhaps the worst. August Willich, the gifted Prussian army officer who led the unit in which Engels and Kinkel fought, found himself, Othello-like, without an occupation in peaceful London. The very conditions which made England the only refuge for a fleeing rebel—its liberal laws of asylum—were bound up with others —a stable financial, social, and political system unlikely to be easily undermined—which rendered Willich's one talent useless. After three years of futile armchair planning for the next German revolution (in which he would take Cologne and thus control the Rhine[75]) in Schärttner's German pub in Long Acre, he left for America in 1853, where he was later to give distinguished service on the Northern States side during the American Civil War.[76]

Life in exile was disorienting also for the many scholars (Gelehrte) in the group. As an early psychoanalytic observer, Dr Oscar Blum, noted in 1916, loss of profession is a horror for the bourgeois, resulting in 'something abrupt, sectarian, even maniacal in the émigré psychology'. The excessive scorn so often observable in refugees is, according to Blum, nothing but a 'disguised subconscious revenge for the sudden violent derailment from the previous professional path' of the victim. Hence the phenomenon, so clearly visible in the lives of the European exiles after 1848, of fierce infighting.[77] It often seems that Prussia was less of an object of hatred to the refugees than they were to one another. Marx caricatured the splits in the German colony as 'the war between the frogs and the mice',[78] but his insight into the absurdity of exiles with so much in common pulling so violently in different directions could not prevent him from crowning such absurdity with his own lengthy and obsessive denunciations of Kinkel, Ruge, Willich, Blind, and the rest in 'The Great Men of the Exile' (1852).

The condition of being an exile produces, it seems, larger-than-life tendencies in its victims. Marx and his friend Wilhelm Wolff reacted to the financial instability of their London existence with excessive pride and secrecy. Marx went to great lengths to hide from well-off visitors like Ferdinand Lassalle and Georg Weerth the real state of his affairs, and Wolff allowed himself to reach almost starvation point before asking Engels for help. Others, like Liebknecht, were, so to speak, liberated from shame by the horrors of near-destitution. Liebknecht, along with a host of beggars, frauds, and cheats, became rather shameless in his despair. He used his wife's state of health, and the English climate as its cause, at once to excuse his failure to send newspaper copy to Cotta and to ask for further advances on his salary. When Cotta finally dropped him from his staff after more than ten years of irregular and indifferent articles, begging letters, and Micawberish hopes of future solvency, Liebknecht asked him to insert in the very *Augsburger Allgemeine Zeitung* from which he had been sacked the following advertisement:

> A journalist, settled in London for twelve years, closely acquainted with English conditions, among other things contributor for several years to one of the first political journals of Germany, desires a permanent post as English correspondent of a liberal, pan-German, preferably Austrian newspaper.[79]

Such extremes of pride, bitterness, or shamelessness as the exiles showed in response to their situation must, of course, be taken into account when their responses to Britain are assessed. As Theodor Fontane noted in the case of Lothar Bucher's negative work on the British parliamentary system, *Der Parlamentarismus wie er ist* (1855), whatever England's faults, 'it is not England that is so black, but the glass through which it is being viewed'.[80] We have to pay attention to the difficulties faced by the refugees: their loss of occupation, problems with language, financial situation, and prospects, and the foreign customs and traditions of the country which they knew to be the most advanced and most liberal in Europe and which yet was strange and often disappointing to them. We must also know something of the situation from which they had fled and their reasons for choosing, inasmuch as a choice was involved at all, England as their second home.

I

The Road from Germany to England

One of the wittiest accounts of exile life in London came from Alexander Herzen, the wealthy Russian *émigré* who was German on his mother's side and who employed a remarkable German exile, Malwida von Meysenbug, as governess to his children. He had a further connection with Germany through his wife's having had a well-known love affair with the German poet Georg Herwegh.[1] Hence, perhaps, the malicious tone of his otherwise not unfair account of the German refugees in his memoirs. While he was shrewd about the difficulties that French refugees had in settling down in England ('the Frenchman cannot forgive the English, in the first place, for not speaking French; in the second, for not understanding him when he calls Charing Cross Sharan-Kro, or Leicester Square Lessestair-Skooar'), he was even sharper when assessing the 'forty times forty German schisms in London':

> The German emigrants were distinguished from the others by their ponderous, prosy and cantankerous nature. There were no enthusiasts among them, as there were among the Italians, no hotheads nor sharp tongues, as among the French.
>
> The other emigrants had little to do with them; the difference of manners, of *habitus*, kept them at a certain distance: French arrogance has nothing in common with German boorishness. The absence of a commonly accepted notion of good manners, the heavy scholastic doctrinairism, the excessive familiarity, the excessive *naiveté* of the Germans hampered their relationships with people who were not used to them. They did not make many advances themselves . . . considering, on the one hand, that they greatly excelled others in their scientific development and, on the other, feeling in the presence of others the awkwardness of a provincial in a *salon* at the capital and of a civil service clerk in a coterie of aristocrats.
>
> Internally the German emigrants displayed the same friability as their country did. They had no common plan; their unity was supported by mutual hatred and malicious persecution of each other.[2]

Herzen's point about German provincialism and bad manners is probably exaggerated, though many of the German exiles, coming from small provincial towns like Detmold (Malwida von Meysenbug, Freiligrath, Weerth, and Friedrich Althaus all came from that small town), were impressed by the size of London and the sophistication of its society. His remark about their 'scientific development', though only grudgingly conceded, reinforces the views of both English and German observers, as we have seen. That the German colony in England was more bitterly divided than other national groups, which also had their rival factions, is undisputed. For—and this may be seen to bear out Herzen's view of the Germans' naïvety—the Germans themselves advertised their internecine struggles, carrying on their petty warfare not only in their clubs and pubs around Leicester Square, but also in the columns of the German-American press, which was in turn much quoted by a gleeful conservative press in Germany. The Prussian and Austrian governments need not have employed so many spies as they did to find out the doings of their exiled nationals and thence assess the probable threat to their own security. Almost nothing that such agents reported back, from the squalor of Marx's home to the split in the Communist League in 1850 with its division into plotters versus swotters—the so-called 'action party' of the military-minded exiles under Willich versus the followers of Marx who advocated education before revolution—was not already widely available in print, being avidly reported by the squabbling factions themselves.[3] If Marx and Engels had been able to find a publisher in 1852 for 'The Great Men of the Exile', a task which they entrusted to the shady Colonel Bangya whom they later found to be a spy (Marx announced his suspicion and discovery of the fact in a letter to Gustav Zerffi, who was himself spying for the Austrian police![4]), they would merely have added to the mass of information and gossip circulating in England, Germany, and America about the doings of such 'great men' as Ruge, Blind, Kinkel, Struve, and Marx himself.

As Herzen says, such divisions in London reflected on a personal level the divided state of the Germany they had left. There had been a pulling together of the separate petty principalities at the beginning of the century in the effort to expel Napoleon, and when this had been achieved, some kind of German unification, along with a much-promised constitution, might have been expected. Instead, the Congress of Vienna in 1815, under the influence of Metternich, divided 'Germany' into thirty-four separate states, all with reactionary unconstitutional governments and loosely connected in a 'German Confederation'. As Disraeli put it in the history lesson he delivered in the narrative part of his novel *Coningsby* (1844), 'All that remains of the pragmatic arrangements of the mighty Congress of Vienna is the mediatisation of the petty German princes'.[5] Autocratic rule and press censorship went on as before. But the desire for unification and a measure of constitutional reform had been nurtured and, as an astute observer wrote in the *Westminster Review* in 1851, 'the spirit of liberty thus violently banished from civil life, found an asylum amid the altars of science, and was exclusively fostered in the universities, where a young generation was growing up to recover the lost liberties of their fatherland'.[6] Professors from their platforms and students in their Burschenschaften clamoured for reform throughout the 1820s and 1830s, and were rewarded by dismissal from their chairs and heavy prison sentences, respectively. As Kinkel told an audience in Edinburgh in 1854, when he lectured on the history of German literature, Ernst Moritz Arndt's poem 'The German Fatherland' ('Was ist des Deutschen Vaterland?', 1841)

> became the very national anthem of Germany: the device of all those who were and are striving for a centralization of our nationality; the rallying cry of the patriotic students of our universities, the war-yell of our last revolution, which certainly will never be silenced, until, as the song runs, all the country, as far as the German tongue is heard, will be united in one great powerful and independent Empire.

For combining German patriotism, acceptable enough during the Napoleonic Wars, with the continued call for a constitution, Arndt was dismissed from his Bonn professorship in 1820, and 'Arnold Ruge, then a student in Jena and now an exile in Brighton, was confined in a Prussian fortress for five years for having joined the German Burschenschaft'.[7]

Hopes of a more enlightened dispensation in Prussia, which had become the largest of the German states and to which many nationalists looked to lead a united Germany, rose in 1840 with the accession to the Prussian throne of Friedrich Wilhelm IV.[8] He was a weak, vacillating man, who flirted with, and teased his people with, the idea of a liberal constitution, but who drew back from the brink and began to talk instead of the divine right of kings. As Queen Victoria, writing to her uncle King Leopold of Belgium in 1850, observed, 'that everlasting "backwards and forwards", as you say of my poor friend the King of Prussia is *calamitous*'.[9] During the 1850s Friedrich Wilhelm became more and more irresponsible and was finally declared insane. He earned the regular jibes of *Punch* for his hesitation between neutrality, a pro-Russian, and a pro-British stance during the Crimean War. *Punch* harped on his drunkenness, called him 'King Clicquot', and noticed a French proverb

> *Travailler pour le roi de Prusse*, which means that, work as you will, you are likely to have your labour only for your pains. We are afraid that the Western Powers, in inducing FREDERICK WILLIAM to join the Alliance, have already found out the truth of this Proverb, for depend upon it their laborious diplomacy has been but so much useless work thrown away upon the KING OF PRUSSIA.[10]

'Travailler pour le roi de Prusse' was, it happens, one of Marx's and Engels's favourite phrases for at once insulting an enemy and describing the state of their (non-existent) income from their writings.[11]

Under Friedrich Wilhelm the authorities responded to the journalistic and poetic protests of 'Young Germany' with more and more censorship. Freiligrath left the country in 1844 on the eve of publication of *Ein Glaubensbekenntnis* (*A Confession of Faith*), a collection of political poems for which he knew he would be arrested if he stayed. The volume was hardly objectionable; it included some vague nationalist rhetoric, much quoting from and reference to Schiller, and some adaptations from such British poems as Burns's 'Is there, for honest poverty' and Thomas Campbell's 'England to Germany'. As Mary Howitt noted in a letter of 1845, 'Ferdinand Freiligrath, the German poet and our dear friend, has been now for some time an exile from his country, on account of what we English should call very innocent writings, but what the Germans term seditious'.[12] At the same time Ruge and Marx were hounded from city to city with their political journals. Ruge's free-thinking *Hallische Jahrbücher* was suppressed in 1841, so he moved to Dresden to edit the *Deutsche Jahrbücher*, which was in turn prohibited a year later. Marx's *Rheinische Zeitung*, published in Cologne, came to an end in 1843 for the same reason. Both men left for Paris: 'A continuation in Germany would be foolish while this police fury lasts', wrote Ruge in January 1843.[13]

As a result of the universal suppression of dissent in Germany, the 1848 revolution, when it came, found many of the leading German radicals already in exile in Paris or Brussels or Zurich. They hurried back, some, like Engels (and Moll and Schapper from London), to join the armed fight, and others, including Marx and Freiligrath, to resume their oppositional journalism. But the German revolution was a partial affair. There was, both because of the system of political repression and because of the number of small states involved, no unified opposition, no recognized leadership, and no proper preparation. Men like Kinkel in

Bonn and Struve in Baden were catapulted into local leadership. (When the exiles gathered in London two years later, it was small wonder that they viewed one another with jealous suspicion, each having had his hour of glory in his own pocket of Germany.) The uprisings were put down—though Metternich fled briefly to London from Vienna as Louis Philippe had done from Paris—and the business of trying to make political gains out of revolutionary action began. Friedrich Wilhelm IV had been forced to promise a constitution, and a preliminary Parliament was set up in Frankfurt. But, as Monckton Milnes pointed out in his *Edinburgh Review* article on Germany, there was no practical parliamentary experience to draw on. The opposition was diverse, composed of liberals, radicals, and socialists; those in favour of a united Germany to include Austria, and those favouring a smaller German state under the leadership of Prussia; convinced republicans and sincere constitutional monarchists. A constitution of sorts was drawn up, but it was both a compromise and a sham. In Moritz Hartmann's words, the Frankfurt Parliament 'committed suicide'. He quoted a poem current in Frankfurt in January 1849 in a letter to his friend Amely Bölte in London:

> 75 Bureaukraten —
> Viele Worte, wenig Thaten.
> 95 Aristokraten —
> Armes Volk, du bist verrathen.
> 130 Professoren —
> Armes Deutschland, du bist verloren.
> Und dazu die Clerisei —
> Deutschland, du wirst nimmer frei!
>
> [75 bureaucrats—many words, few deeds.
> 95 aristocrats—poor people, you're betrayed.
> 130 professors—poor Germany, you're lost.
> And add to that the clerisy—
> Germany, you'll never be free!][14]

Very little was achieved immediately in Germany by the events of 1848–9. In the short term there was a flurry of political activity. Marx and his friends made straight for Cologne, which, having previously been under Napoleon's rule, had attained a greater degree of political and industrial progress than other parts of Germany. Even after 1815 the Rhineland had retained the practice of trial by jury. As the third largest town in Prussia and the centre of the most industrialized part of Germany, Cologne was the obvious place to set up a revolutionary newspaper, the *Neue Rheinische Zeitung*, and to revive the Communist

League.[15] W. E. Aytoun reported for the conservative periodical *Blackwood's Magazine* on the state of Cologne in November 1848. Professing himself 'right sorry' to learn 'that quiet Germany had lighted her revolutionary pipe from the French insurrectionary fires', he went on: 'Always a nest of rascality and filth, Cologne now presents an appearance which is absolutely revolting. Its streets are swarming with scores of miscreants in blouses, belching out their unholy hymns of revolution in your face. . . .' Aytoun proceeded to describe a meeting with a member of Young Germany, got up in a green blouse, 'rusty Hessians', and 'a broad beaver hat, with a conical crown . . . garnished with an immense cockade of red, black, and gold, and surmounted by a couple of dingy ostrich feathers!' This youth began to sing 'a hymn of Freiligrath, which, it struck me, might have been improved by the omission of considerable bloodthirstiness'.[16] These happy days of the *Neue Rheinische Zeitung* were, however, like those of the Frankfurt Parliament it watched and criticized, numbered. Though it survived a court case in February 1849, Marx successfully appealing to the jury to observe the leniency of the Code Napoléon, the paper was forced to close in May 1849, when the police expelled Marx from Prussia.[17] The last number, printed in red with a flamboyant poem of farewell by Freiligrath, appeared on 18 May 1849. Marx fled to Paris, Engels set off for Baden to join the new uprising there (with Willich and Kinkel), and Freiligrath stayed behind, keeping a low profile, winding up the affairs of the *Neue Rheinische Zeitung*, and helping the printers and typesetters to find new jobs.[18] By the autumn of 1849 the Baden uprising had failed; and Marx, with Blind, Seiler, Rasch, and others, had been expelled from Paris. Brussels and Zurich were no longer possible refuges; though King Leopold had cannily offered his people a constitution in 1848 and had survived when other monarchs had to flee, he made sure that revolutionary elements were removed from Belgium in 1848–9. England was the only place open to them, and to England the exiles duly made their way.

England could afford to welcome them, or at least allow them right of entry, for England alone had been unaffected by the February Revolution. Of course, Chartists and communist workers and Harney's Association of Fraternal Democrats had rejoiced at the news from Paris in February 1848. Thomas Frost, a Chartist printer and member of the Fraternal Democrats, remembered being at a meeting of the Association, in company with Harney, Schapper, and groups of Hungarian and Polish patriots:

> Suddenly the news of the events in Paris was brought in. The effect was electrical. Frenchmen, Germans, Poles, Magyars, sprang to their feet, embraced, shouted, and gesticulated in the wildest enthusiasm. Snatches of oratory were delivered in excited tones, and flags were caught from the walls, to be waved exultingly amidst cries of '*Hoch! Eljen! Vive la République!*' Then the doors were opened, and the whole assemblage descended to the street, and, with linked arms and colours flying, marched to the meeting-place of the Westminster Chartists, in Dean Street, Soho. There another enthusiastic fraternization took place, and great was the clinking of glasses that night in and around Soho and Leicester Square.[19]

The Chartists sent Jones and Harney to Paris to observe events and convey brotherly greetings to the revolutionaries. Middle-class liberals, too, rejoiced at the news. Dickens wrote letters in French, signing himself 'Citoyen Charles Dickens'; George Eliot (as yet Mary Ann Evans) was jubilant and expressed her impatience with 'people who can find time to pity Louis Philippe and his moustachioed sons'. Richard Monckton Milnes, among others, dashed to Paris to have a look for himself, and was taken to task by his friend de Tocqueville for treating the post-revolutionary confusion as an amusing spectacle.[20]

At home, press and politicians of all persuasions looked on with detached interest, mixed with some *Schadenfreude*, at the overthrow of the French monarchy and the unseating of political figures like Metternich which followed. One head of state after another wrote to Queen Victoria complaining of his lot and appealing to her sense of monarchical solidarity. Friedrich Wilhelm IV characteristically adverted to his, and her, divine right to govern, and Tsar Nicholas urged a new union between Britain and Russia to weather the disaster and perhaps even 'save the world'. Meanwhile, Victoria's throne remained unshaken. Moreover, Lord John Russell informed her that public opinion—that force so strong in Britain and so marvelled at by the refugees from countries in which it had no voice—would not allow her to offer the fleeing Louis Philippe more than the asylum which 'the sacred duties of hospitality' would require to be available to 'persons of all opinions'.[21] So it was that the King of France arrived at Newhaven in the early hours of 3 March, 'disguised, his whiskers shaved off, a sort of casquette on his head, and a coarse overcoat, and immense goggles over his eyes', according to the British consul at Le Havre, who helped get Louis Philippe on to a steamer for England.[22] *Punch* gloried in the embarrassment of the crowned heads of Europe: '"I hold France in my hand; I know how to manage them", said LOUIS-PHILIPPE, according to the

Morning Post, on the day previous to his overthrow. He certainly did hold France in his hand—for he has let her slip through his fingers.' There follows a mock advertisement for Mivart's Hotel, 'House of Call for Ex-Emperors, Ex-Kings, and Ex-Royalty in General . . . Omnibuses (in correspondence with the hotel) continually running from the Dover Railway. N.B. Beds at any hour. Porter sits up all night.'[23]

England's stability amid reports from Paris, Berlin, and Vienna called forth private and public expressions of relief and self-congratulation. Charles Greville, Clerk to the Privy Council, noted in his diary in March how grand a tribute it was to 'our Constitution' that 'we stand erect and unscathed' in the midst of 'the roar of revolutionary waters that are deluging the whole earth'; and Macaulay, writing the second volume of his great *History of England*, paused at this historic moment to draw the convenient political lesson that England stood firm now because it had already undergone its glorious (Whig) revolution in the seventeenth century.[24]

There was, to be sure, a brief period of anxiety in the weeks before the Chartist demonstration of 10 April. The huge police operation was an indication of official nervousness, as was the swearing in of between 80,000 and 150,000 special constables for the day. Any 'gentleman in London' qualified; one of them was Louis Napoleon, who was to return to France and rule, at first constitutionally, then autocratically by means of a *coup d'état* in December 1851. (Events in France were again on that occasion to affect the hopes and movements of the German exiles. Many of those who, like Willich, remained in London merely in the hope of returning to Europe to take part in a new revolution became disheartened and emigrated to America.) In the event, the forces of law and order outweighed the demonstrators by about ten to one. Dickens, who could not, of course, know the figures, which were, in any case, much disputed, sensed the disproportion. 'I have not been special constableing myself today', he told Bulwer Lytton. 'Thinking there was rather an epidemic in that wise abroad, I walked out and looked at the preparations, without any luggage of staff, warrant, or affidavit.'[25]

The Times summed it up on the day after:

> The 10th of April, 1848, will long be remembered as a great field day of the British Constitution. This is a season of trial, and the Governments of Europe have had their days of reckoning one after another with more or less damage. Powerful armaments have failed to rescue the sovereign or the law from the suit of an oppressed or offended people. This empire, we may confidently say, has now had its share in the European crisis. Disastrous results were hoped or

feared . . . The day has come, and is gone. As far as it is possible to estimate and to reckon upon any human event, it will only augment to a most incalculable degree the confidence of the British public in their existing institutions. The spectacle will not be lost on those nations which are yet in the vortex of change. They will know where to look for the stability they long for. Happily they will find in one of the ancient European sisterhood of nations a safe method of constitutional freedom.

Confidence and the constitution are here the key words. But there is some caution and concession too: 'No one can pretend that our representative system is free from abuses and scandals, which demand a continual rather than a final reform.'[26] *The Times* forbore to consider in detail the abuses, nor did it see anything to criticize in the severe prison sentences imposed by one of Britain's vaunted institutions on Ernest Jones and others for speeches made on or after 10 April. The idea of 'continual reform' was one which was often preached at European countries in difficulties by spokesmen for the superiority of Britain. In *Blackwood's Magazine* Archibald Alison rejoiced in the upholding of order on 10 April and went on to say, rather comically, 'When England became a man, she put away childish things.' Germany, in particular, could learn a lesson:

. . . in two hundred years she may possess the mingled freedom and stability which now constitute the glory and happiness of England. England has preceded other nations by two centuries in this glorious path; it would ill suit the masters to recede, and imitate the follies of such as are only becoming tyros in the attempt to follow it.[27]

This was the note generally sounded, though more diplomatically, by British governments of the period. Mindful of British public opinion, with its mixture of chauvinism and genuine horror at repressive measures abroad, but ever intent on keeping the present balance of power in Europe favourable to Britain, even such an apparent supporter of foreign revolutions and nationalist struggles as Palmerston was careful to give more verbal and symbolic support than actual aid to the Polish, Hungarian, and Italian movements for national freedom.[28] In the words of Max Schlesinger, an unpolitical German living in London, Palmerston performed the necessary function of a British Foreign Minister and was in consequence loved at home and hated abroad. 'He is appointed for the very purpose of barking and snapping all round the house, to keep off intruders and thieves.'[29] Or, as Marx put it, strikingly and provocatively, in an article on Palmerston in Jones's *People's Paper* (October 1853):

> *Ruggiero* is again and again fascinated by the false charms of Alcina, which he knows to disguise an old witch—Sans teeth, sans eyes, sans taste, sans everything, and the knight-errant cannot withstand falling in love with her anew whom he knows to have transmuted all her former adorers into asses and other beasts. The English public is another Ruggiero, and Palmerston is another Alcina . . .
>
> Yielding to foreign influence in facts, he opposes it in words. Having inherited from Canning England's mission to propagate Constitutionalism on the Continent, he is never in need of a theme to pique the national prejudices, and to counteract revolution abroad, and, at the same time, to hold awake the suspicious jealousy of foreign powers. Having succeeded in this easy manner to become the *bête noire* of the continental courts, he could not fail in being set up as the truly English minister at home.[30]

Palmerston and public opinion reacted to the arrival of numbers of fleeing refugees after the restoration of reaction in Europe in 1849 in a way perfectly consistent with their response to the arrival of Louis Philippe, the Prince of Prussia, and Metternich in 1848. Just as they were willing to allow dethroned kings asylum but were not prepared to give them a special welcome, so with that much-vaunted English impartiality they accepted crowds of reputed rebels without doing anything to smooth their paths. In one of the several debates held in both Houses of Parliament during the 1850s on the 'refugee question', usually in response to complaints from the French, Austrian, or Prussian authorities irritated by the activities of their exiled nationals, the Earl of Aberdeen in 1853 referred proudly to 'our general hospitality'.[31] Harney, who through his Association of Fraternal Democrats was concerned to help the refugees—most of them in straitened circumstances—to find a lodging and a means of subsistence (problems not faced by Louis Philippe or Metternich), viewed the English 'open door' policy differently. 'The exile', he wrote in his journal, *The Star of Freedom*, in September 1852, 'is free to land upon our shores, and free to perish of hunger beneath our inclement skies.'[32] The irony of British impartiality, or indifference, depending on one's point of view, was not lost on the refugees themselves. In her autobiographical novel *Hans Ibeles in London* (1860) Johanna Kinkel sketches a scene in which an English hostess innocently introduces a reactionary minister hunted out of his country by a popular uprising in 1848 to a socialist who had been involved in the expulsion of that very minister and who had, in his turn, had to flee during the reaction of 1849.[33]

To England, then, the German exiles came in 1849–50, followed by

Kossuth and his Hungarian nationalists in 1851 and the French victims of Louis Napoleon's *coup d'état* of December 1851. In most cases, England was the last choice of refuge for the Germans. Though its liberal laws of asylum made it the safest refuge and, in the end, the only one (except, of course, America, which some refugees aimed straight for, with more following in 1852 and 1853 after political or economic disappointments), most Germans, even Anglophiles like Freiligrath, tried other European countries first. It is not hard to see the reasons for this. Chiefly, the 'Channel mentality' which has long been attributed to Britons could operate the other way too. Until expulsions became rife in Europe, it was easy to move from country to country on the Continent. Marx, Engels, Blind, Ruge, and others shifted not only from city to city during the 1840s to agitate and print their journals, but also from country to country. They would have preferred to be in Paris, Brussels, Geneva, or Zurich when the next revolution looked like breaking out, rather than across the sea in London. Links with workers' groups and radical sympathizers at home in Germany were easier to maintain from such centres too, though Schapper and Engels were able to send messages from London to German cities in the 1840s by means of Georg Weerth, a communist who was also a travelling salesman based in Bradford.[34] Moreover, though there were connections between refugee groups and such radical English movements as the Chartists and the Fraternal Democrats, as well as some middle-class liberal and radical circles (like that surrounding Mazzini in England), it must have been clear to most refugees after 1848 that there was little opportunity for revolutionary activity in Britain itself.

But if England was a last resort physically for most exiles, it was for many of them the admired land of industrial progress, free institutions, and representative government. By no means all the Germans arriving in London were communists or socialists; many were admirers of the British constitution. Moreover, several, including Kinkel, Tausenau, and Struve, wanted nothing more on arrival in England than, as Ruge complained in 1851, to put the upheavals of 1848–9 behind them and settle down to a 'purely private life'.[35] They came to England with a mental picture formed by reading Shakespeare, Byron, Shelley, and Dickens, as well as the numerous travel books about England by previous German visitors like Prince Pückler-Muskau, who published his English travel diary in 1831 and was immortalized as 'Count Smorltork' by Dickens in *Pickwick Papers* (1837).[36] As a young man preparing to go into business, Freiligrath translated poems by Burns,

Scott, Wordsworth, Coleridge, Keats, Byron, and Shelley as well as writing his own poetry.[37] *Ein Glaubensbekenntnis* (1844) contained free translations from Burns and Campbell. He had hopes of business and literary trips to England in the 1830s, though he did not in fact make the journey until 1846, when he came as a political exile. The young Theodor Fontane made his first visit to London in 1844 with his head full of images of the great city gleaned, as he recalled, from his reading of 'Boz'. Despite knowing about the pallid workers and hungry Ireland, he viewed England 'as the Jews in Egypt viewed Canaan', because of the rule of law and the freedom of the individual tolerated there.[38]

A great many of the refugees who landed in Britain after 1849 wrote accounts, often for immediate publication in German newspapers, sometimes as an opening to autobiographies written half a century later, of what they saw and felt on arrival. Heine had preceded them by twenty years and set the ambivalent tone for many later German observers:

> I have seen the most remarkable sight the world can show, I have seen it and am still amazed—in my memory there still rises up this stone forest of houses and between them the pressing stream of living faces with all their dreadful haste, with all their varied passions, of love, hunger, and hatred—I mean London.[39]

What Heine saw he grasped as a set of contradictory symbols for the political, economic, and social condition of England. Like him, the exiles could not fail to be impressed by the size and busy activity of London's streets and waterways. Arriving on boats along the Thames, they peered at warehouses and ships of all sizes carrying every kind of freight, proclaiming by their flags the most far-flung geographical origins: 'From all corners of the world the ships congregate here in order to lay the products of their regions before the feet of the "ruler of the seas", and in all directions the English ships set off to take the products of English industry to their markets', as Wilhelm Liebknecht wrote in his article on England for the readers of Cotta's *Morgenblatt* (1851).[40]

But the streets of London also exhibited—graphically, because of the extreme contrast—the worst poverty and misery. Liebknecht and the others followed Dickens and Carlyle (via Engels) in the description and interpretation of this visible contrast. Engels, in *The Condition of the Working Class in England*, had paid homage to the 'marvel of England's greatness' along the Thames, only to press on to analyse the 'cost' of this greatness. Finding something ulterior even in the orderly British habit of walking down one side of the pavement and up the other—a phenomenon also remarked on by Weerth—Engels drew a picture of 'social war' on London's streets:

> The hundreds of thousands of all classes and ranks crowding past each other, are they not all human beings with the same qualities and powers, and with the same interest in being happy? And have they not, in the end, to seek happiness in the same way by the same means? And still they crowd by one another as though they had nothing in common, nothing to do with one another, and their only agreement is the tacit one, that each keep to his own side of the pavement, so as not to delay the opposing streams of the crowd, while it occurs to no man to honour another with so much as a glance. The brutal indifference, the unfeeling isolation of each in his private interest, becomes the more repellent and offensive, the more these individuals are crowded together, within a limited space ... The dissolution of mankind into monads, of which each one has a separate principle, the world of atoms, is here carried out to its utmost extreme.[41]

What was a new arrival to think? In Germany in the 1840s there had been a universal cry for a constitution, with England as the obvious model. But Heine, Engels, and an increasing number of observers poured scorn on too naïve an acceptance of the idea that England was the modern promised land. When the novelist Fanny Lewald came to England in 1850 with a view to writing about her experiences, her friend Hermann Hettner wrote from Heidelberg urging her to give a balanced view:

> Until recently we had nothing but constitutional pictures, according to which England was of course, despite Ireland and the proletariat, an Eldorado; now we get nothing but socialist views, and these, in their justified dissent from the apotheosis of English conditions, cloud the view too much *vis-à-vis* the genuinely great and impressive features.[42]

When Fanny Lewald did publish her travel diary, *England und Schottland* (1851), she came out in favour of English institutions on the whole:

> English institutions are almost always more free-thinking, more far-reaching, than the theories one hears developed in conversation. The English are strictly church-going, but they would not deny a Muhammadan, a heathen, or the most peculiar Christian sect the right to a church and freedom of worship. They abhor the idea of a republic, but the banned republicans of all lands find a safe refuge under the protection of the English sceptre.[43]

But Fanny Lewald, though shrewd and sensible, was in England for a matter of months only and she moved in well-known English literary and social circles, breakfasting at Richard Monckton Milnes's house, frequenting the Prussian ambassador Bunsen's residence at Carlton House, and meeting progressive but not radical figures like Dickens, G. H. Lewes, Geraldine Jewsbury in Manchester, and Robert Chambers in Edinburgh.[44] Foreigners who became domiciled in Britain and who were less well furnished with letters of introduction to people of note often took a less rosy, if sometimes, as we have seen, too dark a view of English life.

What were the vaunted freedoms enjoyed by Britons and denied to Germans in their own country? The first, and the most immediate, was the freedom to set foot in the country of their choice and stay there without fear of expulsion. While few exiles can have felt quite as joyful as the Earl of Malmesbury imagined—'I can well conceive the pleasure and happiness of a refugee, hunted from his native land, on approaching the shores of England, and the joy with which he first catches sight of them' (House of Lords, 1852)[45]—many did feel relief at being let into a country with so little ado. Karl Heinrich Schaible was a doctor who had been imprisoned in Rastatt for nine months in 1847 for his liberal journalism, had fled to France in 1848, was arrested in Paris in 1851, escorted to the Belgian border, then allowed to stay in France, only to be exiled without reprieve two years later. He wrote in 1895 of arriving in London in 1853 'with a heart full of hope and a light purse', not knowing a soul but feeling at least that he was free from spies for the first time for years.[46] After the harassment she received in Berlin for merely associating with critics of the Prussian state, Malwida von Meysenbug experienced 'a pleasant feeling of freedom' when no passport was demanded of her on arrival in England in May 1852.[47]

Not only were customs officials not menacing; the English police were less in evidence than the Prussian. The Berlin police and military were notoriously active, even before 1848. Adolf Stahr (who married Fanny Lewald in 1855) remarked in 1846 on the pedantry of the Berlin police who 'thought the world was coming to an end every time a cigar burnt on the street in Berlin or Potsdam'. When Fontane first visited London in 1844 he noticed the lack of police presence compared with Berlin.[48] After 1848 the Prussian police became even more active. Friedrich Max Müller, a non-political German who had gone to London in 1846 to pursue his Sanskrit studies in the library of the East India Company, was expelled from Berlin during a brief visit in October 1849. The grounds given were that he had associated with his fellow Sanskrit scholar, Theodor Goldstücker, who was under surveillance for his liberal opinions. (Goldstücker came to London in the summer of 1850, and was appointed to the Chair of Sanskrit at University College London in 1852. Max Müller became Professor of Modern European Languages at Oxford in 1854.[49]) Carl Schurz, the Bonn University student who organized and effected Kinkel's escape from Spandau and accompanied him to England in 1851, noticed the liveliness of London's streets compared to those of Berlin with its large military presence.[50] English travellers in Germany were equally struck by the contrast. G. H. Lewes complained to the liberal critic Varnhagen von Ense, the grand old man of literary Berlin whose criticism of Prussian politics was tolerated by the authorities (he called himself 'a barbarian tamed in Courts'[51]), of the excessive police presence in Berlin in 1855. Monckton Milnes's cousin Charlotte Williams-Wynn, a frequent visitor to Germany who had once—in 1839—been proposed to by Varnhagen, found the state of Germany in 1851 'most disheartening':

> At Frankfurt the people are completely soldier-ruled, and the grossest instances of oppression occur each day without possibility of redress . . . I have been repeatedly assured by different Germans that the system of espionage is carried on to such a degree that no man likes to speak to a neighbour he does not know.[52]

The Prussian and Austrian government spy networks extended, of course, into France, Belgium, and Switzerland, often with the tacit blessing and sometimes with the active co-operation of the domestic authorities. As Marx and Engels told readers of the *Spectator* in June 1850:

> Some eight years ago, when we, in Prussia, attacked the existing system of government, the official functionaries and press replied, why, if these gentlemen do not like the Prussian system, they are perfectly at liberty to leave the country. We left the country, and we knew the reason why. But after leaving it, we found Prussia everywhere; in France, in Belgium, in Switzerland, we felt the influence of the Prussian Ambassador.

What they were now suggesting was—and it was a charge which English public opinion and Parliament wished to be regularly assured was not true—that, through the Prussian Embassy in London, the Prussian spy system was operating in Britain too: 'Really, Sir', they admonished the editor of the *Spectator*,

> we should have never thought that there existed in this country so many police-spies as we have had the good fortune of making the acquaintance of in the short space of a week. Not only that the doors of the houses where we live are

closely watched by individuals of a more than doubtful look, who take down their notes very coolly every time any one enters the house or leaves it; we cannot make a single step without being followed by them wherever we go. We cannot get into an omnibus or enter a coffee-house without being favoured with the company of at least one of these unknown friends. We do not know whether the gentlemen engaged in this grateful occupation are so 'on her Majesty's service'; but we know this, that the majority of them look anything but clean and respectable.[53]

All classes of Britons were sensitive on this point. Rulers and ruled agreed in priding themselves on their country's observance of the sacred right of the individual to go about his business without harassment. This was partly what made Britain such unpromising material for a revolution: its people might be largely unrepresented, the majority might be the exploited slaves of the capitalist system of production, but they cherished the idea that they were free from direct interference. It was partly in order to enshrine the principle of the individual's freedom from interference that John Stuart Mill set about writing *On Liberty* in 1854. But Mill also criticized British complacency about the freedoms assumed to exist. Fontane shrewdly observed in 1857 that reports in the Continental press of an English revolution being imminent were absurd. The English, even the English poor, felt themselves under no oppression, for though 'the state does nothing *for* the people, neither does it do anything *against* them'.[54] One of the arguments on which British governments repeatedly rested in all their delicate dealings with outraged Continental governments on the subject of the refugees was the argument from moral superiority, though it was based on prudence too. In response to urgings from Paris, Berlin, or Vienna, the reply always was that Her Majesty's Government disdained to stoop to 'act the spy, to play the eaves-dropper, to dog the heels of every person of political character who arrived here from a foreign country' (Lord Beaumont in the House of Lords, April 1852).[55] What was always also complacently observed on these occasions was that Britain had no need to act, covertly or overtly, against the refugees, for they posed no threat to British security and very little to the security of their native countries.

The Home Office could be sure of this precisely because it did sanction a modest amount of police surveillance of the refugees during the 1850s. At the same time as Prussian agents, having infiltrated the German workers' clubs, wrote home about the comic disarray of the German Communist League, an English Home Office official called J. H. Sanders was reporting that the European refugees' activities were relatively innocent.[56] However, the government was cautious in its use of agents, for it did not want a repetition of the case of the Post Office's opening of Mazzini's letters in 1844. Sir James Graham, who had ordered this breach of the individual's liberty, was then attacked in the House of Commons for introducing 'the spy system of foreign states', which was 'repugnant to every principle of the British Constitution, and subversive of the public confidence'. *Punch* produced a cartoon of Graham as 'Paul Pry', and Carlyle thundered in a letter to *The Times* (15 June 1844):

> Whether the extraneous Austrian Emperor and miserable old chimera of a Pope shall maintain themselves in Italy or be obliged to decamp from Italy is not a question in the least vital to Englishmen. But it is a question vital to us that sealed letters in an English post-office be, as we all fancied they were, respected as things sacred; that opening of men's letters, a practice near of kin to picking men's pockets, and to other still viler and far fataler forms of scoundrelism, be not resorted to except in cases of the very last extremity.[57]

What is certain is that British secret policing was not nearly so rife as its Continental equivalent. Nor was the British Government easily rattled. When the Prussian Prime Minister, Manteuffel, sent a report to the Foreign Office that Marx was planning the assassination of Victoria and Albert in May 1850, the British authorities paid no attention to it.[58] There was a stepping-up of all kinds of police activity in the months before the opening of the Great Exhibition in May 1851, but it seems to have been chiefly undertaken with regard to keeping the large numbers of visitors from outside London in order and deterring gangs of pickpockets who might take the opportunity of unwonted crowds to step up *their* professional activities. Foreign authorities, of course, sent more political spies, and quaked at the thought of the opportunities such a large public event—so soon after 1848—would offer to those plotting another revolution. Friedrich Wilhelm IV of Prussia thought it foolhardy, and hesitated to allow his son and grandson to attend the grand opening by Victoria and Albert. Some ultra-reactionaries and pessimists at home, noticeably Colonel Sibthorp in the House of Commons, prophesied assassination attempts on royalty and the proclamation of a red republic.[59] But the general feeling seems to have been one of confidence, tempered by some caution, that the opening would go off smoothly. Dickens characteristically picked up the public mood. On 26 April 1851, less than a week before the opening, he wrote in mock-fearful fashion in *Household Words* of his anxiety at the two-faceted threat posed to the British Constitution by the imminent invasion of London. The native threat took the form of 'gangs of burglars from the counties of Surrey, Sussex, and Lancashire', while the foreign threat emanated from nests of European exiles:

> Conspiracies of a comprehensive character are being hatched in certain back parlours, in certain back streets behind Mr. Cantelo's Chicken Establishment in Leicester Square. A complicated web of machination is being spun—we have it on the authority of a noble peer—against the integrity of the Austrian Empire, at a small coffee-shop in Soho. Prussia is being menaced by twenty-four determined Poles and Honveds in the attics of a cheap *restaurateur* in the Haymarket. Lots are being cast for the assassination of Louis Napoleon, in the inner parlours of various cigar shops.

After the event, *Punch* immediately came forward with a cartoon bearing the caption 'HER MAJESTY, as She Appeared on the FIRST of MAY. Surrounded by "Horrible Conspirators and Assassins"'. The sketch depicts Victoria and Albert with one of their children, surrounded by sweet-looking bonneted ladies, with much waving of hats, handkerchiefs, and flags in the background.[60]

At no time did the exiles feel they were being watched or followed by English police spies, except for a period when Marx thought Palmerston was having him watched.[61] Herzen, who was not an uncritical observer of British conditions, wrote feelingly after years of being followed round Europe:

> The confidence that every poor fellow feels when he shuts the door of his cold, dark, damp little hovel transforms a man's attitude . . . Before I came to England every appearance of a policeman in the house in which I lived gave me an irresistibly nasty feeling, and morally I stood *en garde* against an enemy. In England the policeman at your door or within your doors adds a feeling of security.[62]

Though the exiles from time to time feared the renewal of the Aliens Bill depriving them of the right of asylum, which had been enacted in 1793 in the aftermath of the French Revolution, then not implemented again, though it was reintroduced as a possible sanction in 1848, the combined dislike of Parliament and public for the Bill ensured that it was never enforced. Marx's and Engels's letter to the *Spectator* in June 1850 was prompted by their belief that Prussia, through its Ambassador Bunsen, was pressing for its enforcement. When the question was raised in Parliament in April 1851, the *Leader* attacked the proposal to renew the Bill, mockingly presenting a scene in which the Austrian Ambassador produces 'a few *coupons* of the famous Mazzini loan, as a conclusive proof that the mine stretching all the way from Piccadilly to the Vatican only awaits the application of the lighted end of Mazzini's cigar':

> Whereupon shall Her Majesty's Secretary of State [the Foreign Minister], still all flushed with his Excellency's liquors, proceed at once to the Foreign-office, and issue a warrant for the ignominious expulsion of a man whose offence, for aught that has been proved to the contrary, may go no further than being found tranquilly smoking the terrible cigar aforesaid?[63]

The tone is the familiar one of moral outrage at the threat to individual liberty mingled with the amused superiority of the sophisticated British observer of foreign antics.

The *Leader* article went on to tell the Austrian Ambassador 'to seek redress before English judges and juries'. In fact, it was common for British politicians and diplomats to dissuade foreign powers from doing just that on the grounds, both proud and perplexed, that you could never be quite sure what a British jury would do in any given case. This was amply borne out in the famous Orsini case in 1858. Felice Orsini attempted to blow up Louis Napoleon near the Opéra in Paris in January 1858. He was arrested, tried, and executed in France. During the trial, it emerged that Orsini's bombs had been manufactured in England. The French thereupon pressed for the enactment of an Aliens Bill in England. Palmerston reluctantly framed one, which was rejected by the Cabinet. However, a court case was brought for conspiracy in the plot against Simon Bernard, a Frenchman living in England. An English accomplice, Thomas Allsop, who was later to join Marx on a relief committee for French refugees from the Franco-Prussian War and the Paris Commune in 1871, escaped to America. When Bernard came to trial in April 1858, he was acquitted by the jury, with the full support of most sections of the press, including *The Times*. It was a case of a British jury refusing to bow to French pressure in a trial which it deemed political rather than criminal. Malwida von Meysenbug attended Bernard's trial and 'shared the jubilation of English national feeling when the defendant was acquitted and the advantages of the institutions of this island of freedom had been gloriously upheld'.[64]

That British public opinion, including that portion of it still unrepresented in Parliament, was a force which had to be reckoned with by those in power, was well understood by the English. It struck the refugees from Europe as something remarkable. When the Austrian General Haynau, known for his brutality to women and children when putting down uprisings in Hungary, visited the London brewery of Barclay, Perkins & Co. in September 1850, he was set upon by the brewery's draymen, who instantly became national heroes. Marx and Engels, in their résumé of current affairs for the *Neue Rheinische Zeitung. Politisch-ökonomische Revue* (May–October 1850), explained the event for their German readers as 'a striking display of [the British people's] foreign policy'.[65] Queen Victoria regretted the display, as she did also the huge welcome given to the Hungarian patriot Kossuth in 1851, and that accorded to Garibaldi on his arrival in Britain in 1864, but there was nothing she could do but protest privately to her ministers and endure it.[66] In any case, she was well used to suffering criticism and embarrassment from the public and the press. Albert had been ignominiously attacked in broadsheets during the Crimean War on suspicion of conniving with Prussia, and Victoria herself was hissed at as she rode to the state opening of Parliament in February 1867 during the height of activity concerning the second Reform Bill.[67]

Freedom of speech, of the press, and of association impressed the refugees in England. Liebknecht wrote of the freedom to associate (of which the refugees, of course, availed themselves instantly by forming their various clubs and unions):

> We on the Continent have no concept of the extent of [this freedom], and the tumultuous public meetings during the blissful days of March [1848] offer points of comparison only in their lack of restraint. Each party makes the most extensive use of this right, and the same hall which echoed yesterday with the speeches of Cobden and his friends on the blessings of free trade contains tomorrow a revolutionary Chartist meeting which discusses the red republic and the rule of the proletariat. Even the Queen's Consort does not disdain to appear at meetings and speak to citizens about civic matters.[68]

As for freedom of the press, that was attested by the very fact that Marx and Engels could publish letters like their mildly provocative one in the *Spectator* in 1850. It was from the English press, too, that Engels, Weerth, Liebknecht, Bucher, and others took examples of urban distress and institutional indifference to illustrate their criticisms of England. Editors from the great Delane of *The Times* to the radical writers Harney and Jones and the contributors to the many scurrilous papers of the time, criticized British institutions with great freedom. Delane regularly castigated Queen Victoria directly for her reclusiveness in the years after Albert's death; the royal princes were, then as now, fair game for public criticism. *Punch* made the Duke of Cambridge and the size of his annuity a target of attack in 1850. And W. J. Linton, a radical printer and ardent republican, published regular anti-odes on royal births in his short-lived journals:

Another Guelph! methought I heard a Poor Law Bishop cry—
God bless our Queen and long increase her progeny
And over-population? My Lord Bishop's very sure
There'll be plenty for the Prince, howev'r they starve the poor.[69]

On the other hand, there were checks on these freedoms of speech and publication. One was the obvious 'natural' regulation of the minority press by lack of funds and small circulations. Linton, Jones, and Harney, as well as Ruge, Marx, and Kinkel, who all attempted to get newspapers off the ground, were constantly in financial difficulties. Their radical papers regularly failed. The law assisted such failures until 1857 by prohibiting unstamped newspapers from printing news, a measure which was effective in ensuring that radical newspapers did not survive. Called 'taxes on knowledge' by their critics, these stamp duties were used to prosecute owners, editors, and sellers of newspapers which could not afford the duty but carried news. Harney managed to keep one step ahead of the law and so avoid prison sentences of six months at a time by frequently changing the names of his unstamped papers.[70] Dickens made the new supplement of his periodical *Household Words* a test case, which he won, in 1851. The situation was perhaps far removed from that on the Continent, where the oppositional press was unceremoniously silenced, but as the *Leader* put it in January 1851, 'the English press is subject to a censorship less visible but not less efficient than any that exists on the Continent. Instead of openly curbing the exuberance of the writer it lays a tax which puts down the *poor* reader.'[71]

Similarly with free speech. It was still quite possible to be convicted of blasphemy, as George Jacob Holyoake, the atheist and socialist, found in 1842. He was imprisoned for answering a question at a public meeting in Cheltenham about the place of religion in society to the effect that it had none, and that the Church, which cost the country a lot of money at a time of great national debt, should be removed. Despite a spirited defence conducted by himself, in which he suggested that Shakespeare, Milton, Byron, Shelley, and Southey were among the authors whose works ought to be prohibited if the government were consistent in its prosecution policy on blasphemy, Holyoake was sentenced to six months in prison. In this case, it was to Prussia that Holyoake drew the court's attention as a model. Exaggerating slightly to make his point, he remarked that Dr Strauss, author of *The Life of Jesus*, which George Eliot translated anonymously in 1846, was rewarded for his de-mystifying of the Scriptures with a professorial chair.[72] Holyoake's description of his trial, *The History of the Last Trial by Jury for Atheism in England*, was published in 1850 by James Watson, one of a clutch of radical publishers who were frequently prosecuted under the Stamp Act. George Eliot's translation of Strauss's *Life of Jesus* found a publisher in John Chapman, editor of the *Westminster Review* and promoter of radical and progressive literature.

In the months after the Chartist demonstration of April 1848, Ernest Jones and five other Chartist leaders experienced the penalties sanctioned by the law for excessive freedom of speech. Jones was imprisoned for two years, much of it spent in solitary confinement on a poor diet, for a speech at an open-air meeting in London, in which he was deemed to have spoken seditiously. Jones's speech was certainly a fighting one, but it fell short of rabble-rousing. Indeed, it was couched in rather careful, if suggestive, language, with more negative than positive emphases:

> All that I say is this, stand fast by your colours, do not shrink from the Charter and the whole Charter—do not mind the nonsense of the half and half men—do not pay any attention to the DISPATCH, and if you see any bodies of police, coming near to this meeting—marching on to this meeting—stand your ground, shoulder to shoulder. Do not run, there is danger for those who run, there is safety for those who keep together. Dare them to strike you, and my word for it, they dare not strike a blow. If they were to strike a blow, bad as the laws are now they are still sufficiently stringent to punish those men who assault peaceable citizens in the peaceable execution or performance of their duty . . . Steer clear of all political outbreaks and partial rioting . . . Rest assured that I shall not preach a miserable, namby pamby doctrine of non-resistance and passive obedience. But at the same time I shall preach a doctrine of manly firmness and not hot-headed impetuosity.[73]

When Jones came out of prison in 1850, he carried on with his agitation. For a speech in St Martin's Hall in 1856, in which he described the British constitution as 'one of the vilest shams, and greatest legislative curses ever inflicted on a people', he was not prosecuted, but *Punch* took him to task in an 'Ode to Ernest Jones':

> REMEMBER, ERNEST JONES, while you abuse,
> In frantic terms, the British Constitution,
> That it permits you to propound your views
> Tending to unbelief and revolution.

In any other country could you wag
Your tongue according to your mere discretion?
What Government would fail your jaw to gag,
Though mildly you remarked on huge oppression?[74]

This was, in its way, a fair enough point. Criticism of the constitution had long been permitted—in 1817 Bentham had written scathingly of 'this constitution of ours; the envy of nations! The pride of ages! Matchless in rotten boroughs and sinecures'[75]—but speeches made to the working class in the aftermath of a mass demonstration and in the context of European affairs were to be treated more severely.

As with speeches and the press, so also with the admired jury system in Britain there were negative as well as positive aspects. When the jury acquitted Bernard in the 1858 trial, it seems to have been acting from a combination of liberalism and chauvinism (in this case anti-French and anti-Napoleon). In most cases, as several observers pointed out, a jury would act out of class interest. Engels was quick to make this point in an article in *Vorwärts!* in 1844, in which he corrected the naïve German view of British freedom and equality under the law. The right of habeas corpus, he wrote, was a privilege of the rich. 'The poor man cannot offer surety and therefore must go to prison.' (Dickens had shown his disdain of the so-called privilege when he had Sam Weller refer to it as 'have-his-carcass'.) When he comes for trial, the poor man finds he is not to be tried by his equals but by his 'born enemies', the rich, for only householders paying certain rents are eligible for jury service. How, in Engels's view, can a poor man, a worker, or a radical, expect a fair trial when the jury belongs exclusively to the middle class which he, whether he knows it or not, is determined by history to oppose? W. J. Linton had made the same point about the legal system enabling the rich to judge the poor in 1838,[76] and Dickens hammered it home in novel after novel with a ferocity born of his own unforgettable childhood experiences of being victimized, as he saw it, by the laws on debt with which his unfortunate father was all too acquainted. On the other hand, Engels and the other German critics of British law knew well enough that the jury system, though flawed, represented a stage in civilization which most European countries, with their secret and summary administration of justice, had not yet attained. And Marx, for one, was glad to make use of the English magistrates' courts when collecting evidence and affidavits for two cases involving communists from Germany—the Cologne Communist trials in 1852 and the Vogt affair of 1859.

Perhaps the one aspect of the British system upon which foreigners looked with most admiration and envy was its parliamentary system of elections and representation. Visitors to England could scarcely omit a visit to the public gallery of the House of Commons to observe a debate and, if they were in the country at the right time, a trip to the hustings to watch the British vote. (An afternoon at the Old Bailey was also *de rigueur*.) While most onlookers, including Heine, Fontane, and Marx, were impressed by the debates they heard, they also found elements amusing and absurd. Marx said in 1854 that whole speeches of Lord John Russell could be 'boiled down to just the 2 words: "Now, SAR!"' On the whole, however, German critics were more respectful of what went on in the House of Commons, perhaps because some of them had been themselves, in Marx's words, 'giants of the comedy of the Imperial Constitution' at Frankfurt in 1849, than were many English observers. 'Boz', for one, gave an unflattering sketch of the coming and going, lounging, coughing, laughing, and talking which went on during debates, so that Parliament seemed to vie with 'Smithfield on a market-day, or a cock-pit in its glory'.[77]

As for elections, the novels of Dickens, Disraeli, Trollope, George Eliot, and others offered vivid representations of the bribery, tricking, and treating which went on, despite the reforms of 1832. From the innocent Mr Pickwick's observation of the Eatanswill election to the bumbling Mr Brooke's candidature in Middlemarch, the scandalous aspects of parliamentary elections provided material for the wit, anger, and imagination of Victorian authors. As Marx explained to his *New York Daily Tribune* readers in 1852, British election days had traditionally been 'the bacchanalia of drunken debauchery', when those without an official voice were allowed to let off steam by hearing election speeches and voting by a show of hands before the 'real' election, by the eligible minority, took place.[78] The show of hands was still taken, and in the 1840s and 1850s Chartists and radicals who had no hope of being elected often won overwhelmingly at these impromptu sessions. Harney managed to embarrass Palmerston in 1847 by standing in his Tiverton seat, debating against him before the crowds, and defeating him in the show of hands by the unrepresented. Even after the further extension of the franchise in 1867, radicals would win the show and fail to get the seat. As Engels reported tersely from the Manchester election of 1868, 'Ernest Jones nowhere, despite the cheering'.[79] In general, Europeans were both impressed and amused by the mixture of sophistication and primitiveness, of liberty and powerlessness, which an English election of the mid nineteenth century exhibited.

Indeed, all the British institutions—Parliament, elections, trial by jury, a free press, freedom of speech and association—could be seen to have their limitations. John Stuart Mill felt he ought to explain the English, in this connection, to Mazzini in 1858:

> The English, of all ranks and classes, are at bottom, in all their feelings, aristocrats. They have some conception of liberty, and set some value on it, but the very idea of equality is strange and offensive to them. They do not dislike to have many people above them as long as they have some below them.[80]

Here was an explanation for the unrevolutionary state of Britain, despite the much-publicized inequality of its society. Foreigners shook their heads at the way even those who had nothing defended the rights of property enjoyed by others. British phlegm was in evidence here. Heine saw in 1828 that the Englishman was satisfied with that species of freedom which guaranteed the protection of 'his person, his property, his marriage, his faith, even his whims'. In short, the Englishman's watchword was, appropriately, 'my house is my castle'. If a man could be master in his own house, he had no objection to the existence of an aristocracy. 'What does the court comedy of St James's matter to the freeborn Englishman', wrote Heine, 'since it never intrudes on him, and since no one prevents him from acting out his own comedy in his own house?'[81] Thus public opinion, that force so palpable and yet so hard to define and analyse, could work, like the constitution itself, both for and against liberty and equality. If 'the people' could chastise Haynau for Palmerston, stop the enactment of an Aliens Bill, refuse to convict a conspirator against tyranny, cheer Kossuth and Garibaldi and boo at Prince Albert, it could also acquiesce in the maintenance of a status quo which favoured small sections at the expense of the masses. Public opinion, 'that nasty tyrant' as Amely Bölte called it when she observed her countrywoman, the Countess Hahn-Hahn, flout sexual convention in 1846,[82] might simply be another name for prejudice. Mill thought so, and wrote *On Liberty* to attack the power of prejudice. Engels had come to the same conclusion; he admonished readers of the *Deutsch-Französische Jahrbücher* in 1844:

> You good Germans are told year in, year out by the liberal journalists and parliamentarians what wonderful people, what independent men the English are, and all on account of their free institutions, and from a distance it all looks quite impressive . . . [But] the English Constitution . . . has not made independent men of the English. The English, that is, the educated English, according

to whom the national character is judged on the Continent, these English are the most despicable slaves under the sun . . . The rule of public prejudice is everywhere the first consequence of so-called free political institutions, and in England, the politically freest country in Europe, this rule is stronger than anywhere else . . . The Englishman crawls before public prejudice, he immolates himself to it daily—and the more liberal he is, the more humbly does he grovel in the dust before his idol.[83]

Exaggerated though the passage is—probably deliberately so, as Engels wanted to rouse the German worker by pointing to the need for revolution, even in a 'progressive' society like England's—it highlights an important element in the 'condition of England', one which was noticed and combated by Mill, Dickens, Lewes, George Eliot, and others. Exiles could add interestingly to the stock of criticism of English society not because they came from countries and communities which were free from prejudice, but because they were alert to nuances of difference and similarity, and because so many of them put their thoughts about living in Britain on paper, whether in the form of articles for German readers or in private letters and journals.

Apart from political prejudice, a topic to which Marx and Engels warmed, naturally enough, but which struck less revolutionary-minded exiles less forcibly, the areas of prejudice which refugees identified were religion, social class, and sexual mores. As Engels had pointed out in 1843, 'not a single "respectable" book publisher wanted to print' Strauss's *Life of Jesus*. 'Declare you do not believe in the divinity of Christ, and you are done for; if moreover you confess that you are atheists, the next day people will pretend not to know you.'[84] This scarcely seems overstated when one considers the careful planning, even secrecy, involved in the setting up of the *Leader* in 1850. The title originally intended for the paper was 'The Free Speaker', and, as Lewes wrote in his draft prospectus in February 1850, 'the principle of this journal will be the Sacred Right of Opinion and the Right to its *Free Utterance*'. Though this might seem to be merely claiming a right already recognised by English law, Lewes and his colleagues Thornton Hunt, Linton, and Holyoake were conscious of having to combat prejudice related mainly, though not exclusively, to religious opinion. As Lewes wrote to Robert Chambers (anonymous author of the pre-Darwinian *Vestiges of Creation*, 1844):

Most persons who have reflected freely and maturely on the vital questions of the day entertain opinions considerably in advance of those they avow, or are permitted to avow. The tyranny which keeps down the expression of opinion in our time, though less *dangerous* than it has been in times past, is more domesticated, more searching and constraining. The real opinions that exist will therefore seldom come out, bear little fruit and do not know their own strength.[85]

It is probable that the title of the paper was changed to *The Leader* because of the suggestion of free thinking associated with 'The Free Speaker'. And though free thinking was, of course, the creed embraced by Lewes, Hunt, and Holyoake, and though the *Leader* did advocate frankness of opinion and freedom of conscience, and carried advertisements for all kinds of 'fringe' political and religious societies and publications, Lewes was careful to ensure respectability, and with it financial backing, by courting clergymen at the outset. He wrote to Hunt from Manchester, where he was seeking subscribers: 'Great weight is attached to our having Clergymen with us.' The reference relates chiefly to Edmund Larken, a colleague with whom Hunt was considering sharing the editorship. To this proposal Lewes exclaimed: 'No; no; Thornton dear; it won't do.'[86] A clergyman might support the paper with £1,000, he might write in it to illustrate its reflection of a broad spectrum of opinion, but that he should edit it was out of the question.

German exiles, most of whom had become agnostic from reading Strauss and Feuerbach at the same time as they became political rebels through reading Hegel, found themselves up against English religious prejudice, especially those who sought teaching posts in English schools or with English families. Malwida von Meysenbug and Amely Bölte, both governesses and both free thinkers, had difficulties in being accepted as suitable governesses in England.[87] Johanna Kinkel noted that anti-Catholicism, at its height after the setting up by the Pope of an English Roman Catholic hierarchy in 1850, vied with abhorrence of atheism in the minds of English ladies interviewing prospective governesses. Nevertheless, as Johanna also pointed out, England's superiority over Germany, even in this matter, was not in question. Narrow-minded as the English were in matters of faith, they tolerated those who did not share their views. They might decline to let one teach their children, but they made no attempt to interfere with one's beliefs. (Johanna and her husband had been subjected to pressure by the authorities in Prussia to abjure their atheism.) Nevertheless, Malwida had a manuscript novel returned by an English publisher on the grounds that it 'did not correspond with the prevailing religious view' in England.[88] And there were almost as many comments from the exiles about the dullness of an English Sunday, with its devotion to prayer and

Bible-reading, as there were references to the bustling streets and thick fogs of London.

On the English prejudices with regard to social class, the refugees were able to add particular experiences to the general awareness they shared with such British critics as Carlyle and Dickens. As foreigners and refugees they belonged to no recognizable class. Those who taught for a living found their social position lower than that of a tutor or governess in Germany. Amely Bölte complained to Varnhagen von Ense in 1850 that she was only just tolerated in 'good' society—she and her friend Fanny Lewald had just quarrelled because she was unable to open the doors of the most fashionable houses to the visiting novelist (though she did introduce Fanny Lewald to the Carlyles).[89] As Charlotte Brontë made painfully clear in *Jane Eyre* (1847), and as *Punch* corroborated when it took up the governesses' case in 1850, the position of governess was an ignominious one. Malwida described her position in an English family as that of a kind of social 'polyp', belonging neither above nor below stairs. Both Amely Bölte and Johanna included in their autobiographical fiction examples of middle- and upper-class English girls marrying their German tutors, to the horror of their families. (George Eliot later used Herr Klesmer, the music tutor in *Daniel Deronda*, to comment on English social prejudice. He, too, marries the English heiress.) The differences between England and Germany were summed up by Fontane in 1854: 'We have classes, but not a Chinese caste system like the English.'[90]

An English prejudice *not* singled out by Engels, perhaps because he himself fell in with it—in keeping his semi-secret life with the working-class Irish girl Mary Burns strictly separate from his business and civic social life in Manchester—was that relating to sexual relationships. The women among the exiles tended to remark on it. When the novelist Countess Hahn-Hahn travelled in England in 1846 with her male companion, unaware that she was raising English eyebrows, both Amely Bölte and Monckton Milnes reported the event to Varnhagen von Ense. Milnes described her with amusement as 'encumbered with a *Reisegefährte* [travelling companion], whose name she did not bear, and who was thus difficult to place in an intelligible position in England'.[91] Fanny Lewald, who dealt openly, in imitation of Goethe and George Sand, with sexual matters in her novels, and who pleaded for more liberal divorce laws (she lived with the married Adolf Stahr for some years before he obtained permission to divorce his wife and marry her, in 1855), was told by Johanna Kinkel that her novel *Wandlungen* (*Trans-*

formations, 1853) would be unlikely to find a translator and publisher in England because it 'insulted the prejudices of the English on the subject of divorce'.[92]

Many an Englishman, too, wrote feelingly on both the laws on divorce and the social pressure prevalent in England. Dickens, Linton, the unitarian preacher W. J. Fox, and Richard Hengist Horne, among others, all of whom had unhappy marriages they wished to dissolve, wrote publicly on the subject. Even after the passing of the Divorce Act in 1857, which made divorce less expensive than hitherto, the law was scarcely liberal or equal. As *Punch* pointed out in September 1857, men might sue for divorce if their wives 'went astray', but women had to prove special cruelty or inexcusable absence for more than two years. And social prejudice still inhibited many from seeking a divorce. Dickens did not; and when Horne found that to obtain one he would have to declare himself a deserter and an adulterer, he, too, gave up the idea.[93] Malwida von Meysenbug's energies were much taken up during 1857 with an attempt to obtain a divorce for her friend Mrs Bell, who was being kept prisoner in her own home by her husband. Malwida procured legal advice from William Ashurst, the lawyer friend of Mazzini and Garibaldi, and she does seem to have saved Mrs Bell from her husband's attempts to get her certified insane.[94] George Eliot and G. H. Lewes made discreet enquiries about the possibility of a divorce for him—his wife had borne four children to Thornton Hunt since 1850—but because he had endorsed his wife's adultery by registering the first child as his own, divorce was not a possibility for him either.[95] George Eliot felt the full impact of society's disapproval of her liaison with Lewes.

Indeed, George Eliot and Lewes began their life together in 1854 not in England, but in Germany, where Lewes was researching for his *Life of Goethe* (1855). They divided their time between Weimar and Berlin. In the former place they were accepted wholly by the small courtly society surrounding the Duke of Weimar. Goethe, after all, had flouted convention by living there with Christiane Vulpius, and Liszt was now cohabiting with the Princess Carolyne von Sayn-Wittgenstein in Weimar, where he was kapellmeister. The Leweses' best friends in Berlin were Adolf Stahr and Fanny Lewald, who were enabled to get married in 1855. George Eliot's journal records that she and Lewes called at Stahr's house on 6 February 1855, to find that 'he was gone to be married at last to Fanny Lewald after 9 years of waiting'. 'The Germans', she wrote in the same journal at the same time, 'are at least free from the bigotry and exclusiveness of their more refined cousins.' Johanna Kinkel, who became obsessed with husband–wife relationships (the subject of her novel *Hans Ibeles*) and with sexually motivated crimes, and who probably committed suicide partly from sexual jealousy in 1858, went so far—no doubt it was too far—as to suggest in a letter to Fanny Lewald in May 1856, at the time of the trial in Stafford of William Palmer for the poisoning of his wife, that 'religious England practises poisoning and throat-cutting as a substitute for divorce'.[96]

In the story of her life (and death) Johanna Kinkel provides a dramatic example of the light refugees can throw on English society in the 1850s. She combined a fresh eye for the details of English life, such as the style of the buildings, the shopping habits, or the behaviour of the English at concerts, with a view distorted in certain respects by her particular domestic and marital experiences. Refugees, like anyone else, saw what they were likely to see, given their character and circumstances, and what they wanted to see, given their political views. But unlike other groups, they had the opportunity to compare life in two countries, and the nature of the work many of them did in Britain—journalism, teaching, running political clubs—involved them in making constant observations on the society to which they now uneasily belonged. When considering their view of England, we must take full account of their peculiarities. Some were, as a recent historian of the German emigration to America in the 1930s has put it, 'bei unsers' or 'ach so specialists': i.e. they either compensated for their feelings of uprootedness and neglect by dwelling nostalgically and unrealistically on the superiority of the home country (Amalie Struve was one of these); or they rationalized their loss of professional status by emphasizing what heights they would have achieved, in their profession or in politics, had circumstances permitted them to stay in Germany.[97] Several of our exiles fall into the latter category: Kinkel, Ruge, Struve, the architect Semper; there is even a touch of this in Marx. Of course, in many cases this was true. Kinkel and Semper had been professors. Ruge had been, briefly, a member of the Frankfurt Parliament. Marx, known to his followers in England as 'Papa Marx', would clearly have been a professor if what he professed had not been unpalatable. Here, though, lies the illogicality of the exiles' complaint about their inability to pursue their preferred professions in England. Not only were they in most cases unknown in English professional circles—and many of them sighed about the English habit of relying on 'references'—but their political views made them at least dubious possibilities for professorial or Civil Service posts. Freiligrath had this explained to him, very kindly, by Bulwer Lytton, who tried to help the 'red' poet find a post corresponding to his sense of his own worth. (Even in America, where Freiligrath's friend, the poet Longfellow, put his name forward for a professorship at Columbia, Freiligrath found no acceptance.[98]) A variety of factors, both external and psychological, came into play as the exiles tried to make room for themselves in the 'narrow stable' of English society in the mid nineteenth century.[99]

2

Three Communist Clerks: Engels, Weerth, and Freiligrath in Manchester, Bradford, and London

Engels

By the time of his death in London in 1895, Engels was recognized widely in Britain and Germany as the grand old man of socialism. He corresponded regularly with the founders and leaders of English trade unionism and socialism—William Morris, Ernest Belfort Bax, H. M. Hyndman, George Bernard Shaw—as well as advising the German Social Democratic Party of Liebknecht, Bebel, and Bernstein. A reviewer of Edward Aveling's English translation of Engels's *Socialism, Utopian and Scientific* (1892) looked at the work of Marx and Engels on industrial society and concluded, in a more conciliatory tone than had usually been adopted towards Marx and Engels, when their works were noticed at all in Britain during their forty years of residence:

> [Marx and Engels] carry us past the truth; but they leave us nearer to it than they found us. That being so, we can say with all sincerity that we are glad to see the Marx–Engels literature getting into the hands of English readers; and we hope that every fresh translation will have a fresh preface, no less vivacious and suggestive than this latest utterance of the sage of Regent's Park.[1]

It would seem that Engels had become so acceptable a member of English society that this *Daily Chronicle* reviewer now counted him amongst the privileged few, the licensed critics of English society. First there had been the sage of Highgate (Coleridge), then the sage of Chelsea (Carlyle), now there was the sage of Regent's Park (Engels lived in Regent's Park Road).

It is fitting that Engels should have been accepted as an honorary Englishman. Not only was he one of the first exiles to come to England—his first visit was in 1842—but he was remarkable for the speed with which he learned to speak and write idiomatic English, and he adapted easily to English ways. One part of his social life in Manchester was spent among the businessmen and journalists of that city, while another was shared with his Irish working-class common-law wife, Mary Burns. His was a love-hate relationship with England. He adapted, yet he criticized; he defied social convention, but he did so secretly—his companions in Manchester's Anglo-German Albert Club, of which Engels was a founder-member in 1858, knew nothing of either his life with Mary or his communist journalism. When his father came to inspect the firm of Ermen and Engels in 1853, Engels temporarily moved out of the modest lodgings he normally kept so that he could send regular amounts of money to Marx, in order to 'remove to select LODGINGS, buy select cigars and wines, etc., so that we can impress him'.[2] He appears to have moved frequently, often renting accommodation under false names, sometimes as Mr Burns, sometimes, having his private joke, as Frederick Boardman. Even Marx had to write and ask for his private address on one occasion. In more ways than one, Engels led a double life.[3]

Early on, Engels was forced into dealing duplicitously with his family. He was born in 1820 in the small industrial town of Barmen, where his father ran a cotton yarn factory and was a staunch member of the puritanical Protestant church. The family were Calvinists, strict Sabbatarians, who disapproved of frivolities like dancing or reading novels, and were stubbornly loyal to the Prussian royal family.[4] When the young Engels read Hegel, Strauss, and Feuerbach, as all his contemporaries did, he had to do so secretly. Destined to join the family firm, he studied philosophy and wrote juvenile poetry in his free moments during his office apprenticeship. He jumped at the chance to go to England to join the two Ermen brothers who ran the Manchester branch of the firm, not because he relished his future career, nor because he wanted to please his father, but because it was a chance to escape from the stifling influence of home and because he knew that in England he could study the most advanced industrial country and the most acute social problems in Europe. This first visit lasted from November 1842 to August 1844, and he was scarcely off the boat before he started sending back articles on the condition of England to Marx's *Rheinische Zeitung*.

Part of his father's intention in sending Engels to England was to get him out of the 'bad company' he had begun to keep—the 'Young Hegelians', notably Moses Hess. In fact, Engels took the opportunity to have his first personal meeting with Marx on his journey through the Rhineland on the way to England. The family hoped Engels would become 'respectable' in England, and were greatly disappointed when, on his temporary return in 1844, he retired to his room to write *The*

Condition of the Working Class in England. Engels reported to Marx from his domestic captivity in March 1845:

> Since I am going away in a fortnight or so, I don't want to cause ructions; I never take umbrage, and not being used to that, they are waxing bold. If I get a letter it's sniffed all over before it reaches me. As they're all known to be communist letters they evoke such piously doleful expressions every time that it's enough to drive one out of one's mind. If I go out—the same expression. If I sit in my room and work—communism, of course, as they know—the same expression. I can't eat, drink, sleep, let out a fart, without being confronted by this same accursed lamb-of-God expression.[5]

This family comedy had its pathos too. Engels's mother mediated between him and his father, hid letters received from his mistresses, sent him money, expressed the family's shame at the warrant for his arrest in 1848 and her own concern for his safety and health as he moved from Brussels to Berne in the months after the revolution:

> I will bless the day when you return to us again and once more consent to be our child and walk the same path with us.
>
> Now that you have got the money from us, I entreat you to buy yourself a warm overcoat so that you will have it when the weather turns colder as it soon will; also to provide yourself with drawers and a bed jacket so that you will be warmly clad should you catch a cold, as can very easily happen. I only wish I had occasion to send you some warm socks. Your father, however, thinks it would cost more than they are worth and says I ought to keep them and everything else until you are closer to us again.
>
> What more can I say to you, dear Friedrich? That I love you as only a mother can love her child, you know. May God shine His light upon your heart that you may know what will bring you peace.[6]

On his English visit of 1842–4, during his intermittent residence in Manchester and London between 1846 and 1849, and when he settled in England for good in 1849, Engels wrote not only for German papers about English affairs but also for radical English newspapers on European events. He contributed two articles on European communism to Robert Owen's *New Moral World* in 1843, and was European correspondent of Harney's *Northern Star* between 1845 and 1850. Harney remembered being visited in the editorial office in Leeds by 'a slender young man with a look of almost boyish immaturity, who spoke remarkably pure English and said that he was keenly interested in the Chartist movement'.[7] When Marx and Engels broke with Harney in 1851 because he was fraternizing with exiles of all political opinions and because he was willing to compromise with the middle class, they referred to *his* immaturity: 'our dear', 'our EXDEAR', 'the little HIPHIPHURRAH Scotsman' (Harney had a domineering Scottish wife), and 'Rhadamanthus Harney' were among their descriptions of him.[8]

But in the early days Engels was the inexperienced one and Harney the editor of a radical journal and a man with years of Chartist activity behind him. Engels's early works, especially his 'Outlines of a Critique of Political Economy', written at the end of 1843 and published by Marx and Ruge in 1844 in the first and only number of the *Deutsch-Französische Jahrbücher*, show the young man's openness to current ideas and practice. The essay bears the stamp of Moses Hess's Hegelian socialism, Proudhon's attack on property, and also the newly encountered arguments of English Chartists and Owenites. John Watts, who became a close friend of Engels, was a Manchester Owenite whose book *The Facts and Fictions of Political Economists*, published in 1842, probably influenced Engels in its attack on competition and its arguments about social utility. Engels lectured in Elberfeld in February 1845 in the spirit of Owenite communitarian socialism, though he soon came to disagree with the doctrine, espoused by the Owenites, of peaceful, evolutionary change, and he saw the collapse of practical Owenite example in the failure of Owen's experimental community at Harmony Hall. His association with Chartists, including Harney, led him to more radical views, based on class antagonisms as opposed to Owen's benevolent paternalism.[9] Engels looked in hope to Chartism to effect the social revolution which was so desirable, until Chartism, like Owenism, lost its way by a combination of wrong ideas, wrong tactics, and inability to gain sufficient support among the working class.

However, in 1842 Engels dashed off articles predicting imminent revolution in England on the grounds that a financial crisis would trigger off massive social unrest (he went on making such predictions, as did Marx, during the economic crises of the 1850s), and when writing *The Condition of the Working Class in England* in 1844, Engels still showed incurable optimism about the proximity of a workers' revolution. Harney wrote to Engels in March 1846, showing greater caution and foresight:

> Your speculations as to the speedy coming of a revolution in England, I doubt. Revolutionary changes in Germany I think certain and likely to come soon. Such changes are not less certain in France and likely to ensue soon after the death of that old scoundrel Louis Philippe, but I confess I cannot see the likelihood of

such changes in England, at least until England is moved from *without* as well as within.[10]

Of course, part of Engels's intention in his writings was to rouse German workers and socialists by suggesting that their English counterparts were on the point of seizing power. Yet his optimism was genuine too. As Marx wrote in 1863, when he was re-reading *The Condition of the Working Class*, 'How freshly, passionately, and incisively you grasped things, without any scholarly or scientific reservations. Even the very illusion that results would appear tomorrow or the day after gives the work a warmth and a humorous *joie de vivre*.'[11] Engels was always an optimist—'the Prince of Optimists' Harney called him as late as 1892—and his optimism entailed a certain intellectual crudeness which Eleanor Marx called 'that terrible optimism of his'.[12] Thus he put his hopes, as Marx was to do during the years of the first International in the 1860s, in the trade unions, which he saw, provocatively and prematurely, as 'schools of war'. When considering the past he was as cavalier as he was when prophesying the future. His analysis of the conditions out of which industrial society grew is over-simple. Thinking in crude 'Hegelian' terms, he drew a parallel between the lot of the serf in medieval agrarian society and that of the worker in present-day urban society:

> In short, the position of the two is not far from equal, and if either is at a disadvantage, it is the free working-man. Slaves they both are, with the single difference that the slavery of the one is undissembled, open, honest; that of the other cunning, sly, disguised, deceitfully concealed from himself and every one else, a hypocritical servitude worse than the old.

He found himself agreeing, he noted, with 'philanthropic Tories' like Disraeli, from whose *Sybil* he quoted in the book, when they 'gave the operatives the name white slaves'.[13] We might add that in the interests of putting across the horror of the workers' conditions, he came close to viewing the Middle Ages, as Carlyle unashamedly did in *Past and Present*, through rose-tinted spectacles. This, no doubt, was a calculated exaggeration. Where Engels made his greatest misjudgement was in his over-schematic view of the history of the classes in England. It is a topic which still baffles the foreigner. Engels, and taking their cue from him Weerth, Liebknecht, and Marx, wrote uncomprehendingly in the early years about the landed aristocracy and the moneyed middle class which they tended often to lump together as 'the English bourgeois'. Or sometimes they were classed together under the heading 'aristocracy'.

In his review of *Past and Present* for Marx's and Ruge's *Deutsch-Französische Jahrbücher* in 1844, for example, Engels wrote sweepingly: 'The aristocracy—and nowadays that also includes the middle classes—has exhausted itself.'[14] Engels's 'bourgeois' and later Marx's 'capitalist' were abstract fictions carrying some elements of truth to life, but they could not compare as representations with the 'felt life' of those fictional portraits of factory-owners and upper-class gentry in, say, *North and South*, *Dombey and Son*, *Bleak House*, or *Daniel Deronda.*

But if Engels was blithe in his treatment of history and debonair about the future, his observations about the present were powerful but not exaggerated. Though he was not the first to see in Manchester the 'classic type of the modern manufacturing town'—General Sir Charles James Napier had called Manchester 'the chimney of the world' in 1839[15]—Engels used his intimate knowledge of the town to show that, even in its very geography, the city was symbolic of the condition of England. He described how the wealthy businessman could travel daily from the healthy heights outside the city to the crowded centre without seeing the squalor which nestled close behind the shop-fronts which he passed on his way. Like the pictures of the crowds jostling in London's streets and the homeless sleeping on park benches 'close under the windows of Queen Victoria', this description serves to point to the unjust gulf between the classes, while also tending to give weight to Engels's prediction that the result of such distance-in-proximity would inevitably be revolution.[16]

On one question Engels's prediction was correct. Accusing the Anti-Corn-Law agitators of being middle-class hypocrites pretending to want abolition in the interests of the working man, he explained that

> the Corn Laws keep the price of bread higher than in other countries, and thus raise wages; but these high wages render difficult competition of the manufacturers against other nations in which bread, and consequently wages, are cheaper. The Corn Laws being repealed, the price of bread falls, and wages gradually approach those of other European countries . . . The manufacturer can compete more readily, the demand for English goods increases, and, with it, the demand for labour. In consequence of this increased demand wages would actually rise somewhat, and the unemployed workers be re-employed; but for how long? The 'surplus population' of England, and especially of Ireland, is sufficient to supply English manufacture with the necessary operatives, even if it were doubled; and, in a few years, the small advantage of the repeal of the Corn Laws would be balanced, a new crisis would follow, and we should be back at the point from which we started.

Corn Laws or no Corn Laws, the worker's lot remains dire. In 1850, four years after abolition, Kingsley put a related point in the mouth of an agricultural worker in *Alton Locke*: 'If the loaf's cheap, we shall be ruined; but if the loaf's dear, we shall be starved.'[17]

If Engels's sense of the nuances of middle- and upper-class society was deficient when he treated the question of class in his writings, it soon became more secure in fact as he began to experience the life of a middle-class businessman in Manchester. He liked good wine. Whenever he heard from Marx that Jenny Marx was ill, he promptly sent a case of port or sherry to aid her recovery, as well as money to cover the doctor's bill. His 'idea of happiness' as entered in Marx's daughter Jenny's album in 1868 was 'Château Margaux 1848' (no doubt the date was chosen for reasons not solely to do with wine). Though he worked long hours in the Ermen and Engels office and spent his evenings writing articles for German, English, and American journals, including the articles Marx sent as his own to the *New York Daily Tribune* from August 1851 until August 1852, Engels also found time to pursue his favourite study of military history, and to go horse-riding. He was a member of the Cheshire Hunt; 'it's the greatest physical pleasure I know', he wrote to Marx in 1857. Engels also belonged to Anglo-German gentlemen's clubs such as the Albert Club, the Schiller Anstalt, and the Brazenose Club, of which Charles Hallé was also a member.[18]

So 'Anglicized' had he become by 1861 that he wrote to the directorate of the Manchester Schiller Anstalt complaining about the 'Prussian' tone of a letter he had received from its librarian setting out the rules for borrowing books. The tone 'differs from that which is usual among educated people', he wrote:

> Indeed, when I read the piece I thought myself suddenly transported back home. Instead of a letter from the Librarian of the Schiller Anstalt, I thought I had received a categorical summons from some German commissioner of police, in which I was ordered, on pain of punishment, to put right some offence 'within 24 hours' . . .
>
> Many members could hardly have dreamt that 'the German spirit in the fullest sense of the word', which it was agreed the Schiller Anstalt was to promote, included among other things that spirit of bureaucracy which unfortunately still holds political power at home.

This tone, he concluded, was hardly the right one for an English club which had English as well as German members.[19]

He had two sets of drinking companions, Manchester worthies, whom he invariably called 'philistines', and the few other German exiles who had settled in Manchester. Among the first group was Jeremiah Garnett, editor of the *Manchester Guardian*, whom Engels described as 'a kind of oracle in the eyes of a number of philistines' but whom he appreciated as 'a teller of dirty stories and a moderate carouser'.[20] The second group consisted of Wilhelm Wolff, nicknamed 'Lupus', Weerth, who came over from Bradford regularly, Dronke for a time, Heinrich Heise, and Louis Borchardt, a German doctor who practised in Manchester. Engels seems to have acted as a benevolent father-figure to the hapless Wolff, a much-loved crusty bachelor who got into drunken scrapes—in March 1854 he was set upon and robbed while drunk—and to the others. Engels told Marx of an incident in a pub in May 1854, in which Wolff and Heise had criticized the British handling of the Crimean War and were nearly attacked by the Englishmen they were talking to: 'One or both of them will get a beating before long; yesterday they came close to it, whereupon I suddenly began talking in a Lancashire accent, which made the philistines [i.e. the English] laugh and provided the opportunity for a dignified retreat.'[21]

The combination of Engels's circumstances (i.e. his relatively high income) and his generosity resulted in his being the person to whom his fellow exiles automatically turned when in trouble. Just as he got his friends out of pub scrapes, so Engels helped them out of financial difficulties. He saved Dronke from bankruptcy in 1876 by acting as guarantor for a life-insurance policy.[22] He kept not only Marx, his wife, and three surviving children from 1850 until Marx's death in 1883, but also the three feckless husbands (Lafargue, Longuet, and Aveling) of the three Marx daughters until his own death in 1895. Letters from Dronke, Pieper, Liebknecht, Wolff, Lessner, and many other refugees harp on the theme of need, thanks for gifts or 'loans' received, and renewed need, over the whole period of Engels's life in England. (On one single occasion, before the refugees came to England, Engels, whose father was withholding his allowance, borrowed money from Marx.[23]) The exiles were, indeed, a society of borrowers and lenders, with Engels as the chief lender and all the others as the borrowers. Marx, who had the opposite of a Midas touch with money, described one particular 'economic hindrance' in terms which show both the precariousness of many of the refugees' lives and the reliability of Engels in coming to the rescue. Marx, writing to Engels in 1869, explained why he and Tussy (Eleanor) were unable to visit Manchester as planned. Mrs Marx and Tussy had just returned from a trip to Paris which had 'naturally caused me some extra expenses'. Then came demands from those in need totalling £14: Marx gave £6 to Dupont, who was unemployed and whose wife was seriously ill; to Lessner, whose wife had just died, he gave £5; finally Liebknecht wrote to Eccarius telling the latter to pump Marx for £2 or £3 to pay his rent and avoid eviction. 'So 14£ out of pocket.' Marx still had £15 left, but next came someone from the City with a letter from Herr Zitschke in New York, who had lent Marx £15 '*thirteen years before*' and now demanded payment. In short, Marx concluded the complicated tale, 'I'm broke'.[24] Engels responded, as usual, with cash.

'Uncle Angels', as Marx's children called him, punning obviously but also aptly on his name, was indeed the 'protective angel' of the refugees generally and of Marx in particular. The services he rendered his closest friend were not confined to finance; without Engels's constant prompting, encouraging, and flattering, it is doubtful if Marx would have produced many of his works. For, as Ruge had noticed when he collaborated with Marx in Paris in 1844, Marx was not a finisher. 'He reads a lot', Ruge told Feuerbach, 'he works with unusual intensity, and has a critical talent which sometimes degenerates into over-bold dialectic, but he never completes anything; he keeps breaking off and diving back into an endless sea of books.'[25] Engels's adopted role *vis-à-vis* Marx was like G. H. Lewes's *vis-à-vis* George Eliot: to encourage, praise, and cajole, reminding the other that there was no need to become a walking encyclopaedia about a subject such as Renaissance Florence, in order to write *Romola*, or political economy, in order to write one article for the *New York Daily Tribune*. When Marx began writing his articles for the *Tribune* in English, instead of having Engels or Pieper translate them from German for him, Engels immediately responded: '*Je t'en fais mon compliment.* The English isn't merely good; it's brilliant.'[26]

Engels more than once gave Marx an idea for a book. His notes entitled 'Principles of Communism' were worked up by Marx into the arresting *Communist Manifesto* in 1848, and Engels gave Marx a hint for the striking opening of *The Eighteenth Brumaire of Louis Bonaparte* (1852). Writing to Marx on 3 December 1851, the day after Louis Napoleon's *coup d'état*, Engels wittily invoked Hegel: 'it really seems as though old Hegel, in the guise of the World Spirit, were directing history from the grave and, with the greatest conscientiousness, causing everything to be re-enacted twice over, once as grand tragedy and the second time as rotten farce.' The remark, made briefer and more trenchant, duly appeared at the beginning of Marx's work. Engels wanted no credit for such gifts of ideas, any more than he did for money given. Indeed, he often insisted to Marx that only Marx could work up the ideas satisfactorily. Referring to another such case, which had resulted in Marx's *Holy Family, or Critique of Criticism* (1845), Engels reminded Marx, 'I similarly wrote a few sheets because a pamphlet was envisaged, and you turned it into a full-blown book of 20 sheets in which my trifle looked strange indeed. Once again you would assuredly do so much to it that my contribution, in any case hardly worth mentioning, would quite disappear before your heavy artillery.'[27] Engels's modesty here serves both to flatter Marx and to keep him at work.

No doubt Engels himself felt relieved that he could give Marx the financial and moral support he needed to complete important works, especially the great work on capital, and thus evade the direct responsibility himself of painstakingly laying the scholarly groundwork for future action. He was, on his own admission, happy to play second fiddle to Marx. And he was in certain ways more impatient, more irresponsible even, than Marx. On the one hand, he was 'protective angel' to Marx's 'Dalai Lama' in the London section of the Communist League—the description is Eduard Müller-Tellering's, an obsessive enemy of Marx's after Marx had removed him from the German Workers' Education Association in London in 1850.[28] On the other hand, he was boyish and impulsive. It was at least partly because he was itching for some military excitement that he went off to join Willich and Kinkel in one of the obviously doomed uprisings of May 1849, though his explanation to Marx, who disapproved of such naïve actions, was that he did not want the 'action party' among the Communist League—Willich, Schapper, Moll, and the others already established for some years in London—to be able to point to Marx and Engels and their friends as mere scholars who were only willing to *talk* revolution.

Though living 'respectably' as a member of the Manchester Exchange, he had one brush with the law which illustrates his occasional hotheadedness. In 1859 he was involved in a pub brawl:

> At a drunken gathering I was insulted by an Englishman I didn't know; I hit out at him with the umbrella I was carrying and the ferrule got him in the eye. The chap immediately put the matter in the hands of his LAWYER. . . . However I still hope to get round the JOBBING LAWYERS; if all goes *really well* the DRUNKEN BRAWL will cost me forty or fifty pounds. . . . Needless to say these blasted English don't want to deprive themselves of the pleasure of getting their hands on a BLOODY FOREIGNER.

Engels went on to say that his English friends were 'behaving very honourably and instantly took the thing up', but 'I'm going to be bled, that's certain'. He ended with a promise to send Marx £5 (this letter being a reply to a request for money), apologizing that it could not, under the circumstances, be more.[29]

While Marx, as Ruge had pointed out, was more suited to be a scholar than a journalist because of his habit of reading exhaustively on any subject he intended to discuss, Engels was temperamentally the ideal journalist. His chief characteristic, he wrote in Jenny Marx's album, was 'knowing things by halves'. The description might well represent his own later criticism of his early articles on Britain and *The Condition of the Working Class in England*. But the other side of the coin was the ability he had to absorb information quickly and analyse contemporary events. His study of military history bore fruit on the occasions of the Crimean War, the Austro-Prussian War, and the Franco-Prussian War. In March 1854 he wrote a letter to H. J. Lincoln, editor of the *Daily News*, offering his services as regular military correspondent on events in the Crimea. The letter is remarkable for its skilful combination of truthfulness and concealment of his political views:

> I beg to state . . . that my military school has been the Prussian Artillery, a service which, if it is not what it might be, yet has produced the men who made 'the Turkish Artillery one of the best in Europe' as our friend Nicholas has laid it down. Later on, I had an occasion of seeing some active service during the insurrectionary war in South Germany, 1849. For many years the study of military science in all its branches has been one of my chief occupations . . . An acquaintance, more or less familiar, with most European languages, including Russian, Serbian, and a little Wallachian, opens to me the best sources of information and may, perhaps, prove useful to you in other respects.

Mindful of the need for references, Engels named his friend John Watts, who was himself a contributor on educational subjects to the *Daily News*.[30] The editor replied encouragingly; Engels sent an opening article, 'The Russian Army', which was set up in proof. Engels rejoiced, believing that regular newspaper work would enable him to leave the firm and settle in London. 'Things seem to be working out with *The Daily News*', he told Marx. 'I didn't write until last week, when I had observed the English proprieties by obtaining a REFERENCE from father Watts. . . . If all goes well, in the summer, when my old man comes over, I shall chuck up commerce and move to London.' Marx responded jubilantly, doing an imitation of Lord John Russell: 'I HOPE, SIR, YOU WILL LEAVE MANCHESTER, SIR, FOR EVER,

SIR.'[31] Unfortunately, exile gossip saw to it that the new job came to nothing:

Pieper . . . must have been talking big about it and thus, by the well-known telegraphic medium of émigré gossip, the story came to the ears of Kinkel or some other wretched German blighter acquainted with *The Daily News* and then, of course, nothing was easier than to represent Engels, the MILITARY MAN, as no more than a former one-year volunteer, a communist and a clerk by trade, thus putting a stop to everything.[32]

Marx absolved Pieper in his reply, but Engels did not on this occasion become a regular correspondent of a respectable English newspaper.

This was a pity, for Engels had more than half-knowledge where military history was concerned. His assessment of Wellington, for example, though it would not have found favour in England, where Wellington was revered well above royalty (Fanny Lewald noticed statues to him everywhere she went in 1850, and his funeral in November 1852 was the greatest event of the decade, commanding more attention even than the Great Exhibition[33]), was shrewd. Engels explained Wellington's success and popularity to Marx in 1851 in terms of his quintessential Englishness, almost John Bullishness:

A self-willed, tough, obstinate Englishman, with all the *bon sens*, all the resourcefulness of his nation; slow in his deliberations, cautious, never counting on a lucky chance despite his most colossal luck; he would be a genius if COMMON SENSE were not incapable of rising to the heights of genius. All his things are exemplary, not one of them masterly. . . . And he knows his army, its self-willed, DEFENSIVE DOGGEDNESS, which every Englishman brings with him from the boxing ring, and which enables it, after eight hours of strenuous defensive fighting that would bring any other army to its knees, to launch yet another formidable attack in which lack of élan is compensated by uniformity and steadiness.[34]

Much later, in 1866 and 1870–1, Engels did write on military matters for English papers. He contributed articles to the *Manchester Guardian* on the Austro-Prussian War in 1866—H. M. Acton wrote to him from the editorial office to say the articles 'will suit us exactly'. Acton wrote again in 1871 to ask if Engels could give any hints or letters of introduction to the *Guardian*'s correspondent, who was going to Karlsruhe to cover the Franco-Prussian War.[35] Engels himself was at this time regular war correspondent for another English journal. He contributed about sixty articles on the Franco-Prussian War to the *Pall Mall Gazette*, showing unrivalled knowledge of the historical background to the war. *The Times* and other newspapers quoted and borrowed from these articles, and Queen Victoria (not knowing the author's identity) wrote to her daughter Vicky, 'The Pall Mall has excellent articles. You should take it in.'[36] This is another index of the acceptableness in England of at least one facet of Engels.

After Marx's death, Engels naturally became the elder statesman of the communists and socialists in London. Only a couple of the original German exiles in the party remained: Lessner and Liebknecht (in Germany), and they joined with the new generation of English socialists, with Eleanor Marx as the connecting link between Germany and England. Without Marx, Engels seemed to lose his good humour somewhat. The history of his relations with William Morris and other young disciples is one of partial co-operation and disappointment. He responded sourly to the socialist paper *Justice* in 1884, finding it 'terribly empty':

> But what can you expect from a society of people who make it their task to lecture the world on subjects they themselves don't understand? . . . Hyndman combines internationalist phraseology with chauvinistic actions, Joynes is a confused ignoramus . . . Morris is all right when he gets hold of something, but he doesn't do so very often, and poor Bax gets all tied up in German philosophy of a rather antiquated character.[37]

But he accepted the role of custodian of Marx's ideas, dividing his time between editing Marx's fragmentary notes for vols. ii and iii of *Capital*, supervising their translation by Edward Aveling and Engels's long-standing Manchester friend, Samuel Moore, and corresponding with young socialists in England, France, and Germany.

He also reminisced, naturally, about his early days in England. In 1890 he visited Harney, with whom he had corresponded intermittently since Marx's break with the latter in 1851. Harney had given up national politics when he lost a battle with Ernest Jones for control of the Chartist movement in 1852—Marx described their 'cock-fight' as descending 'to the level of German émigré polemics'[38]—and had gone first to Newcastle, then to Jersey. Engels visited him there in 1857, when he was recuperating from an illness and helping Conrad Schramm, an old member of the Communist League who had settled in Jersey and was fatally ill. Harney was now deep in local petty 'politics'; Engels reported to Marx that Harney was enjoying being the one-eyed king in the kingdom of the blind, 'on his right THE FIRST GROCER, on his left THE FIRST TALLOW-CHANDLER IN THE TOWN'.[39] After Harney's departure to America in 1863, the correspondence became less frequent, though Engels, unlike Marx, retained a certain fondness for 'old Harney'. Perhaps this was because Harney had given him journalistic work during his first years in England. Certainly, Engels looked back forty years later at Harney's Chartist newspapers and recognized their historical significance. In reply to a letter from Petr Lavrovich Lavrov from Paris in 1885 asking for information about the history of Chartism, Engels explained that his own papers from the 1840s had gone missing during the 'storm of 1848–9'. He added that the chief source of information, the *Northern Star*, had become rare, and that Harney was now touring the north of England looking for a complete set. 'It is a pity, for if Harney does not write his memoirs, the history of the first great workers' party will be lost for ever.'[40] (Harney did not write his memoirs, but he appears to have found a complete set of the *Northern Star*. The modern editors of Georg Weerth's works in English note that only three complete sets of the newspaper are known: Harney's, which is in Moscow; Weerth's—of which Weerth boasted in an unpublished article of 1848, 'History of the Radical Reformers from 1780 to 1832'—which is now lost; and the set in the British Museum.[41]) Finally, when Harney returned to England, old and ill, Engels visited him regularly in Richmond in 1892. As ever, Harney was hard up; as ever Engels 'lent' him money.[42] In the event, Harney outlived Engels by two years.

Engels also looked back in the English editions in 1892 of two of his works originally published in German much earlier. Remembering his strictures about English religious and political prejudice in *The Condition of the Working Class in England*, he thought he could detect, nearly fifty years on, an improvement in both respects. In *Socialism: Utopian and Scientific* (1892, first written in German in 1877), he recalled the difference in attitude between educated Englishmen and Germans on the question of religious belief:

> About the middle of this century, what struck every cultivated foreigner who set up his residence in England, was what he was then bound to consider the religious bigotry and stupidity of the English respectable middle-class. We, at that time, were all materialists, or, at least, very advanced free-thinkers, and to us it appeared inconceivable that almost all educated people in England should believe in all sorts of impossible miracles, and that even geologists like Buckland and Mantell should contort the facts of their science so as not to clash too much with the myths of the book of Genesis; while, in order to find people who dared to use their own intellectual faculties with regard to religious matters, you had to go amongst the uneducated, the 'great unwashed', as they were then called, the working people, especially the Owenite Socialists.

This account may seem exaggerated, but it is certainly true that English agnostics and atheists were, on the whole, discreet about their lack of belief in the middle of the century. Dickens paid lip-service to conventional Christianity in his novels; George Eliot was praised for the 'Christian morality' inculcated by her works but regularly castigated by critics for not representing active Christian faith; and Lewes and his colleagues on the *Leader* were cautious about cultivating too free-thinking an image, as we have seen. As Fontane pointed out, Thackeray may have lost the Oxford election contest in 1857 partly because of his 'enlightened, or as others would say his indifferent, views on religion'.[43]

Slowly, after the publication of Darwin's *Origin of Species* (1859), the climate changed. Jenny Marx took her daughters to free-thinking meetings in St Martin's Hall in 1866, and related to a friend in Geneva, J. P. Becker:

> In religious matters there is at present a great change in process in stuffy old England. The chief men of science, Huxley (Darwin's pupil) at their head, with Tyndall, Sir Charles Lyell, Bowring, Carpenter, etc. etc., are giving in St Martin's Hall . . . highly enlightened, truly bold, and free-thinking lectures to the people, and moreover on Sunday evenings, at exactly the time when previously the lambs went to the Lord's pasture. The hall was so chock-full and the rejoicing of the people so great that on the first Sunday evening, when I was there with the girls, 2,000 people were denied entry to the room, which was already full to bursting.[44]

Interestingly, it was by means of a Darwinian metaphor that Engels explained in his preface to the English edition of *The Condition of the Working Class in England* (1892) a corresponding change in the climate of political opinion in Britain. Pointing to the existence of the International since his book was first written, he sees his youthful work as representing an early phase in the growth of socialism:

> Modern international Socialism, since fully developed as a science, chiefly and almost exclusively through the efforts of Marx, did not as yet exist in 1844. My book represents one of the phases of its embryonic development; and as the human embryo, in its early stages, still reproduces the gill arches of our fish ancestors, so this book exhibits everywhere the traces of the descent of modern Socialism from one of its ancestors, German philosophy.

He goes on to claim, with characteristic verve, that socialism has now 'not only become respectable, but has actually donned evening dress and lounges lazily on drawing-room *causeuses*'. For evidence to substantiate Engels's suggestion that in 1850 'socialism' had been distrusted, one might look, for example, at an article by W. R. Greg in the *Edinburgh Review* (January 1851), in which he patronized socialism and 'put his trust', as he said, in political science, not socialism, advocating 'wisdom, self-control, frugality, and toil' on the part of the working classes to prove that they deserved a share in decision-making. The Chartist Thomas Frost recalled having been refused lodgings by a Tory landlord in the 1840s because he professed socialism.[45]

Perhaps Engels half-regretted the new-found respectability of socialism. It meant that the sage of Regent's Park no longer needed to live a double political life, as he had done in Manchester. Nor did he now have a secret personal life. After the death of Mary Burns in January 1863, Engels and her sister Lizzie lived openly together as man and wife. When Eleanor Marx set up house with the married Edward Aveling soon after Marx's death, she knew she was doing nothing to shock Engels. She could scarcely have taken the step during her parents' lifetime, for the Marxes were, in some respects, as bourgeois as the English middle class they criticized. Mrs Marx had refused at first to meet Mary Burns, and had never accepted invitations to stay with Engels and Mary in Manchester. Eleanor once praised Engels to her sister Jenny: 'Truly there is not another like him in the world—in spite of his little weaknesses.' No doubt she was referring here to Engels's known fondness for drinking and to his sexual adventures, one of which was supposed to have resulted in the birth of Freddie Demuth, the son of Marx's housekeeper, Helene Demuth, in June 1851. Eleanor was to discover, to her shock and discomfort, on Engels's death-bed that Engels had assumed paternity to save Marx, who was Freddie's father, from scandal. Freiligrath had once commented in a letter to Weerth's brother on Engels's 'noble outrageousness'.[46] It was a combination of qualities which made him the perfect friend for Marx, the perfect acquaintance for hard-up exiles, and the perfect naturalized Englishman.

Weerth

Georg Weerth travelled to England in December 1843 for reasons similar to those of Engels. He wanted to widen his experience as an apprentice businessman, and he was interested in learning about the political and social condition of England. While Engels made for Manchester, Weerth, two years younger than Engels, settled in Bradford for two years, after which he travelled on business throughout Europe, South America, and the West Indies, where he died of fever in

1856, aged 44. Like Engels, therefore, he was not at first a political exile, but, also like Engels, he escaped to London in 1849 after a warrant had gone out in Germany for his arrest in connection with his contributions to Marx's *Neue Rheinische Zeitung* in Cologne. And he became one of Marx's and Engels's first political disciples. If studying Hegel and Feuerbach, working in Manchester, and reading Carlyle were among the chief influences which combined to produce *The Condition of the Working Class in England*, then reading the latter itself, as well as studying Feuerbach, working in Bradford, and reading Dickens were the corresponding shaping influences on Weerth's early articles and fragments.

When Weerth left Germany in 1843, he was not yet very politically minded. He was born in 1822, the son of a clergyman in Detmold, the small town from which no fewer than three other prominent London exiles came: Freiligrath, Friedrich Althaus, and Malwida von Meysenbug. All of them belonged to the very large German class of civil servants. Althaus's father was the 'highly respectable' clergyman who confirmed Freiligrath and who succeeded Weerth's father as general superintendent of Detmold, as Freiligrath told Engels in 1857 when he wrote asking Engels to help get another Althaus brother, a musician, a job in England.[47] Like Engels, Weerth was half-disowned by his family for his speedy 'lapse' into irreligion (he read Feuerbach in Bradford in 1844 and underwent 'a complete revolution' as a result[48]) and left-wing politics. The stimulus to the latter change was Engels himself. Weerth wrote to his mother from Brussels in July 1845, saying he belonged now to the class of 'Lumpen-Kommunisten' which wanted to help the poor and oppressed. His 'very dear friend Friedrich Engels from Barmen', Weerth went on, had just written a book about the English working class, for which his family had disowned him. Weerth warned his own mother not to do the same to him. Her letters to him, like Elisabeth Engels's to her aberrant son, are full of bafflement and anxiety: 'How you people storm through the world these days—hardly had I imagined you safe and sound in Brussels than you are whirling about in Paris with your friends and catching a cold in Holland!'[49] After Weerth's early death, his family seems to have destroyed Marx's and Engels's letters to him.

Weerth's earliest reports, in letters and articles for German newspapers (only some of which were published), show him responding to Bradford much as Engels did to Manchester. Arrival in Bradford, he wrote in an unpublished sketch, was like descending into hell; one was assailed by darkness and smells: 'Every other factory town in England is paradise compared to this hole; in Manchester the air lies on your head like lead . . . In Bradford, however, one feels as if one has been locked up with the devil alive.' There are echoes of Heine's insolent playfulness and Dickens's sentiment and satire in his descriptions for the *Kölnische Zeitung* in 1844 of 'a factory town'. Like Heine, he is facetious about England and at the same time about the German character:

> A Frenchman would live in an English factory town for three days and then—die; an Italian would stick it out for about a fortnight then put a bullet through his head; a Polish Jew would say after three weeks: 'It is enough!' and would hang himself by his beard; only a German would not be ashamed to stay longer than a full year without once going thoroughly mad! An English factory town looks from the outside like a great molehill, from the inside it looks filthy.

And, like Dickens, he admires and fears the restless industry:

> Whole rows of chimneys, which rise above the roofs of the houses as slim as minarets, indicate that this is the place where the whirring of the wheels and the humming of the looms mingle with the sighs of the tormented workmen, that this is the spot where that mass of wares is produced which Britain sends in its fleets through all the world.[50]

During his regular 'shuttling' between Bradford and Manchester to see Engels, Weerth became infected, it appears, by Engels's optimism about a speedy revolution in England. He wrote to his brother Wilhelm in December 1844 that socialist ideas were becoming 'astonishingly prevalent' in England, and that all that was needed were two bad harvests in a row for there to be a collapse of commerce and a 'revolution against private property'. Like many another observer, he noticed that the English working man, though completely uneducated in the formal sense, was a good practical politician—'he knows what he wants!' But he was also aware, like Engels, that the English reform movements were in disarray in the 1840s. He visited the ageing socialist Robert Owen at his experimental Harmony Hall, and he met local Chartists in Bradford. Chartism, he saw, had lost its momentum and was, wrongly, joining forces with middle-class Anti-Corn-Law agitation. In an essay in 1848, 'History of the Chartists from 1832 to 1848', Weerth took the same line of analysis as Engels and Marx, whom he also now knew. The Chartists had made a mistake and betrayed their class by sharing platforms in Manchester in 1845 with John Bright, Richard Cobden, and other Anti-Corn-Law speakers:

Hired drinkers drank to the future of free trade. Hired boxers boxed for the repeal of the Corn Laws. Hired poets dedicated the feeblest of verse to the defeat of the bread tax; and hired shop keepers wrapped up every pound of butter in a treatise on the necessity of free trade. Prizes were offered to all and sundry for the best distortions not only of the sublime science of political economy but of philosophy and religion, in short of anything and everything that the wide world can afford, if only the subject can be made to serve the League. Even sweet delicate womankind had her place in the grand parade; the ladies of Manchester entered the arena on more than one occasion in the name of the cause.[51]

Weerth could speak as strikingly as he could write. Attending the Free Trade Congress in Brussels in September 1847 with Marx and Engels, he gave an anti-free-trade speech which infuriated delegates and which Engels translated for the *Northern Star.* Weerth told his middle-class audience that they could not claim to speak for the working class, whereas he, who had 'spent several of the most pleasant [!] years of my life' amongst English working men, could and would. He turned delegates' attention away from the question of finance towards the people themselves:

Look wherever you like; to the banks of the Rhone; into the dirty and pestilential lanes of Manchester, Leeds, and Birmingham; on the hills of Saxony and Silesia, or the plains of Westphalia; everywhere you will meet with the same pale starvation, the same gloomy despair, in the eyes of men who in vain claim their rights and their position in civilised society.[52]

The speech caused, as Engels noted, a 'great sensation'. The conference was hurriedly brought to a close and Marx's intended speech was not given.

In an unpublished fragment of a novel, Weerth indicated how important the influence of Engels's *Condition of the Working Class in England* was on his thinking. Written in 1846–7, Weerth's fragment combines—not altogether successfully—Dickensian social satire and straightforward political propaganda. It deals with the three classes in Germany: the benevolent but outdated aristocracy, the thrusting, ruthless capitalist class, and the proletariat. The chief representative of the last class is a young man called Eduard, who has spent two years learning the mechanic's trade in Manchester. Rather as Felix Holt, George Eliot's eponymous hero, returns to Treby Magna politicized by having worked in Glasgow, Eduard comes back from England to plunge into organizing the sheep-like workers in the local factory. He reads them passages from Engels's work, and he tells them about English union activity. Echoing Engels, he praises the English workmen who strike without hope of immediate success, insisting that the inevitable result of strikes will be a mass uprising. Weerth paints a picture, as Mayhew was to do in 1849, of young mothers returning to factory work with 'breasts threatening to burst, because they have left at home a tiny baby which has been stretching its arms in vain for its mother'.[53]

Weerth also commented on English religious prejudice. He told his brother in 1845 that the aristocracy used the 'mask of religion to hide their sinful faces' and that the hypocritical middle class concealed 'the meanest money-grabbing behind a lying Christianity, which they come out with at every opportunity'.[54] (A modern historian estimates that there were about fifty chapels and churches in Bradford in the 1840s to seventy brothels.[55]) In a rather rambling, loosely Pickwickian piece impersonating a German lodger in an English household, Weerth wrote around the same time (the lodger having been caught out one Sunday reading *Tristram Shandy* under cover of the Bible): 'Farewell, you Britons, who like thousands of your ilk are still stuck in the most terrible prejudices, and who are in this "land of freedom" still so intolerant!' Weerth complained in letters and articles about the English habit of keeping Sundays—'the English run the risk of becoming faint from sheer praying and Bible-reading'—and he linked Sabbatarianism with another phenomenon also noticed, like the dreary Sundays, by several exiles—the long, hard working week of the English. 'The whole population keeps hard at work all week, then spends Sunday in zealous church-going. They only know prayer and work.'[56]

Weerth was here anticipating the protests by such 'establishment' critics of society as Dickens and *Punch*. When Parliament passed a series of unpopular measures in 1855, including outlawing Sunday trading and throwing out Sir Joshua Walmsley's bill which would have opened museums and art galleries on Sundays, Dickens came to the defence of those most affected. These were, of course, the working poor, who had no leisure during the week to shop or to view works of art. The English, 'the hardest-worked people on whom the sun shines', who are 'born at the oar' and 'live and die at it', have been insulted, wrote Dickens in *Household Words* in August 1855, by Parliament's reluctance to trust them 'with the liberty of refreshing themselves in humble taverns and tea-gardens on their day of rest'. *Punch* noticed that once again only the poor were affected by such bills, and added that art galleries might as well turn their pictures to the wall, since the mass of people had no chance of seeing them. Marx, who attended two mass meetings in Hyde

Park in June and July 1855 in protest against the Sunday Trading Bill, made the same point as *Punch* and Dickens, though characteristically he looked harder for political and class motives than they. In an article for the *Neue Oder-Zeitung* just after the first demonstration, he wrote:

> The first measure of religious coercion was the Beer Bill, which shut down all places of public entertainment on Sundays, except between 6 and 10 p.m. . . . Then came the Sunday Trading Bill, the third reading of which has now taken place in the Commons . . . In both cases there is a conspiracy of the Church with the monopoly of capital, but in both cases religious penal laws are to be imposed on the lower classes to set the conscience of the privileged classes at rest. Just as the *Beer Bill* did not hurt the aristocratic clubs so the *Sunday Trading Bill* does not interfere with the Sunday occupations of genteel society. The workers get their wages late on Saturday: it is for them alone that trade is carried on on Sundays. The new bill is therefore directed against them alone. The French aristocracy said in the eighteenth century: for us, Voltaire; for the people, the mass and the tithes. The English aristocracy says in the nineteenth century: For us, sanctimonious phrases; for the people, Christian practice.

However, Marx was glad to report to his German readers that the people had held a mass demonstration against this injustice. 'We saw it from beginning to end', he continued, 'and do not think it an exaggeration to say that the *English Revolution began in Hyde Park yesterday*.' To Engels Marx reported more cautiously: 'The demonstration in Hyde Park on Sunday afternoon had quite a revolutionary air.'[57]

Though Weerth, introduced to Marx by Engels in 1845, became, as did Liebknecht, and Freiligrath for a time, very disciple-like in his letters to Marx between 1846 and 1848, the relationship did not develop after that. He moved his business duties to Brussels in 1846, where he worked with Marx in the local branch of the Communist League.[58] After the 1848 revolution he joined Marx in Cologne and wrote on Chartism for the *Neue Rheinische Zeitung.* But when the paper was prohibited and the warrant went out for his arrest, he loosened his connections with the Communist League and subsequently engaged in no more radical journalism. A combination of factors was at work here. Firstly, when he returned to Britain in September 1849 it was not at first to filthy Bradford but to London, which he found stimulating, and where he had good job prospects. Secondly, he lost hope after 1848 of another German revolution, as he told Marx in 1850, and he felt writing to be 'superfluous' in the face of 'world history'. Thirdly, and his remarks to Marx may well be an excuse for this, he was now more concerned with pursuing his business, an unrequited love affair, and better health, than continuing as a revolutionary. He avoided becoming one of Marx's group, as Marx saw clearly enough. 'Weerth left this morning for Holland', Marx reported to Engels in February 1852. 'Where will he go from there? I do not know and neither does Weerth himself perhaps . . . He maintains that he can't stand the English climate.'[59]

Marx was to feel even sourer about Weerth when the latter stayed with him in September 1852. The Marxes were too proud to tell Weerth how hard up they were and resented his genteel expectations (the same was to happen when Marx's colourful German disciple, Ferdinand Lassalle, visited England in 1862). In a letter to Engels, Marx complained, using a foreign language, as he often did, to express his shame with regard to his financial situation, that Weerth 'has *plus ou moins* monopolised my evenings which are usually given over to writing':

> As you know, I'm very fond of Weerth, *mais* it's embarrassing, when one's up to one's neck in trouble, to have to face so fine a gentleman, *auquel il faut cacher les parties trop honteuses*. Such a relationship creates twice as much *gêne* and I hope he will leave for Manchester tomorrow and will on his return find me in circumstances that will enable me to consort with him *franchement*.

The last straw for Marx was when Weerth visited him in December 1852, while Marx was furiously completing his pamphlet on the Cologne Communist trial, and 'asked me "what did I propose, actually, to write about the Cologne affair?"—this in somewhat superior, nasal tones. I asked, "what did he propose to do in the West Indies?" and, after a quarter of an hour or so, he made off.' Marx concluded that Weerth had become 'damned bourgeoisified'.[60]

Nevertheless, Weerth was of some use to Marx. He lent Marx money from time to time, and he gave Marx material for his pamphlet against Kinkel, Ruge, and the rest, 'The Great Men of the Exile' (1852). In 1850, against Marx's advice, he had returned voluntarily to Germany to serve the three-month prison sentence passed on him in his absence for his part in the *Neue Rheinische Zeitung*. He wrote to Marx from prison in Cologne in June 1850, saying he had seen Kinkel, who was serving a life sentence and had been brought to Cologne for a second trial in May. Disapproving of Kinkel's treacherous self-defence, he gave Marx a cruel comic sketch of Kinkel and Johanna which Marx was to use in 'The Great Men of the Exile':

> His wife, a completely mad woman, greeted him through the bars in verse; he replied, I believe, in hexameters; thereupon they both fell down on their knees

before one another, and the prison inspector, an old army sergeant, who was standing near by, didn't know whether he had idiots or comedians on his hands. He later told the chief prosecutor, who had asked what the conversation was about, that though they had both spoken German, he had not understood a word of it, whereupon Mrs Kinkel is said to have replied that no man ought to be made an inspector who was so totally ignorant of literature and the arts.[61]

Probably the last pieces of political writing Weerth did were two essays on English history, extracts of which were published in the *Neue Rheinische Zeitung* in November 1848. They were 'History of the Radical Reformers from 1780 to 1832' and 'History of the Chartists from 1832 to 1848'. Both show more traces of Weerth's acquaintance with English radical works than with those of his friend Marx. The former consists almost entirely of quotations from Weerth's Bradford friend, the self-educated wool-comber John Jackson, and quotations from Samuel Bamford's *Passages in the Life of a Radical* (1841–3). The second article draws on Jackson's pamphlet attacking Feargus O'Connor, *The Demagogue Done Up*, which was published in Bradford in 1844. Though Weerth, in his criticism of the Chartist support of the Anti-Corn Law League, was close to Marx and Engels, he was far less dubious than they about the merits of the two leaders, Harney and Jones. Weerth describes Harney as 'the life and soul of the *Northern Star*' and Jones as 'the Demosthenes of his party'. He voices as a positive fact what unfortunately remained only an attractive potential asset—Jones's knowledge of German and his education at a German university. If what Weerth said had been true, Marx and Jones would surely have had a more fruitful relationship than they did. In Weerth's words, Jones 'was able to combine and to communicate the profundities of German learning with the power of British energy'.[62]

Influenced by the Chartist poetry of Jones and of Thomas Cooper and by the poems of Burns, Shelley, and Hood, Weerth wrote, in German, some 'Songs of Lancashire' around 1845. Though not original, they conveyed some of the spirit and anger of their models, and some of them were published in English in 1888. James Leigh Joynes, the socialist master at Eton who was sacked for his views on Ireland and who edited and contributed to socialist journals like *To-Day*, *Commonweal*, and *Justice* (of which Engels complained in 1884), published *Songs of a Revolutionary Epoch* (1888), in which he included poems by Weerth, 'one of the most remarkable of the poets of the German Proletariat'.[63]

In a sense, Weerth belonged to no party and went his own way. Engels's assessment, made as early as 1847, while it was no doubt coloured by the fact that Marx's speech had been banned as a result of the dramatic effect of Weerth's at the Brussels Free Trade Congress, was probably sound: 'A man who was always too lazy, until pitchforked by his *succès d'un jour* at the Congress. And who, to boot, wishes to be AN INDEPENDENT MEMBER.'[64] No doubt Weerth was, at bottom, more capitalist than communist. Nevertheless he left behind a critical picture of industrial England, particularly Bradford, in the mid nineteenth century which has at least some of the interest of Engels's portrait of Manchester.

Freiligrath

Ferdinand Freiligrath, whose poetry was represented alongside Weerth's in Joynes's *Songs of a Revolutionary Epoch*, is the third communist clerk among the exiles. On the face of it, he ought to have been the most successful of all the German exiles in England. In fact, he had difficulty in getting, and keeping, a job; his aspirations to a high position in academic life were unfulfilled; and his relations with his fellow exiles were tense. He returned to Germany, amnestied, in 1868, and became the unofficial poet laureate in the years when Bismarck was making Germany into a power to be reckoned with.

Like Engels and Weerth, Freiligrath had been bred for business. Ten years older than Engels, he was sent to Amsterdam in 1833 to work in a branch of the family firm. But his letters home to friends indicate that he felt he was not cut out for commerce. He wanted to be a poet, and his models were the poems of 'Albion'. 'Between Shakespeare and Byron, the Alpha and Omega of English poetry, there lies a rich, splendid alphabet of poets', he wrote enthusiastically to his friend Ludwig Merckel in October 1833. Then he went on to name them: 'the quiet, pious Cowper', 'the pictorial Moore', Hogg the Ettrick Shepherd, 'the gentle Wilson', 'the imaginative Coleridge', 'correct Campbell', 'the spellbinding Walter Scott', 'the intelligent Bulwer'. Though this is merely a list, it is an impressive index of Freiligrath's acquaintance with recent and contemporary English literature. Freiligrath's first ventures into writing poetry were translations and adaptations of single poems by Burns and the Romantic poets, which he got published in Cotta's *Morgenblatt* from 1835. In the same year he had high hopes of joining his uncle's business in Edinburgh, consoling himself that, his 'prosaic profession' notwithstanding, he might visit the home country of the 'Wizard of the North'.[65] The plan came to nothing, but Freiligrath carried on working in finance and at the same time writing both his own poetry and translations from English to make up a volume which Cotta published in 1838. (Engels is said to have had Freiligrath's example in mind when he sat at his desk in Bremen in 1838 and wrote verses.[66]) He achieved a great enough success with this volume of poetry to make him feel able to give up business, at least for the time being. Another plan to visit Britain was hatched in 1838, when Freiligrath's friend Heinrich Künzel set off to London to found and edit the *German Review*. Again, in 1841, Freiligrath hoped to join Künzel in publishing a periodical called *Britannia*, but neither journal got off the ground. Freiligrath was to see Künzel briefly in London in 1852, when Freiligrath was the domiciled one and Künzel the visitor. The latter managed the visit to England of a German theatre company and sent his friend tickets for, among other things, Schiller's *Kabale und Liebe*, to which Freiligrath took Jenny Marx. (Queen Victoria and Prince Albert attended the company's first performance, of Goethe's *Egmont*, on 2 June 1852.[67])

Freiligrath's poetry was at first unpolitical, even anti-political. In 1841 he wrote a high-minded poem attacking Georg Herwegh's revolutionary verses, of which the refrain was:

> Der Dichter steht auf einer höhern Warte,
> Als auf den Zinnen der Partei!

[The poet stands on a higher vantage point than on the battlements of party.][68]

He even accepted a literary pension from Friedrich Wilhelm IV in 1842. But like Kinkel, whom he soon came to know, he was horrified by the Prussian King's increasingly repressive measures, particularly his curbing of the freedom to publish, which was to affect his own volumes of poetry. He became caught up in the cries for reform, and renounced his pension in 1843, in order to be free to write political verses.[69] There followed his volume of 1844, *Ein Glaubensbekenntnis*, and his flight from prosecution.

Had he not by now become involved in the political struggle in Germany, he would most probably have gone straight to his much-admired England. But it is likely that he wanted to be on hand for new events in Germany and he probably also wished to become closer to the Marx circle which he had previously avoided. At any rate, he went to Brussels, where he met Marx in February 1845, reporting his first impressions to his friend Karl Buchner: 'Marx has been here for a week now; a nice, interesting, modest chap . . . His and Ruge's expulsion from France at Prussia's request is a real scandal!'[70] During 1845 Freiligrath moved to Zurich to try to get work in a bank. He was now a married man and a father, and needed to earn a living apart from poetry and politics. Unsuccessful in Zurich, he came to London in the summer of 1846, where his friends William and Mary Howitt had found a clerkship for him. He had met them on the Rhine a few years earlier, and they were very helpful to him now. Both Howitts were prolific authors, minor but well-connected figures in liberal literary circles. They had published their translations of poems of his in the *Athenaeum* in 1843 and 1844, and William Howitt had praised his translations, particularly that of *The Ancient Mariner*, in his book *The Rural and Domestic Life of Germany* (1842). Howitt told Harney in a letter of August 1846:

> I have lately been trying hard to fix Freiligrath, the celebrated German poet, in London, and hope to succeed. I have got the interest of the first Bankers, Merchants, & money-lenders in London, Gurney, Baring, Grotes and others engaged for him (*keep this in confidence*) and everything bids fair. He is now staying awhile with us.[71]

Eventually Freiligrath was found a job with the City firm of Frederick Huth & Co., which, like the Barings and Grotes and others, was a merchant business set up by German financiers who had come over to England during the eighteenth century.[72]

The Howitts did their best for Freiligrath the poet as well as Freiligrath the bank clerk. For he still dreamt of giving up commerce and living by his pen. In his letters to friends in Germany and America he dramatized his position, quoting from Charles Lamb: 'A Clerk I am in London gay', and declaring himself a 'slave' to the 'drudgery' of business.[73] Several literary figures exerted themselves for Freiligrath. Richard Monckton Milnes helped with finding him his job, and later lent him money, and Bulwer Lytton, who knew and admired Freiligrath's poetry, wrote to him in January or February 1847, offering hospitality at his home in Hertfordshire, and inviting Freiligrath to use his services to 'soften' his life as an exile. Freiligrath replied gratefully, speaking of the monotony of business life and regretting that 'the City lies far from Parnassus'.[74] An exchange of letters then took place from which it is clear that Bulwer took some trouble to try to place Freiligrath in either an academic or a civil service position which would be financially secure and also leave him free to write. Freiligrath had hopes of a chair of German or a position as curator of a library or museum, or at least a regular reviewing job with a reputable journal. Bulwer's reply was disheartening for him, but shows both how hard he was trying to help Freiligrath and how difficult it was in practice for an educated refugee to find a position which suited him, even when he had influential Englishmen to turn to, and when the competition for jobs among fellow refugees was much less than it was to be after 1848.

Bulwer wrote to Freiligrath on 20 May 1847:

> Of the various ideas you suggest, I think those which refer to literary labour are the most feasible. Let us look at them all seriatim.
>
> Professorship of German Literature at an University. I fear that no such professorship exists at Oxford or Cambridge. At the last (the more politically liberal of the two) German *tuition*, attended with public lectures, sanctioned by the Heads of the University, might however assume the dignity of an endowed and regular Professorship and procure you an honourable and adequate maintenance with all requisite social consideration . . . King's College and the London University [i.e. University College] *may* have German professorships, but is there any vacancy? Or likely to be one?[75]

Both University College and King's College in London had had German chairs from the beginning. The former had, in 1828, appointed an early political exile, Ludwig von Mühlenfels, who had fled from Prussian arrest for his Burschenschaft activities in 1821. Mühlenfels had been enabled to return to Germany in 1831, and the chair lapsed, though there were two teachers of German language at the College during the 1830s and 1840s. At King's College, Adolphus Bernays, author of German grammar books, was professor from 1831, when the College opened, to 1863. Oxford and Cambridge had as yet no German chairs. Even private tuition in the latter two universities was difficult to get: Fontane, more 'respectable' politically than Freiligrath, and with Ambassador Bunsen using his influence for him, failed to obtain a tutorship in Oxford in 1852.[76]

To Freiligrath's notion of trying for library work, Bulwer's reply is interesting, throwing light on certain differences between England and Germany. Firstly, he notes that there are few vacancies in public libraries and museums, and that such vacancies are much sought after. (It was an Italian republican exile, Antonio Panizzi, who was Keeper of Printed Books at the British Museum at this time.) As to private libraries, Bulwer points out:

> Very few indeed amongst us [i.e. the English aristocracy] have collections that warrant a librarian. Public men, it is true, have secretaries—usually their own relations, party politicians, whose researches are amongst statistics and Parliamentary Debates &c. It is a defect *perhaps necessary* to free Constitutions under a Representative system, that the more intellectual of the Aristocracy turn towards the practical ambition of public life—the heats and contests of party,

rather than to letters and the Arts. Few amongst the Great are the elegant and thoughtful Scholars, which Despotisms rear amongst an educated Nobility; the princes of Continental Europe might vie with each other to afford a Home to Voltaire; in England they would say, if Voltaire were living now and wanted a Home; 'He has not even a vote for a borough!'

Finally, reviewing German literature for the *Foreign Quarterly Review* or some such publication might be a possibility, but would hardly yield an adequate income on its own. Bulwer ends his long and helpful letter with a promise to ask Professor Whewell at Cambridge for help there, and mentions such London literary personalities as Lewes, John Forster, and Abraham Hayward (translator of *Faust* in the 1830s and now editor of the *Law Magazine*), as possible contacts for Freiligrath.[77]

In spite of Bulwer's efforts, Freiligrath succeeded in none of the fields discussed in their letters, though during his second stay in England, after 1851, he did do some writing for the *Athenaeum*. To Freiligrath's subsequent request for a reference for some kind of civil service post, Bulwer responded that Freiligrath should 'by all means' use his name 'with Lord P.', but he anticipated a political objection to Freiligrath's joining the Foreign Office. Freiligrath seems to have been unable, too, to put into practice his plan for a volume of his poetry to be translated by Mary Howitt with an introduction by Milnes or Carlyle (it was Bulwer who suggested them).[78] The one introduction which Bulwer arranged which bore fruit—though not for some time—was that to the German bookseller in London, Bernhard Tauchnitz. In 1861 Freiligrath edited a volume in Tauchnitz's 'Collection of British Authors': it was an edition of Coleridge's poetry, with a biographical introduction by Freiligrath.

With all this activity on his behalf, it is likely that Freiligrath would eventually have found something which suited him. Soon after his arrival in London, he had shaved off his beard—always an index of a refugee's willingness to conform and merge into the host society, at least until British soldiers began returning to England from the Crimea with beards, which then became the fashion. In April 1847 he wrote to a friend in Germany that he had met Milnes, Tennyson, Bulwer, and other notables, and that he had recently been at a soirée given by the President of the Royal Society, Lord Northampton, where he met Chevalier Bunsen—'bestarred and beribboned, smooth and obese like a Christian German eel'—and even Prince Albert himself.[79]

But in the same letter he complained that his tiredness after long days in the office and the great distances one had to travel in London kept him away from London society on the whole. Amely Bölte reported to

Varnhagen von Ense that Freiligrath was really rather discontented with his lot. Her remarks are somewhat malicious, but probably contain some truth:

> Freiligrath is not very happy here, and finds that tyranny in Germany was far less oppressive than the social pressures here. Among the Germans in London [i.e. the community of well-off Germans established in banks and businesses] he finds no approval. They are all busy making money and they think him a fool for having given up a secure position at home in order to sing songs of liberty which have never contributed to the improvement of any state . . . Instead of respect, admiration, and recognition he finds everywhere the opposite, and this wounds him deeply; for though he sings about communism and praises the proletariat, nevertheless it would flatter his vanity if London took notice of him, which it doesn't.[80]

Amely Bölte herself made Freiligrath's life in London even harder when her foolish gossip in Cotta's *Morgenblatt* led to his losing his job with Huth at the end of 1847. She had written that Freiligrath was overworked and underpaid by Huth. When Freiligrath was sacked, she was overcome by guilt, and got Monckton Milnes to help him financially. Soon, however, she decided that Freiligrath's own politics and Bunsen's pernicious influence had been to blame. (The one thing which seemed to unite Germans in London—no matter what their politics—was hatred of Bunsen.[81])

Thus by the beginning of 1848 Freiligrath was out of the job which he hated but which kept his growing family, and he had not found a niche in literary circles. At this point he began asking Longfellow to push for him in America. But just as it seemed that he had completely given up thinking political thoughts and writing political poetry (he wrote only three poems during this time in London—one on Ireland and two translations from English, including one of Thomas Hood's famous 'Song of the Shirt'), the February Revolution occurred in Paris, and Freiligrath was once more politicized. Unlike Engels and Weerth, he had written very little about the evils of industrial England. The nearest he had got to social criticism, apart from translating Hood's poems, was a rather lofty dramatized reference in a letter to his having passed through Shoreditch with its 'miseries and sins' on the way back from the glittering soirée at Lord Northampton's.[82] Now the fact that Freiligrath had no job in England made it easier for him to return to Germany, as he did in May 1848, to work for the revolutionary side.

Freiligrath now became a hero of the revolution. He shouldered no arms, but he published poetry in Marx's *Neue Rheinische Zeitung*, including an inflammatory poem 'Die Todten an die Lebenden' ('The Dead to the Living'), for which he was arrested in September 1848. The poem had included a vision of the (Prussian) throne going up in flames, the princes fleeing, and the people becoming sovereign. It was immediately popular; 9,000 copies were sold; and Freiligrath was prosecuted for incitement to revolt against the state. On this occasion, among others, the Rhineland jury, taking a leaf out of the book of many an English jury, acquitted. Freiligrath was borne from the Düsseldorf court shoulder-high, and made for Cologne, where Marx and Engels welcomed him back to the editorial board of the *Neue Rheinische Zeitung*, which had been suspended during Freiligrath's arrest and trial. Freiligrath was now their star contributor. For a few months in 1848–9 the little group of Cologne communists worked happily together to produce their journal. Weerth wrote on English Chartism; Marx and Engels discussed German politics as they were being played out, farcically as Marx reported, in Frankfurt; Müller-Tellering, not yet an implacable enemy, sent correspondence from Vienna; and Freiligrath provided the popularity and the poetry. Marx was twice acquitted by Cologne juries of offences connected with the journal.[83] But by May 1849 the authorities had won the battle. The paper was prohibited, warrants went out for the arrest of most of the participants, and the contributors fled from Cologne. Though Freiligrath featured prominently in the last number of all, the May issue printed in red, with his poem 'Abschiedsworte' ('Words of Farewell'), the authorities thought it prudent not to arrest him. So it was Freiligrath who stayed behind in Cologne, winding up the affairs of the *Neue Rheinische Zeitung*, while Engels went to fight in Willich's regiment, Marx fled to Paris, from which he was soon expelled to London, Weerth went to Brussels, then London, and Wilhelm Wolff fled to two years of poverty in Switzerland.

Freiligrath used his (temporarily) unassailable position as a popular poet and celebrated public figure to act as helper and mediator between his scattered friends and colleagues. On 29 May 1849 he asked Johanna Kinkel, who was editing the *Bonner Zeitung* in the absence of her husband, even then fighting with Willich and Engels against Prussian troops, if she could take on one of the *Neue Rheinische Zeitung*'s redundant typesetters. He also undertook to tell the Cologne family of the London watchmaker and Communist League member, Joseph Moll, of his death in the Baden uprising. In a letter to Wilhelm Wolff of October 1849, he reported on the plights of their various colleagues: Schapper was in prison in Wiesbaden awaiting trial for his communist activities, his wife having just died after bearing her fifth child; Freiligrath was looking after the eldest Schapper daughter, who had infected two of his own children with scarlet fever; Ferdinand Wolff (known as 'Rufus') and Dronke were almost starving in Paris; Marx was now in London, and hard up. Only Weerth was in relatively good circumstances—'the fellow is said to be making an incredible amount of money in Australian wool and rabbit skins'.[84]

Though his friends had high hopes for him, Freiligrath realized that if he wanted to stay in Germany, he must not tax the authorities' patience with further popular insurrectionary verses. He lay low in Cologne, then in Düsseldorf from June 1850, and published no more poetry for the time being. The police watched him; a Düsseldorf sculptor named Grass was expelled from the city for engraving a model of Freiligrath, the 'poet of the people'.[85] But he, too, was hard up; Amely Bölte visited him in Cologne in December 1849 and found him 'much altered' —poorer and more left-wing in his views.[86] He stuck it out until May 1851, when he repeated the pattern of 1844, by absconding to London on the eve of publication of a new volume of political poetry: *Neuere Politische und Soziale Gedichte* (*New Political and Social Poems*).

Freiligrath's motives in returning to London may have been mixed. For one thing, it was all very well being a popular poet in Germany, but frustrating not to be able to publish one's popular poems. For another, he had no secure income. As he wrote to Longfellow on his arrival in London, 'There is no liberty of the press more in Germany—so much so, that, if I print up my new things, I may be sure to be imprisoned, and that, if I print them not, I can starve. Rather a difficult position for a man who depends entirely upon his pen.'[87] Moreover, all his colleagues from the Cologne Communist League had found their way to London by now. Kinkel's example was a heartening one from the point of view of showing it was possible to achieve success in London, for Kinkel had escaped from prison in Spandau in November 1850 and was reputed to be doing very well in England. Might not Freiligrath himself return to England better known since his own trial? Certainly, his case received some notice in England. Lewes's and Hunt's *Leader* carried an article in February 1851 headed 'Pleasures of Prussian Citizenship. The impending Expulsion of the Poet Freiligrath.' The article gave an account of his trial and acquittal, and claimed that the Prussian authorities were illegally refusing to renew his passport. Again on 3 May 1851, a week before Freiligrath's flight to London, the *Leader* drew attention to his plight. Finally, Freiligrath may have got wind of the fact that the

Prussian police, which had been amassing evidence, some of it fabricated by spies, about the Cologne Communist League, was on the point of making mass arrests.[88]

On his return to London, Freiligrath faced, if anything, greater difficulties than on his first arrival in 1846. English friends again helped him to find a banking job. His fellow clerk Andrew Johnson put him up until he found accommodation. His family came over in September 1851, and they settled in Hackney, at that time a pleasant semi-rural area inhabited by people who worked in the City.[89] But despite this, and though it must have been flattering for him to be wooed, as Kinkel had been six months before, by the various groups of German refugees who had gathered in London during his absence, he soon found that he was being drawn into petty quarrels of little interest to him. Summer 1851 was the time when new German clubs and newspapers were being launched in deadly competition with one another: Ruge set up his German Agitation Club in August, and promptly asked Freiligrath to join. Kinkel's rival Emigration Club had been founded in July. Marx looked on spitefully at this 'war between the frogs and the mice', and naturally expected Freiligrath to remain loyal to him and their other *Neue Rheinische Zeitung* friends. Ruge had addressed Freiligrath from Brighton on 4 July: 'We are projecting a kind of club or union which will suspend all private concerns and will exclude no one from the revolutionary social democratic party except anyone who wants to be exclusive and who has made himself impossible by his character and antecedents'. This 'anyone' was, of course, Marx. Freiligrath refused to join, showing Ruge's letter and his own reply to Marx, who in turn sent both letters to Engels, complaining of Freiligrath's 'smarmy' way of being polite in his refusal.[90] Meanwhile, Freiligrath embarked on the impossible task of keeping aloof from the squabbles and falling out with no one, while he tried to get on with earning a living once more. As Herzen noted shrewdly, Freiligrath, a man of 'gentle disposition', 'hid behind' the fact of his City work and of his home being far from the other exiles, who were clustered mainly in Soho or the St John's Wood area. Friedrich Althaus, in his reminiscence of the 'German colony' in England in 1873, thought that Freiligrath's main aim was to settle down in England and work hard to give his family financial security; he quoted from the poem Freiligrath wrote on his first journey of 1846, 'To England', in which Freiligrath had addressed himself as 'wage-earner and poet'.[91]

If Engels lived a double life, as communist and capitalist, Freiligrath's way of coping with his situation was to attempt, chameleon-like, to merge with whichever society he found himself in. Thus his letters to Marx and Engels in the early 1850s, when he was engaged in helping Marx to build the defence case, and wage the propaganda war, on behalf of the arrested Cologne communists, show Freiligrath as tough, committed, adopting the tone of *bonhomie*, camaraderie, and crude satire of opponents which characterize Marx's and Engels's correspondence. In particular, he joined in their denigration of Kinkel, resenting, as they did, the Kinkel 'cult' which existed in London in 1851. As he wrote to Marx in July:

> The Kinkel cult is in its prime, according to a Swabian who recently visited the great man. The two adjutants: Schurz the liberator and Furz the biographer ['Furz' means 'fart', and refers to Adolf Strodtmann, admirer and recent biographer of Kinkel] swing the censer, Princess Lieven [wife of a Russian diplomat and thought by many, including Marx, to be a spy] sprinkles the incense, and Johanna sings the psalm of praise. Damned conceit![92]

But the satirical tone did not come naturally to Freiligrath. Though he helped, out of a sense of duty to his imprisoned Cologne colleagues, to administer the relief fund for their families (his carefully kept account book shows a contribution from the Bermondsey Chartists of 1*s*. 6*d*.[93]), he was unable to satisfy Marx's desire to use him as the *poet* of the London communists. Marx urged him to write something for his friend Joseph Weydemeyer's new paper, *Die Revolution*, in New York. What was wanted was an attack on Kinkel, particularly on Kinkel's ill-fated money-raising tour of America from September 1851 to March 1852. Marx flattered and bullied Freiligrath into producing a satirical poem on the subject, but Freiligrath admitted to having had difficulties. He had 'thrown perhaps a dozen stanzas down on paper' by 12 January 1852, but found they contained 'nothing but personal malice, which isn't true poetry'. He managed to produce the poem, 'To Joseph Weydemeyer', but was clearly unhappy with it, for he never reprinted it in collections of his works. His proper vein in poetry, as Marx knew and Heine pointed out with a superior smile, was the grandiosely declamatory, the vaguely spiritually rousing, which had been so successful in 1848–9, not the sharply satirical, which was now required.[94] Freiligrath may also have felt some shame at ridiculing Kinkel's loan venture when he knew that Marx had tried much the same thing himself. In January 1850 Marx had written to Freiligrath in Cologne asking him to collect money to send Conrad Schramm, a colleague who had been imprisoned for his part in the revolution but had escaped to London in September 1849, on a money-raising mission to America. Freiligrath had replied wryly that he was having no success with 'the collection for the collection', and the plan was dropped.[95]

Freiligrath wrote nothing more for Marx's party. As early as July 1852 he answered a request from the Leipzig publisher Brockhaus for a résumé of his life, explaining that though he still 'held fast to the Revolution', he did not think it necessary to join in the 'self-aggrandizing' and the 'market cries' of the German emigration in London. A 'very happy family life' was his chief concern now. He used his poetic vocation as an excuse—to Marx as well as to Ruge—not to get entangled in political wrangles. His desire was to remain 'unbefangen' ('impartial') so as to be true to himself as a poet. When Marx tried in 1859 to enlist Freiligrath's aid in a complicated propaganda war against Karl Vogt, an exile in Switzerland who had attacked the communists, Freiligrath stayed aloof. As he wrote to a friend in Düsseldorf: 'There is nothing more hateful to me than such frictions between cliques. They are all one needs to make exile, without them so sweet, even sweeter!'[96] In a way, this was a return to his early position before 1844, when he had thought the poet stood above 'the battlements of party'. Marx saw that Freiligrath could not be counted on, but he kept friendly because he 'liked the chap', and because he needed to have Freiligrath on his side, or at least not on the opponents' side, in the squabbles with the Willich group of communists and the Kinkel and Ruge bourgeois radical circles. He also found Freiligrath's City connections 'indispensable' at times in arranging loans for him.[97] Probably the last friendly gesture on Marx's part was his presentation of a copy of his *Zur Kritik der Politischen Oekonomie* (*Contribution to the Critique of Political Economy*), published in Berlin in 1859, to Freiligrath with the inscription 'To his friend F. Freiligrath, K. Marx, London, August 1859'. The copy, now in the library at the London School of Economics, bears a further inscription, but not in Marx's hand. Just underneath the original dedication one reads 'Given to me by Freiligrath, as "unreadable for him," Karl Blind'.

Freiligrath's friendship with Marx could not last. Freiligrath took Mrs Marx to the theatre in 1852, as we have seen; in September of the same year Mrs Freiligrath fetched free medicine for Mrs Marx from the German Hospital in Dalston (established in 1845 on Bunsen's initiative to provide free medical care for the large numbers of poor Germans working as sugar-bakers, furriers, and skin-dressers in the East End[98]); Freiligrath helped Marx's friend Pieper get a tutoring job with a businessman from Mexico in 1854; he was generous with his time and money when an impoverished refugee, Louis Heilberg, was taken into hospital, and his wife and children had to be cared for. Freiligrath's five children were friendly with Marx's daughters: a letter of Marx's to Freiligrath in January 1852 encloses 'a *billet* from Miss Jenny to Master Wolfgang'. But Freiligrath also began to cultivate friendly relations with Kinkel. He appears to have attended a Lord Mayor's Banquet with Kinkel in July 1853.[99] By 1855 Kinkel and Freiligrath were visiting one another's houses; in 1859 they joined forces with Karl Blind to arrange a Schiller centenary festival at Crystal Palace—an event derided by Marx. When Johanna Kinkel died in 1858, Freiligrath wrote a poem which was read at her graveside. Marx noted bitterly that he had written nothing to commemorate deaths in 'his own party', such as that of the Cologne communist Roland Daniels. And Freiligrath was best man at Kinkel's second wedding in 1860. Though Freiligrath felt somewhat uneasy in Kinkel's company—he 'can't help going on stilts', he complained to Ruge in 1866, using the same expression as Herzen in a letter to Malwida von Meysenbug some years earlier[100]—he found Kinkel easier to get on with than Marx. The tone of his letters to Kinkel has none of the roughness of his letters to Marx. Freiligrath became for Marx the 'fat philistine', the 'mercantile poet', and by 1866 Marx was applying the scatological language to Freiligrath which was so prominent a feature of his attack on Kinkel, Ruge, and the other 'great men of the exile' in 1852.[101]

Freiligrath was friendly not only with Kinkel, but also with such non-political Germans in London as the journalist Max Schlesinger, the oriental scholar at the British Museum, Emanuel Deutsch, and businessmen like Isidor Gerstenberg.[102] (Gerstenberg was the man who suggested, and put up much of the money for, a telegraphic cable between England and the Continent in 1851.) He must also have kept up some of his English acquaintances, though there is no evidence that he contacted either Bulwer or Milnes during his second stay in England. It was probably through the Howitts that he began writing on German subjects for the *Athenaeum* around 1855, and his hopes of surviving on literary earnings alone led him to give up his banking job in that year. He tried for a chair in America once more, and sounded out a friend, Dr Siegfried, in Dublin about a librarianship post, but nothing came of these efforts. In June 1856 he succumbed to another banking job, this time a well-paid post with the Swiss General Bank in London.[103]

As in 1846, Freiligrath came close to becoming established in the literary world of London, but did not quite manage it. The *Athenaeum* had been friendly to his works since 1841, when it carried a notice of the intention of Künzel and Freiligrath, 'one of the most original of the rising generation of German poets', to set up a periodical (*Britannia*) in Darmstadt to be devoted to English literature. The Howitts praised and translated his poems for the *Athenaeum* in 1843 and 1844, and they also drew attention to his excellent translations from the English Romantic poets. Inasmuch as Freiligrath's fame was spread at all in Britain, it was naturally on account of his translations rather than for his original poetry. He did not publish a volume of his verses in England, though his daughter Kate, who remained in England after her marriage to a German businessman based in London, edited *Poems from the German of Ferdinand Freiligrath*, which was published in 1870 by Bernhard Tauchnitz and warmly noticed in the faithful *Athenaeum.*[104] His poems were not only, as the *Athenaeum* reviewer pointed out, impossible to translate well; they were frankly second-rate. He rhymed excessively, internally as well as at the ends of lines (a habit which issued in some success in his translation of *The Ancient Mariner*); his rhetoric was lofty but vague and clichéd; and he indulged in heavy stresses and alexandrines, both of which are notoriously difficult to render in English without pathos or bathos. Freiligrath's poem of 1844, published in *Ein Glaubensbekenntnis*, 'Am Baum der Menschheit drängt sich Blüt' an Blüte', illustrates both the attractions and the limitations of his verse. William Howitt's decent translation of it in *German Experiences* (1844) is given here after the original:

Am Baum der Menschheit drängt sich Blüt' an Blüte,
Nach ew'gen Regeln wiegen sie sich drauf;
Wenn hier die eine matt und welk verglühte,
Springt dort die andre voll und prächtig auf.
Ein ewig Kommen und ein ewig Gehen,
Und nun und nimmer träger Stillestand!
Wir sehn sie auf, wir sehn sie niederwehen,
Und jede Blüte ist ein Volk, ein Land!

On manhood's tree springs crowding flower on flower;
By an eternal law they wave thereon.
As here one withereth in its final hour,
There springs another full and glorious one.
An ever coming and an ever going—
And never for one hour a sluggish stand!
We see them burst,—to earth then see them blowing,
And every blossom is a Folk—a Land![105]

Though one might not wish to be so cruel as Müller-Tellering, for whom Freiligrath had become an enemy for siding with Marx against him in 1850 and who abused him as a 'mayflower-and-buttercup poet, a Tyrtaeus lying in mud', and a versifier 'pensioned off by Cotta',[106] it is true that Freiligrath was more a versifier than a poet. He was well suited to firing off provocative poems in the *Neue Rheinische Zeitung*, and occasional verses such as those on the death of Johanna Kinkel, in which he waxed morosely lyrical about the 'battlefield of exile', or the poem to celebrate Schiller's centenary. It is perhaps not surprising, though, that during his uneventful life in London he found no inspiration or ability forthcoming. He shielded himself behind exile and daily routine; as he wrote to Longfellow in 1857: 'I am in good health and tolerable spirits; plodding at the Bank, writing for the *Athenaeum*, doing now and then a little in the way of rhyming; but alas very little! Business and London are too much for the *poet* Freiligrath.'[107]

As a translator, Freiligrath's achievement was more significant. He translated poems by Burns, Campbell, Scott, Wordsworth, Coleridge, Keats, Shelley, Moore, Byron, Hood, Mrs Hemans, Longfellow, Whitman, Tennyson, and others, publishing them separately in magazines from 1835 onwards and in groups in volumes also including his own poetry. His performance is uneven: Tennyson's *Locksley Hall* becomes even more of a mouthful in German than it is in English, and his version of Keats's sonnet on reading Chapman's *Homer* is very poor. Hood's *Song of the Shirt*, on the other hand, is both well and closely translated; and Freiligrath's greatest success is his rendering of *The Ancient Mariner*. He capitalizes on possibilities in German for internal rhyming, using it in verses where Coleridge does and also where Coleridge would have done if he could; for example:

Der Hochzeitgast fährt auf in Hast,
Er kann nicht von der Stelle.
Und so sprach dann der alte Mann,
Der graue Schiffsgeselle.

Vor bösen Geistern schütz' dich Gott,
Du alter Schiffsgenoss!
Was stierst du? — mit der Armbrust mein
Schoss ich den Albatros!

[The Wedding-Guest he beat his breast,
Yet he cannot choose but hear;
And thus spake on that ancient man,
The bright-eyed Mariner.

'God save thee, ancient Mariner!
From the fiends that plague thee thus!
Why look'st thou so?' With my cross-bow
I shot the Albatross.][108]

Coleridge became a special interest of Freiligrath's. While he was working on his biographical memoir of the poet for Tauchnitz in 1860, he became interested in why Coleridge's translation of *Wallenstein* in 1800 differed in some respects—not to be put down merely to 'free' (or bad) translation—from the published *Wallenstein* of Schiller. As he reported in the *Athenaeum* in May 1861, a German professor had just published for the first time 'the hitherto unknown stage manuscript' of Schiller's play, and this version coincided almost exactly with Coleridge's translation. Freiligrath wondered aloud whether the manuscript from which Coleridge translated was still in this country? This elicited a reply from James Gillman, son of the Dr Gillman who had supported Coleridge in his Highgate home during the last years of his life. Yes, the manuscript did exist; he had it. Freiligrath borrowed the work and collated it with the recently published stage version. Not only did they coincide, but Freiligrath thought he had found evidence that Schiller (or someone else) had prepared the manuscript Coleridge used specially for a foreign translator, as it was not written in German script. Could Schiller and Coleridge have corresponded on the subject? Might they have met when Coleridge was in Germany in 1798–9? This query brought no reply, though a Mr Henry Marks of Highbury wrote to say that he owned a manuscript copy of the second part of the *Wallenstein* trilogy, 'Die Piccolomini'. The correspondence ended there, somewhat inconclusively, but at least Freiligrath had done Coleridge the service of pointing out that his deviations from Schiller were an accident of publishing history rather than an act of wantonness.[109]

The biographical introduction Freiligrath wrote for Tauchnitz's volume of Coleridge's poetry in his 'Collection of British Authors' is a fine example of intelligence and affinity with one's subject. Freiligrath praises Coleridge as an 'inquiring spirit', a 'pilot', and a 'pioneer', as well as paying tribute to his wonderful gift for poetry. Coleridge, through his studying in Göttingen and his reading of the new German philosophy, was the first Englishman 'that ever burst / Into that silent sea':

. . . it was Coleridge, also, who first introduced Kant, and it was he, who first introduced Fichte and Schelling to the English nation; and although he did not carry on or diffuse their systems; nay, although, towards the close of his life, he even disclaimed them, and returned, a strict Trinitarian, into the bosom of the

Church of England: yet, what he has written upon metaphysical subjects, has proved highly suggestive to 'inquiring spirits' of a later generation. Much of the ferment in theology and philosophy, at present going on in England and America, originates in Coleridge.

As the *Westminster* reviewer of the volume pointed out, Freiligrath was the ideal author of such a memoir: Coleridge's 'intellectual obligations to German literature are here very properly alluded to, but by no means in that spirit of national exaggeration which would most probably have been the case with a less intelligent and well-informed editor'.[110]

In spite of Freiligrath's connection with the *Athenaeum*, he seems to have made little progress in becoming a man of letters. Perhaps the fact that the Howitts went bankrupt in 1852 after a foolish speculation and William Howitt went off to Australia in search of gold, returning disappointed at the end of 1854, contributed to Freiligrath's lack of success.[111] Maybe his connection with Marx and the German communists in London was known of, and disapproved of, by those who had previously befriended him. Again, the number of refugees from the Continent who came to England in the 1850s was so large that the relatively small group of sympathetic English men and women in a position to help them was probably too stretched to do much. Although, as Althaus pointed out in his memoir of the German exiles, Freiligrath was one of the few refugees 'who did not run down the country which gave them sanctuary',[112] he was not quite contented. If he wrote robustly to Marx and Engels, loftily to Kinkel, and as a naturalized 'Englishman' in his *Athenaeum* articles, he was capable of writing German national sentiment to friends in Germany. To Karl Buchner he wrote in 1857 that he found exile from home only just bearable:

> As for our children, of course they must become Englishmen in England. And that, if things remain as they are, is no bad thing! Even here there are social evils and oppression enough, but on the other hand there is freedom and national greatness, and the individual feels free and great as a part of the free and great whole! May they, then, make their own way as free citizens of a free country, and later—in the schoolroom or at their desks, on trains or in ships, in Australia or at the Cape or in India—forget that their father was a bit of a German poet and gave them, through his renunciation of his homeland, a great new homeland.[113]

The effort to be fair to England's greatness, and the involuntary recognition that his children's horizons are as wide as the expanding English empire (Johanna Kinkel noticed with excitement that English people, unlike Germans, could talk of having relatives in

Australia, India, or Egypt[114]), vie with self-dramatizing and nascent nationalism.

Ten years after this, Freiligrath was preparing to return to a Prussia proud of its rising status as a great power, conqueror of Austria, and soon to be victor in the Franco-Prussian War. Freiligrath found his poetic voice again in writing patriotic poems celebrating Prussia's victory in the Austro-Prussian War of 1866. One of these, 'A Westphalian Summer Song', which his daughter Kate translated for the *Athenaeum*, prompted Marx to refer to the more ignoble bodily functions: 'Freiligrath has dropped a little melancholy lyrical turd on the "war between brothers"', he told Engels in July 1866.[115] Later, when his oldest son Wolfgang voluntarily left England to join the Prussian army fighting the French, and so gave the lie to Freiligrath's earlier prediction about his becoming an Englishman, Freiligrath was moved to write a poem addressing him, 'An Wolfgang im Felde' ('To Wolfgang on the Battlefield'). Marx's sour comment on this was that Freiligrath was turning historic catastrophes to his own account by singing of his own 'brats'.[116] Only two years before, Wolfgang and his brother Otto had been visiting their good friend Eleanor Marx, though their fathers had long since ceased to communicate. And a few years before that, in August 1863, Freiligrath had written, rather awkwardly, to Marx to tell him that Wolfgang had just won 'three prizes and two honourable mentions' at University College School,[117] the school to which a number of exiles' sons went, as well as the sons of several German Jewish businessmen in London. (Like University College London, in which it was housed, the school was founded in the late 1820s to allow Jews, Roman Catholics, Nonconformists, and atheists to have a school education. The Freiligrath, Kinkel, Blind, and Althaus boys all attended UCS in the 1860s, most of them winning prizes, as did the sons and grandsons of Gerstenberg and Sir Isaac Goldsmid, one of the founders. English liberals and free-thinkers, such as Holyoake, Beesly, Professor Faraday, Thomas Hood, and Huxley, also sent their sons there.[118])

Though Freiligrath remained in Germany until his death in 1876, he made frequent visits to London, where both his daughters were married to German businessmen. His daughter Kate Kroeker, his two grandsons Bernhard and Hermann Wiens, and his own widow Ida Freiligrath are all buried together in Ladywell Cemetery in Brockley.[119] Though Freiligrath wrote less than either Engels or Weerth about English social and political life, he experienced various aspects of it as an exile who was also a literary man. And he contributed to Anglo-German culture by his translations. He was neither wedded to England nor critical of it, though he was disappointed at not being lionized. Unlike Engels and Weerth, he had a family to bring up, and he was not prepared, or not able, to sacrifice himself and his family to a particular political ideal. In any case, as Ruge had noticed with some astuteness in 1846, Freiligrath was 'a man of some depth; philosophically, he is not properly oriented, but he has an instinct for freedom'.[120] He showed the instinct in his two flights from Germany, and also in his partially successful attempt to keep clear of the 'market cries' of the bickering parties in London. In a poem called 'Hackney Downs' he celebrated its (and by implication his) apartness from the hustle and bustle of London, which included the squabbling German colonies of Soho and St John's Wood:

An der Weltstadt nördlichem Saum,
Fern von ihrem Gebrause,
Bei der Pappel, dem Ulmenbaum,
Ländlich steht meine Klause;
Liegt eine Wiese, genannt die Downs,
Grün und wallend dahinter,
Grünt im Schatten des Weissdornzauns
Lustig Sommer und Winter.
Dort im Grase, das wellig weht,
Weiden Füllen und Rinder;
Dorten wandelt der stille Poet,
Dort auch spielen die Kinder.

[On the northern edge of the metropolis, far from its hurly-burly, by poplar and elder in the countryside, there lies my hermitage. Behind there lies a meadow, known as the Downs, green and luxuriant. In summer and winter the meadow flourishes in the shadow of the whitethorn hedge. There in the grass that blows in waves, the foals and cattle graze. There the silent poet wanders, and there the children play.]

3
The Communist Intellectuals: Marx and his Party

Marx's Isolation in London

Of all the exiles who found their way to Britain after spells in France, Belgium, or Switzerland, Marx was the one who minded least either the loss of home, of the familiar, or the shock of the new and the strange. I can think of no nostalgic utterance in all his writings and correspondence. It is true that on one occasion, in 1861, he visited Berlin to ask for the renewal of his Prussian citizenship, which he had renounced in 1845 in Brussels to avoid being expelled at Prussia's request. He hoped to set up a journal with Lassalle, but their plans foundered and the Prussian authorities refused his request for a passport. However, the idea of returning to Germany had nothing to do with sentiment. He had been led to make the attempt because of his hopes of Lassalle as a (subordinate) colleague and expectations of greater press freedom after the announcement of an amnesty for political exiles in January 1861.[1] There is perhaps the slightest hint of fondness for Germany, possibly rather dissembled, in his uncharacteristic letter in 1866 to M. Lafargue, father of Paul Lafargue, who had recently become engaged to Laura Marx. Thanking M. Lafargue for a gift of wine, he added, showing also the social snobbery which surfaced occasionally (particularly where his daughters were concerned), 'As I come from a wine-growing area and am an ex-vineyard owner, I know very well how to appreciate wine.'[2]

Not that Marx was a convert to English ways, however. Unlike Johanna Kinkel in her happier moments, or Friedrich Althaus or Karl Tausenau or Ferdinand Wolff, who all became 'Englishmen', he felt little gratitude or warmth towards Britain. On the one occasion on which he applied for British nationality, in 1874, taking advantage of a recent relaxation of the regulations for aliens, he did so simply in order to be able to travel to German health spas without fear of being arrested. As we have seen, the request was turned down because Marx was by now known as the communist leader of the International.

Much has been said about Marx's isolation in England, and about his remaining largely unknown in Britain 'to the end of his life'.[3] The view needs modifying in two ways. Firstly, Marx was, at least in the early 1850s and in the mid 1860s after the founding of the International, in quite close contact with English journals and radical politicians. Secondly, Marx's relative isolation, particularly in the years in which he was working on *Capital*, was largely self-imposed. Marx himself boasted of living in 'complete retirement' in Soho as early as February 1851, for he was disillusioned with Harney's hob-nobbing with Ruge and the Schapper–Willich faction of the Communist League as well as with Marx and his friends. He rationalized his disappointment to Engels:

> I am greatly pleased by the public, authentic isolation in which we two, you and I, now find ourselves. It is wholly in accord with our attitude and our principles. The system of mutual concessions, half-measures tolerated for decency's sake, and the obligation to bear one's share of public ridicule in the party along with all these jackasses, all this is now over.[4]

But only a few days before, Wilhelm Pieper, the one friend Marx was seeing at this time, wrote Engels a note urging him to reply quickly to Marx's last letter expounding his theory of land rent. 'Marx leads a very retired life', wrote Pieper, 'his only friends being John Stuart Mill and Loyd [i.e. Marx was reading books by Mill, for there is no evidence that they knew one another], and whenever one goes to see him one is welcomed with economic categories in lieu of greetings.' Engels responded immediately with a casually enthusiastic letter to Marx: 'your new thing about land rent is absolutely right'.[5]

Marx's proud loneliness was a product both of his quarrelsome nature and need to lead (a need unfortunately shared by Willich, Ruge, Kinkel, and other heroes of the German revolution), and of the misfortune of his not having Engels in London with him after November 1850. The friends were caught in a bind. Marx still spoke 'very little English', as Engels reported to Dronke in July 1851, and so 'our connection with Harney and the Chartists' had made 'little headway'.[6] Perhaps Marx's somewhat longer connection with Ernest Jones was due partly to Jones's ability to speak German. At any rate, Engels could have given Marx valuable support in the battle against the German 'philistines' in London, and even more useful help in liaising with British Chartists and radicals. But Engels was obliged to go to Manchester to earn enough money to keep the Marx family and himself, after his and Marx's attempt to keep the *Neue Rheinische Zeitung. Politisch-ökonomische Revue* afloat had failed. Thus opportunities for work with English colleagues were lost. Another factor in the situation was Marx's family misfortune. The first letter Marx sent to Engels after the latter's removal to Manchester carried the news of the death of Marx's son Guido, 'our little gunpowder-plotter, Fawksy' (so named because he was born on 5 November 1849) on 19 November.[7]

Indeed, Marx's situation was often desperate in the early 1850s. By 1855 two infants had died, as well as the beloved Edgar, aged 8. Living in cramped conditions in densely populated Soho, where they shared a house at 28 Dean Street inhabited by thirteen people, including an Italian cook and an Italian confectioner, the Marx family were vulnerable to the outbreak of cholera in the summer of 1854. Marx wrote to Engels in September:

> *Dans ce moment* the total absence of money is the more horrible—quite apart from the fact that FAMILY WANTS do not ease for an instant—as Soho is a choice district for cholera, the MOB is croaking right and left (e.g. an average of 3 per house in Broad Street), and 'victuals' are the best defence against the beastly thing.[8]

Add to this Marx's being, as he wrote to (the spy) Hermann Ebner in August 1851, the chief butt of attacks by the London Germans and by the German-American press, and his gall at seeing the 'champion drivel' of Kinkel and others in the London-German paper *Kosmos*, which seemed to be succeeding in 1851 where his own paper had failed.[9] His hopes of Weydemeyer's New York journal *Die Revolution*, for which he dashed off his lively work on Louis Napoleon's *coup d'état*, *The Eighteenth Brumaire of Louis Bonaparte*, in December 1851, and for which he drummed up the Kinkel poem from Freiligrath and articles from Engels and others, were also disappointed when the paper failed after two belated numbers in June 1852. He came close to self-pity in his account of his life to Weydemeyer in June 1851. While he worked every day at the British Museum, on 'damnably involved' material, 'from 9 in the morning until 7 in the evening', the 'democratic "SIMPLETONS" to whom inspiration comes "from above" need not, of course, exert themselves thus'. 'It's really all *so simple*, as the doughty Willich used to tell me', he continued in annoyance, 'All so simple to these addled brains!'[10]

It is hardly surprising that Marx's ready contempt for other would-be leaders of the German workers in London won him lifelong enemies. On his earliest visits to London with Engels before 1848 he had attacked the leadership of the Communist League and the German Workers' Education Association, set up by Karl Schapper in 1840. The workers had come under the influence of the talented but Messianic artisan, Wilhelm Weitling, who preached what Engels, in his *History of the Communist League* (1885), called 'primitive Christian Communism'. Marx discredited Weitling, who also advocated community of women and an immediate armed revolution by assorted bandits, at a meeting in Brussels in 1846.[11] It was the first of many confrontations among the German *émigrés* based in London between 'Gelehrte' ('scholars', or 'educated men') and 'Straubinger' (a term originally applied to the travelling journeymen of the Middle Ages, and now used to describe those followers of Weitling, and later Willich, who looked for a solution to social problems in the return to feudal small handicrafts).

When Marx came to London for good in August 1849, he found the German workers and communists without their leader Schapper, who was awaiting trial in Germany on a charge of high treason. However, Willich arrived in London in October, admired for his exploits in leading a revolutionary army in Baden, and a Willich-cult quickly grew up round the colourful 'Capitano', who lived a bachelor, army-style life in a commune, or 'barracks', and 'tippled gratis' in Schärttner's German pub in Long Acre. For the ousted Weitling's brand of communism, Willich now substituted, in Engels's words, 'a kind of communistic Islam'.[12] As before, the objection was to Willich's belief that a new revolution in Europe could be embarked on without delay. He plotted uselessly but publicly in the pubs and clubs, while Marx swotted privately in the British Museum in an attempt to chart and predict the right social and political conditions for the next revolution.

Willich became an attraction to be visited by curious Germans coming over to London for the Great Exhibition. Marx drew a caricature in 'The Great Men of the Exile' not unlike Dickens's tongue-in-cheek sketch of foreigners plotting revolution in back rooms in Soho:

> . . . when the burden and labour of the day, the dutiful inspection of the Exhibition and the other sights had been completed in the sweat of his brow, the German philistine could recover at his ease at the Hanau landlord of Schärttner or the Star landlord of Göhringer, with their beery cosiness, their smoke-filled fug and their public-house politics. Here 'one could meet the whole of the fatherland' and in addition all the greatest men of Germany could be seen gratis. There they all sat, the members of parliament, the deputies of Chambers, the generals, the club orators of the wonderful period of 1848 and 1849. . . . This was the place where for the price of a few bottles of extremely cheap wine the German citizen could discover exactly what went on at the most secret meetings of the European Cabinets. This was the place where he could learn to within a

minute when 'it would all start'. In the meantime one bottle after another was started and all the parties went home unsteadily but strengthened in the knowledge that they had made their contribution to the salvation of the fatherland. Never has the emigration drunk more and cheaper than during the period when the solvent masses of German philistines were in London.

Fontane, too, reported gleefully on his visits to '27 Long Acre' (Schärttner's pub), where he found Willich and his 'corps', pale and shabby, dreaming wild dreams and poring nostalgically over the past. 'You German governments', Fontane concluded, 'put aside your childish fear of such a hollow spectre, and don't pay an army of spies' to follow such 'pathetic goings on'. The threat to Germany from such men, as many a Prussian or Austrian spy also reported back, was nil.[13] The so-called 'Action Party' consisted of mere beer and bluster.

Marx devoted a disproportionate amount of time to exposing the ridiculousness of Willich and his followers, in letters to Ebner which found their way into German police files; in 'The Great Men of the Exile' (1852), for which another spy, Colonel Bangya, was supposed to be finding a publisher, but never did; in *Revelations Concerning the Communist Trial in Cologne* (published in Basle in 1853); and in a pamphlet on Willich entitled *The Knight of the Noble Consciousness*, published in 1854 in New York, where Willich now lived. Marx's motivation was partly jealousy of Willich's popularity, for a larger number of German workers had stayed with Willich and Schapper than had joined Marx's and Engels's faction in the splitting of the Communist League in September 1850, and partly annoyance at Willich's foolishness, which he felt brought the whole German colony in London into disrepute. This view, he might have been cheered to know, was endorsed by the Berlin police spy who reported on the aftermath of the split:

. . . the Willich/Schapper party has never been particularly notable for unity; its meetings were the occasion for the most unpleasant scenes; they hurled accusations at each other and the disreputable activities of their leaders as well as the wildness of their plans and ventures has gradually discredited them even among the supporters of communism, so that more recently members of the League have tended to look more to the former leaders Marx and Engels . . . the Marx Party stands head and shoulders above all the *émigrés*, agitators and Central Committees because it is indisputably in possession of much greater knowledge and qualities of mind. Marx himself is personally known, and it is evident that he has more brains in his little finger than all the rest have in their heads.[14]

Marx used, or misused, his superior intelligence in writing satirically, often in mock-heroic vein as the title of his pamphlet on Willich indicates, about the petty exploits of the little men of the exile. His was the problem which generally faces the writer of mock epic: how to ridicule one's opponents by the satisfying application of grandiose names for petty doings without running the risk of paying so much attention to them as to make them seem more significant than they are. No doubt Marx was letting off necessary steam; he enjoyed finding literary nicknames and allusions for people and events (for this he used Dante, Shakespeare, Dickens, Pope, and Heine most often[15]); and, as we have seen, he was not one for writing briefly on any subject. But he had a sense of grievance not merely personal against Willich in 1851–2, for the police prosecuting Marx's communist friends in Cologne in 1852 used material gleaned from Willich's mad, boastful scheming in order to incriminate the defendants. They seized on Willich's own sense of the importance of his plans to suggest to the court a serious threat to the Prussian state, a threat which they knew, as their secret reports show, did not exist.[16]

Nevertheless, Marx allowed himself to be deflected more than once from his chosen course of study and publication to join the hurly-burly of recriminatory polemics with his enemies. His pamphlet *Herr Vogt* (1860), replying to accusations by Karl Vogt (in Switzerland) that Marx kept money supposedly raised for revolutionary causes, took over a year to write and ended up as a book of nearly two hundred pages. Marx had affidavits sworn before a London magistrate's court and got involved in lawsuits for libel against the Berlin *National Zeitung* and the *Daily Telegraph*, which had repeated accusations from the German press. Karl Blind and another exile, Karl Heinrich Schaible, a teacher and journalist in London, were also involved in what was really an affair of personal malice rather than political differences, though Marx's accusation that Vogt was in Louis Napoleon's pay was later shown to be true. Marx's suit against the *Daily Telegraph* was dismissed for lack of evidence. He had written to the editor on 6 February 1860 demanding a retraction 'for the recklessness with which you dare vilify a man of whose personal character, political past, literary productions, and social standing, you cannot but confess to be utterly ignorant'. The paper was unrepentant and named its solicitors.[17]

The affair prompted Marx to seek advice on what to do from two Englishmen with whom he had earlier had contact. One was C. D. Collet, who edited the *Free Press*, a paper to which Marx had contributed in the mid 1850s and which supported the fanatical David Urquhart in his crusade against Palmerston and Russia, in whose pay he thought Palmerston was. (Marx knew Urquhart was 'an utter maniac' and 'a romantic reactionary', but he shared Urquhart's hatred of Russia and something of his conspiracy theory of history.[18]) Collet told him to get a lawyer, but predicted that the *Telegraph* would not budge: 'Of course you recollect seeing its ungentlemanly libel on Mr. Urquhart and its equally ungentlemanly retraction. They disavowed the slander but would not give up the slanderer.'[19] In fact Marx had already sought legal advice from Ernest Jones, with whom he had broken off relations nearly two years earlier. Marx appears to have written to Jones to ask his legal opinion of whether to go to law, for Jones replied, half in German and addressing Marx with the familiar 'Du', on 10 February 1860. He invited Marx to visit him the next evening and 'make me au fait with the whole affair'. Probably at Marx's prompting during their meeting, Jones then wrote an apparently spontaneous letter dated 11 February and addressed to Marx, in which he strongly took Marx's part in the whole Vogt business:

> My dear Marx
>
> I have read a series of infamous articles against you in the National Zeitung, and am utterly astonished at the falsehood and malignity of the writer. I really feel it a duty that every one who is acquainted with you should, however unnecessary such a testimony must be, pay a tribute to the worth, honor & disinterestedness of your character. It becomes doubly incumbent in me to do so, when I recollect how many articles you contributed to my little Magazine, the 'Notes to the People,' & subsequently to the 'Peoples Paper,' for a series of years, utterly gratuitously . . .

Marx was able to use this letter of Jones's as an appendix to *Herr Vogt*, in vindication of his character.[20]

When we turn to consider Marx's contacts with English radicals during the 1850s, we have to do so against a background of difficulties and failures which were not entirely of his own making. He had hardly any success in getting his works published, or if they were published, they often did not circulate widely. Thus 'The Great Men of the Exile', entrusted to Colonel Bangya, did not get published until it was included in the Russian edition of Marx's works in 1930. *The Eighteenth Brumaire* was published in New York in the short-lived *Revolution* in 1852, but only a few hundred copies found their way into Germany, and no German publisher would touch it until 1869. Pieper translated it (badly) into English in 1852, and Engels corrected the translation, but no

English publisher was found. In the same year Marx produced his *Revelations Concerning the Communist Trial in Cologne*, which he obviously wanted to reach a German audience. It was published in Basle, but was confiscated at the Swiss–German border, as Jenny Marx wrote bitterly to Adolf Cluss in Washington in March 1853. Finally, *Herr Vogt*, which had taken so long to write and which again could have been of interest only in Germany, was never distributed in that country.[21] Marx's attempts to set up German-language journals in London failed. Their fate was not much different from that of rival German papers or the English journals begun by radicals like Linton, Harney, and Jones, though Kinkel's paper *Hermann*, set up in 1859, against which Marx started the rival *Volk*, lasted for several years.

Yet Marx wrote many articles over the years which did reach an audience, particularly those which he, and Engels for him, sent to Dana of the *New York Daily Tribune*, who published them anonymously and often as editorial leaders. His output, in spite of his wasting his energies on *émigré* polemics, most of which interested few readers and reached even fewer, was huge. It is true that he was the only one among the German exiles who never went out teaching or tailoring to make a living for himself and his family. Only once, in 1862 when he was particularly desperate, did he propose exchanging the British Museum for a railway office, but he was turned down for the job of clerk because of his illegible handwriting.[22] It follows that Marx's journalistic work, on English affairs as well as the too-engrossing topics of Willich, Kinkel, Ruge, and other 'mice and frogs', was more voluminous than that of any other exile.

Marx on England and the English

During his first year in England, from August 1849 to autumn 1850, Marx was, understandably, chiefly concerned with writing articles for his and Engels's continuation of the *Neue Rheinische Zeitung*, and with carrying on the battle against Willich for the hearts and minds of the German workers and communists in London. One of his first articles on English topics was the review, written jointly with Engels, of Carlyle's *Latter-Day Pamphlets* (1850). Engels had already praised Carlyle's criticism of social conditions and political do-nothingism in *Past and Present*, though he had rejected Carlyle's neo-feudalism. Now Carlyle exhibited, according to Engels and Marx, 'the decline of literary genius in historical struggles which have reached a point of crisis'. For in *Latter-Day Pamphlets* Carlyle had submerged his sympathy for the poor in a hysterical cry for strong rulers to come forth and govern them, even if the whip and the gun were needed to force the three million 'vagrant Lackalls and Good-for-nothings' to 'obey, work, suffer, abstain'. Marx and Engels related Carlyle's hero-worship to the cult of genius to be found in Fichte and other German philosophers whom Carlyle, as they knew, had read. Then they wittily showed that Carlyle's 'pantheistic mode of thinking' (also inspired by his German reading) had led him to believe in the process of history as determined 'not by the development of the living masses themselves', but 'by an eternal law of nature'. For Carlyle, they concluded, the 'historically produced distinction between classes thus becomes a natural distinction which itself must be acknowledged and revered as a part of the eternal law of nature, by bowing to nature's noble and wise: the cult of genius'.

As for Carlyle's fury at the new 'model prisons', in which the undeserving poor were better fed and housed than the deserving poor in hovels or workhouse, Marx and Engels deliberately speculated *ad absurdum*:

> Just as in the first pamphlet ['The Present Time'] Carlyle erects a complete hierarchy of Nobles and seeks out the Noblest of the Noble, so here ['Model Prisons'] he arranges an equally complete hierarchy of scoundrels and villains and exerts himself in hunting down the *worst of the bad*, the *supreme scoundrel* in England, for the exquisite pleasure of hanging him. Assuming he were to catch him and hang him; then another will be our Worst and must be hanged in turn and then another again, until the turn of the Noble and then the More Noble is reached and finally no one is left but Carlyle, the Noblest, who as persecutor of scoundrels is at once the murderer of the Noble and has murdered what is noble even in the scoundrels; the Noblest of the Noble, who is suddenly transformed into the Vilest of scoundrels and as such must *hang himself.* With that, all questions concerning government, state, the organisation of labour, and the hierarchy of the Noble would be resolved and the eternal law of nature realised at last.[23]

The passage bears the stamp of Marx, with his love of following ideas to their extremes, of mentally turning the tables, as for example he had done when he gave his critique of Proudhon's *Philosophie de la Misère* the title *La Misère de la Philosophie* (1847).[24] It is excessive, of course. But Marx here points seriously to a tendency in the British to think of the class system, and of the government of the lower by the higher, as an immutable law, a *given.* This was his objection also to John Stuart Mill, who was far to the left of Carlyle in his political views, but who appeared to think of the capitalist mode of production as the norm, almost as a law of nature. The tailor Eccarius, under Marx's tutelage, wrote a refutation of Mill's political economy in 1869, *Eines Arbeiters Widerlegung der national-ökonomischen Lehren John Stuart Mill's* (*A Worker's Refutation of John Stuart Mill's Doctrine of Political Economy*), in which he accused Mill of hoping to remove the social injustices he saw and abhorred by moral pressure rather than by considering the possibility of changing the system.[25] Marx put his own position strikingly in his postscript of 1875 to the *Revelations Concerning the Communist Trial in Cologne.* Alluding indirectly to Kant, who claimed in the *Critique of Pure Reason* (1781) to have achieved a 'Copernican Revolution' in philosophical thinking with his argument that objects depend for their validity on the mind perceiving them rather than the other way round, Marx wrote tersely: 'The fact is that Society will not recover its equilibrium until it rotates around the sun of labour.'[26]

In his early articles on Britain Marx showed to the full his curious quality of mind and personality. The revolutionary poet Georg Herwegh had said of him that he 'would have been the perfect incarnation of the last scholastic'; his one-time mentor Moses Hess had noted that he combined 'the most profound philosophical earnestness with the most biting wit', that he was a 'fusion' of Rousseau, Voltaire, Holbach, Lessing, Heine, and Hegel. Marx himself declared in his daughter's album in 1867 that his motto was 'De omnibus dubitandum' (Engels's, entered in the same album in 1868, was 'take it easy'). More negatively, Heine himself is supposed to have said of Marx in 1851, 'When all is said and done, a man is very little if he is nothing but a razor.'[27]

Thus when he set out, with Engels, to explain to German readers of the *Neue Rheinische Zeitung* in 1850 the British class system as it was represented in politics, his tendency to think in opposites and in supervening stages, as well as his habit of finding literary analogies for political personalities, resulted in a highly characteristic, witty, but not quite apposite portrait of Sir Robert Peel, who had recently died:

> . . . the statesmanship of this son of the bourgeoisie who rose to be leader of the landed aristocracy consisted in the realisation that nowadays there remains only one real aristocracy, and that is the bourgeoisie. Having this in mind, he continually used his leadership of the landed aristocracy to force it to make concessions to the bourgeoisie. Thus it was with the Catholic emancipation and the police reform, by which he increased the political power of the bourgeoisie; with the bank laws of 1818 and 1844, which strengthened the finance aristocracy; with the tariff reform of 1842 and the free-trade laws of 1846, by which the landed aristocracy was positively sacrificed to the industrial bourgeoisie. The second main pillar of the aristocracy, the 'Iron Duke', the hero of Waterloo,

stood like a disappointed Don Quixote loyally by the side of the cotton-knight Peel.[28]

This is almost to equate 'aristocracy' with 'Tories' (and, by implication, 'bourgeoisie' with 'Whigs') and to ignore the complicated history of Roman Catholicism in Britain and its crossing of class boundaries. As with Engels and Weerth earlier, such thinking is probably partly the genuine view of a German educated in Hegelian philosophy and partly that combination of wishful thinking and exaggerated propaganda with which the German communist observers sought to persuade German readers that English social revolution was just round the corner.

Even for American and English readers, Marx pressed the same point. In August 1852 he wrote an article on the Chartists in the *New York Daily Tribune*, part of which was later published in Ernest Jones's *People's Paper.* Adapting Hegel's view of history to suit his own preferred timetable, he wrote of the British bourgeoisie as having the aristocracy as their 'vanishing opponent' and the working class as their 'arising enemy':

> They [the bourgeoisie] cannot avoid fulfilling their mission, battering to pieces Old England, the England of the Past; and the very moment when they will have conquered exclusive political dominion, when political dominion and economical supremacy will be united in the same hands, when, therefore, the struggle against capital will no longer be distinct from the struggle against the existing government—from that very moment will date the *Social revolution of England.*

The upshot of this social revolution would be '*the political supremacy of the working* class'.[29] In the meantime, as Marx went on to explain, the working class voted for its leaders in the show of hands at elections, but had no vote in the poll. He quoted Ernest Jones's election speech at the recent election in Halifax. Standing as the Chartist candidate, Jones was nominated by the unrepresented crowd, but did not get the seat. Jones's speech is interesting, as will be seen, because it suggests that Marx was exercising an influence on him at this time. Certainly, their relationship was quite close in 1851–2.

Marx and Engels wrote articles, at first mainly on European politics, in both Harney's and Jones's Chartist journals. By the end of 1851, however, Marx was disillusioned with Harney, whose Fraternal Democrats were associating with Ruge, Mazzini, Kossuth, and other refugees whose views were non- or anti-communist. Marx was invited by John Pettie, an English representative of the Fraternal Democrats, to a banquet in December 1851, but he had no desire to fraternize with 'the Harney clique' and the other great men of the exile. He and Engels transferred their allegiance to Jones, who was German-educated and German-speaking, having been born in Berlin the son of Major Jones, equerry to the Duke of Cumberland.[30] Jones was also, according to Jenny Marx, a 'marvellous' lecturer, 'and, by English standards, advanced, though not quite *à la hauteur* for us Germans who have run the gauntlet of Hegel, Feuerbach, etc.' Marx, too, praised Jones's ability as a lecturer, and Engels reported to Dronke in July 1851 that Jones 'is wholly on our side and is at present expounding the [*Communist*] *Manifesto* to the English'.[31] (In fairness to the now denigrated Harney it should be said that he published the *Communist Manifesto*, translated by Helen Macfarlane, in *The Red Republican*, in November 1850.[32]) Marx got Jones to contribute to Weydemeyer's *Revolution* in March 1852. He and Engels observed the struggles of the Chartists at that time: O'Connor had 'definitely gone mad', Harney was selling out to middle-class interests, but Jones, according to Engels,

> is moving in quite the right direction and we may well say that, without our doctrine, he would not have taken the right path and would never have discovered how, on the one hand, one can not only maintain the only possible basis for the reconstruction of the Chartist party—the instinctive class hatred of the workers for the industrial bourgeoisie—but also enlarge and develop it, so laying the foundations for enlightening propaganda, and how, on the other, one can still be progressive and resist the workers' reactionary appetites and their prejudices.[33]

In 1864 Marx looked again at some of Jones's articles on economics in his *Notes to the People* in 1851 and 1852, and claimed that they 'had been written in the main points under my direction and in part even with my close participation'. Certainly, Jones's Halifax speech as reported by Marx in August 1852 bears witness that Jones had benefited from conversations with Marx on economics, though it shows signs of his having read Carlyle closely, too. Addressing the voters and non-voters, he gestured to his rivals, the Tory, the Whig, and the 'money-monger' (one of the so-called 'Manchester group' in favour of free trade and financial reform, led by Richard Cobden and John Bright):

> Whig, Tory, and money-monger are on my left, it is true, but they are all as one. The money-monger says, buy cheap and sell dear. The Tory says, buy dear, sell dearer. Both are the same for labour. . . . Labour is a hired commodity —labour is a thing in the market that is bought and sold; consequently, as labour

creates all wealth, labour is the first thing bought—'Buy cheap! buy cheap!' Labour is bought in the cheapest market. But now comes the next: 'Sell dear! sell dear!' Sell what? *Labour's produce*. To whom? To the foreigner—aye, and to *the labourer himself*—for labour, not being self-employed, the labourer is *not* the partaker of the first fruits of his toil. 'Buy cheap, sell dear.' How do you like it? 'Buy cheap, sell dear.' Buy the working man's labour cheaply, and sell back to that very working man the produce of his own labour dear! . . . Competition abroad is constantly increasing—consequently cheapness must increase constantly also. Therefore, wages in England must keep constantly falling. And how do they effect the fall? By *surplus labour*. How do they obtain the surplus labour? By monopoly of the land, which drives more hands than are wanted into the factory. By monopoly of machinery, which drives those hands into the street—by woman labour which drives the man from the shuttle—by child labour which drives the woman from the loom. Then planting their foot upon that living base of surplus, they press its aching heart beneath their heel, and cry 'starvation! Who'll work? A half loaf is better than no bread at all'—and the writhing mass grasps greedily at their terms.[34]

The rhetoric is close to Carlyle's in *Past and Present*, or Kingsley's in *Alton Locke*; the stress on the alienation of the worker from the product of his labour and on the uses of surplus labour is, of course, a significant feature of Marx's theory of capital.

But even as Marx publicly approved of Jones's utterances, he was becoming disillusioned with the latter's 'egotism' and ingratitude. 'Since, however, the paper is the only Chartist organ', Marx told Engels in September 1852, 'I shall not break with him but LET HIM SHIFT FOR HIMSELF for a few weeks.' Jones remained loyal, signing Marx's appeal, to be sent to German workers in America, for aid for the Cologne communists in November 1852.[35] He also published Marx's letters on the trial in his paper. But Jones, like Harney before him, annoyed Marx by consorting with foreign refugees holding unacceptable views and later by flirting with middle-class radicals instead of remaining true to the working-class ethos of Chartism. By 1855 there was little close contact between Marx and Jones, though Marx did respond to an invitation to speak at the anniversary dinner of the *People's Paper* in April 1856. In 1858 Marx broke with Jones, who had sold the *People's Paper* and, according to Marx, had 'DECIDEDLY SOLD HIMSELF (BUT AT THE LOWEST POSSIBLE PRICE) TO THE BRIGHT COTERIE. The idiot has ruined himself politically without rescuing himself commercially . . . the laddie is preaching UNION OF THE MIDDLE AND WORKING CLASSES.'[36] The demise of the paper and Jones's return to his original career as a lawyer in 1859 heralded the end of Chartism, which had long been declining as the middle-class financial and reform movements gained momentum.[37] Marx broke off relations with Jones, and next approached him in February 1860, when he wanted legal advice in the Vogt affair. Thereafter, the relationship was carried on intermittently, and more socially than politically, until Jones's death in 1869.

In fact, Jones became Marx's chief resource when matters of social and legal propriety arose. As the three surviving Marx daughters grew up and made middle-class English friends at South Hampstead College for Ladies, the Marxes found themselves conforming, without much sense of irony, to English middle-class expectations. Marx paid £8 a quarter for Jenny's and Laura's schooling in 1858, and hired singing and piano teachers for the girls, though he was still 'borrowing' from Engels to try to make ends meet. Although he could ill afford these expenses, Marx wrote to Engels in July 1858 that a 'SHOW OF RESPECTABILITY' was necessary to avoid complete collapse. 'I for my part wouldn't care a damn about living in Whitechapel . . . But in view of my wife's condition just now such a metamorphosis might entail dangerous consequences, and it could hardly be suitable for growing girls.'[38]

Marx often referred obliquely to his wife's more-than-bourgeois pretensions (she came from an aristocratic family, the von Westphalens), for he undoubtedly felt guilty towards her about the life they led in consequence of his activities. But he shared the pretensions, too. He talked snobbishly of Ruge's wife speaking a 'Saxon patois', and one of his objections to Harney had been that he was a 'plebeian'.[39] When Marx told Engels in 1863 that his financial situation was hopeless and he would have to declare himself a bankrupt, his tone was one of threat and self-dramatization:

> My two oldest children will get governess posts through the Cunningham family. Lenchen [Helene Demuth] must go as a servant to some other family, and my wife and little Tussy and I will go and live in the same model lodging-house where red Wolff once lived with his family.

Not only Ferdinand Wolff, but also Dronke, Eccarius, and Liebknecht had lived at one time in one of the cheap model lodging-houses in Soho. Malwida von Meysenbug, from an upper-middle-class family, did not hesitate to earn her living as a governess, though she sometimes objected to the treatment she received from her employers. But Marx, as well as his wife, hated the idea of his own daughters becoming governesses. When young Jenny went off and found herself a post as one in

1868, Marx wrote to Engels in horror at her action: 'the child will have to teach children almost all day' (Jenny was 24 years old).[40]

Mrs Marx worried about her daughters having religious and political views different from those of their friends. 'They have been brought up with notions and views that form a complete barrier to the society in which they move, and at the same time they are not materially independent', she wrote to Liebknecht's wife in 1866. The girls were bridesmaids in the same year to the daughter of the above-mentioned Cunninghams, 'an eminent and aristocratic family' with whom the Marxes were acquainted. When the time came, in 1867, to announce Laura's engagement to Lafargue, Mrs Marx asked for Ernest Jones's advice about a civil wedding, and also wondered how to explain it to English friends. Engels, who passed on Jones's information about the registry office procedure, told Marx: 'your wife can tell her philistine neighbours that you are choosing this method because Laura is a Protestant and Paul a Catholic'![41]

It is thus on several fronts that Marx practised a middle-class 'vice' when his greatest theoretical care was to advance the decline of that class and its habits. He was a social snob; he shielded behind Engels when he had fathered his servant's child; and he and Jenny Marx were occasionally snide about Engels's relationship with Mary, and later with Lizzie Burns, thus combining social snobbery with sexual hypocrisy.[42] The nearest Marx and Engels ever came to breaking off their friendship was when Marx responded to the news of Mary's death with a cursory expression of sympathy, followed by a catalogue of his own financial misfortunes, as if they were of the same order as the loss of a mate of nearly twenty years. He clearly viewed Engels's relationship as an optional extra in Engels's life: 'It is exceedingly tough for you seeing that with Mary you had a home, free and removed from all human muck, whenever you felt like it.'[43] On the question of money, there is, of course, irony in the fact that the man who studied economics and produced the most detailed analysis of the money relations of industrial society should have been so spectacularly incapable of managing his own household, even when, after he had received various family legacies, his position was in theory no longer desperate. He is reckoned to have got through about £500 a year in the mid 1860s, when an unskilled worker earned £50 a year, and a frugal family of five might have managed on about £200. But though he lived precariously, 'swinging like a pendulum between champagne and the pawnshop', as a spy reported in 1859,[44] it was on Marx, 'Papa Marx', that a whole group of disciples depended, if not for money—though he helped them, or got Engels to help them, financially—then for moral support and intellectual nourishment.

Marx's 'Party' in England: Ferdinand Wolff, Schramm, Pieper, Wilhelm Wolffe, Dronke, Imandt, Liebknecht

In spite of Marx's bold words in 1851 about preferring proud isolation and letting the squabbling factions get on with it, he was, of course, the chief spirit of a group of assorted refugees and workers. A minority of the members of the Communist League went with him after the split with Schapper and Willich in September 1850, and some new arrivals from the Continent who had previously been associated with the *Neue Rheinische Zeitung* in Cologne, like Wilhelm Wolff and Dronke, remained loyal to him in England too. Marx counted on their support in amassing evidence to help the Cologne communists in 1852, but thereafter he became rapidly disenchanted with the calibre of his 'party'. In March 1853 he reviewed them critically in a letter to Engels:

> What milksops these chaps are! With their idleness, lack of stamina and inability to sustain any PRESSURE FROM WITHOUT, they are absolutely hopeless. We must recruit our party entirely anew.... Pieper would not be without his uses if he possessed less childish *vanité* and more *esprit de suite.* Imandt and Liebknecht are tenacious, and each is useful in his own way. But that doesn't add up to a party. ... Lupus [Wilhelm Wolff] GROWS FROM DAY TO DAY OLDER AND BECOMES MORE CROTCHETY. Dronke is and ever will be a 'congenial loafer'.

A few months later he complained that Wolff, Dronke, and Freiligrath, whom he occasionally counted as one of his party, were wasting their time in idle gossip and leaving all the work to him. In 1852, when he had been organizing them all to send contributions to Weydemeyer's *Revolution*, Marx had represented himself as standing 'at their backs, WHIP in hand' till they came up with the required articles.[45]

For one reason or another, they all failed to keep up to Marx's exacting standards. None of them had money—in fact, Wilhelm Wolff almost starved on one occasion—and their most pressing need was to find some occupation to keep them, and their families if they had them, alive. This necessity, coupled with some laziness and lack of commitment, and exacerbated by the frequent dispersal of the group, as one member found a job in Manchester, another in Bradford, a third in Dundee, led to the party's relative lack of cohesion and of propaganda achievement. But there is an interest in following their careers in order to build up our picture of refugee life in Victorian England. The lives of

Marx's friends serve also to show how any society, however small, is made up of those who lead and those who depend, the idle and the industrious, the serious and the light-hearted, those who succeed and those who fail.

Among Marx's friends in London in the early days were two who very soon defected. One was Ferdinand Wolff, known as 'Rufus', who had helped Marx to edit the *Neue Rheinische Zeitung* in Cologne in 1848. He accompanied Marx to Paris in June 1849 after the suspension of the paper. In October Dronke reported from Paris that Wolff was going round 'like a ghost' and entirely destitute.[46] Soon after this he came to London, lived in a model lodging-house, and sided with Marx after the split in the Communist League. But he soon went his own way, became an honorary Englishman, and was lost sight of by Marx and Engels. The latter wrote of him in some amusement in July 1851: 'Red Wolff has gone through various phases of being an Irishman, a worthy bourgeois, a madman and other interesting states, and has completely abandoned *Schnaps* in favour of HALF-AND-HALF [a mixture of ale and porter].' This tell-tale sign of the chameleon, on a par with the shaving of one's beard, was soon followed by an even more outward and visible sign of adaptation. In October Wolff appeared again in Marx's circle, having 'crept back again all unobtrusively' and having in the meantime '*married* an English bluestocking'.[47] By April 1853 he was 'a husband and father' who took 'his wife and child out on jaunts' and seldom put in an appearance among his fellow exiles. Wolff disappeared to the north of England to teach for a salary of £60, as Marx discovered in 1856, and the last that was heard of him was in 1877, when Dronke told Engels that Wolff now had his own boarding school in Blackburn which he advertised, complete with the necessary references from clergymen.[48] Ferdinand Wolff had become integrated into British life.

Conrad Schramm had arrived in London a few days after Marx, in September 1849. He was a member of the Communist League in Cologne who was arrested in May 1849, charged in connection with his revolutionary activities, and sentenced to two years' imprisonment.[49] He escaped from prison and came straight to London. Here Marx hit on the plan—the same, in many respects, as the Kinkel plan a year later—to send Schramm to America to raise money for the London continuation of the *Neue Rheinische Zeitung*. Schramm's 'daring escape' from prison was to be used, as Kinkel's was, as an advertisement.[50] As we have seen, the scheme was abandoned because Schramm's fare could not be raised. Marx later described Schramm as the 'Percy Hotspur' of his party, for when the Communist League split into two groups, it was Schramm who fought a duel for the Marx group against the equally pugnacious Willich. They crossed to Belgium to carry out the duel, as duelling was illegal in England. A French *émigré*, Emmanuel Barthélemy, who acted as Willich's second, fought a duel in England in 1853, for which he was (leniently) sentenced to two months in prison. As Marx pointed out in *Herr Vogt* (1860), Barthélemy was hanged in 1855 for the murder of a policeman in London, while Schramm's second, the Polish officer Miskowsky, was burnt to death in a fire at his wooden barracks in Whitechapel in 1854.[51]

But Schramm failed to come up to the mark. He nearly compromised the Communist League by getting arrested in Paris in September 1851, and Marx referred to him as 'that rascal' and 'this dissolute character'. Schramm was one of those, like Willich, whose carelessness and indiscretion helped the Prussian authorities to build up their case against the Cologne communists. In May 1852 Schramm emigrated to America, presumably to try to earn a living there, pursued by an unflattering curriculum vitae from Marx to Weydemeyer. Strangely enough Schramm came back to Britain, in an advanced stage of consumption, in 1857, and ended his days as a friend of Harney's in Jersey, where Engels visited him just before his death in 1858.[52]

Others of Marx's friends stayed loyal for longer. Chief among the rogues in Marx's rogues' gallery was Wilhelm Pieper, the Lothario of the German exile. He began by being useful to Marx as a 'spy' at meetings of Ruge's Agitation Club in 1851; he and Schramm were unmasked and nearly 'Haynau-ed' at a meeting in February 1851, at which Harney ('Our DEAR'), Willich, and assorted democrats were gathered.[53] Pieper also acted as Marx's secretary during the Cologne Communist trials, and in 1852 he translated *The Eighteenth Brumaire* into English. The translation, 'swarming with mistakes and omissions', was corrected by Engels, who complained of Pieper's 'gross carelessness' and 'Cockney's petty-bourgeois floridity of style'.[54] The articles he should have written for Weydemeyer's *Revolution*, and some for Ernest Jones's *Notes to the People*, in 1851–2, never materialized. In 1852 Engels was sending Pieper £2 a month.[55] The rest of the time he managed to make a living from teaching, at first as a resident tutor with the Rothschild family, and later at boarding schools in Kent and Sussex.

During his time with the Rothschilds (the English branch of the family), he tutored the children, including Nathaniel or 'Natty', who was to become the first Lord Rothschild in 1884, in general subjects, including foreign languages. He travelled with the family to Frankfurt, then Brussels, in October 1851. But he was given notice as resident tutor in December, after a row with Baroness Rothschild, the children's mother, with whom he had been having an affair. Pieper was a cynical, worldly, carefree young man, whom Marx, with a stroke of allusive genius, dubbed 'Tupman' from the self-regarding, ingratiating, responsibility-ducking character in *Pickwick Papers*. As Marx noted, 'the silly lad mistakes his lack of principles for genial high spirits'.[56] Pieper was known to the Marx children as 'Prince Charming', but he presented a less charming face when he wrote to Marx in worldly-wise high spirits from Brussels about his quarrel with Lady Rothschild. Pieper wrote, in English, of himself as 'Fridolin':

> Fridolin has never troubled himself about saving a penny and after paying his debts would be quite as destitute as any of his friends, if he could not get some extra in the final settlement and specially if he could not secure his 'livret'. . . . Fridolin's story ends, as all stories from daily life, smooth round prosaic. He is to have plenty of recommendations, some money and no 'scene'. . . . Next Thursday I shall see you in London.[57]

Once back in London, Pieper was employed in various jobs. Engels tried to get him a clerkship in Manchester in 1853; he had a brief spell as a 'businessman', selling sun-ray lamps in a French shop in the City; and Freiligrath found him a tutoring post with a Mexican businessman in March 1854, which brought him 15*s*. a week.[58] His habit of visiting brothels then going to live with the Marxes with, as Marx put it, 'both his purses equally depleted', resulted in his landing in hospital more than once with syphilis. Marx took him to St Bartholomew's Hospital for free treatment on one occasion, and Pieper became a familiar inmate of the German Hospital in Dalston. 'SERVES HIM RIGHT', wrote Marx on hearing that Pieper was once more hospitalized in February 1859. Apparently, syphilis was a common disease amongst the Germans treated at the German Hospital, most of whom were poor workers living in the East End of London, for in 1856 the Hospital Committee decided to restrict the number of syphilitic patients admitted and to charge sixpence a week for their medicine, in order to make room for cases 'more deserving of charity'.[59]

In October 1854 Pieper was appointed resident master at a school in Eltham, Kent. 'SERVANT FOR ALL WORK', wrote Marx of his duties, bemoaning his loss of a secretary but relieved, too, to have got rid of Pieper with his irresponsible ways and smug sense of his own delightfulness. Pieper kept in touch, letting Marx know of the slavery of school-teaching in England: 'Pieper has to work in his institution from 6 in the morning until 9 at night and to pray some 20 × during that time, which "does him good". No smoking or drinking. Takes the boys to church, etc.'[60]

After another spell in London, living in Marx's rooms while Marx was in Manchester and his family on a visit to Germany in June 1856, Pieper took another school-teaching job in Bognor. He wrote more lively letters to Marx, in which he emulated Marx by making Dickensian references and wrote about his single-handed efforts to improve the lot of the schoolmaster-slave. Not only was Marx, hardly appropriately, 'dear Pickwick', but the people Pieper encountered at the school were viewed through a Dickensian lens. Mrs Richmond, the wife of the headmaster, was described in Pieper's idiomatic English as

> a little woman in the Dorrit style whose superhuman efforts at kindness and universe-embracing looks conveyed to me an unmistakeable warning to let her servant-maids alone—which after inspection of the three unhappy spinsters who delight in that capacity, I think I shall not find too difficult to do.

Pieper reported that he had won a tremendous battle to be allowed a free beer each day and so impressed 'a poor simpleton of an usher whose chief services appear to consist in the ringing of a large bell about a dozen times a day—with the wholesome idea that I am a tremendous swell'. The next battle he intended to fight was 'to get a Sunday for myself every fortnight'.[61]

Soon, however, Pieper gave up such unprofitable work. His main aim was to raise some capital, preferably through a prudent marriage. Marx told Engels the unsavoury story of one such attempt in April 1856:

> Pieper, thanks to his genius, has again been living a freebooter's existence since January and, despite the not inconsiderable SUBSIDIES provided by me, has been daily on the *qui vive* vis-à-vis his LANDLADY. Now it has suddenly occurred to him that all he requires to become a great man is a little capital. Seiler's [Sebastian Seiler, who had come to London with Marx in 1849 and had recently gone to America leaving unpaid debts in London] SISTER-IN-LAW, the GREENGROCER'S 2nd daughter, a tallow-candle in green spectacles, has long been mortally in love with the said Pieper. . . . Pieper has nevertheless discovered that she is not without intelligence, of which she gives incontrovertible proof by regarding our Hanoverian lambkin as a German Byron *manqué.* So, the day before yesterday, therefore, Pieper, to whom this person clings, not simply like a burr but like a CATERPILLAR, resolved to pour out his heart to Seiler's father-in-law. He did not wish to do so in front of his 'beloved' for fear

he might have to kiss her, which indeed is HARD WORK for an occidental unaccustomed TO FEED UPON TALLOW. But in true Pieper-fashion, the declaration of love was combined with—a touch for a loan. . . . On the grounds, that is, of his needing a little capital, SAY 20–40 POUNDS, TO CREATE HIMSELF A POSITION as a FASHIONABLE tutor. Meanwhile he intends to let his 'beloved' enjoy the pleasures of widowhood while still betrothed, nor will his compassion *ever* permit him to marry her.

Marx concluded the story with comments from his own household: 'Little Jenny called him "BENEDICK THE MARRIED MAN", but little Laura said: "BENEDICK WAS A WIT, HE IS BUT 'A CLOWN,' AND 'A CHEAP CLOWN' TOO." The children are constantly reading Shakespeare.'[62]

By May 1859 Pieper had left England, and was school-teaching in Bremen. Marx hardly heard from him again, though he received a card in 1864 announcing Pieper's engagement to the daughter of a professor in Bremen. Years later Engels told a correspondent that Marx had bumped into Pieper on the street in Hanover in 1867, when Marx was taking vol. i of *Capital* to his publisher, and found him 'a bloated philistine'.[63] Pieper had written nothing, and had more or less avoided exile politics, though he acted off and on as Marx's secretary in London, but he had seen the inside of English brothels and English schools and—many times—the German Hospital at Dalston.

Wilhelm Wolff was as different from Pieper as might be. Marx's and Engels's favourite amongst their 'disciples', Wolff was a prematurely crusty bachelor who had been born in 1809 the son of a Silesian peasant, but who had managed to get a university education. A leading member of the Burschenschaft, he had been imprisoned, like Ruge, for five years in 1834 for indulging in forbidden student activities. As a result of his prison experiences, followed by years of near-starvation after 1848 in Brussels, Paris, and Zurich, his health was poor. He died in Manchester in May 1864, mourned by Marx and Engels as their 'truest friend',[64] and by a large community of English and German businessmen, clergymen, and drinking companions in Manchester.

Marx and Engels had been keen to persuade Wolff to join them in England. After the closing down of the Cologne *Neue Rheinische Zeitung*, to which Wolff had contributed, in 1849, he had gone to Zurich and taught classics and modern languages. But he was unable to procure enough teaching to survive, and was planning to emigrate to America in 1851. Engels wrote to him in May 1851 advising him to try England first. He would be sure to get some teaching, since he could speak English and could bring the necessary testimonials with him (Wolff did bring some warmly commendatory references from four professors at Zurich University[65]). Moreover, Wolff must not believe the reports in the Continental press that during the period of the Great Exhibition the British government was 'not admitting any more refugees'. 'You know that no one is ever stopped at a port of entry here, and despite all the empty chatter in the reactionary press, I hope to see you in London for the Exhibition.'[66] Engels was right, although, as we have seen, some minority voices were raised in Parliament and the press about the likelihood of undesirable arrivals and revolutionary plots during the Exhibition. And William Howitt wrote indignantly in *Household Words* in June 1851 about his recent experience on arriving in London after a visit to Germany. He had come home with a boat-load of foreigners, mainly German, on their way to visit the Exhibition, and suffered a long delay at customs, while foreigners were asked to produce their passports:

> When you ask the meaning of this, you are told it is done at the request of the Foreign Powers themselves, to prevent the entrance of dangerous characters. But why should we stoop to become the tools of foreign surveillance? Why not leave our law and police to protect public order, as they have always done?[67]

Actually, Marx and Engels believed at this time that English police activity might well have been stepped up at Prussia's request and regarding themselves. 'Something's *décidément* amiss with the English mails', Engels wrote to Marx on 8 May 1851. He suspected 'dirty tricks' at the Post Office and proposed a plan to 'catch Grey in the act, just as Mazzini once caught Graham'. In fact, enquiries of the Manchester Post Office brought the reply that delays were caused by Marx having addressed his letters to Engels in the German way, with the town coming before the street, and Marx himself admitted he had made a mess of sealing one 'suspicious' letter, so they had to conclude that the Post Office was, on this occasion, 'innocent'.[68]

In any event, Wolff did come to England, arriving in London in June 1851 without adventure. After eight weeks, however, he had found no teaching job. Not all the German refugees were lucky enough to find teaching work; Johanna Kinkel noted in March that Gustav Struve, a democratic republican, was moving on to America after being unable to get proper work in London, and in September she told a friend in Germany that the refugees were 'a whole colony of teachers seeking pupils'.[69] Wolff was saved, as were other refugees such as Kinkel's friend and biographer Strodtmann and Malwida von Meysenbug, by becoming tutor to the children of better-off exiles. While Strodtmann taught the wealthy, aristocratic Frau von Bruiningk's children and lived in her house in St John's Wood, and Malwida was governess to Herzen's children, Wolff got a job with Count Oskar von Reichenbach, a Silesian landowner who had been a left-wing member of the short-lived Frankfurt Parliament and had come to London in 1850. So dependent was Wolff on this source of income that he almost starved after Reichenbach, disillusioned by Louis Napoleon's declaration of himself as Emperor of France in December 1852, left Europe in April 1853 for a new life in America, in company with Willich. Like Willich, Reichenbach had hoped for military action. As Jane Carlyle, who knew Reichenbach, wrote to her brother-in-law in September 1853, 'he has bought a large farm within 15 miles of Philadelphia, ... but he looks forward, I think, with secret desire, to a war, in which he may take part and get himself handsomely killed, rather than drain land in America.'[70]

Meanwhile, Wolff eked out a bare existence, too proud to ask Marx for help, having fallen out with him because Marx appeared to trust Colonel Bangya long after Wolff and others had begun to suspect him as a spy. Marx complained to Engels in May 1853 that Wolff was 'sulking'. Wolff noted in his diary on 21 June, his forty-fourth birthday, that he was 'in almost dreadful distress'. He finally wrote to Dronke in August, asking for help, and Dronke, who now had a clerkship in Bradford, immediately passed on the news to Engels.[71] The latter encouraged him to come to Manchester, finding tutoring work through his doctor, Louis Borchardt, a liberal who had spent three years in prison for his activities in 1848–9 and had been prohibited from practising medicine on his release. He had settled in Manchester in 1852 and built up a good practice, so he was able to introduce Wolff to English and German families in need of a tutor.[72] Engels had to smooth over the ruffled feelings of Marx and Wolff, who had parted on bad terms over a book Marx had borrowed and lost. Marx was grumpy about Wolff's behaviour, even from 'an old man in his dotage, who has become venerable as a party tradition'.[73]

Part of Marx's impatience with Wolff related to his inactivity for the 'party'. Like Pieper, he had produced nothing for Weydemeyer's *Revolution* in 1852, nor did he write anything for *Das Volk* in 1859. He was more an honorary member of the party than anything else, and, once established in Manchester, he settled down to the life of a careful, valetudinarian bourgeois, thoroughly respectable but for the odd skirmish when drunk. Marx thought he spotted a description exactly suited to Wolff in the *Illustrated London News* in 1856: 'Symptoms of being a confirmed old Bachelor: When a man cannot go anywhere without his umbrella, that's a symptom. When a man thinks every one is cheating him, that's a symptom. When a man does all the shopping himself etc.' Engels reported Wolff's rows with his landlady and his violin-playing neighbour, and his propensity to get into confrontations after a few drinks at his regular pub, the Chatsworth. Wolff emerges from Engels's description as a cross between Don Quixote and Tristram Shandy's irascible father:

> Lupus has had another adventure, this time with a parson who swapped travelling bags with him. The deadly earnestness of the affair was, however, alleviated by the fact that the bag that had been left behind contained the said parson's MAIDEN SERMON which he was due to rattle off the following day. This lent the thing certain humorous *extérieurs*, otherwise Lupus was again on the point of exclaiming: 'There are so many rogues in this country, and not of the working class, but of the middle class.'[74]

Wolff and Engels remained good friends and drinking companions, Marx being rather jealous of their companionship and conviviality,[75] and Wolff became a prominent member of the local Schiller Club when it was founded in 1859 in connection with the celebration of Schiller's centenary. Engels, who became a member of the board some years later, kept aloof from the centenary plans, reporting negatively on them to Marx, who was equally caustic about the philistine doings of the London Schillerians at Crystal Palace.[76] Diplomatically, Engels did not mention Wolff's involvement when writing to Marx. Wolff left £100 to the Schiller Club in his will.

When Wolff died in May 1864, Marx and Engels felt they had lost their best friend. Wolff had been much loved in spite of his crotchets (he had once suggested to Freiligrath that they make a joint trip to the tropics to set up a plantation of some kind[77]), and Marx, who attended the funeral in Manchester, noticed how many people attended:

> Borchardt, Gumpert [also Engels's doctor], Engels, Dronke, Steinthal, Marotzki (the Protestant clergyman in whose house Lupus was tutor and who came as a private friend), Beneke (one of the chief businessmen here), Schwabe (ditto), another three businessmen, a few boys, and about 15–20 people of the 'lower classes', among whom Lupus was very popular.[78]

To Marx's surprise and gratitude, he discovered that Wolff had saved over £1,000, in spite of never having been well of, and had left most of it to the Marx family. He had always taken an interest in the Marx girls' successes at school, where they won all the prizes, and his legacy was intended to help Marx complete the first volume of *Capital* in relative comfort.[79] Marx showed his gratitude by dedicating the volume to Wolff's memory. Wolff had not been much use as a 'party' member, but he had been loyal to his friends, despite tiffs when times were hard. He had also become a minor institution in Manchester, beloved of Germans and English, bourgeois and workers, and quarrelling with his landladies and with chance drinking fellows. In the collection of his papers kept in the International Institute for Social History in Amsterdam there is—besides his testimonials from Zurich, his passport, his Manchester bank book, and his last will and testament, all carefully kept together—an unsigned English valentine card from 1861. In his own way, Wolff had become a bit of an Englishman.

Yet another of Marx's colleagues from the Cologne days of 1848–9, Ernst Dronke, found his way to England, via near-starvation, arrests, and imprisonment in Geneva and Paris. He wrote to Weydemeyer from Paris in October 1849 in despair, though he was able to joke too; having asked Weydemeyer to arrange a loan to pay his rent and buy some food, he added, 'I send greetings to you and your wife with as much longing as the memory of the fleshpots of Egypt holds for a completely weakened stomach.' From Geneva in August 1851 he wrote to Weydemeyer again, not knowing that the latter was also in desperate straits and about to emigrate to America. Dronke was, he said, living a 'miserable vagabond existence' and going round 'in a kind of perpetual fever'. If a new revolution had not broken out by the beginning of 1852, he, too, would be 'forced to go to boring America'. The democrat Eugen (later Anglicized to Eugene) Oswald, who became a teacher and author in England, recalled in his chatty *Reminiscences of a Busy Life* (1911) that he met Dronke in prison in Paris in December 1851, when they had both been arrested as members of a supposed 'Franco-German plot' after Louis Napoleon's *coup d'état.*[80] Like Oswald, Dronke was released and expelled from France, arriving in London in April 1852.

Dronke, called 'pixie', 'the little sprite', and '*piccolo*' by Marx and Engels, was in his own way as unreliable a character as Pieper. When Engels heard he was coming to Britain, he warned Marx: 'If the little man does come, you will have some difficulty in restraining his pugnacious temperament, surely much exacerbated by prolonged "toil and trouble"; in this country fisticuffs and brawls cost too much money for him to be permitted to indulge in them.' Engels was referring obliquely to Dronke's having fought a duel with a Russian refugee in Geneva in

August 1851. The remark was prophetic, for when Dronke was living in Bradford as a clerk in 1854, he visited Manchester frequently for drinking sessions with Engels, Wolff, and Heise, and soon got into trouble. Engels told Marx in June that the aptly-named Dronke, 'drunk as usual, was run over by a CAB'; and a month later he was in trouble with the law:

> . . . when he was here [in Manchester] 4 or 6 weeks ago he got drunk and, at one o'clock in the morning or thereabouts, made a grab at a female in the street; she, a married, middle-class woman, boxed his ears, whereupon he KNOCKED HER DOWN. . . . The husband arrived on the scene and went to fetch the police, who didn't want to get mixed up in it. The business was protracted by Dronke's spurious excuses and now he has finally received an ATTORNEY'S letter demanding an APOLOGY AND COMPENSATION, failing which the FOREIGNER is to be made an example of.[81]

The upshot would be, of course, that Engels would have to pay the fine for Dronke.

As useless to Marx's research and propaganda as Pieper was (Dronke was 'idle as a *grisette*', wrote Marx in October 1853), Dronke soon lost regular contact with his friends. He moved between Bradford, Liverpool, and Glasgow, where his fortunes as a businessman rose and fell. His friends had little hope of his settling down and becoming responsible. Imandt wrote to Marx from Dundee in 1857 with the news that Dronke was living in Glasgow with a woman, and had 'started a small business', 'which means', he continued, 'that his boss has sacked him. What the small business is, he didn't say, but a small business it will certainly be.'[82] When business was good, as in 1861 and 1863, Dronke lent Marx money; when it was bad, as in 1876, he borrowed from Engels.[83]

The last time Marx appears to have heard from him was in 1882. A sad letter arrived from Dronke in January, from the German Hospital in Dalston: 'Dear *père* Marx, I'm lying ill in the above hospital and would like to see you.' Marx, whose wife had died in December 1881, wrote of his sorrow and ill health. Dronke's reply expressed his sympathy and added, 'I myself had the unhappiness sixteen months ago to lose my oldest son, Richard. He was a ship's apprentice.' Richard, aged 18, had been on the way home from Hong Kong when his ship was wrecked. Dronke told Marx not to trouble himself to visit him; his bronchitis was getting better, and he would not bother Marx with any more letters.[84]

Peter Imandt, a teacher in Krefeld until the revolution, then a refugee in Switzerland before going to England, differed from the rest of Marx's party, for he began by being a supporter of Kinkel, and was won over to the communists in London in the summer of 1852. While in Switzerland he became a guarantor of Kinkel's American loan, but by August 1852 he was 'spying' for Marx at meetings of the loan committee, at which the democratic refugees argued about what to do with the disappointingly small amount of money Kinkel had raised.[85] (Herzen recorded delightedly that the refugees deposited the money in a London bank 'and chose as trustees Kinkel, Ruge and Count Oskar Reichenbach, three irreconcilable enemies.... One or two of them had only to sign a cheque for the third to refuse to do so. Whatever the German emigrants' society might do, one signature was lacking.'[86]) Though Imandt defected to Marx's group, he still found it useful to use Kinkel's name as a referee when applying for the post of French and German master at a school in Dundee in 1857; his other referee was Freiligrath, whose name was known in Dundee 'as a great poet'.[87]

From 1852 to 1855 Imandt lived in Camberwell, tutoring in languages among the large colony of wealthy German businessmen who lived there, including 'Charles Fleury', a so-called 'democratic businessman' and Prussian spy, whom Marx unmasked, with Imandt's help, as he wrote in *Revelations Concerning the Communist Trial in Cologne*. Imandt, like Freiligrath, supported Marx more in theory than in practice, for he appears to have done no writing at Marx's behest. But he did help Marx out of financial scrapes. The whole Marx family escaped to his Camberwell house in July 1855, partly to enjoy the fresh air and try to get over the death of Edgar a few months earlier, but more pressingly to avoid Marx's creditors, including his doctor, Hermann Freund.[88]

While the Marxes lived in Camberwell, Imandt was in Scotland visiting Heise, and he announced in September 1855 that he was off to Arbroath to what Marx called 'a highly dubious prospect of a post'. He seems to have started a coal-merchant's business on his arrival in Dundee, and to have found five pupils who would bring him £4 a quarter. In February 1856 he told Marx he was 'longing for London'. His business was not doing well, owing to the proverbial meanness of the Scots. But he stayed in Dundee, succeeded in his bid for a language-teaching post in 1857, and married his landlord's daughter in 1859.[89] He appears to have had his nephew, Carl, living with him, for Carl wrote to 'Herr Marx' from Dundee in 1858, reporting on the school he was attending. 'English schools are much better than German ones', he thought, though of course he meant *Scottish* schools, 'the best thing about them being that you don't have to do detention or write homework every day.' Carl hopes the Marxes will visit Dundee next spring, and that 'the redhead' (Laura) and 'black-haired Jenny' will come too.[90]

Though their correspondence was irregular, Imandt was one of the few former friends to whom Marx sent a copy of *Capital* in 1867. Imandt replied belatedly, in February 1870, rather ashamed of his long silence. He found *Capital*, he said, difficult to come to grips with. The introduction was 'a very hard nut indeed', even to one, like Imandt, who had studied Hegel.[91] It must have been a disappointment to Marx to meet with such a poor response from one of his erstwhile disciples.

As for Wilhelm Liebknecht, the most loyal and responsive of all Marx's little group, he was unsatisfactory too. Marx and Engels had a low opinion of him and they failed to take him seriously, even after Liebknecht returned to Germany in 1862 to a life dedicated to socialist politics and journalism at a time when both activities were rewarded with frequent arrest and imprisonment. It is true that Liebknecht had a limited intellectual capacity and suffered from (or enjoyed) an irritatingly Micawberish temperament. He was never financially solvent, always asking for 'loans' and prophesying the coming of better times. He was so hard up in Berlin in 1865 that he contemplated returning to England to try teaching in Manchester. 'Can one get a cottage with a garden for £20–£30 a year in Manchester?' he asked Engels, who expostulated to Marx, 'what notions Liebknecht has about Manchester! He's got nothing to eat and asks me what a house "with garden" costs here! The chap's mind has completely gone to seed.'[92] Despite his innate disadvantages, however, Liebknecht was to become a worthy socialist opponent of Bismarck in the 1870s and 1880s, and in 1868 he founded, with August Bebel, the German trade union movement on the English model.[93] He was also the father of Karl Liebknecht, the victim, with Rosa Luxemburg, of political murder in Berlin in 1919.

Liebknecht had taken part, with Gustav Struve, in the Baden uprising of September 1848, after having had a spell of teaching at Karl Fröbel's experimental school in Zurich. (In 1849 Malwida von Meysenbug was a teacher in the school in Hamburg which Fröbel set up on the same free-thinking principles.) He was imprisoned in Freiburg until summer 1849, when he went to Geneva to join other democratic republicans, including Struve, Schramm, and Amand Goegg. Arrested in February 1850 for his activities in radical clubs in Geneva, he was deported to France, from which country he was further expelled in May. Thereupon he came to London, met Marx at meetings of the German Workers' Education Association, and applied to join the Communist League. He later remembered having been grilled by Marx and Engels, who mistrusted his connection with Struve: 'I was suspected by my two examiners of petty-bourgeois "democracy", and "South German exuberance of feeling".'[94] Liebknecht passed the test, and became a willing student of Marx's theories, which he was soon passing on in his lectures to the German workers.

Of Marx's rebarbativeness, which Liebknecht experienced to the full, being bossed and criticized and alternately grovelling and complaining of Marx's treatment of him, especially after his return to Germany, Liebknecht wrote forgivingly:

> No one is entirely insensitive to thrusts, blows, gnat bites and bug bites, and Marx as he followed his path, attacked from all sides, worried by cares for his daily bread, misunderstood, indeed often rudely rebuffed by the mass of the working people for whose struggle for emancipation he was forging the weapons in the stillness of the night, while they were running after glib-tongued windbags, dissembling traitors, even open enemies, Marx must often have encouraged himself in the loneliness of his poor, genuinely proletarian study with the words of the great Florentine [Dante] and drawn fresh energy from them.

This exhibits Liebknecht's strong sense of loyalty to Marx, and his understanding of Marx's feelings about Willich's popularity with the workers at the time of the split in the Communist League. While Willich and his mates 'made plans for the overthrow of the world and day by day and evening after evening intoxicated themselves with the hashish draught of thinking that "tomorrow it will begin", we', that is, Marx's group, including Liebknecht, 'sat in the British Museum and endeavoured to educate ourselves and to prepare weapons and munitions for the future struggles'.[95]

Apart from supporting Marx at meetings of the German workers, Liebknecht, as we have seen, became London correspondent of two German papers owned by Cotta. But he found the salary too little to live on, so he tried for tutoring jobs too. In January 1853 he borrowed £1 from Engels to redeem his coat from pawn so that he could look respectable when being interviewed by a German businessman, Schuter, who worked for the banking firm of Oppenheim and Co.[96] Liebknecht seems to have lost this post in October 1854, just when he was getting married (to the daughter of one of his prison inspectors at Freiburg). Marx reported to Engels the circumstances of the marriage:

> Liebknecht, as you know, has been vacillating most despondently between an Englishwoman who wanted to marry him and a German woman in Germany

whom he wanted to marry. At last the German descended on him and he married her,—in a religious as well as a civil ceremony. Both of them seem very down-in-the-mouth. His job goes west, since the people are moving away. He spent a wretched honeymoon at No. 14 Church Street in a house where he got himself heavily in debt. But who forced the ass to get married . . .

Liebknecht was to mention his wife, her health, and the births of their children often during the next few years in his uneasy correspondence with Cotta. They were used simultaneously to excuse his failure to send copy and to ask Cotta for a rise in salary in June 1856.[97]

Such naïvety and tactlessness, which finally lost him his newspaper post with Cotta and precipitated his return to Germany, was mirrored in his writings. It must have been vexing for Marx to have had a willing, even slavish, follower who could not help mixing the Marxist doctrine he had learnt with frank admiration of the capitalist society he set out to criticize. Even if we allow for Liebknecht's desire not to alienate the liberal-conservative editor and readers of Cotta's *Morgenblatt*, we can detect in his articles on England a fatal vacillation of attitude. His short article on the Great Exhibition, for example, shows glimpses of a Marxist probing behind the show to capitalist motives, and even more important, to the historical law operating implacably and heralding the end of capitalism:

It is true that this Exhibition does not owe its origin to an enthusiastic upsurge of cosmopolitanism, and if we try to get to the bottom of it we find the most sober calculation and the most blatant motives. We see that English industry has come so far in the course of its incredible development that it must suffocate in its own overproduction unless it can either find new outlets or widen its old ones. The first is impossible, and if the whole social fabric is not to be completely destroyed, there is nothing for it but to enlarge the old markets, that is to make them capable of taking greater quantities of English goods.

So far so good, from the Marxist point of view. But Liebknecht was also the honest layman, wide-eyed with wonder at Britain's industrial achievement, and the article ends on a note entirely at odds with shrewd negative analysis:

If we look closely, we can see that the Great Exhibition is no more than a piece of free trade propaganda. But be that as it may, the idea of this enterprise, and the way it has been put into practice, deserve our admiration, and the admiration with which it has met in every part of the world shows well enough that other nations have grasped its importance . . . And as for the motives behind it, let us not forget that egotism has, albeit unintentionally, done more for humanity than the most humane and self-sacrificing idealism.[98]

The pen thus ran away with Liebknecht. To Marx's and Engels's disgust, he pursued his wavering line once back in Germany, promoting among German workers and in the infancy of the German Social Democratic Party an attitude which veered between parliamentarianism on the British model and a more radical, anti-capitalist view. Constitutionally an optimist despite a life of poverty and imprisonment, he took a rosy view of the success of British trade unions in an article of 1883. Arguing from the Hegelian notion that in all historical struggles between two sides each representing some right a balance will invariably be achieved, Liebknecht concluded that English trade unions, representing the right of workers to oppose the growth of capitalism at their expense, had succeeded in the battle against capitalism, which was exercising its right to remove anything which threatened to hinder industrial development. 'In a word', he added, 'the trades unions have made the English worker into a citizen possessing full rights.'[99]

Still, Liebknecht was Marx's chief link with politics in Germany; Marx pursued the policies of the International with Liebknecht as his German organizer; and Liebknecht was one of the first Social Democrat representatives in the Berlin Reichstag. In a speech there in 1882 he gave evidence of his acquaintance with, and admiration for, capitalist England. Bismarck, he claimed, was the opposite of his English conservative counterpart Disraeli. Liebknecht quoted the latter's early mouthpiece Coningsby, from the novel of that name (1844), to the effect that the job of a good government was to achieve through laws what badly governed peoples achieved only by revolution, as lawful progress had been denied them. This was hardly Marxism, but it indicates that Liebknecht had been affected, as he himself said in 1895, by 'John Bull' in his great world capital, showing the rest of the world the way.[100]

Such were the friends and disciples of Marx. No wonder he wrote in 1853 that they hardly added up to a party. Each had to scrape a living in Britain as well as he could, and none of them had both the will and the ability to dedicate himself to the cause of socialism. As a group, they bear some resemblance to Conrad's anarchists in *The Secret Agent* (1907), who 'mooned about' in a 'delicious and humanitarian idleness'. Conrad divides his group, including a partial portrait of the German anarchist Johann Most, into the 'enemies of discipline', the 'fanatics', and those motivated most by vanity. The first and last of these characteristics, at least, can be seen in many of Marx's disciples. Ironically, the two associates most loyal to Marx in London were two of the German workers, the insolvent tailors Eccarius and Lessner, who will be discussed in a later chapter. With Marx, they played a full part in the founding and furthering of the International. It is to Marx's associations with prominent English workers and socialists in the years of the International that we now turn. But first we might quote Liebknecht again, who offers a glimpse in his reminiscence of Marx of the habit the Marx family and friends had of taking Sunday outings on Hampstead Heath. Equipped with a picnic basket containing roast veal, tea, sugar, and fruit, the party would walk to the Heath from Dean Street, buying bread, cheese, milk, shrimps, watercress, beer, and winkles from stalls on the way and on the Heath itself. There would be singing and story-telling, gymnastics on the grass, hunting for wild flowers, races, and donkey rides. However negative and bleak the prospects Marx had of either financial solvency or recognition for his chosen course of study, Sundays offered a holiday from domestic misery and hard work at the British Museum. 'A Sunday on Hampstead Heath', wrote Liebknecht, 'was one of our greatest joys.'[101]

Marx, the International, and Capital

On 28 September 1864 a meeting was held in St Martin's Hall, the scene of so many meetings of radicals and exiles in the early 1850s. George Odger, Secretary of the London Trades Council, had proposed an international association of workers to further the common interests of the working classes of all nations. The International was thus founded. Marx, who had kept in touch with the German Workers' Education Association despite concentrating on his work in the British Museum, and who had been adviser to Ferdinand Lassalle, the flamboyant leader of the German working-class movement who had died only a few weeks before, was invited to attend. Apart from workers' representatives from France and some Italian and German exiles (including Eccarius), the chief speaker was Edward Beesly, Professor of History at University College London and one of a group of English Comtists. Marx was elected to the committee, and after what was from Marx's point of view a false start, in which his colleagues drew up a so-called 'declaration of principles in which Mazzini was everywhere evident, crusted over with the vaguest tags of French socialism', Marx amended the draft and set out the rules for the International.[102] When the association started its own journal, *Commonwealth*, in 1866, Marx bought five £1 shares, listing himself among the subscribers as 'Dr. Phil.' where the others, including the Germans Eccarius, Lessner, and Hermann Jung, put 'tailor' or 'watchmaker'.[103]

In his inaugural address Marx described the trade unions as an indispensable means towards achieving success for the proletariat in the class struggle, not realizing that in England, at least, the unions were to concentrate their energies chiefly on fighting for better pay and conditions, and would not in the foreseeable future seek to lead a workers' revolution or takeover of power.[104] However, Marx could legitimately claim a practical success on the part of the International when in 1866 it appealed to foreign tailors during the strike of British tailors not to come into Britain and break the strike, as Irish workers had done, for example, during the Preston strike and lockout of 1854. Marx wrote to Liebknecht, asking him to distribute an appeal to tailors in Hanover and Mecklenburg not to answer the call of the tailors' masters in Edinburgh. The tailors were besought on grounds of both self-interest and honour: should they strike-break, the British tailors' conditions would worsen, the poorest of them, including German tailors already established in Britain, being squeezed out of employment, and the strike-breakers themselves, 'completely helpless in a strange country, would soon sink into the position of pariahs'. Moreover, it should be a 'point of honour' with German workers to recognize the 'common interest of their class' and refuse to help the capitalists in their battle with the workers. Marx claimed that it was through the efforts of the International that the London tailors' strike had held solid and achieved improvements in pay and conditions, French and Belgian tailors having heeded the message from the International which was now aimed at the Germans. As Marx told Liebknecht with satisfaction, 'this proof of [the International's] immediate practical importance has struck the practical English mind'.[105]

Through the International, Marx made new contacts with English socialists like Beesly, and renewed old ones with, for example, Ernest Jones. Jones joined the International in February 1865, and promised to try to find a dozen new members in Manchester. But in this he failed (as did Engels), partly because he was himself busy working for the newly founded Reform League. In fact, Jones and Marx renewed a regular correspondence in 1865, each trying to interest the other in his new association.[106] Marx saw that they were using one another; Jones was, he told Engels in May, 'very friendly socially speaking. But between ourselves, *he* is seeking our company, *only* on behalf of his suffrage agitation.' Equally, he added a few days later, '*quoad* E. Jones, it is necessary to march along with him for a while'. Jones flattered Marx a good deal in his letters. 'Advise, be our doctor Politicus—and get up a great Manhood Suffrage meeting in London, if you can', he urged, to no avail. After the passing of the limited Reform Bill in 1867, Jones wanted to stand for Parliament again. He asked Marx to be his election agent in Greenwich in 1868; Marx told Engels, 'I replied that I thought he hadn't the ghost of a chance'.[107] Jones was on the point of winning a seat in Manchester in January 1869 when he died suddenly, his death sending the Marx household into a state of 'deep shock', 'for he was one of the few old friends we had'. Engels attended the huge funeral, in the same Manchester cemetery where Wilhelm Wolff was buried, and agreed with Marx that Jones had been, in spite of his 'bourgeois phrases', the only educated Englishman to have been substantially 'on our side'.[108]

Where Marx had once been welcomed by the Chartists, he was now wooed by the early British socialists. Marx was at first rather suspicious of Beesly and his fellow Comtists, partly because he found Comte's positivist (i.e. 'scientific') analysis of society 'pathetic'. He read Comte's works in 1866, 'because the English and French make such a fuss about the fellow. What captivates them is the encyclopaedic quality, *la synthèse*. But it's pathetic compared to Hegel', he told Engels.[109] Comte had produced a history of society according to his notion of successive stages of belief. After the polytheism of the classical age had come monotheism in early Christian times, maintained throughout the Middle Ages by the Roman Catholic Church, but in a process of dissolution from the Reformation to the scepticism of eighteenth-century Enlightenment thought. The next stage would be the Positive one, in which society would proceed on a scientific basis with a modified, humanistic faith in place of both Christian belief and sceptical metaphysics. A further reason for Marx's suspicion was that the English positivists had a 'fanatical love of France', a sentimentalism about the French Revolution, which made them view France, and even the dreadful Louis Napoleon, with favour. However, Marx also saw the articles Beesly and his fellow positivist Frederic Harrison were writing on political economy and on socialism in the *Fortnightly Review* as signs of some movement in the right direction in England.[110]

By 1867, when vol. i of *Capital* was published in Germany, Marx had become closer to Beesly. He had high hopes that he would get his work reviewed (by Engels, writing anonymously) in the *Fortnightly Review* through Beesly, but the editor, John Morley, decided against carrying a review, on the grounds that *Capital* was 'too dry for a magazine'. Beesly himself, however, responded warmly to Marx's gift of a copy of *Capital*:

I am sorry—ashamed to be obliged to confess that I do not know German. I have long been intending to learn it and your book I hope will supply the final stimulus needed, for I perceive by the notes that it is full of interesting matter and I gather that the diseases of society appear to you in the same light as they do to me. Whether we should agree on the remedy I do not know and probably it is too much to expect. But when the world generally so persistently ignores the disease there must be a wide field for our cooperation.[111]

These remarks of Beesly's draw attention to the peculiar fate of Marx's book. Written in England, using primarily English materials (hence Beesly's sense of its content from the notes), it might have stimulated an English audience, especially as Marx was now becoming known through the International, and as thinkers like Beesly and Harrison (who was 'longing' to read it, Marx was told) were moving at least partly in the same direction as Marx. Yet it was published in German, which these scholars could not read. To cap its misfortunes during Marx's lifetime, the book met with a poor response in Germany, despite several anonymous reviews by Engels.[112]

Still, Marx did become better known and admired among English radicals, if not for *Capital*, then for the addresses he gave at the congresses of the International during the Franco-Prussian War of 1870–1. John Stuart Mill praised Marx's address of July 1870 in which he attacked French militarism,[113] and Beesly congratulated him on his second address of September 1870. Both Marx and Beesly welcomed the abdication of Louis Napoleon and the declaration of a republic in France in that month; both turned against Prussia and for France some months before the atrocities of the Prussian army made English public opinion and that of the 'Prussianized' Queen Victoria swing away from Prussia. Marx criticized British self-interest and hypocrisy in this as in most affairs of foreign policy. In December 1870 he wrote:

Here in England public opinion at the beginning of the war was ultra-Prussian. Now it's the opposite. German singers with their 'Watch on the Rhine' are hissed in the *cafés chantants*, while the French singers of the Marseillaise are accompanied in chorus. Apart from the decided sympathy of the masses with the Republic and the annoyance of the 'respectability' over the obvious alliance between Prussia and Russia and the shameless tone of Prussian diplomacy since their military successes, the method of carrying on the war—the system of requisitioning, burning down villages, shooting *franc-tireurs*, taking civilians prisoner, and other repetitions of the Thirty Years War—has caused general disgust here. Of course, the English did the same in India, Jamaica, etc., but then the French are neither Hindus nor Chinese, and the Prussians are not 'heaven-born Englishmen'.[114]

Beesly so agreed with Marx's analysis in September 1870 that he wrote: 'I now recognise as I never did before the importance of the International and I repent that I have not co-operated with its meetings in the past, though I have always sympathised.' Beesly set about writing a sympathetic account of the International for the *Fortnightly Review*, getting help from Marx—'I shall depend on you for materials for my article', he wrote in September 1870. The article was, accordingly, well informed. Beesly praised the efforts of the 'foreign members' of the International, especially Marx:

> To no one is the success of the association so much due as to Dr. Karl Marx, who, in his acquaintance with the history and statistics of the industrial movement in all parts of Europe is, I should imagine, without a rival. I am largely indebted to him for the information contained in this article.[115]

Even when Marx published his third address 'On the Civil War in France', in which he praised the doomed Paris Commune and drew down on himself the wrath of the English press, Beesly and his colleagues sided with Marx. Though Beesly recognized that Marx was 'radically opposed to us Positivists', he claimed that they had in common an 'indignation against the individualist theories of the propertied classes and their anti-social conduct'. All the English positivists, he assured Marx—himself, Harrison, Bridges, and Congreve—were full supporters of the Paris Commune. Marx, for his part, was not only polite to Beesly, telling him that though he found Comte unscientific, he admired Beesly as the only Comtist who viewed historical crises not from a sectarian but from a proper historical point of view. He was also, more unusually, polite about Beesly to others. To his Hanover friend Ludwig Kugelmann he reported, 'Beesly is a Comtist and as such obliged to subscribe to all sorts of crotchets, but otherwise he's a very capable and bold man.'[116] Beesly himself was aware of Marx's unusual regard for him. In a letter published in the periodical *Christian Socialist* in 1884, he wrote: 'Dr. Marx and I were always good friends; to the end of his life I had a great esteem and regard for him; and I am sure that he considered me to be a well-meaning person—which was more than he was willing to allow with regard to most people who differed with him.'[117]

The Marx and Beesly families met socially quite often at this time, for the two men worked together in the aftermath of the Franco-Prussian War and the Commune. Marx was in charge of the relief committee for the new influx of refugees from France. In December 1871 Beesly sent both advice and money for those in distress, and in February 1872 he announced the startling fact that he had 'found 54 pupils for French exiles'. Not surprisingly, he had 'no more openings left'. The correspondence continued intermittently, with Beesly inviting Marx to dinner with John Morley of the *Fortnightly* in 1874, and advising Marx on a suitable defence lawyer for the recently exiled German anarchist Johann Most in 1881.[118] Presumably, the decline of the International in the 1870s and Marx's subsequent withdrawal from public life to tinker with the rest of *Capital* caused the friendship to lapse, apart from the odd letter, until Marx's death. The relationship seems to have been the least fraught of all Marx's friendships with Englishmen, though no doubt Marx was disappointed at being unable to convert Beesly, whose article on the 'Social Future of the Working Class' in 1869, for example, accepts the gulf between employer and employed, advocates co-operation, and quotes Comte, but not Marx.[119]

Marx's address supporting the Paris Commune also brought a response from a different kind of radical, the 76-year-old Thomas Allsop, who had been involved in the bomb-making for the Orsini plot in 1858. Marx knew of him as the deaf Englishman who escaped to America while the Bernard trial was going on and returned after Bernard's acquittal. In April 1858 Marx quoted the *Daily Telegraph* in a letter to Engels on 'the great danger of being "DEAF" in Paris' as 'all "DEAF ENGLISHMEN" were being hounded by the police as Allsops'. Now Allsop approached Marx in June 1871 from Ramsgate: 'Altho' unknown to you further than having met you with my very good friend and Co-adjutor Dr. Simon Bernard I am induced to address you with respect to the late manifesto of the International Society with which I fully approve and sympathise.' He ended with the hope that he might meet Marx in London one day and with the greeting 'Faithfully and Fraternally, Thomas Allsop'.[120]

Though Marx and Engels referred to him as 'the deaf man' and clearly thought him an old codger,[121] Allsop was very active in the refugee relief effort of 1871. He collected money, gave up tobacco to be able to contribute himself, and sent Marx lists of the refugees' needs and talents, from 'L. Bonis. A Swiss jeweller. Can get some employ when he has clothes and food for a few days to restore his strength' to 'Maret, Guillaume, Artist. Wife and children arrived without resources almost without clothes has a small room but is in other matters totally destitute' and 'Borkhardt. German. Professor. A good Greek Scholar without means. Hopes to get work from a Publisher at present no means.

Starving.'[122] Marx was probably irritated at having to spend time meeting Allsop, as the latter proposed, 'at the German Restaurant in the Strand, famous for its Vienna Beer', to discuss the details of relief. But it was Allsop who paid Marx probably the most satisfying tribute he received from any Englishman, when he wrote in October 1871: 'I congratulate the International to have such a man to *think* for them, since in all the movements I have seen or taken part in during the last 40 years we have had able fluent men, but none who have combined to an equal degree thought and action'.[123] The old radical, and one-time Owenite, whom Herzen called 'good-natured Allsop',[124] was indefatigable, kindly, courteous, and deferential to Marx, who duly sent him a copy of the second German edition of vol. i of *Capital* in 1873. Allsop returned his thanks, saying it had 'interested him deeply. I have only one regret that I cannot give or have it given to our people in English.'[125]

When *Capital*, vol. i, was first published in German in 1867, Marx sent it to Beesly, who expressed the intention of learning German in order to read it. Other notable Englishmen to whom Marx sent the second edition in 1873 responded politely but uncomprehendingly too. Darwin, whom Marx considered as his equivalent in the field of natural science, wrote kindly of the honour he felt at being given a copy of 'your great work on Capital':

> I heartily wish that I was more worthy to receive it, by understanding more of the deep and important subject of political economy. Though our studies have been so different, I believe that we both earnestly desire the extension of knowledge, and that this in the long run is all to the happiness of mankind.

If this was vague, it was at least friendly. The valetudinarian social philosopher Herbert Spencer replied almost rudely:

> Mr. Herbert Spencer is obliged to Dr. Karl Marx for the copy of his 'Das Kapital'. When, presently, Mr. Spencer comes to deal with political-economical questions, as included in Sociology at large, Dr. Marx's volume will have an interest for him; but he fears that his ignorance of German will prevent him from gaining any adequate idea of its contents.[126]

One hopes that Marx was aware of Spencer's crotchety nature and his habit of addressing even close friends in this curious third-person manner.

When the book was finally published in Samuel Moore's and Edward Aveling's English translation in 1887, four years after Marx's death, it met with a mixed response in England. Most reviewers treated it respectfully but in a gingerly fashion. Marx's old enemy the *Daily*

Telegraph carried a curious article in which *Capital* was said—rather prematurely, considering it had only just appeared in English—to be 'the Bible of the working class'. Marx's views might be wrong, the author added, but at least he was 'a good man and meant well; and, moreover, unlike the ruck of contemporary levellers, knew what he wrote and talked about'. But the reviewer declined to go into any more detail than that. The reviewers in the *Guardian* and *Pall Mall Gazette* found much that was abstract, even abstruse, though they admired the descriptive passages. In the *Athenaeum*, Marx was criticized for communicating by means of algebraic symbols (Marx did write, though not obscurely, of commodity *A*, commodity *B*, and the 'equivalent form of value'), and the *Saturday* reviewer thought Marx was 'in love with paradox' and 'careless of the truth of [his] premisses, though astonishingly ingenious in working them out to what seems to be their logical result'. George Bernard Shaw wrote one of the most thoughtful reviews, in the *National Reformer*, which he ended provocatively by exhorting his audience to 'read Marx for the history of the working [of economics] in the past, and the conditions of their application in the present. And never mind the metaphysics.'[127]

Some of these points, though made with the arrogance of the amateur towards an expert, are not entirely inastute. To the lay reader, then as now, Marx's most striking achievement is his picture of the relations between the capitalist and the working class. He turns to English commissions and reports on schools, factories, and workhouses, quoting judiciously and commenting sharply on the injustices of the modern system and the indifference of Parliament and other proud British institutions. Adding to the angry sketches of Dickens, Carlyle, and Engels, he wrote of the English hardness towards the poor who were banished to 'the workhouse, that place of punishment for misery'. If Engels had long ago pointed out that in the law courts the poor man was tried by a jury of (antagonistic) bourgeois, now Marx gave examples to show that bourgeois juries acquitted on the few occasions when a capitalist was brought to trial for contravening the Ten Hours Act or other Factory Acts during the 1840s.[128] The horrors of the schools for poor children were equally laid bare.

And what of those who sought to study the economics of modern society? Here Marx pointed to the weaknesses of his British predecessors with all the wit and righteous anger at his command. Bentham? An 'arch-Philistine', an 'insipid, pedantic, leather-tongued oracle of the ordinary bourgeois intelligence of the 19th century. Bentham is among philosophers what Martin Tupper is among poets. Both could only have been manufactured in England.' (Mill, Bentham's pupil and disciple, had made quite similar points, though much more politely, in his critique of Bentham in the *London and Westminster Review* in 1838.) Harriet Martineau? In her works, Political Economy

very aptly, in the guise of an old maid, puts in the mouth of her 'beau ideal' of a capitalist the following words addressed to those supernumeraries thrown on the streets by their own creation of additional capital:– 'We manufacturers do what we can for you, whilst we are increasing that capital on which you must subsist, and you must do the rest by accommodating your numbers to the means of subsistence.'

Professor Fawcett of Cambridge? Convicted out of his own mouth of 'an uncommonly knowing dodge' in his calculation of circulating capital. Professor Senior? Dispatched to Manchester to learn the economics he professed to teach at Oxford.[129]

The English reviewers had some justification, perhaps, in complaining of abstractness. For the untheoretical Englishman, the chapter on the 'value of labour-power and wages' is hard to make sense of, as it turns on the hypothetical possibility of the capitalist paying 'the value of labour, if such a thing as the value of labour really existed'.[130] Engels saw the difficulty. Though hoping to review the work in the *Fortnightly* in 1868, he wondered how to set about it: 'It's damned hard to explain the dialectical method to the review-reading Englishman, and I can hardly throw the equations W–G–W at the mob.'[131] For Marx, though his stated aim was to demystify the Hegelian dialectic, which he thought was 'standing on its head', chose to do so by means of his own, 'opposite', dialectical method:

To Hegel, the life-process of the human brain, *ie.*, the process of thinking, which, under the name of 'the Idea', he even transforms into an independent subject, is the demiurgos of the real world, and the real world is only the external, phenomenal form of 'the Idea'. With me, on the contrary, the ideal is nothing else than the material world reflected by the human mind, and translated into forms of thought.[132]

So far, so good. However, Marx's attraction to the Hegelian mode of thinking is frequently in evidence, particularly in the passages on 'value', which in *Capital* moves to and fro between abstract and concrete status with an ease bound to bewilder John Bull.[133]

A year or two before his death, fortunately, Marx began to see some attention being paid to his works. His old friend and enemy Harney wrote to Engels from Boston in 1876, regretting the lack of circulation in England of Marx's ideas and offering to subscribe towards the cost of publishing 'a pamphlet or book exhibiting the system or views, or ideas of friend Marx'.[134] When Marx wrote to his friend Sorge to tell him of his wife's death in December 1881, he comforted himself that she had got pleasure out of reading an enthusiastic account of Marx's work in *Modern Thought* just before her death. Entitled 'Leaders of Modern Thought. XXIII. Karl Marx', it was a warm and intelligent essay by the socialist Ernest Belfort Bax. Beginning 'Karl Marx, the greatest living exponent of the economical theory of Modern Socialism' and ending by calling *Capital* 'one of the most important books of the century', Bax gave a careful, thorough, and supportive account of Marx's great work, including several long extracts translated, presumably by Bax himself, from the German. Bax picked up Marx's own hint about the Copernican Revolution and claimed that *Capital* 'embodies the working out of a doctrine in economy, comparable in its revolutionary character and wide-reaching importance to the Copernican system in Astronomy, or the law of gravitation in Mechanics generally'. While 'there is no great discovery that stands absolutely isolated', there are those who can be termed originators by virtue of having recognized a truth, traced its consequences, developed its context, and then fully expounded it. Such a man is Marx. And Bax insists, rightly, on the lack of dryness of the book. Praising its 'fascination and *verve*', he concludes his excellent review by saying that *Capital* 'rivets the attention as well by its humour and readily comprehensible presentation of the most abstract principles, as by the importance of the subject of which it treats'.[135]

Then there was a recent article by John Rae in the *Contemporary Review*, 'The Socialism of Karl Marx and the Young Hegelians'. This article was, Marx rightly thought, 'unsatisfactory, full of mistakes, but "fair", as one of my English friends told me the day before yesterday'. Rae was an English 'Philistine', who knew nothing of the subject, but at least he thought it worth writing about. The review is indeed a vague, rather pompous piece, in which Rae, to Marx's irritation, professed to believe that Marx was activated by 'a thoroughly disinterested' but also a thoroughly 'mistaken zeal' in helping to found the International movement.[136] Marx's work had thus attracted some attention in the periodicals. Mrs Harriet Law, atheist and editor of the *Secular Chronicle*, published a short but glowing account of Marx's work in 1878. A German clergyman living in England, Mauritz Kaufmann, wrote, albeit critically, of Marx's importance to socialism in his book, *Utopias, or*

Schemes of Social Improvement from Sir Thomas More to Karl Marx (1879), in which Marx is so far honoured as to be included in the title. And William Morris reminisced in *Justice* in 1894 how he had learned economics from reading *Capital*, difficult though he found it, and though he thought more information had 'stuck' to him from his conversations with Bax, Hyndman, and others.[137] Finally, the ingratiating H. M. Hyndman had just published his popularizing 'Marxist' book, *England for All* (1881), in which he quoted wholesale from *Capital* without acknowledgement. While Marx was furious at this theft, he had to admit that the 'little book' was good propaganda for his ideas.[138] As so often happens, an unscrupulous and mediocre follower of an important thinker was the means of that thinker's ideas becoming—however debased they might be in the process—known generally to a wide public.

We saw that Marx's great work was received in Germany less comprehendingly than in England, presumably because it dealt with specifically English social conditions and argued its case fully against English political economists. Of Marx's erstwhile 'party', only Imandt seems to have had a copy, and he found it too hard a nut to crack. But an older friend of Marx, who had long been estranged from him, gave *Capital* his full and generous approval. Arnold Ruge, caricatured mercilessly by Marx in 'The Great Men of the Exile' as a second-rate Hegelian, a 'doorkeeper to German philosophy', expressed proper admiration of the work in a letter to a Manchester friend, Steinthal, which somehow got into Engels's, and therefore Marx's, hands. Ruge wrote prophetically:

> It is *an epoch-making work* and throws brilliant, often sharp, light on the development, the decline, the birth pangs and the terrible painful days of the different periods of society. . . . Marx possesses wide learning and a splendid dialectical talent. The book goes above the horizons of many people and journalists; but it will quite certainly win through and, in spite of its broad structure, nay even because of it, it will have great influence.

Marx appreciated the unwonted and unexpected generosity of the old man in Brighton, and he responded with equally unwonted relaxed good humour. Seeing that Ruge was attracted by the very Hegelianism likely to put others off, he commented, 'Ruge clearly could not resist the "negation of the negation"'.[139]

4

The 'Bourgeois' Refugees: Ruge, Kinkel, and the Journalists, Doctors, Artists, and Teachers of the Exile

Ruge

Arnold Ruge, aptly described by Friedrich Althaus as the 'Nestor' of the German refugees in England,[1] was the oldest of the exiles. Born in 1802, he was almost of a different generation from the others, having begun his revolutionary activities and writings while a student in the 1820s. After being arrested in Heidelberg in 1824, he was sentenced to fifteen years' imprisonment for the treasonable offence of leading a Burschenschaft. He served five years, during which he studied classics and wrote poetry not unlike that which Ernest Jones wrote during his two years in prison:

Wo sich der Kerker schliesst um Eure Denker,
Wo Ihr den Freien Ketten schickt und Henker,
Da reisst der Menschheit alter Wahn entzwei,
Durch Fesselträger wird die Erde frei.

[Wherever prison closes on your philosophers, wherever you enchain the free, there mankind's ancient illusions will be stripped away; the earth will be freed by those who carry chains.]

Jones, whose conditions were similar to Ruge's—solitary confinement, little exercise—wrote, apparently sometimes in his own blood, as pen and paper were denied him:

They'll find me still unchanged and strong
When breaks their puny thrall,
With hate for not one living soul,
And pity for them all.[2]

Ruge was released after five years, and became a tutor in philosophy at the University of Halle. Through his teaching and in his journal, the *Hallische Jahrbücher*, founded in 1837, he preached left-wing Hegelianism until stopped by the Prussian censor in 1842. Herzen, who met Ruge in Paris in 1849, remembered that he had learned his 'philosophical radicalism' from 'the celebrated *Hallische Jahrbücher*'. Mikhail Bakunin recalled from prison in 1851 that he had been in Dresden in 1842 and had read Strauss's *Life of Jesus* and Ruge's articles in the *Deutsche Jahrbücher*, which had influenced his political thinking.[3] Ruge moved to Paris in 1843 to collaborate briefly with Marx on the *Deutsch-Französische Jahrbücher*. In 1846 he was in Zurich working with the liberal publisher Julius Fröbel until the long arm of Prussian censorship reached him again. When the 1848 revolutions broke out, Ruge was in Leipzig, and he was chosen as representative for Breslau in the Frankfurt Parliament. His party wanted unity with freedom, and when the Assembly voted for the first without the second, he left Parliament in disgust. Thereafter he travelled from Berlin to Leipzig, trying to publish left-wing and free-thinking journals, and ending up, like many others, in Paris in 1849, from where he was expelled with Blind and Marx in the summer of that year to England.[4]

Ruge stayed some months in London, but seems not to have found employment there. He had become wealthy through his first wife, but had put his money into his radical magazines and had had his property confiscated, so he was as hard up as most of his fellow exiles in London. In September 1850 he went with his recently arrived family to try his luck in Brighton. He and his wife both took pupils, but they were also persuaded to start a business in the hope of making a regular income. His wife Agnes recorded in a memoir of their life in Brighton that they bought a daguerreotype business from a Frenchman, Captain Becquet; worked hard at the dirty, difficult job of cleaning the silver plates, dipping the pictures in a bath and passing a spirit lamp over them; got into a row with the only other daguerreotype specialist in Brighton, whose monopoly and thus livelihood they were threatening; and were finally overtaken by the introduction of photography, which was very much easier and cheaper. Frau Ruge noted that they sold the business at a loss and turned all their attention to their teaching, which was both 'more pleasant and more lucrative'.[5]

Ruge gave lessons and published articles, pamphlets, and translations, making frequent trips to London to lecture and to organize his fellow exiles—as many as would join him—in his 'Agitation Club'. This club was one of the two rival clubs to be founded among the squabbling German refugees in the summer of 1851. Though Marx described the rivalry between the two groups as 'the war between the frogs and the mice', he was worried enough by the support amongst the workers for either Ruge's Agitation Club, frequented mainly by Austrians and

South Germans like Tausenau, Fickler, and Goegg, or Kinkel's and Willich's Emigration Club, which attracted Reichenbach and Willich's large following of ex-soldiers and workers, to set up his own rival group. As he wrote to Weydemeyer in January 1852,

> A *new workers' society* has been formed in London under Stechan's chairmanship, which will keep aloof from 'Emigration', 'Agitation' and Great Windmill Street alike, and pursue a serious line.
>
> *Tu comprends*, *mon cher*, that this society belongs to us, although we only send our younger people there; I refer to our '*heducated people*' not to our workers. They all go there.
>
> *Stechan* [a joiner who had sided with Willich when the Communist League split into two, but whom Marx had now wooed over to his side] has about him something of the solidity of a guild brother and the fickleness of a small master-artisan, but he is educatable and has considerable influence in Northern Germany.[6]

Though it is easy to see why Marx opposed both Ruge and Kinkel as petty bourgeois, muddle-headed, would-be leaders of the people, the enmity between Ruge and Kinkel is less comprehensible. It may well have been largely due to a clash of personalities. Ruge appears to have been almost as difficult to get on with as Marx himself. Even his ally Johannes Ronge expressed relief in March 1851 that Ruge had ended a visit to London and returned to Brighton, for 'he seems to have more of a gift for destruction than for construction'; and his wife admitted that Ruge's English friends told him that he had a 'sledge-hammer' way of talking.[7] Ruge was also strongly anti-communist and therefore mistrusted Kinkel's alliance with Willich. Kinkel, though much more peaceable than Ruge in temperament, was so flattered by the attention he received and the appeals to him as 'the head of the emigration',[8] that he felt a not entirely unwelcome obligation to lead a rival group. Kinkel also looked askance at Ruge's close connection with Mazzini.

In 1850 Mazzini founded the European Central Democratic Committee in an attempt to foster unity between the different nationalities among London's refugees and to further his own aim for a peculiar kind of internationalism centred on Rome and a Roman Catholicism wrenched from papal dominance. Marx was scathing about the 'platitudinous paradise of his cosmopolitan–neo-catholic–ideological manifestos',[9] but Ruge was persuaded, probably because of Mazzini's popularity in England, to join as the German representative. To the delight of malicious observers like Herzen and Marx and to his own discomfort, he found himself putting his signature to a manifesto which urged not only universal democracy but also a social condition having 'God and His law at the summit, the people, the universality of the citizens free and equal at its base, progress for rule, association as means, devotion for baptism, genius and virtue for lights upon the way'. The manifesto was published by the promiscuous Harney in his *Red Republican* in September 1850, and by the *Leader* in October.[10]

That Ruge was unhappy with both the role assigned to God and the emphasis on the 'holiness of work' in the manifesto is made clear by a note he scribbled on his copy: 'You go to church, rule over your slaves, and with that you have fulfilled your duty towards God and men: with that you realize your Christianity, shame on you!'[11] Nevertheless, he signed. Marx and Engels were not slow to point out in their *Neue Rheinische Zeitung* that 'on this occasion' Ruge was 'prepared to pay proper tribute to the distinction between divinity and humanity'. And Herzen wrote to Mazzini from Nice about the Committee:

> It's not an organization—it's mere confusion. . . the first piece ought to be entirely sincere; well, who could read without an ironic smile the name of Ruge (whom I know and esteem) under a proclamation which speaks in the name of God and of providence—Ruge, who has preached atheism since 1838 in the *Hallische Jahrbücher*, and for whom the idea of providence, if he is at all logical, must be rooted in reaction.[12]

Though Ruge was thus discredited among his fellow exiles, he was enabled by his connection with Mazzini to publicize the German democratic movement, with himself as theoretical head, in the *Leader*. For through Mazzini's friend Linton, one of the founders of the paper, it gave a great deal of space to the doings of the European Central Democratic Committee. Marx might make insulting jokes about Ruge's being the 'fifth wheel of European Central Democracy's state coach', but it was Ruge, not Marx, who gained access to the much-admired and much-read *Leader*. He took full advantage of his opportunity in a series of articles in November and December 1850 on the history of the movement for democracy in Germany, which he described in terms of Hegel's philosophy and the writings of two of Hegel's left-wing followers, Ludwig Feuerbach and himself.[13]

Ruge even tried to unite all the (non-communist) German refugees by getting several of them to sign the manifesto of the 'German Central Committee', a national offshoot of Mazzini's international committee, in March 1851. They printed an appeal in German ('To the Germans') to support a vague aim to bring about democracy in Germany by revolutionary means. 'Lend us your thoughts, your purses, and your arms', they exhorted, with particular emphasis on the purses: 'Subscribe ten million francs, and we will liberate the continent!' To show the breadth of support the Committee claimed, the manifesto's signatories were described in terms meant to be alluring: 'The European Central Democratic Committee has sent us Arnold Ruge, the Baden Revolution Gustav Struve, the religious movement Johannes Ronge, and prison has sent us Gottfried Kinkel; we have also asked the social democratic workers to send us a representative.'[14] The manifesto was carefully timed to coincide with the anniversary of the 1848 revolution in Germany, which was also celebrated by a banquet in the Freemason's Tavern. Not only Kinkel, Ruge, Struve, and Ronge were there, but also Mazzini, and G. H. Lewes of the *Leader*, who gave a speech urging that it was the duty of England to promote the cause of liberty in Germany. The *Leader* carried an account of the banquet, as did the *Daily News*, in which Engels in Manchester read of it.[15]

But the unity was fragile and short-lived. Kinkel's name had been put to the manifesto without his permission, as Ruge wanted to use his fame as an escapee.[16] Kinkel withdrew from the Committee and from its offspring, the periodical *Kosmos*, of which only three numbers, full of 'champion drivel', in Marx's words, appeared. The European Committee itself fizzled out in 1852 for lack of funds. Marx's ready comment on Ruge's propaganda was: 'The 10 millions never came in, but the *Kosmos* came to an end and the Central Committee came apart, disintegrating into its original elements.'[17] Ruge ceased to collaborate with either Mazzini or Kinkel and retired, disillusioned, to Brighton. From there, however, he continued to make journeys to London to lecture, to organize, and to quarrel. The Agitation Club, the founding of which he announced in the *Leader* in August 1851, was, according to one of its secretaries, G. L. M. Strauss, not up to much. In his *Reminiscences of an Old Bohemian*, Strauss recalled airily:

> I functioned as secretary to that rather innocuous molehill of which the *timid* German Governments of the period were striving to make a huge mountain. They did me the honour at that time to set a special watch on me, and actually to engage the great Bucket—of Bleak House celebrity—to take note of all my proceedings.

Marx, himself busy setting up his rival workers' society, wrote in February 1852 of 'that idiot Ruge, together with Ronge and two or three other jackasses, who conceal their lazy still-life by calling it "agitation", just as a stagnant swamp might be dubbed "open sea"'.[18]

But Ruge was being active in his own fashion. He was beginning to publicize in as many ways as he could, and for English audiences as well as *émigré* ones, his idea of democracy as the 'new religion' of mankind. He spoke to this effect at a commemoration banquet for the executed democrat Robert Blum in November 1852, and his speech was published by the *Leader*. Jenny Marx went along to the meeting with Imandt and reported on it in tones as sarcastic as her husband's would have been, in an article in a German paper published in Philadelphia. Whereas Mazzini and Kossuth, billed as the stars of the meeting, failed to turn up, she wrote, a mass of secret police and spies did attend:

> Then Arnold rose, stuttering a few words which were impossible to understand, as one could not tell whether they were in English or Low German. . . . Arnold rose once more and edified the English part of his audience with a German speech with surpassed in nonsense, dullness, and stupidity everything he has ever done, and that is saying something.[19]

Ruge had come to the conclusion that Germany held the key to the future of democracy not only in Germany itself, but in Europe generally. His view was logical in its way, since he thought habitually in Hegelian abstract terms, the World Spirit being, for Ruge, on the turn towards democracy as a natural stage following the phase of Prussian autocracy which had, ironically, been embraced by Hegel himself in the 1820s. It was also probably endorsed by his disheartening experience of trying to collaborate with refugees and democrats of other nationalities. In 1853 he wrote to George Jacob Holyoake of the narrow and peculiar nationalism of the Hungarians, 'who have neither principles nor good will for any other emancipation but that of the 4 millions of "noble magyars"', and the Italians, 'who do not pretend that they aim at anything but their *independence* and *a Republic*'. A year later, Ruge was even more critical in a letter to W. J. Linton: 'The Magyars are superstitious aristocrats, the Poles are thorough Catholics, the Italian . . . Augean stable is very full . . . A *German Revolution* . . . is their only chance to arrive at an independent existence.'[20] He reached this conclusion not because social and political conditions in Germany suggested it, but because it was for him logical that, as recent German philosophy had revolutionized thought and as that philosophy took upon itself the task of 'realizing' the ideal, its own realization in concrete historical terms must be the coming of a political and social revolution in Germany.

This was the curious message Ruge addressed to the English in a series of lectures which he delivered in 1853 at Willis's Rooms in

London, in the Albion Rooms in Brighton, and at the Birmingham Mechanics' Institute. He persuaded the radical publisher Holyoake to print the lectures in his series of secularist pamphlets 'The Cabinet of Reason: A Library of Freethought, Politics, and Culture', at one shilling, in 1854. Under the title 'New Germany, its Modern History, Literature, Philosophy, Religion, and Art', Ruge lectured on the 'Catechism of Humanism' as the new alternative religion for the times. Arguing that

> the only way to secure the freedom of the mind is *the critical discussion of all abstract ideas or principles in a system*, or *the logical development of all the ideas which hitherto have formed the principles of scientific systems*, the historical limits of 'human understanding', or the steps of its progress,

he pursued his peculiar path through recent German philosophy until he felt able to conclude that the ideal state, 'a democratic republic', was about to be 'realized' (his favourite verb) in Germany. Not only did Ruge thus argue from theory to social practice as if the latter could follow from the former by a mere fiat of logic and the magic of the word 'realize', but his notion of how the democratic republic would be constituted was a strictly abstract dialectic of traditionally opposite interests: 'The *communistic* element is *labour*, *life*, *intellect*, *thought*—the *social process*. The *egotistical or individual* element is *person*, *property*, *private life*, or the *personal process*.[21]

While Ruge wrote to a friend in Germany that the London lectures had gone well, Herzen, who attended them, reported otherwise:

> The lectures were bad; the Berlin-English accent struck the ear unpleasantly, and besides he pronounced all the Greek and Latin names in the German way so that the English could not make out who these Yofis and Yuno [Joves and Juno] were ... a dozen people came to the second lecture, and to the third, two—Worcell [a Polish exile] and I. As he walked through the empty hall past us Ruge shook me by the hand, and added:
>
> 'Poland and Russia have come, but Italy's not here; I shan't forgive Mazzini or Saffi this when there's a new people's rising.' When he left, wrathful and menacing, I looked at Worcell's sardonic smile and said:
>
> 'Russia invites Poland to dine with her.'
>
> '*C'en est fait d'Italie*', Worcell observed, shaking his head, and we set off.[22]

Undaunted by the disappointing attendance and response to the lectures, Ruge offered them for publication to Holyoake on the grounds that they would 'place the German question on an entirely new basis and enlighten the public'. Holyoake must have been reluctant or slow to respond, for Ruge followed this letter with several more, written in not yet idiomatic English and insisting (also in an un-English way) on the supreme worth and interest of the lectures. Not only was the subject-matter of vital and topical importance, but Ruge would, he wrote, '*be very glad to see my labour rewarded by a small earning from it*'. He urged Holyoake: 'The cause of liberal philosophical principles, which made me an exile to the British shores, I hope shall find an echo in English hearts. Such is the fairest Home a man can have. Help me to it.'[23] Holyoake did publish the pamphlet, though he appears not to have paid Ruge anything, and the latter insisted further that Holyoake should include in his periodical, *The Reasoner*, some passages from the part of Ruge's work which dealt with religion. How better to 'fight the English Christians' than by 'explaining their fancies like those of the Germans'? As it happens, George Eliot's translation of Feuerbach's *Essence of Christianity*, a much more thorough and accessible argument against Christianity, was published in the same year—1854—by Chapman. And as Chapman had George Eliot, G. H. Lewes, John Oxenford, and others to air the social and religious questions knowledgeably in his *Westminster Review*, he had no need of Ruge's services—Ruge complained to Holyoake that Chapman had refused his offers of 'scientific contributions' to the *Westminster*. But Ruge was assiduous in his attempts to come to the notice of radical Englishmen. He sent complimentary copies of *New Germany* to Chapman, Harriet Martineau, Mrs Milner Gibson (wife of the radical MP), and John Oxenford. He also asked Holyoake to get 'Lewes of the *Leader*' to read it. 'Then I hope he would mention it, although he is an enemy of German Philosophy, and rather an adherent of Comte's Philosophy.'[24]

Poor Ruge, isolated in Brighton, felt let down by the lack of interest in his works. He fired off a complaint to Austin Holyoake in September 1854 that his extracts on religion had not been made use of in the *Reasoner*. Austin added at the bottom of the letter, for his brother's attention:

> Dear Geo,
>
> Ruge's article, which is very good, goes in *this* number. The accompanying letter came this morning. Ruge is very impetuous, impatient, and querulous.[25]

He lost his temper again when he read a remark in the *Reasoner* about '*the German moonshine and our want of political freedom*'. The jibe (repeated many years later by Lewes in his correspondence with Ruge) stung Ruge into cataloguing the so-called freedoms of the English:

the English *Theology* I should say [is] the real moonshine that overshines all the sciences and exists in spite of *Geology* and reason in every book as before. *And in political* respect The Atlas must be as blind as the Leader, in order to ridicule the Germans with the failure of their Revolution in the face of . . . a national representation which does not represent the nation at all, in the face of those governing classes who do not dream of the rights of the governed to participate in the government, in the face of their universities, to which nobody except the church people have an entrance and where, if one enters, no science but only the 'theological moonshine' of the mediaeval times is taught, in the face of a justice which no poor man can pay, in the face of a people, where no national education is in existence.

Ruge ends, 'Do not publish my angry remarks.' His wife remembered how difficult Ruge had found it to come to terms with 'English ideas and prejudices' and how impossible it was for him to show consideration for them. He was not exactly blunt, she wrote, but teased people until they were puzzled and thought it wiser not to enter into controversy. This was particularly clear in questions of religion. Endorsing the view of Lewes and Hunt of the *Leader*, Frau Ruge noticed that 'many of the more enlightened men, although they went to church regularly to please their wives and observe custom, confessed their true views in private to Ruge (some of them were clergymen), and it was clear that they respected Ruge all the more because he went his own way, freely and morally, without hypocrisy'.[26] His criticisms were, of course, as Dickens, Carlyle, Lewes, Mill, and Holyoake himself would have been quick to agree, justified. It did not follow, however, that Ruge's version of German philosophy could be translated into social action capable of remedying the wrongs.

Marx had found Ruge's peculiar form of Hegelianism mere 'confusion' as early as 1842 when they were both in Paris, where Heine also ridiculed his 'woolly' thinking. Genuine irritation at Ruge's 'Hegelian phrases' combined, no doubt, with jealousy that 'the Pomeranian thinker' was able, at least for a short while, to propagate his views in the *Leader* and to publish his pamphlet with Holyoake, caused Marx to attack Ruge with particular venom in his polemical writings, the long letter to Ebner of 1851 and 'The Great Men of the Exile' of 1852. Fastening on Ruge's 'mania for manifestos' and his tendency to repeat himself in different lectures and articles, Marx built up a set of metaphors suggesting that Ruge excreted ideas: 'Ruge's daily stint', 'this daily stylistic *diarrhoea*', 'the man besmirching the *Bremer Tages-Chronik* from London with his own guano', 'the *gutter* of freedom; Ruge stands in the German revolution like the notices seen at the corners of certain streets: it is permitted to pass water here'.[27]

The commitment to Hegel did not diminish. While Ruge lived quietly and happily in Brighton among the unenlightened English, he continued to write to fellow Germans both in Germany and in England in an effort to gain a following for his views. Thus he renewed an old correspondence with Varnhagen von Ense, one of the two licensed liberals in Berlin, the other being Bettina von Arnim, tolerated on account of her precocious relationship with Goethe when she was a child. Ruge wrote to Varnhagen in March 1857, asking him to contribute to a new philosophical journal, to be entitled 'Jahrbücher für Wissenschaft und Kunst' ('Annals of Science and Art') and to propound once more Ruge's continuation of Hegelian philosophy. Ruge hoped to persuade Herzen to contribute too. The plan seems not to have succeeded. In 1864 Ruge wrote to Gustav Struve, one of his few allies among the exiles in 1850–1, who had emigrated to America, then returned to Germany, that he was busy writing the first volume of his memoirs, in which he would attack the incorrigibly empirical English and deal 'positively, not negatively, with the misunderstood [German] philosophy and its liberating mission'.[28]

The more he plied his lonely course of post-Hegelianism, the more he also became convinced that Germany would save Europe. Like many a fellow exile, he had expected another revolution in the 1850s. When it failed to come, he became gradually reconciled to the idea of Germany performing the task history meant her to fulfil by a means other than revolutionary. For him Germany meant Prussia, the most advanced state, and excluded Austria as backward, so he could view the outcome of the Austro-Prussian War of 1866 as a step in the right direction. He had come, Hegel-like, to endorse the Prussian status quo. Bismarck became his hero, and he recorded his delight when Bismarck offered him a pension in return for his pro-Prussian writings during the 1860s and the Franco-Prussian War. His odd reading of the latter was that it was 'the war of the bastard Napoleon against the German national revolution'. Marx's comment to Engels was: 'Old Ruge . . . is convinced that the Prussians will declare a French Republic in Paris! Don't you recognize here the old confusion in all its glory?'[29]

Yet despite his pro-German stance and the invitation from Bismarck to return, Ruge preferred to stay in Brighton, where he died in 1880. Though an enemy of English empiricism in general and anti-Hegelianism in particular, he translated Lewes's (despised) *History of*

Philosophy into German in 1871. He had also translated Buckle's celebrated *History of Civilization in England* in 1864, consulting John Stuart Mill in 1867 over a third edition of the translation. As Friedrich Althaus noted in his survey of his fellow exiles in England, it was paradoxical, or pleasantly perverse, of Ruge, of all people, to live out the full term of his exile. So antagonistic towards the practical English, he yet was able to live amongst them. Althaus put this down to England's easy-goingness and to Ruge's happy family life away from the London squabbles.[30]

Marx may have avoided choosing Brighton for the family holiday in 1870, because Brighton was too hot, 'and besides, Arnold Winckelried Ruge makes the place unsafe'. But in 1873, when Eleanor Marx defied her parents' wishes, as her older sister Jenny had done, and got herself a resident teaching job at a girls' school in Brighton, she turned to Ruge for a reference.[31] He may never have viewed Britain other than critically, but he was able to live in the country even after becoming reconciled to German politics. Perhaps he found, as did Jenny Marx, who had lost four children and lived in squalor and poverty, that the very callousness of English society could be an advantage. She wrote to a German friend in 1863 that the girls viewed England as their home and would be horrified to exchange it for Germany, and that even she found herself agreeing with them:

> . . . we have a very cheap little house, and, above all, London is so colossal that you can disappear into thin air. The individual counts for nothing here, and so you stop being essential to yourself and to others—you can withdraw into yourself and your snail's shell—no one bothers about you, whereas in Germany people know the next morning what you had for dinner last night and how much your husband earns.[32]

Though Ruge lived in a smaller city, Brighton, he may have shared some such feelings as these. We know from his wife Agnes's memoir of their life in Brighton that he enjoyed gardening, billiards, and taking long walks by the sea and on the Downs, and that the Ruges had friendly relations with several neighbours and acquaintances in Brighton.

There is a pleasing footnote to the account of Ruge in England. The great-grandson of Ruge's brother Ludwig, having opposed Hitler as a student leader in 1933, escaped from Germany to Spain and thence, on the recommendation of his doctor, to England (he was suffering from a rare form of dysentery). Here he stayed, fought as a major in the British Army, though still an 'enemy alien', in the Second World War, and settled in London, where he still lives, with his grown-up English family around him. This later Ruge expresses his sense of the tradition of 'live and let live' in Britain as one of the strongest elements in his positive feelings for his second home.[33] His great-great uncle no doubt felt the same.

Kinkel

Gottfried Kinkel was the only one among the German exiles whose fame preceded him, like Kossuth's and Garibaldi's, to England. His path to acceptance and economic survival in the new host country was correspondingly smoother than that of most fellow exiles, and his own response to England was, not surprisingly, more generous and grateful than many another's. Yet, for a combination of reasons, Kinkel did not stay in England all his life, as did Ruge and Marx, but returned to the Continent, to a professorial chair in Zurich, in 1866. Among the motives for his leaving England were his increasingly pro-Prussian views, but undoubtedly the chief reason was his failure to be appointed to a prestigious position in England. Like Freiligrath, he felt cheated of a post suited to his abilities, although, also like Freiligrath, he was welcomed and helped by some leading English radicals on his arrival in London in the New Year of 1851. His progress towards integration and the quiet (but successful) life which he sought was severely hampered by his becoming enmeshed against his will in the internecine squabbles of the German *émigrés* in England. If his fame gave him a foothold in England, it was also a commodity which his fellow exiles considered their property and a useful asset for the next revolution.

Kinkel, born in 1815, was a handsome young professor of church history at the University of Bonn in the early 1840s, when, like so many of his contemporaries, he became an atheist on reading Hegel and Feuerbach. As his post was under the direction of the theological faculty, he was unable to carry on professing church history, but his popularity with his students and some of his colleagues made it possible for him to continue lecturing, switching from church to art history. During the 1840s, encouraged by his free-thinking wife Johanna, Kinkel developed as a political liberal in opposition to the increasingly reactionary Prussian state. He was carried along by the growing demand, especially inside the universities, for both German unity and a democratic constitution. Partly because of his rhetorical skills—recognized by, among others, Friedrich Althaus, who recalled that his lectures and speeches always seemed spontaneous though they were in fact very carefully prepared[34]—he was chosen by the student radicals and the workers in Bonn to lead the storming of the arsenal in 1848 and to raise the black, red, and gold flag symbolizing a future united Germany on the steps of the town hall.[35] He edited a local newspaper, the *Bonner Zeitung*, on radical lines, and wrote a pamphlet rather in the sentimental, neo-feudalizing vein of Weitling and Willich: *Handwerk errette dich!* (*Handicraft, Save Thyself!* 1848).

Disappointed by the fiasco of the Frankfurt Parliament in 1849, he rushed to join Willich's corps in the Baden uprising of that summer. According to his fellow enlister, Engels, Kinkel acquitted himself well as a soldier; he was wounded in an engagement with the Prussian army and arrested on serious charges of treason. Engels, who escaped to Switzerland, gave his account to Jenny Marx in Paris in July 1849:

> Willich being the only officer who was any good, I joined him and became his adjutant. I was in four engagements . . . I did not see as many as a dozen men whose conduct was cowardly *in battle*. But all the more 'brave stupidity'. *Enfin*, I came through the whole thing unscathed, and *au bout du compte*, it was as well that one member of the *Neue Rheinische Zeitung* was present, since the entire pack of democratic blackguards were in Baden and the Palatinate, and are now bragging about the heroic deeds they never performed . . . But of all the democratic gentry, the only ones to fight were myself and Kinkel. The latter joined our corps as a musketeer and did pretty well; in the first engagement in which he took part, his head was grazed by a bullet and he was taken prisoner.[36]

Thus Kinkel, unlike Engels, did not emerge unscathed. His treatment while in prison awaiting trial, his natural eloquence (and his good looks) at two defence trials in 1849 and 1850, and the game played with him by the Prussian authorities, who led him to expect the death penalty then commuted the sentence to life imprisonment as a criminal in a fortress—all this brought Kinkel's case to the public eye in Germany. His wife Johanna pulled all the strings she could. Varnhagen von Ense and Professor Adolph Stahr in Berlin published articles in Kinkel's defence, and the redoubtable Bettina von Arnim pleaded his cause with King Friedrich Wilhelm IV himself.[37]

Kinkel's case became widely known. Through Adolph Stahr's future wife Fanny Lewald, who was visiting Britain in 1850, the plight of the professor doomed to spin wool in a cell for the rest of his life was publicized in England. Fanny Lewald herself described Kinkel as a martyr, 'compelled to earn by the winding of wool 10d a day, for which the Government feeds him', in the *Leader* in November 1850. She drew attention to the pathos of 'one of the most beloved professors of the

German universities' being condemned to such a fate.[38] On the same day, 2 November, Dickens carried an even more striking account of Kinkel in *Household Words.* It was written by Richard Hengist Horne, who had met Kinkel in Bonn in 1844 and who was also the 'Commissioner Horne' quoted frequently by Engels on the employment of children in *The Condition of the Working Class in England.* Horne tells the story in Dickensian fashion, beginning with a picture of Professor Kinkel in Bonn in 1844, happy, successsful, and with a promising future. The revolution occurs; Kinkel takes part in the interests of democracy; Kinkel is arrested and made a martyr:

> He who used to toil for thirteen hours a day amidst the learned languages and the works of antiquity, in the study of Theology, and of the arts—the eloquent preacher, lecturer, and tutor—is now compelled to waste his life, with all its acquirements, in spinning. For thirteen hours every day, he is doomed to spin.[39]

In this way Kinkel became an almost mythical figure, as Marx pointed out in one of his wittiest and most venomous *ad hominem* attacks. In the long section on Kinkel in 'The Great Men of the Exile' in 1852, Marx saw Kinkel as the sham martyr thrown up by the peculiar conditions of the times in Germany:

> In the meantime a curious event took place in Germany. It is well known that the German philistine is endowed by nature with a beautiful soul. Now he found his most cherished illusions cruelly shattered by the hard blows of the year 1849. Not a single hope had become reality and even the fast-beating hearts of young men began to despair about the fate of the fatherland. Every heart yielded to a melancholy languor and the need began to be universally felt for a democratic Christ, for a real or imagined sufferer who in his torments would bear the sins of the philistine world with the fortitude of a lamb and whose suffering would epitomise in extreme form the inert, chronic nostalgia of the whole of philistinism . . . And indeed, who better fitted for the task of enacting this great passion farce than our captive passion flower, Kinkel at the spinning wheel, able to emit endless floods of pathetic sentimental tears, who was in addition preacher, professor of fine arts, deputy, political colporteur, musketeer, newly discovered poet and old impresario all rolled into one? Kinkel was the man of the moment and as such he was immediately accepted by the German philistines. Every paper abounded in anecdotes, vignettes, poems, reminiscences of the captive poet, his sufferings in prison were magnified a thousand-fold and took on mythical stature; at least once a month his hair was reported to have gone grey; in every bourgeois meeting-place and at every tea-party he was remembered with solicitude; the daughters of the educated classes sighed over his poems, and old maids, who knew what yearning is, wept freely in various cities of the fatherland at the thought of his shattered manhood.[40]

The portrait, containing many elements of truth—Kinkel's attraction to, and unconscious exploitation of, women; his pathos, self-pity, and self-aggrandizement; his good luck, as it were, to fulfil in his own fate the dreams of many—was motivated partly by jealousy. As Engels's comment in his letter about the Baden uprising to Jenny Marx indicates, there was embarrassment among the communist 'Gelehrte' ('scholars') about their lack of heroic experience in 1848–9. Moreover, when Kinkel arrived in London in 1851, he was immediately surrounded by admirers from among the German refugees Marx was trying to organize and instruct. Sometimes Marx wrote as though Kinkel's life sentence itself were a mere chimera: he and Engels drew understandable hostility upon themselves when they published an article in the *Neue Rheinische Zeitung* in London in 1850 attacking Kinkel's defence speech at his first trial in August 1849. What they alleged was true, namely that Kinkel had defended himself by indirectly incriminating others, including fellow freedom fighters in Baden who had already been executed, in his self-dramatizing speech denying responsibility during the uprising. But they spoke of him as 'the "imprisoned" Kinkel', as though his situation were unreal.[41] In fact, at the time of his speech, Kinkel had spent two months in prison, was on trial for his life, and would face a second trial in May 1850.

The larger-than-life aspect of Kinkel's doings was further endorsed, as Marx saw to his amusement and irritation, by Kinkel's miraculous escape from Spandau with the help of an admiring student, Carl Schurz, and several willing turnkeys less than a week after the 2 November articles in *Household Words* and the *Leader*. 'His escape', wrote Marx, 'was a re-enactment of the story of Richard Lionheart and Blondel, with the difference that this time it was Blondel who was in prison while Lionheart played on the barrel-organ outside.' Marx was reduced at this point to mere insult, as he had been reduced to downright falsification when describing Kinkel's soldiering, against Engels's own firsthand account, as a comically inept affair: 'Gottfried could neither load, nor see, nor shoot, nor march.'[42]

Kinkel's escape was shouted from the roof-tops. In Berlin the people were crying 'Long live Kinkel!' from their windows, according to Varnhagen von Ense. And it was announced in the British press too. In the *Illustrated London News* the question was raised as to whether the Prussian Government itself might have 'connived at his escape' out of embarrassment; and George Hooper, the Chartist poet, published a stirring poem in the *Leader*, which ended

Kinkel is free!
A beaker full of wine,
Fresh from the rocky Rhine!
Brave Kinkel, health to thee!
With beating hearts, and eyes
Moist with glad tears, do we
Shout back the welcome cries,
'Kinkel is free!'[43]

Kinkel and Schurz rode in disguise to the northern port of Rostock, where they embarked on a ship bound for Leith, the port of Edinburgh. Their first experience of British life was, as it happens, a Scottish Sunday. Schurz wrote to Johanna Kinkel in high spirits but with some puzzlement:

> Today we've sauntered around for seven continuous hours looking for an inn, for in England [he meant Scotland, for England was not quite so bad] they are all closed on Sundays, and when we finally found one, we managed just enough English to order a steak, a pudding, and a bottle of beer . . .

(*Punch* noticed in 1854 that 'you [could not] get a dinner on a Sunday' in Scotland unless you ordered a bed as well.[44]) This was 1 December 1850. After a rendezvous with Johanna and their four children in Paris, Kinkel returned to Britain with them in January 1851.

In contrast to those exiles who arrived almost penniless and with no contacts except possibly the address of a cheap German hotel in Soho in their pockets, the Kinkels came well furnished with money and letters of introduction. Adolph Stahr had collected money, including a few coins donated by an apprentice tailor, and Fanny Lewald gave them introductions to some of the people she had met during her stay in 1850. Among them were Anna Swanwick, who had translated Goethe's *Faust* in 1846, and Varnhagen's friend Charlotte Williams-Wynn.[45] Either through Fanny Lewald or through Horne, who wrote to Kinkel soon after his arrival, the Kinkels met William and Mary Howitt, Richard Monckton Milnes, who had been helpful to Freiligrath a few years before, and the radicals Thomas Milner Gibson, George Grote, Richard Cobden, and the Leigh Smith family. The Kinkels went on an outing to Cambridge with several of these friends in May 1851. On one occasion, Harriet Grote, who had patronized Mendelssohn during his many successful visits to London, sent Johanna Kinkel some concert tickets.[46] Johanna's first letter to friends in Germany told of her delight with England and the kindness of everyone she met. Exaggerating slightly, she revelled in the contrast between England's treatment of the Austrian general Haynau in the famous brewery incident in September 1850 and its welcoming of the escaped prisoner Kinkel:

> We have been treated with an obligingness here such as we could never have dreamt of. It's often quite comic to think how many German views are stood on their heads here. Haynau, decorated with medals and stars, gets whipped, and Kinkel, who lost his Prussian national cockade [signifying citizenship], is carried on people's shoulders.[47]

Through the contacts provided by Fanny Lewald, including the Manchester novelist Geraldine Jewsbury, who had, in Jane Carlyle's words, 'sworn eternal friendship' with her German counterpart—both women liked to be rather shocking, George-Sand-like, in their behaviour and both dealt with *risqué* subjects like divorce and triangular love relationships in their novels[48]—Kinkel began to acquire private pupils and to be asked to deliver lectures all over Britain. His fame brought him invitations from the established, rich German communities in Camberwell, Manchester, and Bradford to lecture in German on art history and literature. Engels and Weerth reported to Marx on one such occasion. The former was asked by the secretary of the Manchester Athenaeum Club to subscribe, which he refused to do. In October 1852 he told Marx that Kinkel was in Manchester with 'a RABBLE of local German Jews. However, we have been putting a few ideas in our people's heads and, here as in Bradford, Weerth will make things pretty hot for him.'[49]

Since Kinkel was not a communist, and since he was so obviously a victim of Prussian cruelty, feelings towards him among the non-political Germans in England were warm. Similarly, the English middle-class press had stressed his non-revolutionary nature and his excessive punishment at the hands of an oppressive state. Even Frederick Hardman in the Tory *Blackwood's Magazine*, while regretting Kinkel's revolutionary act as 'unfortunate', had sympathized with his imprisonment in a short introduction to his translation of Kinkel's ironic tale of country life, 'Family Feud', in August 1850.[50] Thus Kinkel was respectable enough, but his recent history also sufficiently exciting, for him to be asked to lecture to English audiences too. He would have been happy to settle down in London and build upon this foundation a successful career as an academic.

But that was not to be. As with Freiligrath, the opportunities for a professorship were lacking. However, in 1852 Kinkel came very near to getting a chair. He applied to George Grote, a member of the Senate of London University, asking for his support for Kinkel's candidature for the Chair of English Language and Literature at University College London. Grote replied kindly but cautiously:

> My sympathy with your past sufferings and sacrifices, my respect for your character, and the idea which I have formed of your literary abilities, alike prompt me to wish you success in any professorial career which you may take up. To your powers as a lecturer in your own language, I can myself bear testimony. Your lectures on the Drama, which I had the pleasure of hearing, struck me most forcibly, from the comprehensive mastery of the subject which they exhibited, as well as from your animated and emphatic delivery.

On the other hand:

> You will not require to be informed that the fact of your being a foreigner will be an obstacle to your success, which it will require a strong conviction of your superiority in other respects to surmount.[51]

The chair went to the excellent candidate David Masson, a friend of Carlyle and of Mazzini, and Kinkel had to be content to carry on teaching at home and giving lectures at several different institutions. But the records of the committee which met to recommend the appointment show that Kinkel was, despite Masson's strengths—he had written essays on Milton and the Pre-Raphaelites which the committee singled out for praise—the favoured candidate. There is a long memo noting Kinkel's attainments and the unanimous praise by his referees, who included Professor Hofmann, 'celebrated Professor in the London College of Chemistry' and a former colleague of Kinkel's in Bonn, George Grote, Dr Leonhard Schmitz, Rector of Edinburgh High School, and Ferencz Pulszky, the Hungarian exile. Professor Heimann, a member of the Committee and Professor of German at University College, also testified to Kinkel's excellence. His career is outlined in the report, and special attention is paid to his oratorical powers. Pulszky, Heimann, and Grote had heard and admired his lecture on the German drama; F. W. Newman, Professor of Latin and a member of the Committee, had been surprised by Kinkel's 'familiarity with Shakespeare' during a private conversation with him. 'Two of us', runs the report, 'testify that his utterance is soft, refined and highly agreeable, in keeping with his other remarkable personal advantages.' The Committee had clearly been as much affected by Kinkel's charm as had the packed court-room in Cologne and as were the ladies who sat at his feet in higher education institutes throughout London. However, the Committee 'happen[ed] to know that in some quarters political prejudices [had] been raised against him', and these prejudices were obviously victorious at the meeting of University College Council two days after this, on 6 November 1852, when it was decided to offer Masson the appointment despite the Senate Committee's unanimous recommendation of Kinkel. The members of the Committee were the Professors of Latin (Newman), Greek (Henry Malden), Jurisprudence (C. J. Foster), German (Heimann), and Mental Philosophy and Logic (John Hoppus).[52] There is no record of the amendment objecting to Kinkel or of its author, and Kinkel himself seems not to have known how close he was to succeeding.

It is highly likely that, with his good start in England, as well as his pleasant manners, good looks, and rhetorical talent, Kinkel would have had great success in his adopted country. However, his reputation not only opened up English society to him, but was also an asset over which the various German exile groups fought. Kinkel had scarcely arrived in England when he was deluged with letters and visits (as Freiligrath was to be when he returned to England in May 1851). Ruge wrote from Brighton on 31 January 1851, asking Kinkel to meet him in London soon. He wanted to win Kinkel for Mazzini's European Democracy movement. Finding Kinkel evasive (Johanna told Ruge that her husband was ill), he used Kinkel's name without securing permission. So also did Willich, who desired to have Kinkel on his side in the battle with Marx for the communists and workers. Willich wrote in February:

> I came to see you to ask you to use your capital—that is, your popularity—which I consider the property of the people, especially the suffering part of the people, to help alleviate the misery of the soldiers arriving from Schleswig-Holstein.
>
> You were not at home; your wife told me you were ill, so I have taken the necessary steps myself. Two respectable merchants and a banker in the City are interesting themselves in the business and will open a subscription to collect the money needed to help refugees emigrate to America.[53]

Others simply wanted Kinkel, whose name was known and who was thought to be wealthy, to help them out of the gutter. C. J. Esser, an out-of-work printer, wrote to Kinkel in August 1851 that he was desperate for 'a small amount' to keep him going until he got another job. He told Kinkel he had a printing press on show at the Great Exhibition, and offered to print something for him. A similar plea came in 1852 from a refugee named Solger, who appealed to Kinkel as 'the head of the emigration' to approach Mazzini's friend James Stansfeld for assistance. Kinkel had already helped Solger in 1851; Johanna had written then to Therese Pulszky, German wife of the well-established Hungarian exile Ferencz Pulszky, asking her to help Solger to a job, stressing his talent and his good English, but also expressing her awareness that Solger was on a tightrope 'between success and the abyss'.[54]

At first, Kinkel tried to keep on friendly terms with all the groups, except that of 'Doctor Great Mogul' Marx.[55] He spoke at a 'German Club' dinner, given in honour of him and two other non-communist exiles, the German liberal Catholic and proponent of the kindergarten system, Johannes Ronge, and the bourgeois democrat, amateur craniologist, and vegetarian, Gustav Struve. It was a meeting of 'respectable' political exiles and non-political Germans like the wealthy businessman Gerstenberg and the London bookseller Franz Thimm. The dinner was reported in the *Leader*, according to which Ronge spoke about freedom in religion and politics, and Struve expressed his republicanism:

> But when Kinkel rose, a fine, almost handsome figure, the burst of enthusiasm was great, and he spoke like a poet; he said he only remembered two evenings of his life—the one when he took leave of his sleeping children to take up the musket for the political cause of his country, and the other the banquet evening, when he took leave of his sleeping children, feeling happy and free, and honoured by his countrymen on a free and foreign soil.[56]

The content of the speech and the effect on the audience were a minor repetition of the events at Kinkel's second trial in May 1850, when, to Marx's disgust, Kinkel had appealed to his audience's sense of pathos by describing his leave-taking of his four children. Freiligrath, Stahr, Varnhagen, and others reported that the court in Cologne dissolved in tears after Kinkel's speech. Marx, fed with information by Weerth, who was in prison in Cologne at the time of the trial, reduced the speech to comic shorthand in 'The Great Men of the Exile':

> 'Members of the Court, Gentlemen of the Jury—the blue eyes of my children—the green waters of the Rhine—it is no dishonour to shake the hand of the proletarian—the pallid lips of the prisoner—the gentle air of one's home'—and similar muck: that was what the whole famous speech amounted to and the public, the jury, the prosecution and even the police shed their bitterest tears and the trial closed with a unanimous . . . weeping and sobbing. Kinkel is doubtless a dear, good man but he is also a repulsive mixture of religious, political and literary reminiscences.

Marx was scarcely being unfair here. In his defence speech, Kinkel had declared himself a democrat and, as such,

> I confess myself a supporter of the revolution for which my blood flowed, and I declare this today again before you; with life and limb surrendered to my opponents I declare it with the pale lips of the prisoner.
>
> . . . I am banished to the far north, to which no sound of my home penetrates; I am not permitted to see my dear wife through the bars of my prison or to bathe my yearning soul in the flower-blue eyes of my children . . . My lords; if the proletarian gives me his hand, that does not degrade me.[57]

As Herzen and Freiligrath, as well as Marx, noted, Kinkel could not help 'going on stilts'. His pathos and self-dramatization succeeded with audiences, whether middle-class or proletarian, German or English. Thus he was again the toast of the evening at the commemorative banquet of 13 March 1851, at which Ruge, Mazzini, and Lewes also spoke.[58] He tried, as Marx saw, to be all things to all men. Egged on by his saviour Schurz, who had settled in Paris,[59] he courted Willich's company in order to win influence over Willich's working men, while at the same time maintaining a respectable face for the Camberwell and City Germans who were paying a guinea each to attend those lectures on the German drama which Grote referred to in his letter to Kinkel.[60] It was Schurz, too, who insisted that Kinkel had a duty to capitalize on his fame by undertaking a begging tour of America to raise money for the German National Loan, a venture similar to Mazzini's Italian one and to Marx's unfulfilled plan to send Schramm to America the previous year. The project gained Kinkel much publicity among German exiles in England and America, most of it hostile. Amand Goegg was sent on a rival tour two months after Kinkel set off in September 1851, and Kossuth, accompanied by Pulszky, swelled the numbers of European fund-raisers in America early in 1852.

Kinkel was later bitter about his experience. He had felt obliged to go, when he would rather have stayed with his wife and family after his long separation from them, and when he could have been consolidating his social and economic position with his lecturing and dining out in London. Instead, he spent six months in America, coming back with an amount too small to be of any use, even if the committee which sent him had had any clear idea of exactly how the money should be spent, which it had not. When he returned in March 1852, Napoleon's *coup* in France had dampened hopes of an immediate revolution anywhere in Europe; several refugees packed up and left for America; the German clubs had disintegrated; morale was low and recrimination louder than ever. The

'Nibelungen treasure', as Friedrich Althaus called it, was an embarrassment and a bone of contention among those who were supposed to administer it. Kinkel finally deposited the money in a bank, and after turning down several applications, mainly from Karl Blind, who wanted money from the fund to set up republican periodicals in 1857 and 1861, he managed to divest himself of the responsibility for a loan which it had not been his idea to collect in the first place and which had brought him nothing but criticism and trouble. Kinkel let his old rival Goegg have disposal of the money after he left for Zurich in 1866, and some of it was used to found August Bebel's Social Democratic Party and its journal,[61] thus ending a saga from which Marx and Herzen and a host of New York German journalists had drawn abundant material for satire. Kinkel had collected, it now came about, for the disciples in Germany of his fiercest adversary, Marx.

On his return to London, Kinkel set about distancing himself from 'London Germany' and getting established as a teacher of German language, literature, art, and history. His diary for 1852 records social visits to the Howitts, the Leigh Smiths, Lady Morgan, and the Milner Gibsons, as well as meetings with Mazzini and dinners with some Camberwell Germans.[62] When he went to Manchester in October 1852 to lecture in German to the Athenaeum Club, the *Manchester Examiner and Times* carried full résumés of the lectures, as well as telling again the famous story of Kinkel's escape and imprisonment. The myth was embellished further:

> A countess, rich and beautiful [Baroness von Bruiningk, who had helped finance Kinkel's escape and who came to live near him in St John's Wood in the summer of 1851], a fellow student of the same *alma mater*, and a kind-hearted innkeeper, were the chief agencies which led Gottfried Kinkel, in the disguise of a Prussian soldier, through the portal and over the drawbridge of the Prussian bastile.

The story was repeated in various provincial newspapers at different times, whenever Kinkel lectured—for example, the *Stirling Journal and Advertiser* referred to his 'rather romantic life' in its account of his lecture on medieval art in Stirling in 1856.[63]

Though his first few lectures were in German, Kinkel achieved great success in a set of lectures on art history which he delivered in English at University College London in April 1853. His friends reported their success. Althaus remembered in 1883 how good they had been, and Malwida von Meysenbug wrote to her mother at the time of the lectures:

I would never have dreamt that Kinkel would have such a brilliant success. The huge amphitheatre of the University, which holds five hundred, was crammed so full that people were sitting and standing on the steps and in the aisles. When Kinkel appeared in the midst of the professors, he was greeted by such an endless cheering that he couldn't get started. After the lecture the upper rooms of the University were opened, where the Flaxman Collections are exhibited. People crowded up there. One met innumerable acquaintances; I myself was amazed at how many I have here; the 'How do you do', 'Guten Abend', 'Bonsoir' seemed as if they would never come to an end. All the professors introduced themselves to Frau Kinkel. The second lecture was even more packed; people had to be turned away. Kinkel spoke wonderfully well; hearing German ideas in a foreign language gave me great pleasure.[64]

Even Herzen, who went to the lectures with his son Alexander, praised Kinkel's talent, but Marx, on hearsay, damned them with that mixture of jealousy, shrewdness, and distortion which he so often displayed when discussing his fellow exiles:

The amiable Gottfried has so far succeeded in ingratiating himself that he has been accorded the use of one of London University's lecture rooms to repeat before a London audience his old series of lectures on Christian art in the Middle Ages. He is giving them *free* and gratis in the hope that he will be able to worm his way into the post of Professor of Aesthetics at London University. He delivers them in ABOMINABLE English, *reading* from a manuscript. Though welcomed with applause at the beginning of the series, he subsequently proved such a complete failure that not even the organised claque of Jewish aesthetics-mongers could save him.[65]

There is every reason to believe that Kinkel's lectures were, in fact, as successful as his friends claimed. His notes for a different series of lectures, on the history of German literature, delivered in Edinburgh in January 1854, survive, and they are quite impressive, being well adapted for his audience. His English was fluent; Kinkel covered the topic from the earliest ages with a broad sweep, describing the sudden flourishing of literature in Germany in the late eighteenth century as the short spring following a long winter of unseen preparation. Mindful of his British audience, he made frequent mention of English translations of, and articles on, German literature. He quoted Professor Blackie, who had translated *Faust* in the 1830s and who held the Chair of Classics at Edinburgh University, on Lessing, and used Blackie's translation of Arndt's rousing song 'The German's Fatherland'. He showed his acquaintance, too, with Carlyle's essays on German Romantic literature. When he reached present-day German literature, he became more 'political', praising Freiligrath and noting that he was once more exiled and 'has quietly and honestly taken a situation in a small counting-house in the City of London'. All the stress was on Germany needing, wanting, and deserving to be united and to have a constitution and proper representation. There was no revolutionary rhetoric, no party line. Kinkel was appealing to his audience's sense of fair play, and in so doing he flattered it. He was careful, too, to add glowing references to the novels of Dickens and Mrs Gaskell on the social conditions in the cities. From his diary it becomes clear that he read all Dickens's novels as they came out; and while in Edinburgh he began a reading of Scott's novels.[66] Kinkel was thus skilful in going some way towards meeting his British host society by acquainting himself with its interests. Marx, Ruge, and other German rivals thought his manner of doing this ingratiating and egotistical. And so it was. On the other hand, many a German exile merely moaned about British society and squabbled with other Germans, thus stranding himself, like Lothar Bucher, who saw nothing at all in a positive light.[67]

Kinkel threw himself into teaching. Johanna taught music at home, and Kinkel gave private tuition in German, art, and history to pupils who came to the house. He also lectured on several subjects at various educational institutions and colleges around London, as well as making lecture tours of the provinces. His notebook for 1853–4 shows that he taught geography at Crosby Hall, Roman history at the recently founded Bedford College for women, geography at Finsbury College and Hyde Park College, sculpture at the Greenwich and Camberwell Institutions, art at Belgrave College, and so on. Johanna Kinkel wrote to Fanny Lewald in 1856 that Kinkel left home between nine and ten in the mornings and did not return till ten o'clock at night, when he had to start marking his students' papers. Often he covered twenty miles in a day, travelling from one London college to another. By 1855 Kinkel was earning an average of between £60 and £70 a month, which was a comfortable income.[68]

The family had moved from St John's Wood to Paddington in December 1852, to be able to attract pupils to the house, St John's Wood being too far from central London,[69] and also to get away from the time-wasting, ungrateful spongers who had attached themselves to Kinkel on his arrival. Many of these were followers of Willich, Prussian ex-officers like Schimmelpfennig and Techow who hung around Kinkel's wealthy patroness, Baroness von Bruiningk, and attended her 'revolutionary' salons just down the road from the Kinkels' St John's

Wood house. Herzen, who viewed Kinkel's vanity with amusement, described his situation with merriment and some sympathy:

> [Kinkel] had lectured publicly on aesthetics in London and Manchester: this could not be forgiven him by the liberators, roaming hungrily and idly about London, of thirty-four German fatherlands. Kinkel was constantly abused in American newspapers, which became the main channel for German libels . . . He was abused by all his compatriots, who never gave any lessons and were constantly asking for loans, never gave back what they had borrowed and were always ready, in case of refusal, to denounce a man as a spy or a thief. Kinkel did not reply . . . The scribblers barked; . . . only now and then a rough, hairy, uncombed mongrel darts out from the bottom floor of German democracy into the *feuilleton* that is read by nobody and bursts out into a vicious yapping to recall the happy times of fraternal insurrections in the various Tübingens, Darmstadts and Brunswick-Wolfenbüttels.[70]

But for the fact that Marx was one of the chief orchestrators of the German-American attacks on Kinkel, this might have been him writing. For he shared Herzen's scorn for, as well as the Kinkels' annoyance with, the idle parading of the Prussian lieutenants and leaders of the next revolution under the command of 'capitano' Willich.

The chief part of Kinkel's income came from his teaching at several of the recently founded colleges for women. He gave the opening lecture at one of these—Hyde Park College—in 1853. His daughter Adela was a pupil there in 1854, and Johanna was full of praise for the 'excellent' ladies' colleges of London.[71] (Unfortunately, Kinkel's attractiveness to women, noted by Althaus and Herzen, who said Kinkel had 'the majestic head of a Zeus',[72] became a torment to Johanna in her increasingly depressed and jealous state. Kinkel seems to have taught almost exclusively girls and women at home as well as in the colleges.) As Marx had guessed, Kinkel always hoped for a full-time, permanent, and exalted position at an educational institution in London. In 1855 he petitioned a fellow exile, the architect Gottfried Semper, who had had the luck to be commissioned to design Wellington's funeral car in 1852 and who was close to Henry Cole, one of the leading spirits behind the building of the Crystal Palace in 1851. Semper had been a lecturer at the School of Design, and Kinkel wanted to apply for a post as lecturer on ornamental art there. Semper gave him a reference to Cole, but warned that there might be 'political objections' to Kinkel. He also said that he himself had not been able to make as much as £400 a year in London and had therefore taken up a post in Zurich, though he would have preferred to stay in London, Zurich being 'too narrow and too pedantic'.[73] Either this put Kinkel off, or he was turned down for the post, for he did not on this occasion get the 'berth' he hoped for. He was to follow Semper to a chair in Zurich eleven years later. Meanwhile, he carried on with his work among the middle-class women and girls who adored him and of whom Johanna Kinkel, as we shall see, was highly critical.

Kinkel also maintained cordial relations with the wealthy, respectable, non-political Germans of Camberwell. He had dissociated himself from most of his fellow exiles after his return from America in March 1852, his Emigration Club of the previous summer having broken up, like Ruge's rival Agitation Club, after Napoleon's *coup*. Now he concentrated on his lecturing and on keeping up friendships with Germans from the financial community, like Gerstenberg and Schwarz, non-political German academics such as Goldstücker of University College, Emanuel Deutsch of the British Museum, the publisher Trübner, and the engineer Siemens. All of these joined Kinkel's German Association for Science and Art, founded in 1864, which met at University College.[74] In 1855–6 he had met Freiligrath at dinners given by the democratic refugee Oppenheim and by Gerstenberg, at which they buried their differences and became friends. Both sent their sons to University College School (as did Karl Blind and, later, Friedrich Althaus). Gottfried Kinkel junior and Wolfgang Freiligrath won prizes at the school in 1861 and 1863, respectively. When Kinkel delivered a memorial address after Freiligrath's death in 1867, he remembered many happy Sundays spent with the Freiligraths in Hackney, 'far from the London fog and the London roar'.[75]

Kinkel also went out to Camberwell, as did Haug and Bucher among others, to lecture to the City Germans who lived there. Fontane reported in the Berlin conservative paper, *Die Kreuzzeitung*, in 1857 on one of Kinkel's lectures to the Camberwell Germans:

> Kinkel's political lapses do not come into the question. For the moment he is Gottfried Kinkel, an eloquent teacher who, as in former times, I won't exactly say unlocks the treasures of special knowledge, but still enlivens his subject and enthralls his hearers with the great power and plastic art of his lecture.

In addition to giving this shrewd analysis of Kinkel's mixture of mediocrity and extraordinary talent, Fontane thought he detected some dejection on Kinkel's part:

> Before me, grown grey with work and worry, stood this man who had such various hopes at various periods of his life. They have all remained equally unfulfilled. Possibly he finds a certain amount of satisfaction in the fate which

has befallen him; but it seemed to me that there sounded from this organ, clear as a bell, homesickness and mourning for something lost . . .[76]

There is certainly some truth in this account, even allowing for Fontane's writing as a servant of the Prussian state and bearing in mind also his own almost fanatical concern with position. Moreover, when Kinkel launched his own German-language journal, *Hermann*, in 1859 in London after his wife's death, the political position it adopted was one of national unity for Germany. His views grew closer to those of German nationalists at home, moving from advocacy of a national republic to that of a Germany constitutionally united under Prussian hegemony. He founded the German National Association in London in 1860, married a second German wife, Minna Werner, in March of that year, with Freiligrath as best man,[77] and generally took a greater interest in events in Germany than he had done at any time since his arrival.

Nevertheless, Kinkel still strove to be fair to England. He pointed out in *Hermann* in 1859, with some justice, that too many exiles wrote negatively about England in German newspapers. These were the very people who had found asylum in 'the only country in Europe which has never expelled a refugee and whose juries have never let themselves be dictated to by a foreign despot'. Some of these correspondents (Lothar Bucher must have been in his mind) wrote as if everything were actually freer in Germany—'even in Berlin!'—than here in Britain. They complained of the Anglican Church and the strict observance of Sundays, but failed to add that the English cleric was, 'of all the clergymen in the world, the least likely to persecute others'. Moreover, Germans attacked the complicated workings of English courts, when in Germany they had not yet reached the stage of having independent judges and a habeas corpus act. Kinkel concluded that such hypocritical criticism was motivated by envy.[78] He himself more than once supported an English cause against his own country and countrymen. On one occasion, he became involved in local Paddington politics. The *Marylebone Mercury* for 3 July 1858 carried an account of a meeting at the Prince of Wales Hotel to discuss the suppression of street noises. After B. Jones, Esq., had moved from the chair that a weekly market be instituted to stop itinerant vendors from crying their wares all day every day, 'Dr Kinkell' [*sic*] rose and said "that he was frequently obliged to wait ten minutes or more, from a man playing an organ under his window, and interrupting him in his studies"; and that, though a foreigner himself, he was quite disgusted with the conduct of some of his countrymen, who were too idle to work in their own country, and then greatly annoyed the inhabitants of this'. In 1861 Kinkel incurred displeasure in the German clubs in London when he took the British side in the odd case of a British army officer, MacDonald, who was arrested for boorish behaviour on a German train.[79]

Kinkel remained polite and grateful to England, despite his failure to obtain a tenured position. He had worked hard and done quite well, helped by his early fame and the recommendations he had to various English people of influence and standing. On the eve of his departure to a professorship in Zurich in 1866, he made a point of addressing the audience at his farewell dinner, most of whom were German, in English. This was, he said, to show his appreciation of 'this noble England, the only country which never denied asylum to the fugitive'. England was a hospitable country:

> . . . it gives elbowroom to every man, a field for his labour and energy, and full liberty to build up his house by his labours, without demanding in return a denial of his principles or the sacrifice of his character. I have not obtained a berth here, and never expected one, believing that my own convictions in religious, political and social questions differ so widely from those of the great majority of the English people; but the difference of opinion has not prevented me, as it would have done in my own country, and might have done in almost every other country, from obtaining through my own labours an honourable position and gain.

Despite the piety, Kinkel was here expressing that sense of liberty to which John Stuart Mill subscribed in his famous work *On Liberty* (1859), in which he was concerned to investigate 'the nature and limits of the power which can legitimately be exercised by society over the individual'. He was also, gently and implicitly, agreeing with Mill (and Engels) in deploring the tyranny of custom and opinion in Britain.[80]

Siemens made a speech of farewell, closely following Horne's sketch of Kinkel's life in *Household Words* in 1850, and hailing Kinkel as a German nationalist. The toast was drunk by the 300 guests (Althaus, who was there, later remembered the number as 500 or 600), then the Camberwell German Choir sang a farewell song. Among the guests and contributors to Kinkel's parting gift were Emanuel Deutsch, Dr Goldstücker, Max Schlesinger, Siemens, and Trübner.[81] Thus Kinkel left England in a relatively bright blaze of glory. His was such a pliable nature that he would have been happy to stay in England, but he was also enthusiastic about his new life in Zurich (though he was undoubtedly disappointed that he was never invited back to Germany as a hero and patriot). He wrote rather hypocritically to his friend Ferdinand Jebens soon after his arrival in Switzerland, saying things were going well. Whereas in England 'the spirit of the country was against me (necessarily, because as a free-thinker, republican, and socialist, I stood against a religious, conservative, and aristocratic society)', here in Switzerland 'the stream flows with me'.[82] 'That's Kinkel for you', as Marx had written in 1851 to Ebner. Kinkel, he said, always moved 'in accordance with the way he believes the popular wind to be blowing'. Marx noticed Kinkel's admiration of a gigantic mirror on show at the Great Exhibition and concluded, 'the mirror is the element in which he exists. He is first and foremost an actor.'[83] Kinkel's vanity is not in doubt, though he seems to have been perfectly sincere in his inconsistency. Herzen thought he had never lost the unction of the former theologian and the egotism of the German professor, and he likened Kinkel, in a flash of genius, to Mr Dorrit in Dickens's novel—'a personage who had no merits other than the physiognomy of a philanthropic patriarch'.[84] It is, however, thanks to Kinkel's vanity that we know so much about his life in London, for the University of Bonn has a huge collection of his carefully kept letters, notebooks, and diaries, as well as his annotated cuttings from German and English newspapers, whenever they contained, as they very frequently did, notices of his doings. And he had, after all, enough talent to impress a committee of professors at University College into almost appointing him to a chair.

Other Refugees: Journalists, Doctors, Artists, and Teachers

Like Kinkel and, in his different way, Ruge, several of the exiles settled down to a new life in England. Many of them had done nothing more revolutionary than refuse to pay taxes in protest at the Prussian reaction after 1848. Some were ex-members of the Frankfurt Parliament, several had published articles critical of the state, and one—Johannes Ronge—was the victim of religious persecution for his pursuance of a liberal Catholic ministry. On arrival in Britain, they looked around for jobs suited to their talents and qualifications. There were doctors (one of them, Karl Heinrich Schaible, estimated that in 1853 there were about forty German doctors in London[85]), artists, musicians, teachers—the largest group—and journalists.

Karl Blind alone managed to make a living entirely, as far as is known, out of writing. He arrived in London with Marx and Seiler in August 1849, and lived in Britain until his death in 1907. During this time, he was German correspondent of the *Morning Advertiser* from 1853,[86] and wrote hundreds of articles on various subjects in the *Fortnightly Review*,

Macmillan's, the *Cornhill Magazine*, and the *National*, *Contemporary*, and *Scottish Reviews*, among others. He was friendly with the Stansfelds, John Morley, John Chapman, and the poets Swinburne and Rossetti. And he appears to have managed the enviable feat of getting his writings into English periodicals (which Marx and Ruge found so hard) and acquiring influential English friends, largely by dint of his quite extraordinary assiduousness, what Marx—for once not unfairly—called his 'genius' for self-advertisement.[87] Friedrich Althaus characteristically put it more kindly in his memoir of the German exiles. What made Blind unique among them, he wrote, was his firm, consistently held republicanism. Not only did he seek a republic in Germany (*not* the autocratic empire which Bismarck eventually built up), but he supported republicanism of every nationality, though he seems to have steered clear of British politics. Thus at different times he wrote pamphlets and articles favouring Mazzini and Garibaldi, lectured in Scotland on behalf of a free Poland, and in 1905 he propagandized for the 'Free Russia' movement.[88]

As Althaus noted, Blind was indefatigable in his propaganda activity. He wrote in English, Italian, German, and American papers. Not only was he foreign correspondent of the *Morning Advertiser* for twelve years, but he also wrote on current affairs for the *Globe*, *The Times*, *Daily News*, and *Morning Star*. Where Kinkel wavered between democracy and republicanism, and Ruge maintained an abstract view on the question until Bismarck's policy beguiled him, Blind stuck to his international republicanism, even to the point of libelling the King of Prussia in his London newspaper, *Der deutsche Eidgenosse* (*The German Confederate*), in 1866. Blind enjoyed the distinction, on this occasion, of having the Prussian government request an English prosecution for libel. No doubt mindful of the jury's view of foreign interference at the Orsini trial, the English government refused the request, on the ostensible grounds that prosecution would only give further publicity to the libel (which is exactly what happened when the government did give way to pressure by prosecuting Johann Most's obscure anarchist journal, *Die Freiheit*, in 1881).[89] Blind was willing to go further than libel. In 1905 he wrote a stirring address 'To the Russian Army', in which he appealed to the ordinary Russian soldiers:

> Sons of the people, you are sent to the shambles in the Far East, not for the benefit of Russia, but for the sake of a corrupt system of government, in which some of the highest members of the Imperial family itself are shamelessly implicated . . . Do not allow yourselves to be made, any more, the butchers of the

champions and supporters of so sacred a cause. If ordered to slay them, turn your weapons upon tyranny itself.[90]

Blind went his own way almost from the first. He was imprisoned in Paris in June 1849 on suspicion of conspiracy, then expelled to England with Marx and others.[91] Before Paris, he had been a republican member of the Frankfurt Parliament and had been imprisoned in Bruchsal for articles written between 1845 and 1848. In May 1849, after spending eight months in prison, he and Gustav and Amalie Struve were freed by the people during the Baden uprising.[92] Once in London, Blind took a room in Grosvenor Square, in which Marx stayed until his family came over from Paris. Their relationship was friendly; when Blind visited Brussels in October 1849 to collect his wife and children, he let Marx stay in his London room, thanked him for the loan of £2 (!), and wrote friendly letters in the name of 'Walter', telling Marx to use his overcoat if he needed it. The following year, in July 1850, Marx was attempting to borrow £20 from Blind, and in 1851 he told Engels that he and Pieper had upset Blind's wife, 'Madame Cohen', a 'vivacious Jewess', with their fierce attack on Feuerbach.[93]

Thereafter, Marx and Blind went their separate ways, Marx marvelling from time to time at Blind's capacity for making speeches and immediately puffing them in a variety of English and German newspapers. On one such occasion in 1870, Marx wrote, 'This is one among thousands of examples of how this "lion" tries to make the English believe he is a kind of German Mazzini.' Ruge, whose wife wrote bitterly of Blind's attacks on her husband, similarly caricatured Blind in 1862 as 'the Baden Garibaldi'.[94] None of his fellow German exiles seems to have liked him much, and perhaps because of this he managed to keep aloof from the 1850–1 squabbles. He secured his job with the *Morning Advertiser*, and had friendly relations—as did all the exiles at one time or another—with Harney, to whose paper, *The Star of Freedom*, he subscribed in 1852, and for whom he wrote some letters of introduction when Harney was preparing to leave for America in 1863.[95]

Blind's friendship with Mazzini was, like most of Mazzini's relationships with other exiles, one of mutual usefulness. While Blind advertised Mazzini's cause in his journalism, Mazzini introduced Blind to his English friends, the Stansfelds, with whom the Blind family became friendly, sometimes meeting up during summer holidays in Eastbourne or Folkstone or Hythe. It was through Blind that Swinburne was able to meet his hero, Mazzini, in 1867, and he was effusively grateful:

> I have no words to thank you for the great kindness you have shewn me. To be permitted to meet face to face the man who from my boyhood has been to me the incarnate figure of all that is great and good, is in itself a privilege beyond price or thanks; that it should be granted to me through and by you, enhances it.

Blind subsequently introduced Swinburne to Louis Blanc, the French socialist exile, too. In 1859 Blanc, a small man with the exile's large ego (he was much lampooned by Marx on both counts), turned to Blind for advice on whether he should accept an invitation to lecture on Rousseau at the Marylebone Institution. Was it a respectable institution? How much should he charge? He also asked Blind to arrange for the *Morning Advertiser* to notice one of his books, thanking his friend 'as a Frenchman, as a friend of liberty, and as a man', when Blind obliged.[96]

In 1857 Blind reopened his correspondence with Struve, Ruge, Ronge, and others, in an attempt to mobilize them to join him in a new republican journal he wanted to found and edit. He told Struve that he was well placed for this task, as he had been for three years a regular contributor to the *Morning Advertiser*, 'the paper with the largest circulation in England, after *The Times*'. He supposed that Struve, who had been living in America since 1851, would be well acquainted with his articles in American papers. The plan, he said, was to get together enough of the German *émigrés*—Ruge, Ronge, Freiligrath, Goegg, for example—to put pressure on Kinkel to release some of the loan money for the venture. However, Kinkel was not to be wooed on this occasion. He wrote to Struve that Blind had sent him extracts from letters by sixteen Germans supposedly supporting his plan. Kinkel noted wryly that all sixteen had different ideas—some wanted money for Swiss periodicals, others hoped to form a club, and Struve himself had the notion of publishing a communally written satire. The only item on which all sixteen agreed was that Kinkel should give them the money.[97]

Though Marx was, of course, not thought of as a possible colleague on a non-communist republican journal, he and Blind had further relations in 1859. It was Blind who passed on to Marx the hint that Karl Vogt, exiled in Switzerland, was in Napoleon's pay (which he was), thus starting Marx off on the long and bitter anti-Vogt campaign. Blind tried to wriggle out of the controversy, but Marx got the English journalist Collet to swear that the information had come from Blind, via Blind's 'tame elephant', Dr Schaible.[98]

In the same year, 1859, Blind became involved in the event which Marx excoriated as a beanfeast of philistines, namely the celebration of the centenary of Schiller's birth. On the face of it, it is strange that

Schiller, the great poet and dramatist of individual, social, and national freedom (having celebrated noble outlaws in *The Robbers* and Swiss nationalism in *William Tell*), should have caused such dissension among those who might plausibly be seen as his national heirs and disciples. But in Marx's view, he had, like Hegel, become the property of bourgeois 'thinkers', an excuse for the German 'philistine' to think elevated thoughts and speak noble words while pursuing in fact a blind, selfish, self-satisfied existence.[99] Blind, Kinkel, and Freiligrath came together, albeit uneasily, to pay homage to their national poet in a festival at the Crystal Palace on 10 November 1859. Freiligrath excused himself grandiosely to the accusing Marx, saying he could hardly, as a poet, 'withdraw sulking into his tent' when Schiller was to be honoured. He wrote a poem for the occasion, which was set to music by the Camberwell musician Ernst Pauer,[100] while Kinkel gave a stirring nationalist speech.

Marx chortled over the arguments on the committee as to whether Schiller's bust should be unveiled during Kinkel's speech or during the singing by the combined German Glee Clubs of London of Freiligrath's cantata, and whether, on advertisements, Kinkel's or Freiligrath's name should come first. The final arrangement was for Kinkel's address, or 'sermon', as Marx called it, to come first, followed by Schiller's 'Lay of the Bell', sung by 'nearly ONE THOUSAND VOICES', then Freiligrath's cantata, during the performance of which 'THE COLOSSAL BUST OF SCHILLER, modelled for this Festival by Herr ANDRE GRASS, will be unveiled', as the advertisement announced. There was also a torchlight procession on the terraces, and tickets for the festival cost a shilling for adults and sixpence for children. Though Blind was less conspicuous than Kinkel and Freiligrath, he, too, was on the committee, and he gave details to Louis Blanc, who wanted to attend, of when and where to leave for Crystal Palace on the day.[101] The 'Herr Andre Grass' who modelled the bust of Schiller was the same Andreas Grass who had been drummed out of Cologne ten years before for striking a medal of Freiligrath. Like so many others, he, too, had ended up in London.

After this, Blind concentrated on his journalism and on enlarging his circle of English acquaintances. In 1864 the *Athenaeum* announced that 'Herr Carl Blind' had become a member of the Shakespeare Committee for the promotion of scholarly editions of Shakespeare's works ('What does Blind understand of Shakespeare?' growled Marx[102]). He made one more attempt to launch a German republican periodical in 1864.

Freiligrath joined him on the editorial board of *Der deutsche Eidgenosse*, which was to be published in London and Hamburg, with Rasch and Struve, now back in Germany, on the German editorial board. The paper's aim was to overthrow tyranny and establish a republican commonwealth. Its motto was: 'Alles durch das Volk! Alles für das Volk!' ('Everything through the people! Everything for the people!') Garibaldi wrote to Blind from Caprera in April 1865, congratulating him on the journal, which he described as the 'organe de l'avenir d'un grand peuple et de la solidarité humaine'.[103] It lasted for two years and was, as we have seen, almost the occasion of a libel suit in 1866.

In 1866, too, Blind's stepson Ferdinand Cohen attempted to assassinate Bismarck in Berlin. He failed, was arrested, and committed suicide in prison. Queen Victoria's daughter, married to the Crown Prince of Prussia and a devout enemy of Bismarck, wrote to her mother on 9 May 1866, 'The poor, well-meaning but mistaken and short-sighted wretch who shot at Bismarck is dead.' Blind and his wife received letters of condolence from Louis Blanc and Ledru-Rollin, and Mrs Stansfeld wrote to Mrs Blind, 'Poor Ferdinand—what a sad fate. I well remember him in our pleasant visit to you at Broadstairs. He looked so quiet and modest and his motives must have been the purest even in this unfortunate affair.' Even Marx was touched, for Ferdinand had been during the early days in London a childhood friend of his son 'Musch' (Edgar), who had died in 1855, aged 8. Ferdinand had also been a pupil, like the sons of Kinkel and Freiligrath, at University College School from 1858 to 1861. Though Marx was moved by the boy's fate, he was hard on his stepfather: 'The strange part of the affair is that Blind has sacrificed on the altar of liberty not his own son, but the Isaac of old Cohen, through his foolish chatter about tyrannicide.'[104]

Blind kept up his friendship with Freiligrath until the latter's return to Germany in 1867, and their sons were friends at University College School during the early 1860s. Otherwise, he carried on writing republican pamphlets, sending articles to newspapers, and giving lectures up and down the country. He made several trips to Bradford to lecture, invited by his friend Dr Bronner, a refugee from events in Baden in 1849 who had set up an eye hospital in Bradford and who founded the Schiller Club there.[105] In January 1870 the Irvine Burns Club, near Burns's birthplace in Ayrshire, made him an honorary member. Later that year John Morley of the *Fortnightly Review* asked him to write an article on the 'probable effects of the consolidation of Germany upon democracy in Europe' after the Franco-Prussian War. Blind replied with a very pro-German piece, which Morley published in the January–June number of 1871.[106] During the next forty years Blind published around thirty more articles in the *Fortnightly* on European history and politics, as well as several in other journals. He ranged over German, French, Russian, Turkish, Italian, and Belgian topics but seldom dealt with English affairs, except in passing. Perhaps this was one secret of his success in English journalism. His uncompromising republican views were acceptable when concentrated on other, generally less advanced, nations. He did, however, publish a pamphlet in German in 1873, entitled *Zur Geschichte der Republikanischen Partei in England* (*Contribution to the History of the Republican Party in England*). In this work, which he seems, wisely, not to have published in English, Blind wrote zealously and with exaggeration of the thriving republican movement in England, counting among English republicans several radical MPs, including Peter Taylor, Henry Fawcett, Sir Charles Dilke, and the late John Stuart Mill and George Grote.

Meanwhile, Blind continued his old practice of sending copies of his articles and pamphlets to the famous and the influential. He courted Max Müller in the 1890s, and wrote to Joseph Chamberlain in 1893 about Gladstone, with whose policies on the Eastern Question he disagreed and of whose religious views he was suspicious.[107] Tireless, terrier-like, he worked for over sixty years in England for his ideal of international republicanism and co-operation. In so doing, he puffed himself shamelessly, as Marx continually noted. Ruge, too, complained to Struve in 1865:

> Blind supports no one but Blind. Even the letter which he wrote to Jena appears in the *Eidgenosse* with the introduction 'The following letter was received in Jena', instead of saying 'was sent there by me'. Have you investigated his head? [a reference to Struve's amateur phrenologizing] or do you know him inside out already?[108]

Blind's ability to survive in exile was no doubt due largely to this undaunted energy, industry, and consistency.

Of the doctors among the exiles, many could not make a living and moved on to America in the early 1850s. Those who stayed, including Blind's friend Dr Bronner, often did rather well. Bronner succeeded in Bradford, where there was a large community of wealthy German businessmen; Engels's friends Louis Borchardt and Eduard Gumpert survived in Manchester, where they could serve a similar community. In London, the Marx family was treated by two German doctors, Freund and Bauer, both of whom threatened to sue him for non-payment of bills.[109] Bauer was an exile who arrived in 1849 and joined the 'bourgeois' circle around Ruge in 1851. Freund had been in England for some years, and was important as one of the chief instigators of the plan for a German hospital in London in 1843.

The Hospital, patronized by Bunsen and Freiligrath's first employer in London, the financier Frederick Huth, was founded in 1845, with Freund as its first Directing Physician. It was an important institution, for it offered free medicine to the thousands of poor German workers living around Whitechapel. Unlike English hospitals, where a reference from one of the patrons was required for admission (thus ensuring that poorer patients went instead to the infirmaries, which had grown up as adjuncts to the poorhouse), the German Hospital admitted patients without ceremony. Several distinguished doctors, English and German, were connected at some time with the Hospital. Hermann Weber, Resident Physician from 1851 to 1853, was later to become a Fellow of the Royal College of Surgeons, and to be knighted by Queen Victoria in 1899. Sir William Jenner, President of the Royal College of Surgeons, was Consulting Physician at the Hospital from 1865 to 1890, as was the Queen's physician, Sir James Paget, from 1878 to 1899.[110]

Of the other German doctors among the exiles, 'Bohemian' Strauss became one of a group of homoeopathic doctors in London, writing articles for the *Homoeopathic Times* in 1853–4, and Julius Althaus, one of three Althaus brothers who came to England in the 1850s because of their opposition to Prussian politics, settled in Manchester Square in 1857, founded a hospital for nervous diseases in Maida Vale, and wrote over fifty books, in English, on a wide range of medical subjects.[111] Dr Schaible made a living from teaching and writing, rather than practising medicine. He taught for several years at the Royal Military Academy in Woolwich, and wrote a successful primer on educational methods, called *Exercises in the Art of Thinking* (1860), which Friedrich Althaus's son, Theodore Frederick, revised and republished as *Seeing and Thinking: Elementary Lessons and Exercises introductory to Grammar, Composition, and Logical Analysis* in 1883.

If it was hard for the refugees to establish themselves in journalism and, in some cases, as medical practitioners, it was, by common consent, hardest of all to succeed in the arts, both because of the large number of musicians and artists among the exiles and because of what most Europeans thought of as Britain's native hostility to art and music, though not to literature. Moreover, those who sought work suffered from the need to find patrons and the intense jealousy of native rivals. Germans may have been particularly vulnerable, as Prince Albert had been regularly taken to task after his arrival as Prince Consort in 1840 for filling the royal household with German servants, artists, and librarians. There was considerable resentment, for example, of Peter von Cornelius, a German artist who arrived in London in 1841 as a protégé of Albert's.[112] Karl Heinrich Schmolze, a refugee from 1848–9, did 'a rather nice set of cartoons' of his fellow exiles in London in 1852, as Marx recounted to Engels. 'Kinkel as King Lear and Willich as the Fool. Also a cartoon in which Willich, as a sloth, squats in a fruit-tree while Mrs. Schärttner on the ground shakes the tree to dislodge him.' Another of Schmolze's cartoons was of Johanna Kinkel leading Kinkel on stage as a dancing bear on a chain. Clearly, though, Schmolze was unable to make a living in England, for he departed to America in April 1853 with Reichenbach and Schimmelpfennig.[113]

One artist who was successful was the portrait painter Rudolf Lehmann, who, though not a political refugee, was nevertheless exiled by the 1848 revolution. For when the revolution broke out in Paris in February 1848, Lehmann, who was studying in Paris and existing by means of giving lessons, lost his livelihood more or less at a stroke. 'Of course', he wrote in his *Reminiscences* (1894), 'all unnecessary expenses, all luxuries, were ruthlessly cut down, and, as is natural in such cases, the fine arts went to the wall.' He thought of America, but stopped in London on the way, in April 1850. His first day was not auspicious, for, like Schurz and Kinkel later that year, he found himself experiencing a British Sunday—though in his case it was in 'aristocratic Mayfair', not Calvinist Edinburgh:

> . . . dead silence reigned on the Sunday morning after my arrival . . . At 11 a.m. all doors opened simultaneously, and out walked solemn gentlemen in black (butlers, as I since learned) with black books under their arms. The doors were slammed to in quick succession. Then came the carriages to fetch the masters or rather mistresses, and finally the servants emerged from the area all with prayer-books; silence followed again until about one o'clock, when the whole party returned in inverse order. That was my first experience of an English Sunday, so different from a Continental one.

Another inauspicious fact was that the revolutions on the Continent had sent several artists in search of work to England. Nevertheless, Lehmann received some commissions to paint the portraits of a few noblemen. After some years in Rome, he settled in London for good in

1867 and became a specialist in society and literary portraits, painting, among others, Browning, Milnes, Dickens, and Lewes.[114] He and his brother Frederick, a merchant, both married daughters of Robert Chambers, and Frederick was to be grandfather to John, Rosamond, and Beatrix Lehmann.

The architect Semper had to fight against British resentment and prejudice when he arrived in 1850, having fled from the Dresden uprisings of 1848–9 via Paris. He had been Professor of Architecture at the Dresden Academy before the revolution, and hoped for recognition in Britain. Through references to Henry Cole, he got some teaching at the School of Design in 1852. Edwin Chadwick, the Public Health Commissioner and champion of proper sanitation and hygienic burial, was planning a large new outer-London cemetery after the alarming cholera epidemic of 1849,[115] and he asked Semper to submit plans for such a cemetery. Nothing came of these, partly because the Treasury made difficulties over financing the project, and partly because Semper's plans, submitted to the Board of Health in June 1851, were rejected as too large and too pagan in style. Though Semper, offended at the rejection, thought of emigrating to Canada, he stayed in England long enough to become distinguished as the designer of Wellington's hearse in September 1852. Prince Albert approved of his plans, and the *Illustrated London News*, which carried lavish engravings of this, the biggest funeral ceremony of the century, described Semper's design as 'splendid'.[116] In spite of this success, the touchy Semper felt dissatisfied, and after much wavering, took up a post at Zurich Polytechnic in 1855, though he soon wished, as he told Kinkel, that he had stayed in less narrow-minded London.

Semper obtained his job in Zurich with the help of Richard Wagner, who, like him, had fled from Dresden after being involved in revolutionary activities. Though Wagner did not become a refugee in England, his story intersects with those of more than one fellow revolutionary who did. For not only did he know Semper, but he was one of those German exiles based in Zurich who answered Schurz's appeal in 1851 to become guarantors of Kinkel's loan.[117] When in 1855 he was invited to London by the secretary of the London Philharmonic Society (George Hogarth, Dickens's father-in-law) to give a series of concerts, Wagner came and spent four months in London, from March to June, during which time he met Malwida von Meysenbug and Friedrich Althaus.

Like his patron in Weimar, Liszt, and Berlioz, who was in London at the same time conducting a season of concerts for the rival New

Philharmonic Society, Wagner was unimpressed by the musical life of London. He hated the cliques, the hostile press, the influential music critics—particularly Davison of *The Times*—who required to be flattered or even bribed with presents of snuff-boxes and shirt-studs, and, most of all, the requirement to conduct third-rate works by British composers such as Potter, Onslow, and Macfarren. Fontane and Weerth had both criticized the bad taste of the English in music. Now Wagner was scornful of the British love of oratorio which had begun with a German—Handel—and been shrewdly appealed to by another —Mendelssohn, the darling of the London musical scene until his death in 1847.[118] Wagner thought English audiences both inattentive and indiscriminate in their applause. Here the ever-watchful *Punch* would have agreed with him (though it joined in the sneering about 'the music of the future' and the gossip about Wagner's unpaid debts during Wagner's visit[119]). Music was made subordinate to social manners, as *Punch* had noted in 1848. It carried a spoof letter from Elysian Fields, signed 'Ludwig van Beethoven', complaining of what had happened at a recent musical festival in Norwich. The orchestra had played the first movement of a Beethoven symphony and was proceeding with the intermezzo when the Duke of Cambridge arrived in the hall. At this point, the conductor (ironically another German who had settled in London in 1835, Julius Benedict) 'stopped the band, and the National Anthem was immediately begun'.[120]

In spite of his disgust with England, Wagner did have some success with his concerts. Victoria and Albert attended one of them, on 11 June, when they heard not only Macfarren's *Chevy Chase* overture but also Wagner's own *Tannhäuser* overture. On 14 May, Malwida von Meysenbug and the Kinkels had been to another concert which included the *Tannhäuser*. Malwida had written Wagner a fan letter in 1852, and now she met her ideal composer (of whom she was to see a great deal more when they both lived in Rome many years later) at the house of Friedrich Althaus. Althaus, in turn, admired Wagner and had foreseen success for him in England, so he begged his friend in Germany, von Bandel, for a letter of introduction to the composer.[121] Though Wagner despised Mendelssohn's music and his success in England, he allowed himself to be entertained by some of the wealthy Camberwell Germans, like Beneke, who had patronized Mendelssohn.[122] Wagner did not meet Marx, but he almost coincided with him in Camberwell, for Marx fled to Imandt's house there in the summer of 1855 to avoid Dr Freund and other creditors. And his life bore one curious similarity to Marx's. His great work, the *Ring* cycle, with its German topic and its characteristically German ambitious scope, was written entirely in exile, just as Marx's *magnum opus*, *Capital*, was.

If Wagner was dissatisfied with England's musical ways, so also was Charles Hallé, who contrasted the excellent music-making of provincial German towns like his home town, Hagen, with the poor standard of execution and appreciation in London and Manchester. (One of the few advantages of the historical and geographical arrangement of Germany was that each princedom had its centre of music and theatre.) Like Lehmann, he was a non-political exile who was in Paris in February 1848, lost his pupils through the 'damnable Revolution', and made for England as the only country immune to the general revolutionary upheaval. He wrote to his parents from London in April 1848:

> The competition is very keen, for, besides the native musicians, there are at present here—Thalberg, Chopin, Kalkbrenner, Pixis, Osborne, Prudent, Pillet, and a lot of other pianists besides myself who have all, through necessity, been driven to England, and we shall probably end by devouring one another.[123]

Hallé called on Berlioz, who was also visiting London and who began his *Memoirs* in London in March 1848 with the following dramatic observation:

> As I write, the juggernaut of Republicanism rolls across Europe. The art of music, long since dying, is not quite dead. They are about to bury it, or rather to throw it on the dung-heap. France and Germany have no further existence for me. Russia is too remote, I cannot go back there. England, since I have lived here, has treated me most warmly and hospitably; but now, with the first tremors from the Continent, flocks of frightened artists come hurrying from all points to seek refuge, as sea-birds fly landward before great storms. Will the British capital be able to maintain so many exiles? Will it wish to listen to their tales of woe amid the vainglorious clamour of its neighbours . . . ?

Berlioz commiserated mock-seriously with Hallé's fate: 'I am very *sorry* to have the pleasure of seeing you, nevertheless I thank you for having come to this house so soon after your shipwreck on the coast of England.'[124]

Despite his reluctance to be in England, Hallé soon settled down to become a popular pianist and conductor, and to 'play a humble but not altogether unimportant part in the development of [England's] musical taste', particularly in Manchester, where he went in the summer of 1848 at the invitation of the 'prosperous and important' German colony there. He worked at the improvement of music-making in Manchester, gave piano recitals in London, and later specialized in conducting concerts to which working-class people were encouraged to come. 'An Operative' wrote to him in 1873, thanking him for giving him such pleasure at a recent concert and enclosing 'two yards of fine white flannel' as a 'small token' of his regard.[125] From 1869 Hallé was a member, with Engels, of the Brazenose Club in Manchester, and in 1887 he was knighted for his services to music, particularly in Manchester, whose most famous orchestra still bears his name.

As for the teachers among the refugees, they found it difficult to get started, unless, like Kinkel, they arrived well furnished with references, or, like Wolff and Pieper, they taught the children of better-off German exile families like that of Reichenbach, or established banking families like the Rothschilds and the Huths. Those who succeeded in making a living from teaching did so in various ways. In Brighton, Ruge and his wife both took in pupils and travelled around Sussex, giving lessons 'to respectable people in elegant houses', as Agnes Ruge wrote in her memoir of her life in Brighton.[126] Kinkel tramped around London, lecturing here and there, as did his younger friend and ex-student Friedrich Althaus, who wrote in 1873 that those exiles who were willing to work hard and travel from job to job usually succeeded in making a decent living.[127] He himself was finally rewarded after twenty years of part-time teaching at different institutions with the chair of German at University College London in 1874. Others, like Eugen Oswald and Karl Tausenau, spent a lifetime teaching and examining here and there in London. One exile, Johannes Ronge, set up a school in Hampstead in 1851, where he successfully started a new movement in English education.

Ronge, a Catholic who had established a 'Freie Gemeinde' ('Free Community') in Hamburg in 1846 and later a non-confessional school on the same lines, came to England in 1849 to escape government oppression. In London he consorted with Ruge, joining his and Mazzini's European Central Democratic Committee in 1850, and he also became friendly with the Kinkels. He attended several of the commemorative banquets in the early 1850s, adding, as Jenny Marx reported, his 'German Catholic organ tones' to the fluent English of the 'sly Viennese' Tausenau and the clumsy 'Low German' accent of Ruge at the Robert Blum banquet in 1852.[128] Ronge appears to have been rather a comic figure, according to enemies like the Marxes—'the modern Luther', 'John the Baptist' to Kinkel's Christ—but also to friends like Johanna Kinkel, who noted wryly that he was doing well in setting up his religious but non-denominational community in London. Amalie Struve reported enviously in March 1851 that Ronge was giving lectures and, unlike the purely political refugees for whom the English showed little sympathy, had found 'a good furrow to plough'.[129]

Not only did Ronge find willing converts to his religious society, but, more importantly and more lastingly, he started the kindergarten system in England which, to borrow his own metaphor, quickly took root and still flourishes today. The system had first been established in Zurich earlier in the century by Friedrich Fröbel, whose nephews Julius and Carl carried on his ideas, Julius in Zurich and, after the revolution, in America (from where he proposed to Malwida von Meysenbug, whom he had not met, in 1850), and Carl in Zurich and Hamburg, then from 1853 in Scotland. The latter, in his *Explanation of the Kindergarten* (1875), described the system as having something in common with established infant-school practice in Scotland and with Robert Owen's ideas for communal living and working. Its creed was 'Christian Humanism', broad enough to be shared by Jews, Muslims, and Hindus. The theory was one of the harmonious development of children's abilities through play.[130]

Johannes Ronge set up the first English kindergarten in his Hampstead house in September 1851. He and his wife Bertha wrote *A Practical Guide to the English Kinder Garten* in 1855, which stressed organized play as 'a means of culture and a useful labour for a child'. Space was important, as was physical exercise. Music was played for its humanizing effect and to inculcate an instinct for harmony. The kindergarten should be, in short, 'a garden in which humanity may bloom'.[131] Whereas the Prussian government had prohibited the schools in August 1851 as 'dangerous to society', the British government gave Ronge financial as well as moral support. He told Kinkel in 1859 that fifteen schools had already accepted the system and that he and his wife had trained about fifty teachers in its methods.[132] By 1853 his own school was doing so well that he had moved it to the more central Tavistock Place. There he was able to find plenty of pupils, including children of some German exiles and visitors. Fontane sent his son there during a stay in London in 1857; Heinrich Bettziech, a refugee and foreign correspondent of various German newspapers (who had been a pupil of Ruge's in Halle in the early 1830s), also had his sons with Ronge; and the children of Kinkel's second marriage, to Minna Werner, attended in the early 1860s.[133]

As one might expect, Ronge offended some English people with the breadth of his views on religion. He must have raised some eyebrows when he brought in the atheist Holyoake to address the Humanistic Association in 1855. And F. W. Newman, brother of John Henry Newman and a leading Unitarian as well as Professor of Latin at University College, and writer on social, political, educational, and religious subjects, quarrelled with Ronge over the latter's having married a divorcee.[134] Ronge's comic image among his fellow exiles was due in part to the atheism which was almost *de rigueur* amongst them, and in part probably to his tendency to be taken in by swindlers. In one letter to Kinkel, he complained that a German shoemaker passed on to him by Kinkel had run off with a new pair of shoes Ronge had paid him for, adding, 'Unfortunately, I have been cheated so often by our countrymen since I have been here that I am hardly surprised at it happening again.' His naïvety exhibited itself again in 1860, when he returned to Germany to establish his system once more. He was soon imprisoned for lecturing on the sexuality of children and for criticizing Catholicism. In a miserable letter from prison in Frankfurt in 1865 he told Kinkel that Bismarck and the Jesuits had combined to persecute him.[135]

However, thanks chiefly to Ronge, the kindergarten system became highly respected in England. The Froebel Society was founded in 1874, and in 1885 its vice-presidents included Mrs Humphry Ward, Oscar Browning, and Lady Goldsmid. A Miss Franks opened training schools for kindergarten teachers in Camden and Baker Street in the same year, and she lectured on the system to the girls of the North London Collegiate School, also in 1885.[136]

The North London Collegiate, founded in 1850, was the school favoured for their daughters by several German merchants in London. Fredericka Seckel, daughter of 'Sigismund Seckel, Merchant', Anna Wiedhofft, daughter of 'F. A. Wiedhofft, Wholesale Manufacturing Furrier', and Elizabeth Jung, daughter of 'Charles Jung, Manager of Colonial Department of Messrs. Fred. Huth & Co', are names in the register for the 1870s. So also is Gertrude Freund, daughter of Dr Freund, and from 1883 to 1890 Ella Oswald, daughter of the exile Eugen Oswald.[137] Oswald's sister Augusta was German teacher at the school from 1871 until her death in 1884, when an Augusta Oswald Memorial Fund was set up and 'sixty-nine volumes' of German works were bought with the money raised.[138]

Eugen Oswald himself was a teacher in England for over fifty years. In his *Reminiscences of a Busy Life* (1911), Oswald recalled his involvement in the Dresden uprising of 1848, his flight to Paris, two months' imprisonment there (with Dronke as a fellow inmate), then his expulsion to Belgium in 1852 and his further ejection after a few weeks to England. A lawyer by training and belonging to no discernible political party, Oswald consorted with Ruge, becoming a secretary of his short-lived Agitation Club, with Pulszky, whose sons he tutored, with Kossuth, whose daughter his sister Augusta taught in 1852, and with Kinkel, whom he succeeded as a teacher at a private school in London around 1860. During the Franco-Prussian War, he drew up a document on behalf of French and German exiles in Britain protesting against the war. Louis Blanc signed it, as did Karl Blind and also Marx, though he refused to do so in the same room as Blind. Marx thought Oswald 'a decent chap, but rather clueless'. Oswald helped Marx to administer the fund for refugees from the war in 1871, bombarding Marx, as Allsop was also doing, with letters about the needs of refugees.[139]

In his memoir, Oswald claimed to have been friendly with refugees of all opinions, including Semper, Schaible, Ronge, Liebknecht, and Malwida von Meysenbug, whom he met more than once during the 1850s on the Isle of Wight, where she went as governess to the Herzen family and he as companion to the Pulszkys and tutor to their children. He also had a genius for collecting famous English acquaintances. While teaching languages at a private school in Cumberland he met Robert Chambers, the Edinburgh friend of Fanny Lewald and Kinkel's host in 1854 when he lectured in Edinburgh. In 1855 Oswald began teaching French at University College School, where the two Pulszky boys were his pupils.[140] He married an Englishwoman in 1860, taught Richard Cobden's daughters for a time, became connected with the Working Men's Colleges established by Kingsley and F. D. Maurice, was an examiner at Greenwich College in the 1870s, and was still teaching German in 1905—to the children of King Edward VII, no less. The German Social Democrat Eduard Bernstein remembered Oswald as an honest, diligent man, who was well respected in England but who, because his appointment at Greenwich had not been tenured, received no pension and thus had to go on lecturing into his seventies in order to live.[141]

Oswald was a prolific writer, too. In 1854 he translated, with Joseph Coulthard, Wilhelm von Humboldt's *Sphere and Duties of Government*, on which Mill drew for sections of his work *On Liberty*. He also wrote the first German 'biography' of Carlyle in 1881. Fontane reviewed it favourably, though it was no more than a patchwork containing snippets from Carlyle's works and extracts from memoirs of Carlyle by, among others, Goethe, Taine, Lewes, and Sterling.[142] During the last thirty years of the century, Oswald was a member of a dozen clubs; he was a Positivist, a member of the F. D. Maurice Society, the Carlyle Society, Holyoake's co-operative movement, and the English Goethe Society, founded in 1886 with Max Müller as its first president. In connection with the last-mentioned society, Oswald compiled a Goethe bibliography in 1900, which Frederic Harrison praised as 'a striking testimony to the great poet's reputation and to your own industry and acumen'.[143] Like Blind, he became involved in Russian affairs, as a letter to him from Ramsay MacDonald in 1908, regretting that the Russian Committee was made up solely of MPs, testifies.[144]

Though Oswald's *Reminiscences* make him seem a rather comic character—he takes pride, for instance, in having collected not only famous friends, but also their belongings, telling his readers that Mrs Stansfeld once gave him a book given to her by Mazzini and his wife a bracelet with a cameo of Kossuth, and that Carlyle's niece passed on to him a pair of silver sugar tongs 'which had belonged to and been used by Mr. and Mrs. Thomas Carlyle'[145]—there is no doubt that his was indeed a 'busy life', and one in which he accepted his exile philosophically, getting on with whatever work came to hand. Moreover, he had started with no advantages except possibly that of being able to remain amicably aloof from party squabbles, because he arrived in London after the dogfights of 1850–1.

Staying away from the exile clubs with their plotting and nostalgia was also the secret of Karl Tausenau's success. He had participated in the revolution in Vienna, spent six weeks in prison in Paris in 1849 with Blind, among others, and joined Ruge's agitation group on his arrival in England. However, he was soon singled out for abuse, not only by opponents of Ruge but also by members of the club. For he used his exceptional fluency in English to flatter English audiences at banquets, to impress English landladies—Gustav Rasch remembered that his landlady would say, when Tausenau visited, 'Indeed, he is quite English'—and to become generally acceptable in London. To his almost accentless English he added a self-deprecating humour attractive to the English, a beardless face, a good English suit, membership of the Whittington Club, and respectable lodgings at which to receive the pupils who, by all accounts, came immediately and continued coming until at least 1873, when Friedrich Althaus noted that Tausenau was still teaching in London.[146] His was the success of the chameleon.

So also was that of the man who, in the professional sense, did best of all in England. Friedrich Althaus was the first of the three brothers from Detmold to arrive in England in November 1853, Julius, the doctor, and Bernhard, a musician, following him in the mid 1850s. In 1854 Johanna Kinkel prophesied, rightly, that Althaus would do well: 'He is just the person to flourish in London. A winning appearance, real gentlemanly manners, full of knowledge, and rather serious and reserved—he'll turn out well.' Kinkel helped to get Althaus some teaching in London, providing him with a reference for a post at Woking Women's College in 1861.[147] Althaus, too, kept aloof from the warring factions. No doubt, as in the case of Oswald, this was easier for him because he first came to England in 1853, after the clubs had split up and many of the quarrellers had gone to America. Having been born in 1829, he was a good deal younger than most of the other exiles and had had little contact with them in Germany (except for Kinkel, who had taught him and his older brother Theodor). He got on quietly with his life in England, and his view was that those who failed to settle happily were themselves at fault. At any rate, he wrote in his retrospect of the exiles in 1873, 'everyone enjoyed equally the protection of the law and the right to the advantages of social and industrial conditions which offered an unlimited field of activity to individual enterprise'.[148]

If he sounds here like the perfect English gentleman, that seems to be indeed what he became. His memoir of the exiles is a model of objectivity, in which he tactfully assesses his countrymen's doings in England in the kindest way. Marx is the only one at whose expense he allows himself some humour, and then only mildly:

> . . . the famous founder of the International still lives in London, and will presumably go on doing so into his old age as the 'last of the Mohicans' among the German exiles, unless (admittedly an unlikely eventuality) the victory of his ideas calls him to become president of some workers' republic somewhere.[149]

In the 1870s Althaus was, with Schaible and Professors Huxley and Tyndall, an examiner in the University of London and in 1874 he became Professor of German at University College London, a position he held till his death in 1897. He lectured on medieval and modern German literature, and in the course of his survey he dealt, of course, with poets of the Revolution such as Arndt, Herwegh, Heine, and Freiligrath. Althaus tactfully avoided political controversy, merely describing the works of these poets, and singling out Freiligrath's translations from English poets for particular praise.[150] In a book published in Germany in 1869, *Englische Charakterbilder* (*English Portraits*), Althaus republished essays written in German periodicals on English literary and political figures. Again, tact and a balanced assessment are the keynote to his accounts of celebrities such as Palmerston, Disraeli, Cobden, Thackeray, Carlyle, John Stuart Mill, and Turner. In his introduction he claimed that he was trying to avoid both Anglomania, which had characterized much German discussion of England up to the mid 1850s, and Anglophobia, which had disfigured many Continental accounts since then. The essays are knowledgeable, detailed, and fair-minded, though seldom exciting. Carlyle, to whom Althaus sent a copy, replied that the essay on Disraeli was, in his opinion, the best: 'something of real Portrait there, though not quite crowned with hemlock, as perhaps it might have been'. 'To others', he added, '(myself not excepted,—nor still less the Cobden, Mill & Co.) you are far too kind; though doubtless that is the safe side to err on.'[151]

Carlyle was, in fact, the living celebrity in whom Althaus was most interested. Althaus was a historian, having submitted his doctorate to Berlin University in 1852 on the writing of history, and he thought Carlyle 'without question' the greatest essayist and historian in Britain.[152] In 1866, after the death of Jane Carlyle, Althaus set about writing a memoir of Carlyle. He wanted to meet his subject, but Carlyle was not inclined to see visitors in the months after his wife's death. Instead, Althaus approached Joseph Neuberg, a German living in Britain who hero-worshipped Carlyle and had become his researcher and amanuensis during the writing of *Frederick the Great*. Neuberg asked Carlyle for certain biographical facts, and Althaus was able to write a remarkably accurate piece on Carlyle, which was published in the periodical *Unsere Zeit* in 1866 and republished in *Englische Charakterbilder* three years later. In the essay Althaus, like Engels before him, was most interested in the confluence in Carlyle of British practical, empirical thinking and German transcendental idealism. Like Engels, he mistook Carlyle for an 'Englishman', though not for a Tory. He called him 'the English journalist', at which point Carlyle, no doubt with both terms in mind, noted in the margin of his own copy 'schwerlich!' ('hardly!').[153] Otherwise, the piece is knowledgeable and interesting. It stresses the importance of *Sartor Resartus* in Carlyle's career as a symbolic statement of Carlyle's 'lament over the decline of the former age of faith' and his 'plea for idealism rather than materialism'.

Althaus also traced without difficulty the German influences on *Sartor Resartus*—mainly from Fichte and Jean Paul Richter—which had puzzled English readers. Of Carlyle's later, illiberal writings Althaus wrote diplomatically but dissentingly. *On Heroes and Hero-Worship* ran 'counter to the democratic *Zeitgeist*', and Carlyle's endorsement in *Chartism* of might as right was, along with Hegel's similar view that what is reality is rational, 'a dangerous, double-edged principle, and, as one can well imagine, doubly repugnant to a people like the English so jealously proud of their ancient birthright of freedom'.[154]

Against the sections where Althaus's liberal political views show through the polite assessment, as in the passage just quoted, Carlyle wrote in the margin, 'empty babble to me every line of it'. Otherwise, Carlyle's comments were mainly additional rather than corrective, and he wrote quite warmly to Althaus in July 1866, after he had received the essay:

> Mr. Carlyle sends his compliments to Mr. F. Althaus; has rec[d] Mr. A.'s Essay; recognises well enough the careful study, the ingenuity and loyalty, the altogether friendly feelings everywhere manifest there; and returns Mr. A. his thanks for the same.
>
> Errors not a few are unavoidable in such an Enterprise; but none of Mr. A.'s are of much importance.[155]

Althaus was to have more to do with Carlyle and to meet him in person, when he was asked to finish the German translation of *Frederick the Great*, begun by Joseph Neuberg, who died in March 1867. The completed translation appeared in 1869. Althaus also translated Foster's *Life of Dickens* into German. These translations, together with his teaching and lecturing, amounted to a genuine contribution to Anglo-German literary relations, while in his domestic and social life Althaus became an honorary Englishman. Carlyle noted in 1866: 'Althaus, I hear, is a man towards 40; some kind of German Teacher in Woolwich Military Academy, and "own Correspondent" of various German Newspapers; a perfectly respectable and quietly diligent Householder and Pater-familias among us.'[156] When Althaus made his successful application for the post of German professor at University College London, he asked Carlyle, who had offered him 'help in cases of this kind', to write a reference for him. Althaus hoped to be given the chair, not for financial reasons, but because, he told Carlyle, 'I should prize it as a means of contributing in my humble way to the better understanding between England and Germany, which, as long as I have been here, has been one of the leading principles on which I have acted in everything I have tried to do.'[157]

Althaus's sons were, of course, sent to University College School.

One of them, Theodore Frederick, went on to Oxford on a scholarship, was tutor in the 1880s to the teenage Rothschild who was to become the first Baron Rothschild, and was the author of several books. In one of these, the brief *Recollections of Mark Pattison* (1885), Theodore Frederick Althaus tells an amusing story about his father's high expectations of an Oxford education and Pattison's prompt deflation of them. The young Althaus told his tutor that his father wanted him to learn Sanskrit, as well as following the official course in classics. To this Pattison replied:

> My young friend, I am very grieved to tell you that if you have come up to Oxford with the idea of getting knowledge, you must give that up at once. It is merely a race to get through the examinations; you have time for nothing else. We have bought you and we're running you for two plates. Yes, we've bought you; tell your father so; tell him you don't belong to him now, and that until you have got your Classes in the Examinations, you have no time for reading what is not connected with them.[158]

Theodore later became a stockbroker, helped by the Rothschilds, who were grateful for his services as tutor, and his grandson, Mr Nigel Althaus, is today a senior partner in the same firm of stockbrokers in the City. Friedrich Althaus has thus a double distinction: he achieved the most permanent and respectable professional position of all the exiles, and he began a line of Althauses who have become, except in name, entirely English. Being, unlike Marx, neither a genius nor a man of unacceptable or dubious politics, Althaus fitted comfortably into English life in the later nineteenth century.

5
The Women of the Exile

Johanna Kinkel

Johanna Kinkel was, according to her friend Malwida von Meysenbug, 'the outstanding woman of the emigration'. In her own words in 1851, half ironic, half self-dramatizing, she was the 'mother of the emigrants', to whom 'our unhappy exiled acquaintances' came with 'a hundred different claims and requests'.[1] Johanna made no secret of the fact that she resented her husband being beset by his fellow exiles, all hoping either to use his name for support for their political schemes, or to get financial help or a job recommendation, or both. She was determined to keep Kinkel to herself, now that she had him back with her after his imprisonment, and all she wanted was to work hard and do well in England, a country she admired in almost all its aspects. As she told Fanny Lewald in a letter of October 1852, she knew that by her hard work and relative success, she was making 'innumerable enemies' among the exiles because she could not satisfy the demands of 'those who *don't* work'.[2]

Her robust view was that the idlers and moaners and dreamers had only themselves to blame if they were unhappy and insolvent in exile. In this she was in agreement with Herzen, though naturally she found her fellow countrymen less amusing than the more detached, less bothered Russian did. In 1854 she wrote:

> One can learn an awful lot in England. Instead of always chewing over their old mottoes and maxims, those who have been forced into exile here ought really to make a thorough study of this land and its institutions, so that, when there is something for them to organize some day back in Germany, they can get started in a more practical way than they did in 1848. Would you believe it?—there are still clubs of Continental refugees . . . sitting around here, not mixing at all with the English, but just carrying on among themselves the squabbles about 1849 [the Frankfurt Parliament fiasco]. Amongst these people it's the fashion to criticize England, and people like us are actually looked on with suspicion, because we reconcile ourselves to our situation and put up with our surroundings.[3]

Johanna was to make this point again and again. In her novel *Hans*

Ibeles in London (published posthumously in 1860), a remarkably interesting work of scarcely disguised autobiography with a flight at the end into neurotic fantasy, she described how Hans Ibeles and his wife Dorothea were accused of feathering their own nests by 'the gentlemen' of the exile who 'dozed around', conspiring among themselves and disdaining to learn English—so brief was their exile to be, as they thought. Yet these same gentlemen, headed by Wildemann (based on Willich), were queuing up to demand some of the fruits of the Ibeles' labours, which they disdained as 'bourgeois'.[4] Her awareness of the hypocrisy of this attitude was as sharp as Herzen's or Marx's, though the latter had, of course, no sympathy for the Kinkels' attempts to survive in England. Indeed, so irritated was he by their genius for making the headlines that he allowed himself some cruel criticism after Johanna's suicide in November 1858. Fanny Lewald published some of Johanna's letters to her from London in a German newspaper immediately after Johanna's death, and these soon appeared in English in the *Daily Telegraph*. Marx read them and commented to Engels on this evidence of how

> the coterie is exploiting the death of the NASTY 'acrimonious shrew' who wrote from London: 'Have you any idea what it is to be looked upon as a sort of mother to all emigrants?' That was what the creature wrote at a time when she and Gottfried, AS A SORT OF BEGGAR, were knocking at the doors of all the Jews in the City.

In fact, as we have seen, Gottfried and Johanna were using introductions from Fanny Lewald to English sympathizers to build up their careers as teachers, though they also had access, through Kinkel's fame, to the wealthy Germans in England. To borrow Johanna's metaphor for the Ibeles couple, they were like 'accomplished swimmers around whose legs a mass of drowning men were clinging'.[5]

When the workers among the exiles taxed the Kinkels with pandering to the aristocracy because Kinkel gave lectures before aristocratic and bourgeois audiences, Johanna turned on them roundly: 'I asked, "What is your job?" They replied, "We make carpets." I cried, "How can you call yourselves members of the workers' party, then? Does the proletariat want carpets for its rooms? Don't you also rather serve the aristocracy and the bourgeoisie?"' She had a point, though she failed to take into account the fact that she and Kinkel were soon able to make a comfortable living from their kind of hard work, whereas the carpet-makers, no matter how many hours they laboured, would never earn enough to live other than precariously. She always took her stand, naïvely, on the importance of one's being willing to work. Thus she viewed the agitation about the Ten Hours Bill, designed to restrict factory working to ten hours a day, with some scepticism. Recounting to Fanny Lewald in 1854 how hard she and Kinkel were working, she described the English proletariat as 'naïve' to complain about working more than ten hours. 'How they would revolt if they were to work as much as we do!' she wrote, rather unimaginatively. Johanna added teachers to the ranks of the British working class, whom, agreeing with Dickens, she saw as the hardest-worked people under the sun. 'If you want to know what white slavery is', she told Kathinka Zitz in 1853, 'come to London.'[6]

And she and Kinkel did work hard. While he spent long days lecturing and tutoring in colleges all over London, Johanna stayed at home organizing the household and teaching music and singing to English pupils who came to the house. Kinkel bought her an Erard piano in July 1851,[7] and she set up a singing school for young children, using a book she had published in Bonn in 1849, which appeared in London in 1852 as *Songs for Little Children.* Johanna noted in her journal at this time that her school was so successful that a group of old ladies, on hearing tiny children sing so well, were fired with enthusiasm to learn singing themselves. When Johanna doubted if their voices were flexible enough, they replied, 'O, if you can teach so little children, you are also able to instruct old Ladies.'[8] One of her compositions, 'The Soldier's Farewell', became a favourite Victorian song.

Apart from teaching music, Johanna also wrote articles on musical life in London, some of which were published, alongside Liebknecht's schizophrenic contributions, as 'Correspondence from London' in Cotta's *Morgenblatt* during the 1850s. On this subject, Johanna agreed with Wagner and others about the woeful limitations of English music-making. She noticed, like him, that the English were oratorio lovers and that their favourite opera was the light Italian kind by Donizetti, Rossini, and Bellini. When German music was played, it was invariably by Mendelssohn or Weber, and even their music would be embellished with 'Yankee-Doodle' variations. In high society, musicians would be hired to entertain guests, but were not allowed to mix with them. Two of Hans Ibeles's pupils who show musical talent are laughed at by their school-friends, and their father apprentices them to the family business rather than let them pursue musical careers. As the authoress comments, the English are willing to pay to listen to music but would be ashamed to practise it at home, except as a hobby. A respectable Englishwoman in *Hans Ibeles* weeps with shame because her sister-in-law has married her piano teacher.[9] English novelists were aware of this form of snobbery too. George Eliot was to satirize the anti-culture attitude of the English landed gentry nearly twenty years later, in *Daniel Deronda* (1876), when she showed the Arrowpoint family responding with horror to their daughter's desire to marry her German music tutor, Herr Klesmer. And in 1860 Wilkie Collins, who topically introduced an Italian refugee, Professor Pesca, into the plot of *The Woman in White*, described the prospective employers of Walter Hartright, the drawing master, making anxious enquiries: 'Is he a foreigner or an Englishman? . . . Respectable? . . . Never mind about his genius . . . We don't want genius in this country, unless it is accompanied by respectability.'

Even teaching piano and singing at home brought problems. Getting started was almost impossible without the precious references which, as many exiles noticed, were required in England, and which, in the nature of things, they very seldom had to show. 'The Englishman doesn't trust his ears', wrote Johanna crossly, 'but he trusts references.' Especially, she continued, if the references came from an aristrocratic family.[10] Like Charles Hallé, she sometimes found teaching music to the English a comic business. Hallé tells how one of the young ladies of Manchester who came to him for piano lessons once omitted several bars of a Mozart sonata. When Hallé asked her why, 'she gave a never-to-be-forgotten answer, "Oh, that is in a minor key, and papa does not like minor."' In 1852 Johanna Kinkel told of giving music lessons in her front room in St John's Wood at the same time as her neighbour, also a singing teacher, did the same in his adjacent front room. On one occasion when their lessons coincided, she was amused to hear his renderings of Rossini finales filling in the gaps in her own teaching of classical German works.[11]

During the later 1850s, Johanna was able to spend some time in the British Museum, researching for a history of music which she left unfinished at her death.[12] When the British Museum's great circular Reading Room was opened in 1857, Johanna described it ecstatically in a letter to Fanny Lewald:

> The Reading Room of the British Museum is now completed, and if London had nothing but this hall of the blessed, scholars would find it well worth their while to make a pilgrimage here. All the sorrows of the outside world disappear in the mighty rotunda, and it is so quiet in this region of eternal spirits that one can follow a thought into one's inmost recesses. Thank goodness there is at last

one place in London where you can have peace and quiet. You only need to step into the Reading Room, and you feel yourself to be pure spirit. How can they possibly have managed to build it so that no sound can be heard from the squares and thoroughfares . . . ? The volumes round the walls look like a delicate mosaic, and gilded galleries go round right up to the glass dome. Never has wisdom been made so comfortable for the student. Each one has his place, with a desk and accessories, and he only needs to signal for the folios to come floating down from every region.[13]

All modern users of the Reading Room will recognize this description, despite the fanciful element; and though Marx left no such record of *his* impressions, one imagines he may have felt something of Johanna's excitement too as he worked diligently on *Capital* at the same time and under the same glass roof.

On the question of education generally, Johanna had quite a lot to say. Not only did she and Kinkel teach, but they also had their four children educated at schools in London. She reported to friends in Germany that her older son Gottfried was to go to University College School in 1854, because it was one of the few institutions in London which was 'free from religious influence'. However, the fees were 'enormous', and the school, though one of the best in London, not marvellous. Gottfried was unhappy at first, and Johanna complained that all the classes took place in one large hall, most of the teachers being merely cheaply hired 'assistant masters' who did nothing more than hear the children read.[14] However, Gottfried remained at the school, attending both the junior and senior sections, until 1862 (winning the school prize for the best English essay in 1861), when he was sent to Zurich University to study classics, later becoming Professor of Greek there. His academic success, like that of the sons of Freiligrath, Althaus, and Blind, suggests that the school did not give Gottfried such a poor education as Johanna feared at the beginning. Indeed, the Kinkels' friend, the Hungarian exile Pulszky, whose sons also attended University College School, noted in his autobiography that the headmaster, Keys, allowed the boys some rights and freedoms which would not have been dreamt of in European schools—for example, one group of boys complained, successfully, about a privilege extended to another group. Pulszky also commented, quite favourably, on the stress in English schools on character-building rather than mere scholarship.[15]

If boys' schools in London seemed a little disappointing, girls' schools, on the contrary, were excellent, according to Johanna. Her daughters attended the children's part of Hyde Park College, a higher education institution for girls and women. As Kinkel taught there and was on the governing committee, he had some say in the running of the college. Johanna admired the organization of such colleges, in which there was continuity from junior school to high school, the whole forming 'a kind of republic'. Whereas University College School was, in her view, more a commercial than an educational concern, the ladies' colleges were owned by an association of shareholders whose own daughters attended and in whose interest it therefore was to employ the best teachers.[16] The two Kinkel girls did well. Johanna junior went on to art school in 1858, as well as taking private lessons with her friend, Herzen's daughter Tata. The younger daughter, Adelheid, attended the Royal Academy of Music from 1861, while the younger son, Hermann, followed his brother to Zurich in 1864, after University College School, to study engineering.[17] The fact that both his sons were in Zurich in 1866 no doubt weighed with Kinkel when he accepted a professorship there.

Closely related to the question of education in England—too closely related, in the opinion of the Kinkels, among others—was that of religion. Not only was it difficult to find a non-religious school to which to send one's sons, but it was hard for tutors and, more particularly, governesses to get jobs with English families if they were non-believers. Meta Braun, a character in *Hans Ibeles* obviously based on Malwida von Meysenbug, finds that the first question she is asked at interviews is, 'What is your religion?' (the second being, 'Are you from a good family?'). Meta manages to get taken on by declaring herself a Protestant and by offering references from a City banker and a clergyman.[18] Johanna shows here that hypocrisy was forced upon the atheist in England by that tyrant, public opinion. It is the same point as that made privately by Lewes when he was helping to found the *Leader* and publicly by Mill in *On Liberty*. This country was 'not a place of mental freedom', Mill wrote.

> Our merely social intolerance kills no one, roots out no opinions, but induces men to disguise them, or to abstain from any active effort for their diffusion. With us, heretical opinions do not perceptibly gain, or even lose, ground in each decade or generation . . .

The result is a 'sort of intellectual pacification' for which we pay the price of 'the sacrifice of the entire moral courage of the human mind'. Mill did not mean to imply that institutional intolerance was preferable to 'our merely social intolerance', but rather that Britain had not yet attained in social practice that degree of freedom supposedly guaranteed by its laws and fondly believed by its citizens to be a unique characteristic of their country. For, 'from the peculiar circumstances of our history', the 'yoke of law' was 'lighter than in most other countries of Europe', while that of opinion was heavier.[19]

Johanna shared Mill's view, but as she and Kinkel had suffered under a repressive regime, which had tried to force Kinkel to make a religious conversion while he was in prison, she was inclined to defend England even while acknowledging its religious prejudice:

> People say so much about the religious narrowness of the English. Yet we had to suffer constant torments in Germany on account of our unbelief, whereas we are left in peace here. Proselytizers in Germany are immoderate, turbulent, like flies which you try in vain to get rid of and which always settle on your nose again. Here, it's true, they all try; they knock at the door to see if they can convert you, but when you send them away they leave you in peace ever after. In Germany, the pious man you send away immediately becomes your irreconcilable enemy, who pursues you wherever you go. Here you can carry on relations with the pious without them ever making you aware of the gulf between you. They accept that we have something in common with them—culture, hard work, or cleverness, and never touch on the points of irreconcilable difference. The Englishman doesn't enjoy quarrelling; he is absolutely the most peaceable, well-meaning type of humanity you can find, and this is certainly the result of long years of political liberty.[20]

Here Johanna was speaking from her comparative experience, though no doubt she was not entirely free from prejudice against her own country on this point. Since the English preferred a quiet life, it was easier if one kept off the sensitive subject of religion, but if it arose none the less, as it did for Malwida von Meysenbug when she was looking for a post as governess and for Mrs Marx when she was faced with explaining Laura's registry office marriage to English middle-class friends, the best way out was to practise a little English hypocrisy and say one was Protestant. (Ruge used to solve the problem by telling his Brighton acquaintances that his *wife* was a Quaker—and indeed he and she shared the Quakers' pacifist views—but he was uncompromising about his own atheism, except in the case, already noted, of his signing Mazzini's European Democratic manifesto.[21])

On the question of freedom under the law, Johanna noticed, as did so many of the exiles, that the police left people to their own devices significantly more than on the Continent. As for the judiciary, though she must have been aware of the inequities eloquently criticized by

Engels, Marx, Linton, Lewes, and others, she also found occasion to marvel at the independence of the judiciary from police and government pressure. Thus, like Marx and Dickens, she exulted in the Hyde Park Riots in 1855 caused by proposals in Parliament for yet more Sunday restrictions. Going beyond Marx's pleasure in the numbers of demonstrators and their 'revolutionary' air, she noticed that when protesters were arrested, they in turn laid complaints against the police, to whom the magistrates turned round and said, 'How dare you arrest these people? Do the police think they are the masters of the public? No, we pay the police to serve us. If a few idiots in Parliament frame a stupid law, it is the police's job to wait and see if the public will allow it to be passed before enforcing it.'[22] Allowing for some dramatic exaggeration on Johanna's part, we can still see some truth in her observation. For indeed pressure from inside and outside Parliament did force such bills to be dropped. This influence on the part of the press, the public, and individuals in Parliament was something quite unknown in most European countries, where, even if there was a Parliament of sorts, there was no such thing as an unmuzzled press or vociferous public opinion. It was, as Johanna saw, the better side of the two-sided coin of public opinion, the worse, tyrannical side of which Mill was attacking in *On Liberty*.

Of course, Johanna's experience of the law in action in Germany had been especially bitter. During Kinkel's imprisonment awaiting trial in 1849, she had bravely set off for Karlsruhe to try to see him and to find out when his trial would be. In a memoir notable for its local detail she described the petty cruelty of almost every level of the bureaucracy with which she was dealing. She waited for hours in queues of unfortunate people ('a genre painter would have a field day!') whose hopes of reclaiming relatives from prison hung on the whim of a series of petty officials. She persisted in her enquiries, as well as getting Kinkel's plight publicized, and—for this Marx could not forgive her—sophistically pleading Kinkel's social position as grounds for his being treated differently from his fellow prisoners. She petitioned the King for his life, promising on Kinkel's behalf that he would steer clear of politics and emigrate to America if released. Knowing this to be a plea in political bad faith, she reasoned that Kinkel's life and freedom were the most important thing to her.[23]

Johanna reacted to her situation with a combination of admirable determination and enterprise and a sentimental self-dramatization which she shared with her husband and for which they were both derided by Marx, Weerth, Herzen, and others. When she was rewarded for her persistence by being allowed to see Kinkel in his cell, she wrote of the blood-soaked cloth on his forehead where before the laurel wreath (presented by their Bonn poetry group) had been. In letters, some of which were published at the time through Fanny Lewald and Adolf Stahr, the Kinkels wrote of their fate as if they were characters in classical tragedy. On hearing of his life sentence in September 1849, Johanna wrote to a friend, 'My suffering is great and tragic, like the Eroica Symphony.'[24] Kinkel was behaving heroically, and she worshipped him as a 'saint'. Kinkel himself wrote remarkably sunny letters, in which he saw himself as a martyr. In December 1849 he wrote from prison to a friend: 'Now I am reaping the benefits of my loving heart—loving not like pious people who despise the world, but loving like a thinker . . . They hate me because I am more pious than they: thus did the heathens paradoxically accuse the early Christians of atheism!'[25] Not surprisingly, Marx fixed on 'Jesus Christ Kinkel' as one of his many terms of abuse in 'The Great Men of the Exile'.

As well as worshipping her husband, Johanna was jealous and fearful of losing him. Obsessed with a sense of his handsomeness and her age and ugliness—she was five years older than Kinkel—and well aware of his attractiveness to women, from the daughters of his prison guard in 1849–50 to his female pupils in London after 1851, Johanna admitted that she was afraid of losing him. Herzen, among others, noted this, and drew a comic sketch of the Kinkel household in London:

> Kinkel always preserved his dignity and she always marvelled at him. Between themselves they talk of the most everyday matters in the style of edifying comedies . . . and moral novels. '*Beste Johanna,*' says he sonorously and without haste, '*du bist, mein Engel, so gut, schenke mir noch eine Tasse von dem vortrefflichen Thee, den du so gut machst, ein!*' ['Best Johanna, be so good, my angel, as to pour me another cup of that excellent tea, which you make so well!']
>
> '*Es ist zu himmlisch, lieber Gottfried, dass er dir geschmeckt hat. Tue, mein Bester, für mich einige Tropfen Schmand hinein!*' ['It is too heavenly, Gottfried dear, that the tea is to your taste. Pour me, my love, a few drops of cream!']
>
> And he lets some cream drip in, regarding her with tenderness, and she gazes at him with gratitude. Johanna persecuted her husband fiercely with her perpetual, inexorable solicitude . . . [she] begged him to protect himself from the wind, from evil people, from harmful food, and *in petto* from women's eyes, which were more harmful than any winds and *pâté de foie gras* . . . In a word, she poisoned his life with her acute jealousy and implacable, ever-stimulated love. In return she supported him in his idea that he was a genius, at any rate not inferior

to Lessing, and that in him a new Stein was being provided for Germany; Kinkel knew that this was true, and mildly restrained Johanna in the presence of outsiders when her praises went rather too far.[26]

Herzen's description is wicked, but as we have seen, there was indeed something larger-than-life about the Kinkels and what happened to them, and if Herzen saw them as characters from literature, that is also how they saw themselves, though no doubt not as the rather Dickensian comic caricatures they appeared to others. If Kinkel ever left her, Johanna told a friend in 1849, she would 'sink into the anger and egotism of suffering'.[27] Kinkel's celebrity was thus in one sense a torture for her. While she adored his manly bearing under stress, so also did many another (particularly Germany's old maids, according to Marx). For instance, the rich Baroness von Bruiningk took up his cause and financed his escape from prison. Her letter to Johanna from Venice on hearing of Kinkel's successful escape must have raised very mixed feelings in the recipient for her joyful phrases seemed to claim Kinkel as her possession as well as Johanna's: 'O my dear, dear friend, *we* need no words, . . . I have—we have—come through . . . It is spring in my heart', and so on. When Marie von Bruiningk followed the Kinkels to London in the summer of 1851 and established herself as 'the queen and godhead of the wandering democracy'[28] (Malwida's description) in a house near the Kinkels in St John's Wood, Johanna's jealousy found a ready object.

Being rich, and having an older husband who did not share her democratic views but who did not attempt to stand in her way, the Baroness presided over an *émigré* salon much frequented by Willich and his friends. Malwida von Meysenbug was critical of her for encouraging these dreamers in their impractical plans. And Johanna was irritated by her time-wasting and conspiratorial ways into causing a breach between the two families which was only partly patched up by the complaisant Baron's diplomacy in letters to Kinkel after the latter's return from America in March 1852.[29] Like a character in a Henry James novel, the Baroness kept up an appearance of dignity while attracting gossip and quarrels. Thus Marx heard on the ever-active exile grapevine that Willich had made a gross pass at her and had been rebuffed. He wrote delightedly to Engels in May 1852:

> Willich has had a rather nice adventure. Mrs. von Brüningk, who provided him with free board, used to enjoy flirting with the old he-goat, as with the other ex-lieutenants. One day the blood rushes to the head of our ascetic, he makes a brutally brutish assault upon madame, and is ejected from the house with éclat. No more love! No more free board! *Nous ne voulons plus de jouisseurs.*

Mrs Marx recalled in 1865 that Willich had made attempts on *her* in the early days in London, trying 'to pursue the worm which lives in every marriage and lure it out', until Marx put a stop to his visits to her.[30] The Baroness raised eyebrows once again when, on her early death in January 1853, she left one of Willich's fellow soldiers, Schimmelpfenning, £1,000 in her will. In her novel, *Hans Ibeles in London*, Johanna portrays the Baroness as a Polish Countess who not only wastes the Ibeles's precious time, but presses her generosity tactlessly on them, has 'an incomprehensible relationship' with one of her servants, and even suggests to the impressionable Hans that he and Dorothea join her in a phalanstery to be run on communistic principles.[31]

Johanna's fears did not end with Marie von Bruiningk's early death. Her moods swung from the euphoric to the depressed (her father was also a depressive and was confined in an asylum during the 1850s), and when a spate of husband-and-wife poisonings occurred in 1856–7, Johanna's imagination was fired along with the rest of the population's by the lurid headlines. She became obsessed by the case of William Palmer, who was hanged in June 1856 for poisoning his wife, and by that of Madeleine Smith, the Glasgow poisoner of her lover, in 1857. She told one correspondent that she feared for 'the whole moral basis of society' as a result of these and similar cases. To another, Fanny Lewald, she described 'the eternal poisonings and throat-cuttings' as 'pious England's substitute' for divorce, which was so difficult, and expensive, to obtain.[32] Excessive though her reaction was, she was not the only commentator to notice some curious marital habits among the English which might be related to the illiberality of the divorce laws. Julius Rodenberg, a bourgeois exile who wrote hack-journalism in German newspapers, described in his collection of 'scenes of everyday London life', *Alltagsleben in London. Ein Skizzenbuch* (1860), how the papers were full of accounts of English men and women declaring their spouses insane in an effort to shake off the loathed partner.[33] Lady Bulwer Lytton was the most celebrated example, but there were others, including a Mr Bell, whose wife Malwida von Meysenbug helped to escape from being incarcerated in a lunatic asylum at her husband's instigation.

Madeleine Smith even makes an indirect appearance towards the end of *Hans Ibeles*, when Ibeles becomes infatuated with a clairvoyant black American woman who turns out to be a painted and disguised criminal on the run. The novel becomes feverish and fantastic at this point, after having moved along naturalistically for most of its course. With some of the intensity, though less of the imaginative ability, of Charlotte Brontë in *Villette*, Johanna lets her morbid neurosis take over at the end of the novel with the dramatic unmasking of the criminal, as her black paint runs down her face during a jealous confrontation with Ibeles's wife.

On 10 November 1858 the unsuspecting Kinkel noted in his diary, 'Johanna finishes *Hans Ibeles in London*.' Five days later the entry was, 'At twelve minutes past two the horror happened.' Johanna had either thrown herself out of an upstairs window or had fallen out during one of her increasingly frequent dizzy spells. The coroner's verdict a few days later was accidental death, but suicide while in a state of depression was strongly suspected by friends, opponents, and her doctor. The last mentioned, a Dr Wilkinson, wrote Kinkel a detailed account of his last visit to Johanna, an hour before she died. She had talked of being sleepless and of enduring 'mental suffering'. She felt guilty towards her family, and also towards 'some persons' whom she had depicted in her novel, the writing of which 'her conscience now repudiated'. She was forty-eight.[34]

To the surprise of friends like Freiligrath, Kinkel went ahead and published *Hans Ibeles* in his periodical, *Hermann*, in 1859, though Johanna had indicated that she did not want it to be published, and though it depicted Ibeles, a thinly disguised portrait of Kinkel, in a dubious light. This seems to have been entirely in character, for that Kinkel was conveniently oblivious of his attractions to women and the pain his unconscious flirting caused Johanna is precisely the element in him which she described and punished fictionally in the novel. Ibeles is a charming, conceited, naïve, innocent yet culpable figure, largely passive, seized on by women who admire or pity or flirt with him, or all three. He is ridiculous but lovable, and he is punished by the plot (as Herzen suggests Kinkel was punished by Johanna's love), for after his embarrassing flirtation with the adulteress and escaped criminal, Livia, he is subjected to the elaborate forgiveness of his wife. True to himself, Kinkel does not appear to have seen all this.

However, there are letters among his papers—it is again characteristic of him not to have destroyed them—from an Englishwoman who attended his classes, which go into some detail about his relations with some of his pupils. Writing in June 1859, the woman told Kinkel of her discussions with Johanna:

> That some persons had made remarks to her upon the ladies of the classes, I feel convinced, for in speaking of Mrs. Bell, to me, she told me, that she had been made acquainted with circumstances in Mrs. Bell's conduct since, and

before her separation from her husband, which if generally known, and they were likely to become so, would make her presence an injury to the class, and that you were fully acquainted with this . . .

She censured what she had seen of English ladies' conduct with respect to married, and unmarried gentlemen . . . She also said that tho' gentlemen so placed did not like them for it, (and no one disliked it more than *you*, when you saw it, but you did not always see it) they were obliged to be polite.

She was excessively afraid of the injury that the Drury family might do you *both* from the part she had taken, and taken by your wish, in speaking to the mother . . . Of the Art Class generally, I told her I had seen nothing in the two seasons I had attended it, that could be found fault with and tho' I was aware of Miss Drury's feelings, I had seen her experience self control.[35]

The Mrs Bell mentioned here was undoubtedly the same Mrs Bell whom Johanna's friend Malwida was innocently helping to obtain a legal separation from her frightful husband, as Malwida reported to the Kinkels in several letters during 1857. She was probably one of the causes of Johanna's coolness towards Malwida from that time.[36] As for the Drurys, Kinkel's diary shows that he often dined at their house in the few years before Johanna's death. His insensitivity to her jealousy matches that of Carlyle, for as Kinkel visited the houses of middle-class female adorers while Johanna stayed at home with headaches and cramps, so during the same years Carlyle was frequenting the aristocratic salon of Lady Ashburton (whose husband was a member of the Barings, the famous banking family of German origin), leaving his wife at home a prey to jealous fears. Jane Carlyle, who also took careful note of murder cases like that of Madeleine Smith, confided to her journal during 1855–7 her resentment at being neglected for a clever and aristocratic woman. For example, on 5 November 1855 she wrote simply, 'Alone this evening. Lady A. in town again, and Mr C[arlyle] of course at Bath House.'[37]

Though Johanna's last years were thus soured by the behaviour of the English ladies who attended Kinkel's lectures at those colleges which she had praised for their educational standards, there were still some enjoyments to be had. The Kinkels had good friends in the prominent shipyard engineer John Scott Russell and his wife, who lived in Sydenham, where they often invited Johanna to visit them for a few days during her frequent bouts of illness in 1856–7. And the Kinkel daughters, like the Marx girls, made respectable middle-class friends. In 1858 Johanna junior was asked to be bridesmaid to a Miss Gibbons, and Mrs Gibbons invited her to accompany her and her younger daughter, Kitty, on a tour of the Rhineland. However, the authorities in

Bonn would not grant the 12-year-old Johanna a permit, so the Gibbonses had to go without her. Johanna Kinkel observed that her English friends could scarcely believe there could be such problems over passports.[38]

With her keen eye for detail, Johanna sent sketches to Germany of happy family holidays in the English fashion in south-coast resorts like Hastings, which she praised for its healthy air, the safe bathing, and the fresh milk, unadulterated, unlike its London namesake, with chalk and water. (In 1850 *Punch* had declared that the difference between London milk and London water was that in the case of the latter, 'you expect to find water at the bottom of the chalk', while in the case of the former, 'you may be sure to find chalk at the bottom of the water'.)[39] In spite of her capacity for sentiment and self-pity, she appears never to have complained about England as a refuge. Her letters and her novel provide one of the fullest records of life in England during the 1850s among the many exile writings of the time. In one of her happier moments, she wrote a long paean of praise for England's, and more particularly London's, cosmopolitanism, sophistication, and broad freedoms. Writing to Auguste Heinrich in June 1852, she declared:

> The dreamy life by the Rhine was suited to our youth, and we enjoyed it to the full. Now, in the height of our life's summer, I praise London, where you feel the pulse of the whole world beating. How much there is to be learned here, my dear friend! What splendid people there are, and what a wealth of ideas from every area of thought jostle one another in a single room when you spend an hour or two with a few people by the fire! The best from all parts of the world meets together here in this great country. People travel with amazing ease to all corners of the globe; one man has a brother in the Australian colonies, another sends his daughter to be married in India, there is constant interaction with those parts of the world. The women are acquainted with the dangers of journeying by land and sea, and become, as a result, indifferent to trivial problems. At tea parties you meet Persians, Egyptians, and so on . . . For observing poets and writers it offers an inexhaustible store of ideas. If only one had time to work it up! . . . I'm ashamed to say that we visit almost exclusively in English society. The Germans here, those who have no work, are terribly demoralized. They complain about England, without considering that it is the only piece of Europe where you can freely think and speak as you like.[40]

Johanna would have been gratified to know that, after her death, her letters to Fanny Lewald were published in the *Daily Telegraph*, and, even more appropriately, in an article on her in Barbara Leigh Smith's newly founded *Englishwoman's Journal*. The Kinkels had known the Leigh

Smiths, and Barbara clearly felt that Johanna was interesting enough to feature in a series of articles on famous women. The second volume of the *Journal*, in January 1859, carried a piece, partly poached from the *Telegraph*, entitled 'Johanna Kinkel', and celebrating her trials and endurance.

Malwida von Meysenbug

Most of the women among the German exiles were wives. Their energies were largely taken up with household duties and bringing up children, though, as the Marxes brought Helene Demuth with them, so also did the Ruges and the Kinkels bring German maids to London to help with the household chores. It seems that the German middle class, like their English counterparts, could not think of doing without servants, however badly off they were (the Carlyles, for example) or however revolutionary their theories of social class. Thus the more robust of them, like Johanna Kinkel and Agnes Ruge, were able to leave the children with a servant and earn some money for the household from teaching; Johanna and Jenny Marx both contributed occasionally to German or American journals; and, fortunately, they all wrote lively, detailed letters to friends in Germany about their lives in England. Johanna also produced the only novel of the exile, which, as Friedrich Althaus confirmed, 'gave an extremely vivid and largely accurate picture' of exile life in the 1850s. And Therese Pulszky, a German woman married to one of the Hungarian refugees, came to the notice of the British press with her book in English publicizing the Hungarian cause, *Memoirs of a Hungarian Lady* (1850), which Johanna Kinkel admired as 'excellent propaganda', wishing one of the Germans would stop quarrelling and idling and do something similar for the German exiles.[41]

Malwida von Meysenbug was unique among the political exiles in being a spinster. Not being rich, she had to make a living in England. The only course open to her was governessing, which she had in any case already contemplated in Germany after her father, a retainer of the Prince of Hessen-Kassel whom the latter ennobled in 1825, had died in 1847. Her family background—pious, titled, arch-conservative—made it all the more remarkable a feat for her to become a political rebel. Like Weerth, Freiligrath, and Althaus, she was brought up largely in Detmold, though her family travelled a lot in Prince Wilhelm's retinue. She rebelled, as they almost all did, first in spiritual matters. As she recorded in her long account of her life, characteristically called *Memoiren einer Idealistin* (1877) and later translated and abridged by her great-niece under the coy title *Rebel in a Crinoline* (1937), she read Feuerbach in 1848 with a group of young local democrats:

> Until now, Feuerbach's work had been absolutely forbidden me. My mother saw in him the expression of complete atheism, and I too had been somewhat timid in approaching the free thinkers. . . . [but] Feuerbach, it seemed to me, called everything by its real name for the first time; he destroyed forever the idea of any other revelation than that made by great minds and great hearts.[42]

Loss of religious faith—though in her case it was replaced by a vague pantheistic humanism—went along with enlightened political views. Malwida soon alarmed her mother, and her brothers, all of whom were employed by the Prussian government, by professing democratic ideals. She fell under the influence of, and in love with, the young Feuerbachian Theodor Althaus, older brother of Friedrich, Julius, and Bernhard, who was imprisoned for three years in November 1849 for an essay inciting the populace to arms. He was released after six months because of his poor health, broke off romantic relations with Malwida, and died in 1852 after much dedicated nursing by her. When the revolution of March 1848 broke out, the Meysenbug family was in Frankfurt, and Malwida followed events with excitement, including the meetings of the doomed Frankfurt Parliament. Hearing of Kinkel's imprisonment, she wrote to Johanna offering enthusiastic support. In one letter, enclosing Christmas presents for the Kinkel children, she unburdened herself to Johanna, telling of her difficult life in the small provincial town of Detmold in a family of conservatives, isolated with her democratic ideals, except for her friendship with the Althaus family. She was quietly educating herself in physics, history, and the natural sciences, in the hope that she would soon be able to teach children, giving them a broad, humane, progressive education. For Malwida, education was the key to progress. Teaching was her mission.[43]

Like Weerth and Engels, but with much more emotional difficulty, she broke away from her pious home in 1850, hesitating over an idealistic offer of marriage from Julius Fröbel in America, with whom she corresponded but whom she had never met, and deciding instead on the less dramatic course of joining Fröbel's brother Carl and his wife in their free-thinking girls' school in Hamburg. Already in May 1851 she reported that one of her brothers, a minister in Baden, had been warned of the government's displeasure at his sister's 'revolutionary opinions'.[44] When official action was taken to close Fröbel's liberal educational establishment early in 1852, Malwida moved to Berlin with her pupil

Anna Koppe (who, as Friedrich Althaus's first wife, was to come to London in 1853) to try to set up a school there. This proved impossible, and when an invitation came, through Charlotte Voss (another friend, who came to England with the Althauses and who became the second Mrs Althaus after Anna's death in 1856), to travel to England as governess to a German family, Malwida was ready to take it. The family turned out to be that of Oskar von Reichenbach, one of the richer political refugees in London. In spite of Malwida's crafty appeals to her mother's snobbery—what could be better for her daughter than to spend a summer in London with an aristocratic family who would introduce her to the best English society?—the Reichenbachs' politics were strenuously objected to. Malwida gave up the idea: 'Dear mother, I have sacrificed my plan to your wishes.' A few days later, however, on 29 May 1852, Malwida wrote to her mother from London. The Berlin police had searched her lodgings, and she suspected her brother Wilhelm's co-operation with them. She had left the country.[45]

On arrival in England, Malwida remembered later, 'a pleasant feeling of freedom came over me when no passport was demanded'. She had a 'sole point of contact in London': the Kinkels, with whom she had continued her friendly correspondence. Accordingly, she boarded an omnibus for St John's Wood:

> We drove through streets and over squares, over squares and through streets, without number and without end. The dismal, high houses, the grey sky, the noise of the never ceasing stream of carriages, the throngs of pedestrians crowding the [pavements] in feverish haste, as though life depended upon their overtaking one another—all this confused and deafened me. My neighbour explained to me that this was the 'City', the centre of the trade and business life of London.
>
> After that we came into more beautiful, broader streets with palatial houses bearing the unmistakable signs of a life of splendour and power, but always covered with the veil of grey, lead-coloured sky; that was the 'West End', the home of the aristocracy.
>
> Finally, after a drive which seemed to me to last an eternity, we reached a part of the great city where everything took on a friendlier and more homelike aspect. Pretty, new little houses, built in the most varied styles of architecture and surrounded by neat gardens, made a friendlier impression . . .

She alighted after this physical (and symbolic) journey past capitalist wealth and upper-class pretension outside the house of the Kinkels, her spiritual companions. On announcing herself, she was warmly welcomed and felt that the compensation for the bitter cup of exile was that those who had never before met immediately recognized each other as children of the same ideals and felt drawn to one another without having to go through the conventional forms which society, whose main purpose is to hide one from another, considers necessary.

The Kinkels, of whom Malwida noted that Johanna's manner was 'coarser' than Kinkel's, which was, in turn, almost 'effeminate' and 'polite to the point of gallantry', helped her to find lodgings near by and set about finding pupils for her.[46]

Malwida had an eye for social details at least as sharp as Johanna's. Thus she noticed the English habit of house-owners letting their houses to landladies who then sublet various rooms to lodgers, keeping the front parlour to themselves, though allowing the lodger in the back bedroom downstairs the use of this parlour 'with the understanding that [he or she] might be subject to momentary interruptions by the landlady who received her visitors there'. Malwida's landlady seems to have been one of that breed celebrated in the novels of Fielding and Dickens. Malwida describes her as 'a marked national type', like 'Mrs. Quickly come to life, right out of Shakespeare's *Henry V*'. She was a widow who had lost her only son and talked incessantly with 'comic, boastful pathos' of her misfortunes. Her red complexion was, 'as I soon noticed, the result of her constant enjoyment of gin and brandy', a god which she worshipped 'along with the God of her Anglican church'.[47]

Amusing though she found this, Malwida soon drew dismal conclusions about the niceties of English social life. One day she innocently asked if she might iron her dress in 'Mrs Quickly's' kitchen. The latter was horrified, telling Malwida that it was 'very unladylike for a lady to come into the kitchen—and to iron a dress besides!' Would Madam please ring the bell in future when she needed anything. Malwida's amusement at the 'tremendous abyss the barriers of prejudice had dug' between a mean little ground-floor room and the kitchen in the basement soon turned to apprehension:

> I became sad because I saw that I, who had gone through so many painful struggles to get away from prejudices, would have to face others even more stupid in this country without being able to conquer them. Having to earn my living, I would be dependent on a society so jealous of its savoir vivre that it looks upon each deviation from convention as a mortal sin.[48]

Though the conclusion may seem exaggerated in relation to this minor example, Malwida here voiced the criticism classically expressed by Mill in *On Liberty*, and she herself had in the next few months sufficient experience in her efforts to obtain a post as governess to an English family to confirm the argument.

The problem was twofold: social and religious. As Charlotte Brontë had made abundantly clear in her refracted experience in *Jane Eyre* (1847), the governess was a despised type, a victim in modern society, who might nevertheless be a remarkable, even superior creature. Malwida saw that a governess in England was a 'social polyp', 'a something between master and servant, with limited social consideration, the narrowest horizon of pleasures and recreation, and an immoderately long list of tasks and duties'.[49] And, she might have added, little chance of escaping from this awful position, because she was so poorly paid. Worse, from Malwida's point of view, was the religious difficulty. One of a governess's jobs was to take the children to church on Sundays; and to obtain a post in the first place, the governess had to profess, as Johanna Kinkel pointed out in *Hans Ibeles*, some religion, preferably Protestantism. *Punch* saw the hypocrisy and injustice of the whole arrangement. In 1850 it quoted an advertisement from *The Times*:

> Wanted, in a gentleman's family, a LADY, who is desirous of meeting with a comfortable home, to undertake the EDUCATION OF TWO CHILDREN, of the ages of seven and eight years, and who would consider *the above as equivalent to a salary*. She would be required to instruct them in an English education, French, and music, without the aid of masters. Must be of the Established Church. Good references.

Punch commented:

> We shall expect to see shortly an advertisement for a pig-driver who will consider the pleasure of thrashing the pig as 'equivalent to a salary'.
>
> The stipulation in the announcement we have quoted, that the lady should be 'of the Established Church', is quite characteristic of the sort of thing, for we always find a little bit of religion dragged in at the end, to tone down the unchristian complexion of the rest of the advertisement.

Matters had improved, but only marginally, by 1874, when Eleanor Marx quoted from *The Times* in a letter to Natalie Liebknecht to illustrate 'the horrible position of governesses here'. This time it was a governess advertising for a post: 'A young lady desires an engagement as governess. She can give good references, and teaches *German*, *French*, *Music* and *drawing* learnt abroad. *Terms 6 shillings* a week.'[50]

Malwida had some good luck, however. After one or two abortive interviews with English families, she wrote to Mrs Julia Salis-Schwabe, wife of a German industrialist and philanthropist in Manchester. Mrs Salis-Schwabe was, like her husband, a Unitarian, an adherent of the 'Manchester School' of Free Traders and friend of Cobden, and a liberal supporter of good causes. Her husband had been one of the wealthy Manchester businessmen whom Lewes had persuaded to subscribe to the *Leader* in 1849, and Mrs Salis-Schwabe was a prominent member, with Mrs Cobden, of the 'Society of Friends of Foreigners in Distress', which raised money, among other things, to help patients of the German Hospital find employment when they were discharged.[51] When Malwida launched into an explanation of her theories of education, Mrs Salis-Schwabe, unlike the English ladies who were put off by her enthusiasm, answered immediately, 'saying that all I wrote coincided absolutely with her own views, that she had long yearned for someone who thought thus, and inviting me to spend two or three weeks with her at her country estate'.[52]

Thus Malwida spent part of August 1852 at the Salis-Schwabe country house in Wales, discussing education and meeting Manchester notables. It was the first of several visits during which she met, among others, Mrs Gaskell, Professor Scott of Owens College, and a philanthropic factory-owner called Pigott. She also observed with a critical eye the Schwabe household, in which the manners and habits of the English aristocracy were imitated, for Mr Schwabe 'had the petty vanity of the parvenu and felt flattered in associating with the nobility'. Mrs Schwabe later, in 1857, asked Malwida to become permanent governess to her children, but Malwida refused on the grounds, also given as the reason for her refusal of a similar offer from the Pulszkys, that she wanted to maintain her independence. She did, however, accompany the Schwabe and Cobden families to Paris for the winter of 1859–60, during which time she taught their children German.[53]

Meanwhile, back in London in 1852, amid 'the sultry atmosphere of a refugee's life', Malwida set about collecting pupils. At Kinkel's and Pulszky's houses she met Kossuth, whose aristocratic demeanour she disliked, and Herzen, with whom she was delighted.[54] Herzen, whose wife had left him for the German poet Herwegh, came to London from Paris in August 1852, followed in May 1853 by his daughters Tata (later the close friend of Kinkel's daughter Johanna) and Olga with their German nurse. Malwida agreed to become their governess, and moved into Herzen's house in Euston Square in December 1853.[55] Here she was able to put her educational theories into practice; she became attached to the girls, particularly Olga, and she had a stimulating intellectual relationship with Herzen, to whom she regularly wrote long theoretical letters while living under the same roof. Through Herzen she met English liberals like Milner Gibson and the Ashursts and Stansfelds, as well as Mazzini and the Italian exiles.

In letters to her mother, Malwida stressed the respectability of the circles in which she moved. She also recounted examples of England's superiority over Germany in political freedoms, while observing that the 'German spirit' was in many ways freer, especially in artistic matters. Thus she described her attendance at Wellington's funeral in November 1852, noting the size of the crowd, the length of the procession, and the splendour of the soldiers' uniforms. After the procession had passed the spot where she was, the crowd indulged in some good-natured fun after its three-hour wait:

> Someone threw something to eat from a window to the soldiers, who had stood to attention for so long. The gesture was appreciated, and now there flew out of every window rolls, cakes, apples, etc., wrapped in paper, and the soldiers, paying no attention to their officers, jumped joyfully this way and that to catch them. This easy relationship between the people and the soldiers was very attractive.

Such a scene would be an impossibility in Germany. But, as she also proudly remarked, it was Beethoven's Funeral March which accompanied the procession, and the magnificent hearse had been designed by the refugee Semper from Dresden. 'I was delighted', wrote Malwida, 'that the spiritual and aesthetic element was German.'[56]

Another high spot during her life in London was the trial of Simon Bernard, after Orsini's attempt to blow up Napoleon, in April 1858. Malwida attended the Old Bailey and 'shared British national feeling' when the jury acquitted Bernard, thereby ensuring that the 'merits of the institutions of this island were gloriously defended'. The Orsini affair, she told the Kinkels two months later, politicized her anew, and she had now become a close colleague of Mazzini's. The latter had encouraged her in her new venture, to run a workers' educational club for poor Germans in Whitechapel. Malwida had thrown herself into relief work in Whitechapel in 1856, after leaving Herzen, who had allowed his Russian friends, the Ogarevs, to stay on a prolonged visit and to interfere with her method of bringing up the children. The separation from the Herzen family caused her agonies of jealousy and loneliness, and the plunge into philanthropic activity saved her from despair and possible suicide.[57]

Malwida's interest in the East End had been stimulated a few years earlier by a visit in a group of Marie von Bruiningk's friends to watch the working class do its shopping on a Saturday evening. (H. M. Hyndman, the popularizer of Marxism, recalled that it was the fashion for the wealthy and the middle class to satisfy their curiosity by group visits to the rookeries and cellars of London's slums.[58]) Like Engels, Mayhew, and many more observers, she invoked Dante's *Inferno* to describe the smells and mists, the 'screaming, scolding, bargaining' of the crowds, 'looking as though they had risen from abysmal depths, creatures changed by misery or crime into caricatures of God's image'. Now, in 1856, she visited the poor Germans of Whitechapel:

> Poor German families are there by the hundreds; they are partly German street musicians [like those Kinkel testified against in the Marylebone meeting], such as organ grinders, partly labourers of all kinds who mostly earn their living by cleaning hides and making coarse slippers,—hard, wearisome, and unhealthy occupations, especially the first, as they have to stand in water to do it. This winter, even such labour brought scant living. Hundreds of men were out of work and this hit first the foreigners whose misery was doubly great as they, the women at least, spoke only very little English and still felt themselves utter strangers. The German woman's club, the pastor and teacher at the German school did their best, but what was that compared with the great need![59]

This was the community which the German Hospital had been set up to serve. Work in the hide factories could be even worse than Malwida describes it. A contemporary newspaper went into greater detail:

> The work is stamping raw pelts at a German fur factory in East London. Imagine a big barrel in a very warm room, filled to the very top with ermine and sable skins. A man climbs into the barrel stark-naked and stamps and works with his hands and feet from morning till night. The perspiration pours from his body in streams. This soaks into the skins and gives them their suppleness and durability, without which they would be useless for more elegant purposes. Thus our rich ladies, with their boas and muffs, though they do not suspect it, are literally clothed in the sweat of the democrats.[60]

Here the author makes explicit the social irony of which Mayhew, as we have seen, showed himself perhaps half-aware in his similar account of the tailoring business.

Malwida set up her club, with Mazzini's help, and joined workers' processions and meetings, hearing Ernest Jones address one of the latter. She also came under the influence of Mazzini's conspiratorial methods, joining him in a secret society to educate the workers for 'the sacred battle' for international democracy. Her activities alienated her from the Kinkels, particularly Johanna, who disapproved of Mazzini's terrorist tactics and 'revolutionary hocus-pocus'.[61] Malwida tried, without success, to induce the Kinkels to join her, assuring them that they could keep their respectability by using her as a medium: 'I will take all the odium *vis-à-vis* the English on myself, as I am an obscure person.' She also, prodded by Mazzini, asked Kinkel to part with some of the German Loan money for Mazzini's society, claiming that it would be better spent than if he gave some to Blind, who was also clamouring for finance, and who was only interested in 'destroying, not creating'. This was in June 1858; after Johanna's death in November, Mazzini himself wrote to Kinkel offering condolences and urging Kinkel, whom he rightly judged to be more impressionable than Johanna, to join forces with him and work for the European cause.[62] Kinkel, however, steered clear of Mazzini, though he did re-enter political journalism by starting his German paper, *Hermann*, in January 1859.

Not realizing Johanna's morbid obsession with unhappy marriages, adultery, and husband-and-wife poisonings, Malwida had eagerly notified the Kinkels in 1857 of the twists and turns of the case of Mrs Bell, whom she had decided to save from her tyrannical husband; whose separation she achieved with the help of the radical lawyer and friend of Mazzini, William Ashurst; and who appears to have been a pupil and admirer, if nothing more, of Kinkel.[63] Undoubtedly, this was, along with her enthusiasm for Mazzini, a cause of Johanna's cooling towards Malwida.

As well as campaigning to improve the position of married women trapped in unhappy marriages like Mrs Bell, whose husband tried to have her certified insane rather than agree to a separation, Malwida busied herself with English female education. In 1859 she helped Mrs Taylor, wife of the radical MP Peter Taylor, to find support from 'influential names' for the prospectus for a female professorship in medicine. 'A lady' had given £5,000 for the purpose of setting up such a foundation, so that a women's hospital could be built and women doctors and nurses be trained to a high standard. The plan had originated with the Langham Place Group of women's rights agitators, led by George Eliot's great friend Barbara Leigh Smith, now Mme Bodichon. The group had invited Dr Elizabeth Blackwell, an Englishwoman educated in America and the only practising woman doctor, to come to London to lecture on medicine as a profession for women. This she did in March 1859 to an audience which included Elizabeth Garrett, who was to qualify as the first British woman doctor, after years of disappointment and exclusion, in 1864. The plan in 1859 was for Elizabeth Blackwell to stay in England and supervise medical instruction for women. To the regret of Barbara Bodichon, Elizabeth was disheartened by the obstacles put in the way of the project by the British medical profession. 'I have no faith in its rapid success', she wrote to Emily Davies, member of the Langham Place Group and later founder and first mistress of Girton College. Elizabeth Blackwell returned to her medical practice in New York.[64] Taking a degree, including a medical degree, was not to become an option for women in England for another ten years.

No doubt Malwida would have continued to work in such circles, keeping herself by teaching and writing—she translated Herzen's memoirs into German in 1859 and contributed articles on Russian literature to German periodicals—if Herzen had not asked her, to her great joy, to come back and look after Olga. She saw it as her duty and her passion to 'save' the child, and was to devote the rest of her long life to Olga. She took both Herzen girls with her to Italy in 1861, and lived there until she died, aged 86, in 1903. During her years in Italy she befriended Wagner, Nietzsche, and Liszt's ex-mistress, Princess Carolyne von Sayn-Wittgenstein.[65] Like so many of her friends, she became an enthusiastic German nationalist, rejoicing in Bismarck's success in the Austro-Prussian War of 1866.[66] But she never lost her firm faith in a kind of spiritual humanism and religious unbelief. On her death, she was cremated, and, at her own wish, no burial service was said.

Malwida was a remarkable woman. In her long life she fell under the spell of a succession of interesting men: Theodor Althaus, Julius Fröbel, Kinkel, Herzen, and Mazzini. She broke free from the religious, political, and social restrictions of a small German town. In England she earned her living by teaching. Even the fact that she lived (platonically) with Herzen was unconventional. She took holidays alone in south-east coastal resorts (as did George Eliot in the years immediately before her unorthodox liaison with Lewes[67]). In a way she was the type of the German governess—plain, earnest, given to flights of sentiment and abstract rhetoric—but she was also shrewd, observant, independent, and resourceful. Her relationship with England and the English was not emotionally close, but it was one of mutual respect and recognition. She admired British institutions and criticized British prejudice. And she managed to survive, largely by her own efforts, on 'this stormy sea of life called London'.[68]

An Unpolitical Exile: Amely Bölte

Amely Bölte was not a political exile, though she met most of her exiled compatriots, including Marx, around 1850. Indeed, she did not get on with any of them, despising their 'delicious vanity' and resenting their disapproval of her brother's taking political office in Germany.[69] But as a governess working in England since 1839, as a close, if rather subordinate, acquaintance of the Carlyles, as Varnhagen von Ense's chief reporter of English society, and as the describer of both English and German exile life in a series of novels and stories—worthless from the literary point of view—she merits our attention.

'Little Bölte', as Jane Carlyle rather patronizingly called her,[70] came to England, with references, in 1839 after three years of being governess with a landed family in Germany. Governessing was, in Germany as in England, the chief resort of young middle-class women of no means. (Amely's father, Bürgermeister of a small town in Mecklenburg, had died in 1827, leaving seven children.[71]) It was quite common for Germans to come to England as governesses, though they found conditions, especially their social status, less favourable than at home. Amely Bölte was lucky, not being unorthodox in politics and having useful references, including one from Dr Hitzig of Berlin to Carlyle, which got her jobs with pleasant families like the Bullers and the wealthy German Jewish philanthropist, Sir Isaac Goldsmid. Nevertheless, despite her tenacious friendship with the Carlyles, and the acquaintance of Richard Monckton Milnes, Bulwer, Geraldine Jewsbury, and other notables, her main feeling towards English society was resentment. As she complained to Varnhagen in 1850, she was 'only tolerated now and again' in the best English society, and only then through friends, being unable ever to act as a hostess or leader herself.[72]

This resentment, born of her insecurity as a single woman, a foreigner, and a governess, shows through every piece of writing she did. It is constantly there in her 'scenes from London', sent to Cotta's *Morgenblatt* throughout the 1840s, in her stories about German artists, musicians, and governesses being snubbed in England, and most of all in her lengthy, indiscreet letters to that arch-gossip of Berlin society, Varnhagen von Ense. She quarrelled with almost everyone. It was she who gossiped about Freiligrath's being treated as a common clerk by Huth in the *Morgenblatt* in 1847, thus causing him to lose his job. Her great friend Fanny Lewald visited England in 1850, and Amely introduced her to the English people she knew, but Fanny showed insufficient gratitude, and the two fell out before Fanny's return to Germany. Though Jane Carlyle tolerated her as a 'fine manly little creature, with a deal of excellent sense, and not without plenty of German enthusiasm', though she seemed so 'humdrum', she pressed herself on Jane and sometimes outstayed her welcome. Carlyle rather sourly remembered her as a 'bustling, shifty little German governess, who in few years, managed to pick up some modicum of money here, and then retired to Dresden, wholly devoting herself to "literature"'. On one occasion, when Jane was staying with Geraldine Jewsbury in Liverpool, the latter wrote a circumstantial reply to Amely's complaints of being neglected. Amely was advised to be gracious enough to accept that Mrs Carlyle's health was poor, and that she was having a much-needed rest from all her duties, including that of not offending Amely.[73]

Though some of Amely Bölte's complaints were justified, as we shall see, the impression she gives in her letters is of finding everyone she met seriously lacking and unworthy of her friendship, at the same time that she felt acutely aware of suspected snubs on their part. Thus in 1850 she met Lewes of the *Leader*, disliked him, and noted that he needed no approbation from others, as he had enough self-approbation to satisfy his vanity. She also mentions that Tauchnitz is about to publish Lewes's novel, *Ranthorpe*, in German, 'which won't be much of a gain for Germany'. Though Milnes invited her to some of his famous literary breakfasts, she found him, too, vain and hypocritical. Excusing herself in the affair of Freiligrath and Huth, she triumphs over Freiligrath's naïvety in thinking Milnes and Bulwer are really intending to help him after the initial round of 'lion parties' to celebrate his arrival. Geraldine Jewsbury is 'a woman who smokes, and falls passionately in love with one man after another, and who writes so immorally, without knowing it, that Mr Forster had to look through her most recent book, *The Half-Sisters*, before it could be allowed to have Mrs Carlyle's name on the dedication page'. The German arrivals are no better. The Austrian poet Moritz Hartmann, whom she introduced to the Carlyles and Lewes, has refused to learn English and has consequently had little success in England. Ruge arrives in 1850, staying in London until his family comes to join him, and Amely notes, with unconscious irony, how he criticizes everything about England.[74]

Because she was so touchy and critical, Amely Bölte reported to Varnhagen all sorts of details which help to fill in the picture of refugee life in England. For example, she noticed that when Freiligrath returned to England in 1851, he had become a communist: 'He recently brought Marx to visit me . . . He looks changed . . . He's consorting with the communists.' In the same letter, in June 1851, she commented that Ruge had managed to have an article on Chamisso's *Peter Schlemihl* published in *Tait's Magazine.* She also provides an answer to the question as to why Carlyle, who had been so interested in German literature and who, whatever he was, was not a Tory or an orthodox Christian, seemed so unenthusiastic about the German exiles who were arriving daily. Though he had befriended Mazzini and some of the Polish exiles during the 1830s, he would have nothing to do with the new arrivals. Amely reported to Varnhagen in 1851 that Carlyle was becoming hardened in his reactionary opinions, and had no time for any of the exiles now.[75]

Again because of her detailed gossip and scant sense of discretion, it is Amely Bölte who extends our knowledge of the strains of the Carlyles' marriage around 1850. Her letters are full of references to Carlyle's illogical enjoyment of aristocratic society, particularly that of Lady Ashburton, and to Jane's unhappiness. In 1881, when she had been back in Germany for thirty years, she sent J. A. Froude, Carlyle's biographer, letters she had received from Jane for inclusion in his edition of Jane's letters and memorials. In his reply, Froude wrote frankly of the difficulties of the marriage:

> I believe—you perhaps can tell me about this—that several times she was on the point of leaving him. I infer from a sentence in her Journal, and the explanation of it which I had from Geraldine Jewsbury, that he was *once personally violent* with her. . . . In writing to you I feel that I am addressing the *last* survivor of her intimate friends, and I therefore run on to you with a confidence which I could not feel in any other human being.[76]

Amely must have felt gratified by this compliment, especially as she had met with some criticism in 1860, when she opportunistically published Varnhagen's letters to her—Varnhagen having just died—including several references to the state of the Carlyles' marriage. Charlotte Williams-Wynn wrote to Varnhagen's niece, Ludmilla Assing, about the 'breach of confidence' Amely had committed:

> . . . the allusion to the Carlyles it is shameful to publish, because it will annoy them and do no good. Your uncle said nothing but what was kind in itself, but all his remarks show that Miss Bölte was in the habit of living intimately with them (the C's) and sending off daily reports of what they said, and did, and of his

singularities and odd opinions,—which we should call neither more or less, than a Household Spy.[77]

Amely herself was aware of her position. She told Varnhagen in 1848 that she wrote so frankly only to him, begging him not to pass on her remarks to others, especially not, as it happens, to 'Miss Wynn', for the English 'have such a pernickety idea of discretion, that one shouldn't tell tales out of school'.[78] It is clear that she wanted to show off to Varnhagen how close she was to the Carlyles, and with that spitefulness which she showed towards most people, she perhaps wished to be harmful even to the Carlyles for treating her patronizingly. For she must have been hurt when Carlyle refused to let her translate *Sartor Resartus* in 1848, because he feared, as she told Varnhagen, that she 'wouldn't do it well enough'. Jane was aware of having used Amely's services—Amely met her once in 1849 in Carlyle's absence, when Jane was returning to London from a visit, and in the same year 'Providence under the form of Miss Bölte had sent a most promising looking servant here the very day we came home'—and also of having been unkind to her. In 1846 she wrote to Carlyle that she had received 'a Packet from—Bölte! at Cambridge,—a pretty little collar and cuffs of the poor thing's own work, with the kindest Letter, after all my cruelties to her!'[79]

Of all the faults she found during her time in England, the most frequently alluded to in her letters, articles, and fiction was 'the horrible tyranny of public opinion'. The social and moral position of governesses exercised her greatly. Presumably she had some unpleasant experiences, though her time with the liberal-minded Buller family, in which Carlyle himself had been a tutor during the 1820s, was a happy one. She stayed with them from 1843 to 1847, when she and the family caught typhoid in Nice. In 1848 both Buller parents and their son Charles died. Things started off well, too, with the wealthy and cultured Goldsmid family. Sir Isaac was a banker who had been active in the founding of University College London and in the agitation during the 1820s for Jewish emancipation. Thanks largely to his efforts, Jewish MPs were allowed to forgo the parliamentary oath 'on the true faith of a Christian' in 1858. The family was socially unstuffy. But in 1848 Amely became the target of the amorous attentions of the Count d'Avigdor, a son-in-law of Sir Isaac Goldsmid, so that by January 1850 she thought it better, with the Goldsmids' agreement, to leave.[80]

Amely's feelings on the subject of the governess's awkward position had been aired, before this experience at the Goldsmids', in her rather crazy short story, *Louise oder die Deutsche in England* (*Louise, or the German Girl in England*, 1846). In it, she poured out her undisguised resentment against the English aristocracy. There is much loving, or love-hating, description of the splendid salons of Belgrave Square, the dressing for dinner, the arrival of the oldest son back from school at 'Eaton' (Amely often misspelt English names in her letters, too), and the snubbing of the governess at dinner. Louise resists seduction by the fascinating but despicable young Lord Glandworth (!), teaches in a girls' school, has a spell at the 'slavery' of needlework, faints at church, and is improbably brought by the German pastor before the Queen, who, delighting in matchmaking, engineers the happy-ever-after marriage of the upright Louise and the aforesaid rake, now apparently reformed, Lord Glandworth.

Two years later the theme was sounded again, though in reverse, in one of her *Erzählungen aus der Mappe einer Deutschen in London* (*Tales from the File of a German Girl in London*). A young upper-class English girl turns down marriage to a lord in favour of her German tutor, whom she finds more cultured than the young nobleman with his conversation about 'politics, dogs, foxes, and horses' and nothing else. Like Engels, Carlyle, and George Eliot, she draws attention to the coarseness of English aristocratic taste, especially in music and art, and the horror a noble family experiences if its son wishes to become a musician. The German artist in her story *Eine deutsche Palette in London* (*A German Palette in London*, 1853) finds himself ostracized at social functions, though he is 'hired' by their patrons for his artistic services.[81]

In 1851 Amely became too ill to carry on with governessing. She returned to Germany to live from writing articles and yet more bad novels and tales, including a two-volume novel published in 1872, *Elisabeth oder eine deutsche Jane Eyre*, which continued the unhappy theme. Not that she had no reason to complain of the governess's lot. We have seen ample evidence, from both German and English sources, of its miseries. Jane Carlyle had exerted herself for Amely in 1843, to help her avoid the even worse fate of 'being made into mince-meat to indiscriminate boarding-school Misses—at "a small salary" too. Ach Gott! Better one good sixpenny worth of arsenic once for all, than to prolong existence in *that* fashion!'[82]

Though Amely, from temperament and situation combined, found little to please her in England, she was there at an interesting time and she met the most interesting people. Indeed, she deliberately collected acquaintances, partly to flatter her own self-esteem and partly to please Varnhagen, who was a well-known collector of famous autographs, and to whom she sent as many as she could. Thus letters to her from celebrities such as Leigh Hunt, Anna Jameson, and Geraldine Jewsbury found their way into the huge Varnhagen collection of manuscripts, kept in Berlin until the Second World War and now in Cracow. She even got hold of a letter from Shelley for him—'Shelley is much sought-after and very rare'—from an old friend of Shelley's who 'could not refuse a lady's request'. Amely was also anxious to keep up with fashions. On one occasion, according to Jane Carlyle, Amely allowed herself to be mesmerized at the Bullers', whereupon Carlyle agreed that the mesmerist had 'stiffened all poor little Miss Bölte there into something very awful'.[83] She was a voluntary exile, and she certainly observed English life with great interest, but paradoxically she felt less at home in England than many of those who came reluctantly or because they had no choice.

The Wives of the Exile: Amalie Struve, Agnes Ruge, and Jenny Marx

If England did not suit Amely Bölte, neither did it please Amalie Struve. She is the most striking example among the German exiles of a 'bei unser', to borrow the term used by refugees from Hitler's Germany who made their way to America. A 'bei unser' ('bei uns' means 'at our house') was one who was constantly making comparisons between home and the adopted country, to the detriment of the latter.[84] In 1850 she published her *Erinnerungen aus den badischen Freiheitskämpfen, den deutschen Frauen gewidmet* (*Memories of the Baden Liberation Battles, dedicated to German Women*), in which she told the story of the part she had played, alongside her husband Gustav, in the Baden uprisings of 1848. They were imprisoned, with Karl Blind, in Bruchsal, from where they were liberated by the people in the uprising of May 1849. Making first for Switzerland, they were soon expelled. There was then no choice but to go to 'monarchical England', though they would rather have remained in 'republican Switzerland', mainly for political reasons, but also because it 'bordered on Germany'. Travelling through France, they met up with Willich, who was also on his way to England.

The group arrived in London in October 1849, and Amalie seems to have been intimidated, like so many refugees, by the size of the city, the inclement weather, and the lack of 'Herzlichkeit' ('warm-heartedness') of its inhabitants. She immediately set about writing her book, prefacing it with the lines:

Empfanget, Schwestern, diese Gabe,
Die an der Themse trübem Strand
Im Stillen ich vollendet habe,
Mit treuem Sinn im Vaterland!

[Receive, my sisters, this gift which I have completed quietly on the gloomy banks of the Thames. Receive it in the fatherland with a true spirit.]

The little book's epitaph is in the same negative spirit:

Der Flüchtling an der Themse Strand
Empfindet tief fürs Vaterland.

[The exile on the banks of the Thames feels deeply for the fatherland.]

Amalie's letters from London played endlessly on the theme of banishment, homesickness, pain, nostalgia for the fatherland, London's unbearable climate, its fogs, and the egotism and lack of sympathy of the English for the ideals of the German refugees. She was busy, however, writing novels to be published in Germany, and planning a women's almanac. For this, she sought famous names. Thus she wrote with a flourish to Bettina von Arnim in Berlin, 'Why do I write to you from exile? In such an important time as the present, women cannot remain idle.' In short, would Bettina contribute to the almanac?[85]

The Struves had no luck in London. Gustav, considered rather a fool by his fellow exiles, from Schurz to—predictably—Marx (who harped on his vegetarianism and amateur phrenologizing in 'The Great Men of the Exile'),[86] was unable to find enough pupils to make a living. This is a little surprising, for, though there was tough competition among the exiles, Struve did have some contacts in England. Milnes apparently gave him hospitality, and he moved in Anglo-German circles. In May 1850 *The Times* reported that Struve and Thomas Fothergill, secretary of a London union set up to help poor German refugees, had approached the acting Lord Mayor of London, Alderman Gibbs, asking him to provide jobs for a hundred unemployed German refugees. Alderman Gibbs refused, saying many English workers were in the same position. Marx and Engels, seeing that the publicity was bad for the exile cause in general, and fearful that public pressure might lead to the enforcement of the dreaded Aliens Bill, had a letter published in *The Times* a few days later, in which they dissociated themselves and the majority of the exiles from Struve's appeal.[87] The Struves could not make a go of it. Hating London, they moved in June 1850 to try life in the country, near York. But here, too, they found neither the pupils necessary to their economic survival nor the fellow-feeling equally necessary to their emotional well-being. Amalie wrote dismally to her Strasbourg friend, Frau von Chézy, about sinking under the burden of a broken heart:

> Among the English we have no close acquaintances yet. These people do not know our fatherland and its struggles. They scarcely know that Prussia is part of Germany or that Austria is ruled by a Kaiser. They have no idea of the freedom-fighting among our people, and exiles are looked upon, at best, as 'enthusiasts' and 'restless fellows'. Here is no sympathy, no spiritual coexistence.[88]

By spring 1851 they were back in London. Struve was consorting with the recently arrived Kinkels, and with Ronge, taking part with them in the March banquet commemorating 1848. Amalie reported Kinkel's eloquence on this occasion, describing how his 'fine German eyes sparkl[ed] as he spoke'.[89] Despite the friendship of the Ronges and Kinkels, who were succeeding in London, the Struves were forced to emigrate to America in April of the same year. Johanna Kinkel told a friend that the Struves had led 'a very sad existence' in London, and simply could not make a living. Presumably they received some of the money given at this time by the British government to help destitute exiles move on to America, for on 10 April Amalie wrote to Frau von Chézy from the Emigrants' Home in Liverpool. As Marx inelegantly put it on 15 April, 'Last Friday [Struve] pushed off, still with Amalia.'[90] In America, Amalie joined the growing women's rights movement, and Struve became a contributor to German-American newspapers. Like Willich, he fought for the Northern States in the American Civil War, returning to Germany in 1863 to continue propaganda for a republic.[91]

Amalie and her husband were unlucky in England. One suspects, however, that they were partly to blame for their lack of success. She seems not to have tried to adjust, and he appears to have been impatient and odd. Marx's pen-portrait of Struve in 'The Great Men of the Exile' may have been less exaggerated than that of most of his targets. Struve and Amalie fitted neatly into his conception of mock-epic: the crazed knight, like a Hudibras or a Don Quixote, accompanied by his sentimental damsel, both looked on askance by the English and their compatriots alike:

> Regarding his own skull as the normal human cranium, [Struve] vigorously applied himself to phrenology and from then on he refused to trust anyone whose skull he had not yet felt and examined. He also gave up eating meat and preached the gospel of strict vegetarianism; he was, moreover, a weather-

prophet, he inveighed against tobacco and was prominent in the interest of the ethics of German Catholicism [Ronge's movement] and water-cures. Given his thoroughgoing hatred of concrete knowledge it was natural that he should be in favour of free universities in which the four faculties would be replaced by the study of phrenology, physiognomy, chiromancy and necromancy.[92]

As for Amalie, she never saw the beloved fatherland again, for she died in America in 1862.

While Amalie and Struve were struggling unsuccessfully to make a living in England in 1850–1, Ruge and his wife Agnes were tenaciously digging themselves in at Brighton. In the memoir which she wrote in old age, Agnes recalled that they decided against London because of the expense of living there, the competition for jobs, and Ruge's failure to obtain regular employment on a newspaper during the summer of 1850, before the arrival of Agnes, the maid, and the three youngest children. (Richard, the oldest son, aged 15, was left behind in Berlin with Ruge's brother, studied medicine, and visited the family in Brighton during the holidays.[93]) They chose Brighton because they had a contact there, a piano-teacher called Franz d'Alquen. Initially they made friends with the Quakers of the town, whom they sought out because Ruge shared their pacifism, having spoken in the Frankfurt Parliament in favour of reducing the standing army. They met William Coningham, afterwards a radical MP, and later Buckle, whose *History of Civilization* Ruge translated in the 1860s. Ruge also became a friend of Thomas Allsop, and, according to Agnes, almost became involved in the Orsini bomb-plot. She describes 'poor Orsini', whom they met in Tunbridge in 1857, and who spoke English with such a strong Italian accent that his audiences could not help laughing, even when he was telling them of the miseries of his countrymen. 'So, for example, he wanted to say "men were hoping, women were weeping", but he spoke too quickly, saying instead "men were hopping, women were whipping".' One evening Ruge was invited to go to Sevenoaks with Orsini, Allsop, and a few chosen friends for a 'party'. Ruge returned saying it had been difficult to get away, but he had not wanted to stay. Agnes later worked out that this had been the night when the plot against Napoleon was hatched.

Agnes Ruge's memoir supplies the details of their day-to-day living which are missing from her husband's surviving writings. It also shows Ruge from the viewpoint of a loving, faithful wife, who, alone of all his audience, thought his lecturing successful, and who presents Ruge in homely situations in which he appears warmer, more human, than he does in the ruthless mirror of Marx's criticism or even in his own anxious, egotistical letters and lectures. Like the other wives, Agnes dwells on the difficulties of making a living: the fiasco of the daguerreotype business, the insecurity of teaching, the lack of payment for Ruge's pamphlets. She noted that constant worries about finances changed her husband's 'otherwise cheerful' nature. He used to walk about at night, unable to sleep. As late as 1854 he still felt insecure, as he could not interest German publishers in his prolific output.

But despite the sourness which was commented on by all the other exiles, including Herzen, who visited his erstwhile mentor in Brighton in 1852 and found him 'a grumbling old man, angry and spiteful, absorbed in slanderous gossip',[94] Ruge survived in Brighton, and seems to have been liked locally. When in 1864 they could finally afford to move from modest lodgings to what Agnes jubilantly called 'Casa Ruge', a smart house in the desirable Park Crescent, Ruge was chosen to be chairman of the crescent's housing committee.

We learn from Agnes about Ruge's love of seaside walks, his gardening, his efforts—successful against his wife's expectations—to make a bed for their youngest child, Franziska. She tells how Ruge would come half-way to meet her and escort her back from her teaching at wealthy houses in and near Brighton, and of how he would pick flowers for her. She represents his Berlin accent from time to time, when he would ask on a fine evening if she would like to go for a walk with him, or whether she would take notes at his dictation ('Schreibste mir e bischen?'). This is the other side to the man so caricaturable for his 'Pomeranian' accent. And Agnes sees that the egotism, the sense of his own importance, and his bitterness at being ignored, have a positive side too. He so wanted to help his country achieve freedom, that he would say, 'I wish I could be there, I could be so useful to them.'

In spite of their disappointments—they had hoped Richard could set up as a doctor in England, but he had to go back to Germany to find work, and their older daughter, Hedwig, had her engagement cancelled by the fiancé, Willie Mason, in 1868—the Ruges made the best of life in England. Agnes would probably not have pursued a career if she had stayed in Germany, whereas here, though at first terribly nervous, she found her teaching rewarding. Like Liebknecht, Weerth, and others, she was impressed by the fact that at public meetings in England, the women also attended and had an equal right to speak. This was 'a fine trait' of English life, she thought. And though her sons studied abroad, Richard in Berlin and Arnold, an engineer, in Zurich, her daughters stayed with her in England, Franziska marrying an Englishman, William

Fargus, and Hedwig living with her mother until the latter's death, aged 84, in Brighton in 1899. Agnes seems to have felt bitterness towards no one but Karl Blind. Even Marx, once Ruge's friend and collaborator, who had attacked him so often, is not criticized by her. She remembers a 'German circle' meeting at the house of Freiligrath's older daughter, Käthe, at which 'one of the daughters of Karl Marx' (it was probably Eleanor, who loved doing amateur theatre) declaimed speeches from Shakespeare. Of course, as Agnes wrote at the end of her memoir, there were bitter experiences she might have recorded in detail, but she preferred to remember the happier times and the fact that, in spite of all, they had made a go of living in England.

Among the exiles' wives, Jenny Marx suffered perhaps the most. She also impressed her husband's friends and disciples greatly. Liebknecht remembered her as someone who had 'perhaps as strong an influence' on his development as Marx himself. He also recalled with a smile an escapade of Ferdinand Wolff's. Wolff was short-sighted and a chaser of women. On one occasion these two characteristics had come together and he had pursued a woman on the street. When he finally caught up with her, he discovered, to his embarrassment, that it was Mrs Marx. Wolff ran away in consternation, and would not visit the Marxes for another six months.[95]

Jenny Marx also wrote a memoir, which was unpublished in her lifetime. Written in 1865, it was called 'Kurze Umrisse eines bewegten Lebens' ('A Short Sketch of an Eventful Life'), and like Agnes Ruge's piece, it provides details of her domestic life which add to the picture we have from the Marx letters. Unlike Agnes Ruge, Jenny gives few details of her husband, though she takes his part in recounting the quarrels and libels of the early 1850s. 'Karl, above all the rest', she complains, 'was persecuted beyond measure, calumniated and defamed.'[96] Again unlike Agnes, she is unable to make the best of things. It is not that she particularly disliked England or the English; indeed, in the relatively less hard-up years after 1860, when her daughters 'were entering the beautiful golden age of their maidenhood', the family made middle-class English friends, enjoyed annual holidays at the seaside—often Hastings—among the English middle class, and lived in a relatively elegant house in Belsize Park. Rather it was that Jenny's life with Marx, whether in France, Belgium, or England, was always insecure financially. When they had money, as when relatives died leaving them legacies, the Marxes spent royally until they had none again. Jenny says of their first move in 1856 out of cramped Dean Street to more spacious

Grafton Terrace in Kentish Town, that though it seemed like moving into a palace (Agnes Ruge used the same words to describe *her* removal to Park Terrace), 'there were still the same little hardships, the same struggles and the same wretchedness, the same intimate relationship with the three balls'.

Added to the financial hardship, and partly as a result of it, were the difficult births and early deaths of some of her children. Most of the exiles had children who died young. Indeed it was, of course, a common occurrence in the mid nineteenth century, but the exiles, like the indigenous poor, seem to have lost more children at an early age than did their English middle-class counterparts. Jenny describes the birth of Fawksy on 5 November 1849, not long after her arrival in England with her 'three small and persecuted children'. While the people outside were shouting 'Guy Fawkes for ever', and 'small boys wearing baroque masks were riding the streets on cleverly fashioned donkeys and all was in uproar, my poor little Heinrich was born'. Fawksy died in November 1850, aged one. In May 1850 she wrote of her troubles to Weydemeyer (who was enduring hardship himself in Frankfurt); of the baby's convulsions, her lack of sleep and painful breasts, the family's summary eviction from their lodgings by an unsympathetic landlady, the bailiffs' repossession of their few belongings.[97] When another child, Franziska, died in 1852, also aged one year, they had no money for a coffin. Ernest Jones would have helped, but was hard up too, and Colonel Bangya promised to, but did not. Jenny ran to a French exile who lived near by and begged him for £2 for a coffin, which he gave 'with the friendliest sympathy'.

Jenny's nerves were shattered by the life they led. Marx showed his awareness of this when he told Laura's fiancé Lafargue that he intended 'as far as lies within my power to save my daughter from the reefs on which her mother's life has been wrecked'.[98] (As it turned out, all three of his daughters married unlikeable, improvident socialists just like himself, except that none of them was a genius.) She got some pleasure out of seeing her older girls acquire the usual accomplishments, hiring French and Italian tutors for them after they left South Hampstead College for Ladies in 1860 having won most of the prizes there,[99] and allowing them to have drawing and singing, and later even riding, lessons. She mentions in her memoir giving 'the first small ball' in the new house in Belsize Park in 1864, following it up with 'several small parties'. Her last pleasure, as we have seen, was reading Bax's praise of Marx's work immediately before her death in December 1881. In the main, however, her life was one of 'sorrows, disappointments, and renunciation', though, as she willingly admitted, that was hardly England's fault.

Thus it is from the women among the German exiles that we can learn many details of social life in England and the exiles' responses to it. This is partly because many of them ran households, saw to the children's schoolings, had dealings with neighbours and shopkeepers (and pawnbrokers), partly because among them were women of intelligence, spirit, and descriptive ability. In letters to friends at home they spent time on the minutiae of life, and in their journals, memoirs, and fiction they gave full expression to the interlocking themes of the present work: life in England in the mid nineteenth century, the life led by the German refugees as a group, and the comparisons to be made between German and English mores at the time.

6

The Proletariat and the Lumpenproletariat of the Exile

The Mad, the Desperate, and the Swindlers

In April 1861 Jenny Marx wrote to Engels:

> *A propos*. I must tell you a little story of London life. Last Wednesday immediately after dinner I saw outside our door a huge crowd gathering; all the local children were clustered round a man who lay stretched out in front of our house with his face on the ground. No Irishman in the worst state of degradation could have looked as bad as this skeleton. What's more, the ragged, dirty man seemed of unusual length. When I went up, the neighbours had already brought food and spirits, but in vain. The man lay there without moving, and we took him for dead. I sent for a policeman. When the latter arrived and had looked at him, he immediately addressed him with 'you mean impostor', gave him a kick, which knocked off his hat, then picked him up like a parcel, shook him, and who did I find staring at me with mad, desperate eyes?—the Laplander. You can imagine my horror. I immediately sent some money after him, as he went off swaying, but he refused it. He said to Marian, 'Please, please, I don't need any money', put it on a stone and shouted to the policeman, 'that's for your attention'. Isn't it sad?[1]

If the English policeman's handling of the poor man, Albert Anders, known as 'the Laplander', a German journalist and member of the Communist League, seems unkind, his view that Anders was shamming was shared by Marx and Freiligrath. They had had occasion to help their fellow exile a few months earlier. In November 1860 Freiligrath wrote to Marx that he would meet Anders on his release from 'the House of Correction' with some money and clothes. But he did not know what to do with him. Hoping to convince the prison doctors of Anders's insanity, he planned to get him into an asylum. However, a week later he reported that Anders's madness had given way to mere coarseness: 'He *demands* that we shouldn't let him starve'; and Freiligrath had come to the conclusion that he was less mad than lazy and work-shy.[2]

Anders was one of many among the exiles who ended up in prison or asylum, or begging and cheating, unable to make an honest living. A Metropolitan Police report of March 1854 stated that out of the estimated 1,970 refugees in London, two-thirds were 'in straitened circumstances', and so it is hardly surprising that some of them found their way to the courts, charged with pathetic offences like the theft of an umbrella or a bottle of sauce.[3] Though there were relief associations, some run by liberal Englishmen and others by better-established Poles, Hungarians, Italians, and others for their countrymen, there was never enough money to go round. The refugees helped one another, as we have seen, but often the problem—chronic and continuous lack of money—was merely pushed from one to another and back again, without ever being solved. As Herzen eloquently expressed it:

> It may well be imagined how many incongruous elements are caught up from the Continent and deposited in England by those ebbs and flows of revolution and reaction which exhaust the constitution of Europe like an intermittent fever; and what amazing types of people are cast down by these waves and stray about the moist, miry bottom of London. What must be the chaos of ideas and theories in these samples of every moral formation and reformation, of every protest, every Utopia, every disillusionment, and every hope, who meet in the alleys, cook-shops and pot-houses of Leicester Square and the adjoining back streets?[4]

Such people, mainly though not entirely working-class rather than middle-class, took to a variety of ways of trying to help themselves out of the mire. Some, like Anders, fell victim to, or feigned, madness. Jane Carlyle took on one such exile in 1844, before her husband had turned against political refugees. As Amely Bölte told Varnhagen, this man, Plattnauer, had been at Berlin University, 'had dreamed a beautiful dream of freedom, and was rewarded with lifelong banishment'. He came to London in the early 1840s, became a tutor in an aristocratic English family, and was befriended by the Carlyles. However, he got into difficulties, and one day in 1844 Jane received a letter from him asking her to take him from the asylum he was in, as he had been pronounced cured but needed someone to collect him. Jane herself described how she went to the lunatic asylum and brought him home with her for a while, how he was 'horribly excitable' but she was confident she could 'keep him from any new crisis so long as he is beside *me*'.[5] Plattnauer was clearly a survivor. In 1853 Jane wrote to her brother-in-law:

> London is as empty as ever I saw it; one was thankful almost for the return of Plattnauer. He made the most particular inquiries after you and your Lady,—is less mad than last year, in fact shows no mad symptoms at present but spending money with a rashness![6]

Others begged. Herzen gives an ironic account of the different tones adopted by those who approached him for 'loans'. There were 'naïve' letters simply asking for, say, a pair of trousers; 'classical' ones written in Latin expressing the 'joy' the writer would experience if Herzen could do something for him; letters 'distinguished by a peculiar method of reckoning' from those who had already borrowed £3 and would now like to borrow a further £2, in order to be able to pay back the £5 'in a *round sum*'; 'business letters' from would-be inventors seeking a backer; and 'purely oratorical' examples flattering the recipient, giving pathetic expression to the writer's circumstances, and ending up, like all the others, asking for money.[7] Kinkel, of course, was often approached for help, and he usually responded with a small amount of money. Poor Johanna described a visit in 1854 from an importunate carpenter, whom Kinkel was helping to emigrate to Australia. He asked for more than she could afford, and she had to say no. 'He then decided to stay put until I gave in', she wrote to Kinkel, who was lecturing in Edinburgh. 'I felt persecuted, and it made me late for an appointment.' Moreover, she felt guilty for days because she had given him nothing. Fortunately the man reappeared a few days later and went away satisfied with a small amount.[8]

Some desperate refugees even approached Marx, who seldom had money to give and who was not always sympathetic to those even worse off than himself. Wilhelm Reiff, one of the Cologne communists who had been put on trial in 1852, came to London after serving five years in prison, lived with Lessner, who had also been imprisoned in Cologne, and begged Marx not to let him 'go under'. To Engels he wrote with desperate self-respect:

> I did not come to England with the idea that the party should support me. I've tried to find every kind of job in London, and finally on the advice of some friends I took a violin and have managed to fiddle my way up to now . . . But it's been a total failure. As a foreigner with a fiddle moving from place to place, you just cannot scrape even a bare existence. I only managed to make 8*d*. or 9*d*. a day . . . As if it weren't already bad enough, my situation gets worse every day, as I can't afford to replace my worn-out clothes.[9]

Engels was also the victim of a piece of desperate insolence by Hugo von Selmnitz, whom the cautious Freiligrath had passed on: 'Freiligrath saddles me with Prussian ex-lieutenants, dabblers in bonds, who spend the entire day trying to borrow money . . . and who, after their departure, send me pawn tickets so that I can redeem their watches at my own expense.'[10] Then there was Carl Göhringer, owner of one of the German pubs in London and a member of the Willich–Schapper faction of the Communist League, who ended up in debtors' prison in 1854, somewhat to Marx's satisfaction, for Göhringer had threatened to send Marx himself there when the latter tried to avoid repaying a loan in 1851.[11]

There were those who sought to avoid prison or asylum by starting imaginative businesses. Thus the refugee Victor Schily, later a member of the First International, tried to interest Engels in 'a fantastic plan' to open a factory in Liverpool in 1852 'for the production of a purported patent soda which would yield 400–500 per cent profit and might, depending on circumstances, produce 4½ million talers a year'.[12] Hermann ('Red') Becker, another Cologne communist who came to London in 1857 after five years in prison, hit on the idea of, as Freiligrath put it, 'selling old England, which is daily growing shorter of foxes for hunting, between fifty and a hundred live young foxes'. Becker had a partner in Westphalia who would supply the foxes, and wanted Freiligrath to find customers for him. The time was right for such an Anglo-German trade, Becker thought, because of the recent marriage, in January 1858, between Princess Vicky and the Prussian Crown Prince.[13]

Such stories, comic and pathetic, appear in the correspondence of those exiles who were themselves able, if sometimes only just, to stay off the 'miry bottom' of London. They are no doubt similar to the histories of many of London's native population of the (deserving and undeserving) poor, as told by Carlyle, Mayhew, and, with less caricature and exaggeration than one might think if one had not read such factual accounts, in the novels of Dickens. But they differed from their English equivalents in being foreigners of more than one class, many of whom had not always been destitute, but might have been employed as carpenters, tailors, journalists, and teachers in Germany if their politics had not driven them out.

The Workers: Schapper, Eccarius, and Lessner

When we move from this glimpse of the most unfortunate group among the refugees to look at the next group up the ladder (or the greasy pole), we must note that criticism of society, as well as mere participation in it, is strikingly to hand among the final émigré group to be studied here—the German workers. Of course, there were many hundreds of workers—from unpolitical German tailors working in London simply as part of their apprenticeship, and sugar-bakers in Whitechapel who came because there was no work at home, to the politicized workers of the Communist League and the Workers' Education Association—who in the nature of things left no testament to their more or less wretched existence. Like their English counterparts, they had neither the education, nor the leisure, nor was it their custom, to write down their experience for posterity. There was, it is true, a kind of 'working-class literature' in England, from novels and tales and memoirs of Owenites and Chartists to the works of William Morris and beyond. But these were chiefly romances and Utopias, rather than accounts of the daily routine.[14] Moreover, they were often written by middle-class sympathizers, just as the most famous 'Chartist' novel (though it was in fact critical of Chartism) was Kingsley's *Alton Locke*. Robert Tressell's *Ragged Trousered Philanthropists*, the first work of fiction by a worker which gave a full, unsentimental 'insider's' account of workers' lives, was not written until the early 1900s, and not published until after the author's death, when it appeared, much edited, in 1914.

The letters and memoirs of a few German communist workers in England survive, largely because they were friends of Marx and Engels, who carefully preserved all the 'socialist material' they generated and received. Thus some idea of the lives of the tailors Eccarius and Lessner, for example, can be gleaned from Marx's correspondence with them and from the articles and memoirs they wrote, usually at Marx's or later Engels's bidding. Both of them led long, active, heroic lives, full of personal loss and impecuniousness. To them may be added Karl Schapper, not a disciple of Marx's but rather his predecessor in the 1840s as leader of the German communist workers in London.

Schapper, like Willich, was not a proletarian by birth but became an honorary proletarian by choice. Born in 1812, he had studied theology in Giessen during the 1830s and had been expelled from Germany for his Burschenschaft activities. He went first to Switzerland in 1834, where Mazzini and his group were. After taking part in a failed uprising in Paris in 1839, he fled to London, where he became leader of the Workers' Education Association. Schapper taught German for a living, married an Englishwoman, and later encouraged his sons to learn trades. With Harney he founded the Democratic Friends of all Nations in 1844; and, though he was later criticized by Marx and Engels for his Utopian ideas about workers' education, he administered a rebuke to the 'primitive communist' Weitling in 1845 which sounds very like Marx's rebuttals of Willich's hot-headed idealism five years later. At a meeting of the

Workers' Education Association he told Weitling that people must be educated before revolution could succeed; the truth could not simply be knocked into their heads with the butt of a rifle.[15] After his rather surprising support for Willich in the split of 1850 with Marx and Engels, Schapper kept up relations with Marx, effecting a *rapprochement* in 1852. As Marx put it, 'Schapper has been sounding me and making contrite admissions through Imandt'.[16]

Marx was consequently less antagonistic towards Schapper than he was towards Willich, who returned his fire in the bitter battles fought in the German-American newspapers. Apart from referring to Schapper's 'hippopotamus belly' and his frequent 'tippling jaunts', Marx left Schapper unharmed by his wit.[17] Having returned to Germany in 1848 to help spread revolutionary propaganda among the workers of Cologne, Schapper was arrested on a charge of high treason, but acquitted in February 1850. He returned to London, but left politics altogether after Napoleon's *coup* and the Cologne Communist trials, and quietly made a living for his children and his second wife through teaching and journalism and continued work with workers' education clubs.[18] Marx had little contact with Schapper over the next two decades, though he enlisted Schapper's help—as he enlisted that of many other old friends and enemies—as a witness to the truth of his obsessive, point-by-point rebuttal of Karl Vogt's accusations that he had betrayed his own party. He quoted a supportive letter from Schapper in part 4 of *Herr Vogt* (1860). When Schapper was dying of consumption in 1870, he asked to see Marx, who was impressed by his composure and his 'true manliness'. Schapper was comforted by knowing that his children were provided for: his daughter was married, his oldest son was a self-employed bookbinder; and the two younger sons were already earning £1 a week as goldsmiths. He said to Marx: 'Tell all our people that I have remained true to our principles. I'm not a theoretician. During the reaction [after 1848] I had enough to do just bringing up my family. I have lived as a hard-working labourer and die a proletarian.'[19]

Of the workers who came under Marx's influence in London in the 1850s, the most prominent were Lochner, Pfänder, and Eccarius and Lessner, all of whom were members of the First International in London in 1864. We know comparatively little about the first two; indeed Lessner recalled that Karl Pfänder had been a man who never pushed himself forward, but who worked tirelessly for workers' organizations in England until his death as an 'unsung hero' in 1876. Engels remembered him as one of 'two men who were considerably superior' to the rest of the Communist League members 'in capacity for theoretical knowledge', the other being Eccarius. Pfänder was, said Engels, 'a man of peculiarly fine intelligence, witty, ironical and dialectical'.[20] But the two tailors are frequently mentioned in the Marx–Engels correspondence, and both published articles, Eccarius some pamphlets, and Lessner an autobiography. In their different ways, they illustrate the miserable life of the tailor in London. Eccarius and Lessner may well have learned something about workers' action from their Chartist fellow workmen at the same time as they were being tutored in economics by Marx. They also undertook, encouraged by Marx, a self-education which included attending lectures on science given at University College London by Professors Tyndall and Huxley in the 1860s.[21]

Eccarius first came to work in England in 1846, and, like Lessner, he was a member of the Communist League and the Workers' Education Association, at that time under Schapper's leadership. Lessner remembered that when they all turned out to take part in the Chartist demonstration of 10 April 1848, Eccarius carried his large tailor's scissors with him.[22] He became a loyal disciple of Marx, to whom he was indispensable as a worker experiencing the actual conditions of the tailoring trade in London. With Pfänder and others, Eccarius attended 'lectures' on political economy given by Marx at his Dean Street house during 1850.[23] Marx published an article written by Eccarius with his help in the *Neue Rheinische Zeitung* in the autumn of that year. Entitled 'Der Kampf des grossen und des kleinen Kapitals, oder die Schneiderei in London' ('The Struggle between Big and Small Capital, or Tailoring in London'), the article embodied Marx's idea of the need for educating the workers to understand the conditions governing their trade before they took action to try to better them. Marx and Engels issued a challenge in their introduction to the article:

> The author of this article is himself a *worker* in one of London's tailoring shops. We ask the German bourgeoisie how many authors it numbers capable of grasping the real movement in a similar manner?
>
> Before the proletariat fights out its victories on the barricades and in the battle lines it gives notice of its impending rule with a series of intellectual victories.

Their intention was not only to shake up the docile German middle class but also to triumph over the 'sentimental, moral and psychological criticism employed against existing conditions by Weitling and other workers who engage in authorship'. These writers' advocacy of primitive communism, involving a return to the 'semi-medieval' guild system as an answer to modern industrial relations, was shown up by Eccarius's article for the hopelessly unrealistic dream it was. Another target was Henry Mayhew, whose accounts of the tailoring trade in his *Morning Chronicle* articles, though sympathetic and factual, betrayed, Marx and Eccarius thought, 'a reactionary tendency' which they wanted to correct (especially, one supposes, because Mayhew's articles were so widely read and admired).[24]

Eccarius's article contains a brief history of the tailoring trade from the Middle Ages up to the complicated conditions of the early Victorian period in England. Like Mayhew, he describes the two halves of the trade—respectable and slop—and gives statistics of wages and prices. He looks forward to the tailor's emancipation, partly through the introduction of new machinery, but chiefly through social revolution. One senses Marx looking over his shoulder when Eccarius wrote the final sentences of his piece. He foresees, in the near future, a crisis in modern industry, after which 'a continuation of production within the existing property relations will become quite impossible' and the social problem will only be solved 'with the complete dissolution of bourgeois society and its property relations'.[25]

In 1866, when Eccarius was, briefly, editor of the International's journal, *The Commonwealth*, he talked among his English friends about the need to correct John Stuart Mill's 'reactionary' political economy in his *Principles of Political Economy*, first published in 1848. His friends asked him to give 'the worker's point of view', which he did in a series of articles for the *Commonwealth*. Eccarius later republished the articles in German as a book, *Eines Arbeiters Widerlegung der national-ökonomischen Lehren John Stuart Mill's (A Worker's Refutation of John Stuart Mill's Doctrine of Political Economy*, 1869). Eccarius's main point was that Mill never saw things from the worker's position, never saw either the need or the possibility for radical change in the make-up of society. Like Plato and Aristotle before him, Mill was trying to keep in existence an outmoded phase of society by appealing to eternal laws of nature. In a reading of history in which he was closely tutored by Marx, Eccarius saw hope in the Reform Act of 1867 which had finally given the bourgeoisie power in the land after six hundred years of fighting the aristocracy for supremacy. The next task would be for the proletariat, only just emerging into 'full self-consciousness as a force on the stage of world history', to take over in its turn. This should take sixty years, not six hundred, wrote Eccarius with the same excessive optimism the young Engels had shown twenty-five years before. Eccarius stressed that he was an informed and credible observer, having worked as a tailor for years and seen conditions on the ground (or in the garret) but having also educated himself in political economy and history. He was convinced a workers' revolution would happen. Eccarius's articles are impressive for their detail and argument, particularly in the section in which, under Marx's tutelage, no doubt, he takes Mill to task for defending property as an essential right of the individual, a position which leads Mill into a *laissez-faire* attitude to society and thus into a defence of the manifestly unjust status quo. Perhaps also under Marx's influence with regard to style, Eccarius writes belligerently and often sneeringly about Mill, as when he more than once finds Mill 'holding two different opinions about the same subject'.[26]

Between these two sets of articles, Eccarius had had little spare time to write, as most of his energies went into the tailoring from which he had to eke a living for his growing family. Despite this he was one of the few among Marx's 'party' to fulfil a promise to produce an article for Weydemeyer's American journal, *Die Revolution*, in January 1852. Marx sent the piece, an account of the machine-building workers' strike organized by the Amalgamated Society of Engineers to agitate for the abolition of overtime and the improvement of conditions (to which the employers responded with a lock-out which defeated the workers), to Weydemeyer. The latter, wrote Marx, would have to correct Eccarius's grammar and punctuation, as he had not had time to do it.[27]

Eccarius's working conditions in the 'Schneiderhölle' ('tailor's hell'), as Marx and Engels called the sweat-shop system, caused his health to deteriorate. In 1859 he became consumptive and wrote Marx a letter which Marx sent on to Engels, who thought it 'heroic'. For the letter was cheerful despite Eccarius's illness and near-destitution. In it, Eccarius asked Marx to lend him some books to pass the time in self-improvement until he got better. Engels sent him some port to aid his recovery, and Eccarius returned to the tailor's hell a month later, before he was really fit.[28] In 1862 Eccarius was devastated by the loss, one after the other, of three of his children from scarlatina. Marx collected money for him; Engels sent £3, and Dronke £2. Poor Eccarius was distraught. When thanking Marx for his and the others' kindness, he expressed his anger at English society—a so-called Christian society—letting unfortunate people like himself go on the parish and then saying to them, 'hence your trouble, it is a visitation of the Lord'.[29] Perhaps Marx had in mind his poor German friend, still living in unhealthy Soho from which

Marx's family had escaped in 1856, when he wrote his biting account of 'primitive accumulation' in *Capital*:

> This primitive accumulation plays in Political Economy about the same part as original sin in theology. Adam bit the apple, and thereupon sin fell on the human race. Its origin is supposed to be explained when it is told as an anecdote of the past. In times long gone by there were two sorts of people; one, the diligent, intelligent, and, above all, frugal élite; the other, lazy rascals, spending their substance, and more, in riotous living. The legend of theological original sin tells us certainly how man came to be condemned to eat his bread in the sweat of his brow; but the history of economic original sin reveals to us that there are people to whom this is by no means essential. Never mind! Thus it came to pass that the former sort accumulated wealth, and the latter sort had at last nothing to sell except their own skins. And from this original sin dates the poverty of the great majority, that, despite all its labour, has up to now nothing to sell but itself, and the wealth of the few that increases constantly although they have long ceased to work. Such insipid childishness is every day preached to us in the defence of property.[30]

When his domestic tragedy struck him in November 1862, Eccarius was already trying to supplement his tailor's earnings with money from teaching pupils. He put advertisements in the London German newspapers, including even Kinkel's *Hermann*, offering to give Germans lessons in English for a shilling an hour, and mentioning that he had written for English newspapers.[31] When Liebknecht returned to Germany in 1862, Eccarius inherited some of his pupils in the Workers' Education Association, but he did not earn enough money from this and found them 'in the main very uneducated people'. He would rather, he said, become a schoolmaster teaching German, like Wilhelm Wolff in Manchester, from whom he asked for advice about German language primers. A few months later he reported to Wolff that he had had no luck; no new pupils were forthcoming, and he was down to his last £2. In that dry, bantering, but not far from desperate tone so familiar in exiles' letters, he told Wolff: 'Your letter came not like "de la moutarde après dîner" but like "de la moutarde sans dîner".'[32]

Though Eccarius was never able to give up tailoring altogether, he was soon to play an important organizing and journalistic role in English labour politics. On Marx's recommendation, Eccarius spoke as the representative of the German workers at the foundation meeting of the International in 1864, and was elected to its first General Council. He attended every conference and reported back to Marx from the congress at Geneva (where 'the dirty pack' of French delegates caused trouble) in

1866 and Brussels in 1868.[33] In 1866 he was chosen as the first editor of the International's newspaper, *The Commonwealth*, and from 1867 to 1871 he reported on the annual congresses for no less a paper than *The Times*, which had decided to inform itself and its readers about this international workers' organization with its base in London. Eccarius got into trouble with his colleagues for these articles, which Engels said *The Times* had edited to conform to its house tone of cynical humour at the expense of the Association. Eccarius had ill-advisedly concentrated in his *Times* articles on the antics of the French delegates at Lausanne in 1867, and, with further editing, his reports appeared highly treacherous to the International.[34] Eccarius seems to have been tactless and insensitive to criticism on this point, for he repeated the crime during the Brussels Congress of September 1868, when the executive gave notice of its intention to censure him at its next meeting and prevent him from acting as a delegate again. Marx, who had defended his rash friend the previous year, felt unable to do so again, but in the event Eccarius's illness prevented him from attending the meeting and he was not in fact censured.[35]

The complaints against him were that he was ironic at the expense of other delegates in his reports, when he did not suppress their contributions altogether. Eccarius's irony was, as irony is, a two-edged weapon in his relations with his fellows. On the one hand, as Marx noted in 1865, he had 'a peculiar, dry, humorous manner of speaking, which [went] down especially well with the English'.[36] On the other, this tendency to irony, fortified by egotism and occasional silliness, led him into tactless and treacherous behaviour. Thus he was accused in 1868 at Brussels of taking very little part in the congress, then representing himself in *The Times* as its 'leading mind'. His unwise activities in these early years of the International brought him enemies; he imagined a conspiracy against him, in which he thought Marx was implicated, and resigned from the Council of the International in 1871 amid criticism of his lack of activity on its behalf.[37]

Much later poor Eccarius was reported to have been a spy for the Austrian government all along. This rumour was partly based on his 'treacherous' reports from the International congresses in *The Times*, and partly on his later connection with a Vienna workers' paper edited by Heinrich Oberwinder, who was exposed as a spy in 1888.[38] But then, what exile was not at some time closely involved with one of the many spies who infiltrated socialist and revolutionary societies in the nineteenth century? Freiligrath was close to Ebner, and Marx to both

Ebner and Bangya. Which of the refugees, if they were to be convicted on the mere evidence of associating with such men, would escape whipping? It seems unlikely that Eccarius was a spy, if only because the evidence of his life, with its chronic poverty, suggests that he had no extra source of income.

The most unfortunate result of the rows on the International Council was Eccarius's permanent estrangement from Marx after 1872. Marx had been relatively patient, being aware of the strains of illness and poverty on Eccarius. Though he saw that Eccarius was becoming involved with English associations for which he had little time, such as the Land and Labour League, founded in 1869 with Eccarius as secretary, he continued to help his disciple. Eccarius asked him for advice about his inaugural speech to the League in November 1869.[39] But Marx had already noticed signs of Eccarius's mind becoming unbalanced. In 1867 Eccarius went on strike with his fellow tailors and suffered the usual extra hardships consequent on that course of action. He then rushed off to try living in Newbury in Berkshire, but he found that though rent was cheaper than in London, he was paid less. A few months later he was back in London, unable to pay his rent, and living temporarily with a friend. In December 1870 Eccarius wrote an incoherent note to Engels, thanking him for £5, and saying that 'an old tormentor', a carpenter, who had 'spared' him two years ago, had appeared again and 'was holding [Eccarius] prisoner'—presumably until he paid his old debt.[40]

The troubles with the International grew. After the London conference of September 1871, someone leaked the supposedly private resolutions to the *Scotsman* and the *Manchester Guardian.* Eccarius was suspected. He in turn thought his erstwhile friends were intriguing against him to force him off the Council. In May 1872 he rashly resigned, apparently in the hope that he would be thought indispensable and would be asked to stay on. Instead, his resignation was accepted, and he was replaced by the Englishman Hales. Eccarius blamed Marx and Engels for intriguing with Hales in a letter to Liebknecht in Germany, from which Engels concluded that he was 'mad'.[41] Marx himself received a curt letter from Eccarius, who wrote, in English, 'Sir, I shall deem it a very great favor if you will kindly furnish me with a copy of so much of the letter, complaining of me, as relates to my culpable correspondence . . . likewise a copy of the indictment, in case you come prepared with one, on Saturday next.' Marx replied, firmly but humanely:

Finally, I shall give you some good advice. Don't think that your old personal and party friends are any the less well disposed towards you because they hold it their duty to act against your freaks. On the other hand, don't delude yourself that the little clique of Englishmen who use you for their own purposes are your friends. . . . And now, *salut.* As the day after tomorrow is my birthday, I don't want to approach it with the unpleasant thought that I have lost one of my oldest friends and comrades. *Salut fraternel.*[42]

Marx had lost Eccarius, however. There was no further correspondence between them. In October 1872 Eccarius applied for, and was granted, British nationality. He declared that he had been living and working in London since 1846, and that he was married, with two under-age children living with him: Henry Sedgley Eccarius, aged 17, and Fritz Marx Eccarius, aged 9. The latter had been born after the deaths of three of his children from scarlatina and before his separation from Marx. Four English householders and trade unionists, including Thomas Mottershead of the International, supported his successful application to become a British citizen. Eccarius now went his way with the leaders of certain trade unions, becoming thereby, in Engels's opinion, a 'traitor to our cause'.[43] After Marx's death, Engels, whose arrival in London in 1870 may have contributed to the worsening of Eccarius's relations with Marx, was bitter about Eccarius. When Hermann Schlüter wrote from Zurich in 1885 asking for Eccarius's address—he wanted to reprint Eccarius's pamphlet against Mill—Engels replied brusquely: 'I am completely out of touch with Eccarius and have no desire to resume relations.' Furthermore, he advised Schlüter to republish the pamphlet as it stood, for if he asked Eccarius, the latter would probably 'correct' it to conform to his new ideas, whereas the original had been written 'with considerable help and cramming' by Marx, and was therefore a valuable document, in Engels's view. In the same year he noted laconically in his 'History of the Communist League' that Eccarius had long since 'devoted himself exclusively to the English trade union movement'. In 1889, the year of Eccarius's death, Engels commented to a friend in Germany on a new split among the English groups into possibilists and socialists. The former, including the opportunist Hyndman, were attacking Marxism with lies and misrepresentations. Hyndman went for his information about the International to 'the malcontents who used to be on the General Council, Eccarius, Jung & Co.'[44]

Though Engels would and could not see it, Eccarius had in fact thrown in his lot with a movement which was to gain momentum and power, not in the way predicted and hoped for it by Marx, but through the industrial means of agitating for improved pay and conditions rather than attacking the capitalist system and so changing the world. The English trade union movement had an uneasy relationship with the International, many of its leaders preferring a practical, industrial-relations approach to problems rather than political theorizing.[45] Eccarius seems to have fitted in well with other trade union leaders in the 1870s. One of them, Robert Applegarth, leader of the Amalgamated Carpenters and Joiners, remembered him as 'a thoroughly able man' who had made considerable sacrifices for the workers' cause. Applegarth's biographer remarks:

> Poor Eccarius died in dire poverty. His had been a hard life. In the 'sixties, a Labour paper, *The Commonwealth*, was started by a group of working men, of which Applegarth was one, and Eccarius related to Applegarth how, on one occasion, in order to finish his leading article he had to pawn his flat iron and so procure money for the purchase of a candle.[46]

Among his own class, Eccarius had become as much an honorary Englishman as had the middle-class Friedrich Althaus.

Like Eccarius, Friedrich Lessner was a tailor who came to London before 1848, and became a loyal follower of Marx. Unlike Eccarius, he remained loyal to Marx and Engels, whom he outlived by several years, and to Marxism as Marx had taught it. His personal loyalty is a tribute to his character, for not only was he one of the few friends of whom Marx was not at one time or another bitingly critical, but he was also —unenviably—Marx's tailor. Though he was often as hard up as Eccarius, Lessner appears to have been patient with Marx's non-payment of bills. There survives one such bill from September 1868, which reads as follows:

Tailor's bill. Dr Karl Marx from Lessner. 24 September 1868

	£	*s.*	*d.*
October 1867 bill delivered	26	13	10
December 1867 money received	5	0	0
	21	13	10

With various items added, the total bill in September 1868 came to £23 14*s.* 8*d.*[47]

Lessner was also one of the many refugees who at difficult times relied on hand-outs from Engels to keep his head above water. One such time was 1869, when his first wife had died, aged 29, and he contemplated leaving his children behind with their grandmother and going off to Brazil to try making a living there. However, he stayed in England after all, and during 1870 and 1871 borrowed regularly from Engels, though he also took a lodger named Salomon (probably another tailor) into his lodgings in Tottenham Court Road to try to make ends meet.[48] When Engels died in 1895, Lessner was one of those, along with Eugen Oswald and the Marx daughters and sons-in-laws, whose debts were nullified in Engels's will.[49] Lessner himself went on both working in English trade union and labour politics and remaining in contact with the German Social Democrats until his death in 1910. He had been in London for more than sixty years, longer than any other exile.

Lessner's life is a fitting one with which to bring this study of the exiles to a close. In one sense he was unusual, since he was a worker who, unlike most of his fellows, wrote an autobiography. His life was, however, in another sense typical of the large group of exiles of whom he was one: he was caught up in revolutionary events, became a communist, spent time in prison for his activities, ate the 'bitter bread of exile', and suffered domestic tragedies as well as economic hardship. Lessner also embodied in his life and work both English and German influences, being a useful member of the International, and a man who echoed Marx, yet one who also co-founded the Independent Labour Party in England in 1893.

By his own account, Lessner would have remained an unsung hero like his friend Karl Pfänder, if his Cologne colleagues had not asked him in 1893 to write his memoirs for the benefit of the Communist Party. Lessner was reluctant, but the death of Engels two years later, leaving him the chief survivor of the old London Communist League, pushed him into publishing his life story, which he dedicated to Engels's memory, in 1898. His autobiographical writings were published in English in 1907 under the title *Sixty Years in the Social-Democratic Movement*, with a foreword by Ernest Belfort Bax, who wrote warmly of 'that old war-horse of the Socialist Party, Friedrich Lessner, probably the oldest living Social-Democrat', whose memoirs were 'bound to constitute in the future a valuable first-hand source to the historian of the Modern Socialist movement'.[50] Lessner tells the story simply and undramatically, though it is not lacking in exciting events.

Born in 1825 in Saxony, Lessner became a tailor's apprentice at the age of 14. Following the medieval custom for craftsmen which still obtained in Germany, he set off on his travels as a journeyman tailor in

1842. After doing part of his obligatory military service in 1846–7, he went to Hamburg to work, and 'from having been a soldier of absolutism I became a soldier of revolution'.[51] For in Hamburg two things happened. Firstly, he found himself working with tailors who had spent time in London and learned communist ideas from that most politicized group of English workers. Secondly, Lessner heard his fellow tailor, the 'primitive communist' Wilhelm Weitling, lecture in Hamburg, and, inspired by this, read Weitling's pamphlet *Garantien der Harmonie und Freiheit* (*Guarantees of Harmony and Freedom*, 1842), which impressed even Marx, who wrote of it as the '*vehement* and brilliant literary début of the German workers'.[52] Fired by Weitling's rhetoric about history being 'one great story of robbery', Lessner decided not to go back to his barracks in Weimar to complete the statutory military duty, but on 1 April 1847 took ship for England instead: 'I left my whole past on the Continent in order to start a new life in England—a life that I decided to devote to the struggle for the emancipation of my class.'[53] There he immediately joined Schapper, Bauer, and Moll in the Workers' Education Association and the Communist League. Lessner thus lived through the take-over of the latter by Marx in 1847, accepted Marx's analysis of the prospects for revolution, and abandoned Weitling's naïve communism for Marx's complex version. He fulfilled at this time the first of his many missions as messenger or lieutenant to the party. 'I took the manuscript [of the *Communist Manifesto*] to the printer', he recalls proudly in his memoirs.[54]

February 1848 excited Lessner along with other communists and Chartists. He remembered Ernest Jones coming to speak to the German Workers' Education Association, and was impressed, as Marx and Engels at first were, both by Jones's knowledge of German and by his understanding of socialism. After the Chartist demonstration on 10 April, in which he took part, Lessner was anxious to go back to Germany to agitate there. Being a poorly paid worker, he had to save up for the journey, and had not made enough money until July, when he set off for Cologne to join Marx, Engels, Wolff, Freiligrath, and the others on the *Neue Rheinische Zeitung.* Like some of them, he was running a conscious risk, since he was open to criminal charges as a deserter from the army. He took an assumed name, Corstens, and distributed pamphlets. On the suspension of the paper in May 1849 and the arrest of Schapper for treason, Lessner helped Freiligrath, who took in Schapper's daughter on the death of his wife while Schapper was awaiting trial. Freiligrath was supposed to attend Schapper's trial in Wiesbaden in February 1850, but Lessner went on his behalf. This lieutenancy seems to have had a comic and a tragic side. Lessner tells us the comic part: Schapper had made a brilliant defence speech and been acquitted to popular acclaim; it was known that the famous poet Freiligrath was coming to congratulate Schapper and escort him in triumph to Cologne. When Lessner turned up, he was treated by the populace to the full hero's welcome, in the belief that he was Freiligrath. What Lessner omits is the fact that he took his fiancée with him, whom Schapper seduced and 'stole' from him, taking her back to England with him.[55]

While Schapper returned to London in the summer of 1850, Lessner went to Mainz to try to establish anew the Communist League there. In June 1851 he was arrested, accused of distributing treasonable pamphlets, bearing a false name, and being a member of the Communist League. He was held in solitary confinement for fifteen months, while the Prussian government set about gathering information, in the dubious ways exposed by Marx, for the Cologne Communist trials. Lessner was finally tried, with the others, in October 1852. He was sentenced to three years in prison, and released in January 1856. Luckily for him, there was a change of ruler in Saxony at that time, bringing the usual amnesty for prisoners. Otherwise, Lessner recalled, he would have been immediately rearrested and convicted on a separate charge of desertion. Instead, he was freed: 'Free! As if Germany was not at that time one great prison!'[56] Seeing that political activity in Germany was now impossible, Lessner returned to London in May 1856.

During his time in prison, the situation among the Germans in London had changed. There were still his old friends Marx, Eccarius, Pfänder, and Freiligrath. But others had moved on to America in 1852 and 1853. The Communist League was split, and new arrivals from Germany, like Liebknecht and Kinkel, had taken their place in the exile community. Lessner allows himself his only bitter comment in the whole autobiography at Kinkel's expense. He found many of his fellow workers of the Workers' Education Association now slavishly following their idol. 'Bourgeoisified', they attended lectures given by Kinkel, 'who was not to be had except for a fee' (while Marx, Liebknecht, and others lectured to the workers for nothing). 'The Professor knew very well how to educate the workers in the cult of personality—his.'[57] No doubt Lessner was influenced in his hatred of Kinkel by Marx, but he must also have felt, though he was too delicate to say so, a sense of anger at the injustice of Kinkel's fame as an escapee after eighteen months in prison, while he (Lessner) and others arrived unsung after serving much longer sentences, and without having compromised their cause to save their skins.

Once settled again in London, Lessner set up his tailoring premises, married a German girl living in England in 1858, helped Marx and Liebknecht build up the communist workers' club again, contributed to the workers' journal, *Das Volk*, in 1859, and joined the Council of the First International, with Marx and Eccarius, in 1864. He also attended the scientific lectures of Huxley, Tyndall, and others at University College. With Marx, he went along to Sunday evening meetings at which Charles Bradlaugh preached free thinking. Like Eccarius, he wrote articles for workers' journals which Marx, and later Engels and his friends, had to correct in point of style and grammar. And he and Eccarius represented the International at meetings of the English Reform Movement of 1866. He also took part in the great tailors' strike of 1866–7.[58] Lessner attended the Lausanne and Brussels Congresses of the International in 1867 and 1868, reporting back to Marx on the association's activities, and on Eccarius's indiscretions.[59]

Like Eccarius, Lessner was involved in the activities of his union, and he went on after Marx's death to play a role in the founding of some of the many socialist organizations which sprang up in the 1880s and 1890s. With Eleanor and Engels, he was a member of the Social Democratic Federation, founded by Hyndman in 1882, seceding with them in 1884 and starting the Socialist League in a move to isolate Hyndman, whom they distrusted for his egotism, jingoism, and lack of commitment to socialism. He co-founded the Independent Labour Party at Bradford in January 1893, at a meeting to which Eleanor Marx went as a visitor and Edward Aveling as a delegate.[60] Lessner was still the good and faithful servant of Marxism. When a German named Walter applied to Engels for support in 1888, the latter replied that he could not help those who were unknown to him and who were possibly political opponents. As Walter had mentioned Johann Most in his letter, Engels concluded he was a fellow anarchist and as such an opponent of the socialist movement in Germany. If this was not so, Walter should 'legitimate' himself with 'my old friend Lessner, 12 Fitzroy Street', after which Engels would be willing to assist him.[61]

Lessner was to perform two more pious acts of symbolic significance both for the history of communism and for the story of the German exiles in England. This modest man, who had begun his autobiography with the words, 'It is not easy to describe one's own life; especially when that life has been full of sorrow and distress, struggle and suffering, such as a rebellious proletarian necessarily endures',[62] was one of the bearers of Engels's ashes to be scattered, at his request, in the sea off the coast of Eastbourne, Engels's favourite resort. Less than three years later, in April 1898, Lessner carried the ashes of Eleanor Marx, which the perfidious Aveling did not claim, to the headquarters of the Social Democratic Federation.[63]

Lessner lived on for another twelve years. As is natural given his occupation, his reticence, and the fact of his having outlived his famous friends, it is difficult to trace in detail his activities during those years. He was to speak at the funerals of other socialist colleagues, including Liebknecht (in 1900) and the jeweller Jung, who had been on the General Council of the International and who was apparently murdered during a political argument in 1901.[64] In fact, Lessner outlived all his old comrades, and spent his last years defending Marx's and Engels's views against criticisms or misrepresentations in both English and German newspapers. The socialist periodical *Justice* published New Year greetings from 'the veteran of the International' in 1900, as well as printing his attacks on Hyndman's anti-Marxism and on Frederic Harrison's criticisms of Marx. Like Marx and Engels themselves, he kept a collection of documents pertaining to his socialist activities. He handed it over in 1905 to J. Motteler of Leipzig, who deposited it in the archives of the German Social Democratic Party. Lessner lived to the age of 85, but he was still poor, and during the last few years of his life he was deaf and blind. Still, through his son Karl and his daughter Kate, he communicated with socialist leaders and contributed to periodicals. He died, the last of all the generation of 1848 exiles, in February 1910. Lessner had experience of working conditions in Germany and in England, he was 'educated' alike by Marx and by 'practical John Bull', as Liebknecht put it, and he no doubt contributed, in ways it would be difficult, if not impossible, to trace, the fruits of his comparative experiences to the growing labour movement in England at the end of the nineteenth and the beginning of the twentieth century.

Typically, Lessner himself paid a moving tribute to his second wife—and, by extension, to the wives and families of many other socialist workers—for her 'silent sacrifices' to the general cause. His praise of his wife modulates into a rallying-call to others to do as he and she have unhesitatingly done with their lives:

> When I joined the Labour movement in early life, it soon became clear to me that women must be drawn into the movement, that without their participation a movement like the proletarian one could never be perfect and victorious. It is to

women and their influence upon the education and bringing up of children that we must look for a better state of social conditions in the next generation.

With my help my wife soon learned to understand my ideas on economical and political questions. From the beginning of our married life I took her to German and English meetings for her to understand the working-class movement. But as years went by, we had to work harder for our living; the family grew, and there was little spare time left for my wife to accompany me to meetings, but, unselfishly, she insisted that I should go. Without her help and goodwill, it would have been impossible for me to do for the cause what little I have done.

. . . There are so many time-servers and place-hunters in this world who consider their interest alone, to the exclusion of all fellow-feeling, that it is imperative for those endowed with intelligence to take their stand in the interest of our common cause. There are thousands of nameless men and women who silently have done their duty. Where would the working class be now without their silent sacrifices? May this fact appeal to everyone to do his duty.[65]

Epilogue

The group of German exiles in Britain in mid Victorian England was, as has been seen, heterogeneous in character, opinion, and profession. The range of experience covered by its members is a wide one, from the occupation of a professorial chair to violin-playing in the streets, from senior factory management to incarceration in a lunatic asylum. Geographically, the German exiles spanned the country from Brighton to Dundee. Nevertheless, as foreigners responding to a strange country and its customs, as political refugees who would probably have broadly agreed in defining their opposition to their home state if hardly at all in describing their positive goals, the Germans evince a number of common responses to Britain. These have been seen to centre on the paradox of an advanced civilization, a complex political system, and a relatively high degree of civic freedom coexisting with an ingrained class system and seemingly unbudgeable prejudices in the areas of religion and sexual relations. The freedom of the individual held equal sway with the tyranny of custom, as many an exile noticed with exasperation. Advanced political awareness on the part of all classes was balanced by lack of formal education for the largest class of all. Britain opened its doors to all comers, but extended a warm embrace to no one.

The interaction between the German *émigrés* and British society also varied according to the temperament and circumstances of individual arrivals. No one exile made an immediate practical impression on British politics, though Marx's impact on the International and on the numerous socialist groups which were formed during the 1880s and 1890s was considerable, and his posthumous influence on world politics enormous. In literature, art, music, and education, German exiles left their mark, though on the whole not in ways which can be measured. The same is true of the doctors, journalists, and businessmen among them. On the other hand, by their articles, pamphlets, lectures, and books, many German exiles added valuably to the total output of Victorian learning in several fields of interest. The value of their contribution lies chiefly in their criticisms, based on comparisons between England and Germany, of English life and culture.

Though some settled in other towns, the vast majority of German exiles remained in London. They lived, studied, held meetings, and enjoyed Sunday recreations in locations which are still used for the same purposes. One can walk round Soho and Leicester Square and think of the cheap hotels, foreign pubs, and model lodging-houses frequented by many on their arrival. To sit in the British Museum, reading the works of Marx, Althaus, Oswald, Freiligrath, Blind, or Johanna Kinkel, is to repeat the experience each of them enjoyed, often daily, during the 1850s and 1860s. Hampstead Heath is still a favourite Sunday resort for families. The German Hospital in Dalston still stands, and though it is no longer serving German patients, it has archives, portraits, and manuscripts of, among others, Florence Nightingale and Bismarck, to remind one of its original purpose and use. Highgate Cemetery includes the graves of Marx and his family, appropriately placed very near to those of George Eliot, G. H. Lewes, Holyoake (who bought the plot next to George Eliot's for himself), and Herbert Spencer, all of whom lie along 'Dissenters' Path'. In Camberwell some of the grand houses where the wealthy businessmen lived remain, and in Sydenham the German Evangelical Church which Freiligrath's married daughters attended still exists, served by a German pastor and attended by a German-speaking congregation. University College London, the institution with which exiles were most involved, either as teachers and examiners, as students, or as members of clubs devoted to the arts and sciences, carries on as a centre of academic research and teaching over a wide range of subjects. Its archives contain valuable sources for the study of exiles, as well as for progressive English Victorians. University College School and the North London Collegiate School continue; both have libraries well stocked with records and registers dating back to the 1850s, in which one can read the names of German exiles' children.

It is with a brief account of some of the activities of exiles' children that I wish to end this book. It has not been possible to trace descendants of all of them. Many returned to Germany; daughters married and lost their surnames; two world wars probably ensured that many more left the country or changed their names. A search through current telephone directories produced some 'exile' names—Lessner and Lochner, for example—but, on application to their bearers, no descendants of the Lessner and Lochner who were Marx's friends. But a letter to the two Althauses and the one Ruge in the London telephone directory brought enthusiastic, helpful letters and friendly personal contacts. Mr Nigel Althaus, great-grandson of Friedrich, unearthed letters from Carlyle to Althaus and a volume of Althaus's lectures given at University College in the 1880s. The Ruge connection, though indirect, led to a correspondence with the German great-grandson of

Arnold Ruge who was kind enough to send me a copy of Agnes Ruge's delightful memoir.

The generation immediately following that of the exiles themselves was rich in writers, academics, and activists, and those who, as first-generation British men and women, moved naturally in interesting British circles. Karl Blind's son Rudolf translated into English the work of the German explorer of Africa Leo Frobenius, *The Voice of Africa*, in 1913. His sister Ottilie moved in women's rights circles and was a friend of Hertha Marks, the daughter of a Polish refugee who was 'adopted' by Barbara Bodichon and who may have been a model for Mirah in *Daniel Deronda.* Their half-sister Mathilde, sister of the unfortunate Ferdinand Cohen, lived with the Madox Brown family, consorted with the other Pre-Raphaelites, and published several volumes of poetry, including a long poem celebrating Darwinism, 'The Ascent of Man' (1888). She wrote the first biography of George Eliot, for the Eminent Women series, in 1883. Though short, the book is lively, confronts the feminist issue boldly but not stridently, and uses some unpublished material by permission of George Eliot's brother, Isaac Evans, and stepson, Charles Lewes. It preceded John Cross's more detailed and official biography by two years. Richard Garnett, in the introduction to Mathilde's *Poetical Works* (1900), remembered her interest in women's rights and her biography of Shelley, published by Tauchnitz, and noted that as a girl of 18 she had written a German ode for the Bradford Schiller Club's celebrations of the Schiller centenary in 1859. No doubt her stepfather's friend Dr Bronner, who was president of the club, had commissioned it. Her interest in women's education led her to leave about £4,000 in her will to Newnham College, Cambridge, to found a Mathilde Blind Scholarship for Languages and Literature. Mathilde was intimate with the Rossettis and Swinburne, and also with an Anglo-German circle in London which met to read poetry. Agnes Ruge remembered visiting London and hearing Eleanor Marx recite Shakespeare to this group, of which Freiligrath's daughter Kate Kroeker was also a member. The latter recalled hearing Mathilde read her own poetry at a dinner given by Dr Julius Althaus.

Kate Kroeker herself played a small part in London's literary life in the 1870s and 1880s, translating her father's poetry and writing articles in the *Athenaeum.* Married to one of the Camberwell Germans, she lived in Sydenham. Her sister Luise also married a German businessman named Wiens, and was a member of the German Evangelical Church choir. Mrs Freiligrath, Kate Kroeker, and Luise's sons Bernhard and

Hermann are all buried in Ladywell Cemetery in Brockley, as Pastor Albrecht Plag of the German Evangelical Church at Sydenham recently discovered.

We have seen that Theodore Frederick Althaus wrote books on education, updating Schaible's work, as well as writing a recollection of Mark Pattison. The Althauses had much to do, also, with the English Goethe Society, founded in 1886. Friedrich Althaus wrote an essay on Goethe and Byron in an early volume of the *Publications of the English Goethe Society* in 1888. In the same number, Mathilde Blind translated some of Goethe's 'Maxims and Reflections', and in 1893 Kate Kroeker published translations of Goethe's poems in the same periodical. Eugen Oswald was secretary of the society from 1891 until his death in 1912, and was helped in his last years by his daughters Lina and Ella. The latter held various offices in the society until her death, aged 94, in 1965.

If Ella Oswald was one of the longest-lived of the exiles' children, Eleanor Marx was possibly the shortest-lived of those who survived early childhood. She committed suicide in 1898, aged 43. But she had an importance for Anglo-German relations which was not merely symbolic, though it was that too. For Marx, the intellectual giant among the German exiles, had bequeathed both Marxism and a daughter who was deeply involved with British politics, education, and culture. Eleanor was the first to translate *Madame Bovary* into English (in 1886), and one of the first translators of Ibsen's plays. She worked with trade union leaders, organizing strikes and educating workers. She knew all of the foremost socialists: Bax, William Morris, Hyndman, and George Bernard Shaw, whom she met in the British Museum. She worked for Furnivall's Early English Texts Society; she lectured on Shelley and Byron. Elizabeth Garrett Anderson was, appropriately, Eleanor's doctor, and Will Thorne, leader of the gasworkers' union and later a Labour MP, remembered her efforts on behalf of women as well as workers. If she had lived, he wrote in his autobiography, *My Life's Battles* (1925), she would have been 'a greater woman's leader than the greatest of contemporary women'. Thus, though the chief legacy of the German exiles of 1848 was their work and writing, their human issue, too, made its mark in a variety of ways.

It is perhaps worth noting that Eleanor Marx's contribution to English life belonged to the field of education and labour organization, rather than the stirring up of a class revolution. England was still, in the 1890s as in the 1850s, 'as slow to be set on fire as a *stomach*', as George Eliot had put it in a letter of 1854 about her translation of Feuerbach's *Essence of Christianity*. Ferencz Pulszky recorded in his autobiography how calm England had been in 1848 when he arrived hotfoot from European revolutionary activities: 'When I came to London at the end of February [1848], I saw to my amazement that everything was going on here in the usual way, as if no Continental revolution existed.' The shrewd Fontane, reviewing a performance of *Coriolanus* at Sadler's Wells in 1857, marvelled at the fact that such an anti-mob play could be put on shortly after a working-class demonstration in nearby Smithfield. As he told readers of the *Kreuzzeitung* in February 1857:

> The people of Islington sat there, sucking oranges, in the stalls and in the gallery, and every time Caius Marcius scorned the Roman people, every time he refused them the corn they demanded, every time he told them to wash their faces and clean their teeth, a great 'Hurrah!' went through the theatre. This is a small matter, but very characteristic. The Englishman feels more sympathy with Coriolanus than with the revolutionaries, the tribunes of the people. Even the common man here has an honest, sincere admiration for rank and wealth. In other capital cities the putting on of *such* a play under *such* circumstances would have been avoided. Here, anything goes. The people are either too well-behaved or, as far as I can see, too stupid. As it is, that is a blessing.

England was not ripe for a people's revolution at the end of the century either. Though Eleanor's friend Will Thorne called his son Karl in memory of Marx, and Engels found himself acceptable as a socialist in the 1890s, the mass of the people were not socialists. Robert Tressell wrote in the preface to his working-class novel, *The Ragged Trousered Philanthropists* (published posthumously in 1914), that socialism was widely mistrusted and misunderstood. His novel was intended 'to show the conditions resulting from poverty and unemployment: to expose the futility of the measures taken to deal with them and to indicate what I believe to be the only real remedy, namely—Socialism'. Engels and Eleanor Marx lived amongst a Bohemian élite, in which unorthodoxy was the fashion in religion, politics, and sexual relations. As regards the latter, there had been no revolution either, though there may have been some slow movement. Eleanor Marx could not have known it, but the proud, earnest, high-minded letters she wrote to her more conventional female friends when she decided to set up home with the married Edward Aveling in 1884 echoed, almost to the letter, those written by George Eliot thirty years before as she planned to become G. H. Lewes's partner under similar circumstances. Both wrote of a marriage true in spirit if not sanctioned legally; both asserted the seriousness of the decision: 'I feel no levity', wrote George Eliot to Mrs

Bray; the step 'was not lightly taken', Eleanor Marx assured Mrs Bland of the Fabian Society. As Pulszky had noticed, Britain was 'the land of freedom, but also the land of form'; Mill had urged in *On Liberty* that the tyranny of opinion must be broken without damage to either the rights of the individual or the welfare of society as a whole. Attaining a balance between these two claims was, and is, a problem peculiarly and indissolubly connected with the development of democracy. The German exiles and their children experienced British life in the nineteenth century and commented valuably on the land of fogs and freedom, of fairness and formality, of progress and tradition.

Notes

INTRODUCTION

1. Engels to Marx, 27 Apr. 1867, *Marx-Engels Werke*, 39 vols. (Berlin, 1956–68), xxxi. 292–3 (henceforth referred to as *MEW*). See also *The Marx–Engels Correspondence, the Personal Letters 1844–1877*, selected and edited by F. J. Raddatz (London, 1981), 125.
2. Ibid.
3. There is in the International Institute for Social History in Amsterdam (henceforth referred to as IISH) a collection of papers relating to Engels's activities with the Cheshire Hunt and his membership of various Anglo-German clubs, including the Albert Club (founded 1858), the Manchester Schiller Institution (founded 1866), and the Brazenose Club (founded 1869).
4. Summer 1849 saw the largest number of European exiles arriving in England, after Prussia, Switzerland, Belgium, and France had co-operated to expel their unwanted revolutionaries. Thus Marx himself arrived from Paris in late August 1849, in company with Karl Blind and the communist journalist Sebastian Seiler; see David McLellan, *Karl Marx: His Life and Thought* (London, 1976), 226.
5. For a lively account of Schapper, Bauer, and Moll in London in the 1840s see Boris Nicolaievsky and Otto Maenchen-Helfen, *Karl Marx: Man and Fighter* (London, 1936, repr. 1983), 113 ff. For the struggle for leadership and the resultant break-up of the Communist League in 1850, see ibid. 211 ff.
6. See Bert Andréas, 'Marx' Verhaftung und Ausweisung Brüssel Februar/März 1848', *Schriften aus dem Karl-Marx-Haus* (Trier, 1978), 10; and Mikhail Bakunin, 'Confession to the Tsar' (1851) in *Michael Bakunins Beichte aus der Peter-Pauls-Festung an Zar Nikolaus I*, trans. and ed. Kurt Kersten (Berlin, 1926), 11, 17.
7. See also Stephan Born, *Erinnerungen eines Achtundvierzigers* (Leipzig, 1898), 99. Born accompanied Jenny Marx and her children from Brussels to Paris and noted the festive spirit among Parisians immediately after the revolution and the establishment of the revolutionary government.
8. *Hansard's Parliamentary Debates*, 3rd ser. (1 Apr. 1852), cxx. 511–2. See Bernard Porter, *The Refugee Question in Mid-Victorian Politics* (Cambridge, 1979), 130–1. Porter's book gives an excellent account of the official political and diplomatic response to foreign refugees in the 1850s.
9. Of the many historical accounts of Chartism, the most lucid are John Saville, *Ernest Jones: Chartist* (London, 1952), A. R. Schoyen, *The Chartist Challenge: A Portrait of George Julian Harney* (London, 1958), and David Goodway, *London Chartism 1838–1848* (Cambridge, 1982).
10. See Engels to Marx, 19 Nov. 1844, 'I am up to my eyebrows in English newspapers and books upon which I am drawing for my book on the

condition of the English proletarians', *Marx–Engels Collected Works* (English edition in progress by Lawrence and Wishart Limited, London, International Publishers Co. Inc., New York, and Progress Publishers, Moscow, in collaboration with the Institute of Marxism-Leninism, Moscow, henceforth referred to as *MECW*), xxxviii. 10. For Mayhew's articles see *The Unknown Mayhew: Selections from the Morning Chronicle 1849–1850*, ed. E. P. Thompson and Eileen Yeo (London, 1971, repr. 1984).

11. For Carlyle's importance in spreading a knowledge of German literature and philosophy in Britain, see Rosemary Ashton, *The German Idea: Four English Writers and the Reception of German Thought 1800–1860* (Cambridge, 1980).
12. Carlyle, *Past and Present* (London, 1843), Bk. I, chap. i, and Engels, 'The Condition of England. *Past and Present*, by Thomas Carlyle', *MECW*, iii. 448.
13. *The Condition of the Working Class in England*, pub. in German (Leipzig, 1845) and in English (New York, 1887; London, 1892), *MECW*, iv. 345, 323.
14. Ibid. 363–4.
15. For Engels's friend Georg Weerth, communist and Bradford businessman in 1843–4, who wrote articles on Bradford for German periodicals, see Chapter 2.
16. Letter of 25 May 1883, in the Marx–Engels Collection in Amsterdam, IISH (folder R66). Amsterdam houses one of the largest collections of Marx–Engels manuscripts and documents, including xeroxed copies of the important holdings of the Institute of Marxism-Leninism, Moscow.
17. Marx, *Capital: A Critique of Political Economy*, i (London, Lawrence and Wishart, 1954, repr. 1977), 20.
18. Paul Lafargue, 'Reminiscences of Marx', *Die Neue Zeit* (Sept. 1870), repr. in Karl Marx, *Selected Works*, ed. V. Adoratsky, 2 vols. (London, 1942), 92; *Punch*, 24 (Jan.–June 1853), 30.
19. 'To the Working-Classes of Great Britain', *The Condition of the Working Class in England*, *MECW*, iv. 298.
20. *Capital*, i. 19, 215, 559n. Isaiah Berlin compares Marx's 'long, mordant and annihilating' footnotes in *Capital* with Gibbon's similar use of notes, *Karl Marx: His Life and Environment* (London, 1939, repr. 1963), 249.
21. More of this later. I cannot agree with Isaiah Berlin that Marx, in his isolation in London, might as well have been anywhere else—say, Madagascar—for all the influence England had on the writing of *Capital*. It is true that he owed nothing intellectually to English thinkers, but England was his subject, the perfect subject for the exercise of his philosophical method, and he could only come to know his subject so well by long residence there and close access, via Engels, to the facts of industrial life (see Berlin, op. cit., 17–18).
22. Shakespeare, *1 Henry IV*, III. i. Marx to Engels, 22 Aug. 1870, 'Lieber wär' ich ein Kätzchen und schrie Miau, / Als solch ein Versballadenkrämer!' *MEW*, xxxiii. 47. The poem 'Hurra, Germania!' was published in an English translation in the *Pall Mall Gazette* (20 Aug. 1870).

23. See H. Collins and C. Abramsky, *Karl Marx and the British Labour Movement* (London, 1965), for a detailed history of Marx and the International. David McLellan gives a briefer account, op. cit., 360 ff.
24. Mill wrote that he was 'highly pleased with the address'; see Collins and Abramsky, op. cit., 178–9. Beesly wrote to Marx several times during 1870 and 1871, expressing his and his fellow positivists' support for Marx's leadership of the International and its attitude to the Franco-Prussian War (letters in IISH, D247 ff.). For the official British reaction and Marx's becoming known as 'the Red Terrorist Doctor', see Isaiah Berlin, op. cit., 259.
25. Home Office document, published in *Bulletin of the Society for the Study of Labour History*, 4 (Spring 1962), 54.
26. Kinkel mentioned his disappointment at not having obtained a berth in England in his speech at the farewell dinner held for him in September 1866. Kinkel's notebook, with the draft speech, is in the large collection of Kinkel manuscripts and newspaper cuttings in the University Library at Bonn (henceforth referred to as UB Bonn), MS S2689.
27. Marx to Engels on Freiligrath ('der fette Reimschmied'), Jan. 1860, *MEW*, xxx. 5; and on Kinkel, Marx to Engels, 31 Mar. 1851, *MECW*, xxxviii. 323.
28. For example, Marx to Engels, 16 May 1870, Raddatz, op. cit., 152, and Marx to Engels, 25 Feb. 1865, *MEW*, xxxi. 83.
29. Wilhelm Liebknecht, 'Friedrich Engels', *Süd-Deutsches Pavillon*, 14 (1895); see Utz Haltern, *Liebknecht und England. Zur Publizistik Wilhelm Liebknechts während seines Londoner Exils (1850—1862)* (Trier, 1977), 44.
30. See Rosemary Ashton, op. cit., *passim.* Mill's essays were republished with an introductory essay by F. R. Leavis, *Mill on Bentham and Coleridge* (London, 1950).
31. Mill to Gomperz, 19 Aug. 1854, *The Later Letters of John Stuart Mill*, ed. F. E. Mineka and D. N. Lindley, *Collected Works of John Stuart Mill*, ed. F. E. L. Priestley, 17 vols. (Toronto, 1963–72), xiv. 238.
32. G. H. Lewes, *Biographical History of Philosophy*, 4 vols. (London, 1845–6), iv. 208, 209.
33. Marx in his witty, spiteful account of his fellow exiles, not published in his lifetime, 'The Great Men of the Exile' (1852), *MECW*, xi. 274, 265.
34. Arnold Ruge to his son Richard, 3 Aug. 1871, and Lewes to Ruge, [1871], *Arnold Ruges Briefwechsel und Tagebuchblätter aus den Jahren 1825—1880*, ed. Paul Nerrlich, 2 vols. in one (Berlin, 1886), ii. 366, 360.
35. Dickens and Henry Morley, 'Mr. Bendigo Buster on our National Defences against Education', *Household Words*, 28 Dec. 1850, repr. in *Uncollected Writings: Household Words 1850–9*, ed. Harry Stone, 2 vols. (London, 1969), i. 192–3.
36. Charles Kingsley, *Alton Locke, Tailor and Poet* (London, 1850, repr. World's Classics, 1983), 241.
37. Richard Monckton Milnes, 'Reflections on the Political State of Germany', *Edinburgh Review*, 89 (Apr. 1849), 537–8. For Milnes's time in Bonn in 1830, see James Pope-Hennessy, *Richard Monckton Milnes: The Years of Promise 1809–1851* (London, 1949), 25 ff.

38. William Howitt, *The Rural and Domestic Life of Germany* (London, 1842), 490–1.
39. G. W. F. Hegel, *Philosophie der Geschichte*, lectures given at the University of Berlin from 1822 to 1831.
40. Moses Hess was the most influential of the left-wing Hegelians; see David McLellan, introd. to Karl Marx, *Early Texts* (Oxford, 1971).
41. Alexander Herzen, *My Past and Thoughts*, trans. Constance Garnett, rev. Humphrey Higgens, 4 vols. (London, 1968), iii. 1157.
42. Arnold Ruge, *New Germany, its Modern History, Literature, Philosophy, Religion, and Art*, pub. in Holyoake's series, *The Cabinet of Reason: A Library of Freethought, Politics and Culture* (London, 1854), p. 51.
43. Marx and Engels, Preface to *The German Ideology*, *MECW*, v. 23–4.
44. *MECW*, iv. 303.
45. Marx, *Contribution to the Critique of Hegel's Philosophy of Law*, *MECW*, iii. 180.
46. *Capital*, i. 380 n. 2. For Marx's welcoming of Darwin's *Origin of Species* as providing a natural historical basis compatible with Marxism but being 'coarsely developed' ('grob englisch entwickelt'), see Marx to Engels, 19 Dec. 1860, *MEW*, xxxiii. 131.
47. Heinrich Heine, *Deutschland: Ein Wintermärchen*, Caput VII, *Sämtliche Schriften*, ed. Klaus Briegleb, 6 vols. in 7 (Munich, 1968–76), iv. 592.
48. Heine to his (understandably nervous) German publisher, Campe, 29 Dec. 1843, ibid. 1013.
49. Ruge to Feuerbach, 15 May 1844, *Briefwechsel und Tagebuchblätter*, i. 343.
50. 'In Prussia . . . the state certainly took the lead in patronizing higher learning, and this ensured a high status for professors and what they taught. But it also subordinated universities to its political aims, and created a class of discontented intellectuals by keeping those aims narrow and archaic', William Thomas, *The Philosophical Radicals* (Oxford, 1979), 450. (Thomas borrows the term 'professor *raté*' for men like Feuerbach and Marx from the German historian Golo Mann.)
51. Dickens, *Household Words*, 1 (6 July 1850), 359, 360; Liebknecht, 'Englische Skizzen', 10 Dec. 1850, Haltern, op. cit., 69.
52. Marx, 1875 Postscript to *Revelations Concerning the Communist Trial in Cologne* (Basle, 1853), Marx and Engels, *The Cologne Communist Trial*, trans. and ed. Rodney Livingstone (London, 1971), 131.
53. Kinkel to Auguste Heinrich, 28 July 1851, Friedrich Althaus, 'Erinnerungen an Gottfried Kinkel', *Nord und Süd*, 25 (Apr. 1883), 66.
54. 'Sie wissen, es ist Flüchtlings-Ton, London und die Engländer entsetzlich zu finden. Ich meine aber damit sei nichts gethan, dass Jemand sich in London als der Flüchtling Kunz oder Hinz hinstellt. Für meine Begriffe giebt es nur geflüchtete Schneider, Schuster, Gelehrte, Künstler, etc. etc.' Johanna Kinkel to Fanny Lewald, 25 Oct. 1852, manuscript in Deutsche Staatsbibliothek, Berlin (Lewald–Stahr Collection).
55. See Bernard Porter, op. cit., 5. If the exiles of 1848 were less assimilable than earlier generations, they were more so than the 'flood' of German clerks in the 1880s and 1890s; see Arthur Shadwell's protesting article, 'The German Colony in London', *National Review*, 26 (Feb. 1896),

798–810. Talk of 'the Foreign Flood' grew with the arrival of Jewish refugees from Russia in the 1890s, and reached a peak in 1905, when a new Aliens Act was put in force; see Porter, op. cit., 218, and Colin Holmes, 'The Impact of Immigration on British Society 1870–1980', *Population and Society in Britain 1850–1980*, ed. Theo Barker and Michael Drake (London, 1982), 172–201.

56. See, for example, Marx to Engels on Eccarius and 'die Schneiderhölle', 18 May 1859, *MEW*, xxix. 437; Thomas Carlyle, *Past and Present* (Bk. III, chap. vii, 'Over-Production'); Mayhew, 'The Tailors', *The Unknown Mayhew*, 217 ff.
57. Eccarius, 'Tailoring in London or the Struggle between Big and Small Capital', introd. Marx and Engels, *Neue Rheinische Zeitung. Politisch-ökonomische Revue*, nos. 5–6 (1850); see *MECW*, x. 485.
58. *The Unknown Mayhew*, 257.
59. Liebknecht to Cotta, publisher of the *Augsburger Allgemeine Zeitung*, 31 May 1858, Haltern, op. cit., 56.
60. See Carl Zaddach, *Lothar Bucher bis zum Ende seines Londoner Exils (1817–1861)* (Heidelberg, 1915), 113–14.
61. See Haltern, op. cit., 16 ff.
62. G. L. M. Strauss, *Reminiscences of an Old Bohemian*, 2 vols. (London, 1882), i. 193 n.
63. *The Leader* printed Mazzini's manifesto of the European Central Democratic Committee in October 1850, Ruge's address 'to the Germans' on behalf of the Committee in November and December 1850, Fanny Lewald's account of Kinkel's prison experience in November 1850, and Marx's and Engels's letter on the Cologne Communist trial in October 1852. Marx's comment on Ruge is in 'The Great Men of the Exile', *MECW*, xi. 266, and his description of Mazzini in a letter to Adolf Cluss, 30 July 1852, *MECW*, xxxix. 142.
64. See Jones's letter of thanks to Marx, 11 Feb. 1860: 'I recollect how many articles you contributed to my little Magazine, the "Notes to the People," & subsequently to the "Peoples [*sic*] Paper," for a series of years, utterly gratuitously' (IISH, D2498, original in Moscow). Marx published an extract from Jones's letter in an appendix to his pamphlet *Herr Vogt* (1860), *MECW*, xvii. 323.
65. For a brief history of Marx's connections with the *New York Daily Tribune* until he fell out with its editor's policy on the American Civil War, see *MECW*, xxxviii. 627–8, and Isaiah Berlin, op. cit., 229.
66. Kinkel taught, for example, at Bedford College and Hyde Park College during the 1850s.
67. See the portrait of Tausenau in Gustav Struve and Gustav Rasch, *Zwölf Streiter der Revolution* (Berlin, 1867), 157 ff.
68. For example, Liebknecht borrowed £1 from Engels in January 1853 to get his coat out of pawn in order to secure a tutoring post with a German merchant's family; Wilhelm Liebknecht, *Briefwechsel mit Karl Marx und Friedrich Engels*, ed. Georg Eckert (The Hague, 1963), 26.
69. *The Life and Letters of Sir Charles Hallé*, ed. C. E. Hallé and Marie Hallé (London, 1896), 92, 229.

70. 'Die Teuerung ist so gross, dass alle Leute ihre Speise an ihrer Bildung absparen', Johanna Kinkel to a friend in Bonn, 1 Feb. 1855, Adelheid von Asten-Kinkel, 'Johanna Kinkel in England', *Deutsche Revue*, 26 (1901), 180.
71. Johanna Kinkel, 'Musikalisches aus London', UB Bonn (S2391). See also Letter to Kathinka Zitz, 25 Sept. 1851, 'Johanna und Gottfried Kinkels Briefe an Kathinka Zitz 1849–1861', ed. Rupprecht Leppla, *Bonner Geschichtsblätter*, 12 (1958), 41.
72. Ibid.
73. 6 May 1854, *MECW*, xxxix. 448–9.
74. *Archiv für die Geschichte des Sozialismus*, 10 (1922), 56 ff. See also McLellan, op. cit., 268–9.
75. Willich's long, detailed, and impractical plan for establishing a revolutionary government from Cologne is contained in a letter to Hermann Becker, a fellow exile in London, 24 Dec. 1850, MS 48, Willich Collection (IISH).
76. See Lloyd D. Easton, *Hegel's First American Followers* (Cleveland, Ohio, 1966), 192 ff.
77. Oscar Blum, 'Zur Psychologie der Emigration', *Archiv für die Geschichte des Sozialismus und der Arbeiterbewegung*, 17 (Leipzig, 1916), 416, 419.
78. See Marx on the 'frogs and mice' of the emigration, *MECW*, xii. 488 and xvii. 87.
79. Liebknecht to Cotta, 5 Sept. 1861, Haltern, op. cit., 59.
80. Theodor Fontane, 'Die Buchersche Schule' (1857), *Sämtliche Werke*, ed. Edgar Gross *et al.*, 24 vols. (Munich, 1959–75), xvii. 580.

CHAPTER 1

1. For a very readable account of Herzen and Herwegh see E. H. Carr, *The Romantic Exiles* (London, 1933).
2. Alexander Herzen, *My Past and Thoughts*, iii. 1157, 1155.
3. The Marx–Engels letters during the 1850s are full of allusions to the German-American press, from which they learned as much about their opponents' doings in London as they did from their own spies sent to rival meetings, see *MECW*, xxxviii and xxxix, *passim.*
4. Marx to Zerffi, 28 Dec. 1852, *MECW*, xxix. 267.
5. Benjamin Disraeli, *Coningsby* (London, 1844), Bk. II, chap. i.
6. 'Revolution and Counter-Revolution', *Westminster Review*, 55 (Apr. 1851), 95. *The Wellesley Index to Victorian Periodicals* does not attribute the authorship of this article.
7. Kinkel Collection, UB Bonn (S2705).
8. For the complex shift of hopes for unification from Austria to Prussia in the first half of the nineteenth century, see Golo Mann, *The History of Germany since 1789* (Frankfurt, 1958; London, 1968, repr. 1974), 97–105.
9. Letter of 10 Dec. 1850, *The Letters of Queen Victoria*, ed. A. C. Benson and Viscount Esher, 3 vols. (London, 1907), ii. 335.
10. *Punch*, 28 (Jan.–June 1855), 54. See also the poem 'Ode to Bacchus', ibid., p. 57:

Oh, CLICQUOT, what a grievous weight,
Must be the crown upon thy pate.
Does that, if nothing else, not make
Thy poor head very often ache?

Surely thy lot would be more sweet,
Wert thou from grandeur to retreat;
And leave that golden load of care
For one of stronger brain to wear.

11. See, for example, Marx to Joseph Weydemeyer, 20 Feb. 1852, *MECW*, xxxix. 41.
12. Mary Howitt, *An Autobiography*, ed. Margaret Howitt, 2 vols. (London, 1889), ii. 34.
13. Ruge to Prutz, 25 Jan. 1843, *Briefe und Tagebuchblätter*, i. 296.
14. Moritz Hartmann to Amely Bölte, 27 Jan. 1849, *Briefe von Moritz Hartmann*, selected and edited by Rudolf Wolkan (Vienna, 1921), 31–2.
15. See David McLellan, op. cit., 194 ff.
16. W. E. Aytoun, 'A Glimpse of Germany and its Parliament', *Blackwood's Magazine*, 64 (Nov. 1848), 516, 521, 522–3.
17. See McLellan, op. cit., 214 ff.
18. See *Freiligraths Briefwechsel mit Marx und Engels*, ed. Manfred Häckel, 2 vols. (Berlin, 1976), i. lvii–lviii.
19. Thomas Frost, *Forty Years' Recollections: Literary and Political* (London, 1880), 128–9.
20. Dickens to John Forster, 29 Feb. 1848, *Letters*, ed. G. Storey and K. J. Fielding, 5 vols. so far (Oxford, 1965–) v. 256–7; George Eliot to John Sibree, 8 Mar. 1848, *The George Eliot Letters*, ed. Gordon S. Haight, 9 vols. (New Haven, 1954–5 and 1978), i. 253–4; Pope-Hennessy, op. cit., 282–3.
21. See letters to Queen Victoria during February and March 1848 from Friedrich Wilhelm IV, the Queen of the Belgians, Louis Philippe, and Tsar Nicholas of Russia, *Letters of Queen Victoria*, ii. 177 ff; Lord John Russell to Queen Victoria, 29 Feb. 1848, ibid. 182–3. See also Dickens to Emile de la Rue, 29 Feb. 1848: 'If the Queen should be marked in her attentions to old Papa Philippe, I think there will be great discontent and dissatisfaction expressed, throughout the country', *Letters*, v. 254.
22. Featherstonhaugh to Palmerston, 3 Mar. 1848, *Letters of Queen Victoria*, ii. 187.
23. *Punch*, 14 (Jan.–June 1848), 96, 97.
24. Greville's diary, quoted by Reginald Pound, *Albert: A Biography of the Prince Consort* (London, 1973), 179. Macaulay, 'It is because we had a preserving revolution in the seventeenth century, that we have not had a destroying revolution in the nineteenth', *The History of England*, 4th ed., 5 vols. (London, 1849–61), ii. 663–4.
25. Dickens, *Letters*, v. 274. Most historians quote the number of special constables on 10 April at about 150,000, which was the figure given by *The Times*, but a recent study has suggested that the true figure was lower, probably between 80,000 and 85,000: David Goodway, op. cit., 130–1.

See also Henry Weisser, *April 10: Challenge and Response in England in 1848* (London, 1983), 55 ff.

26. *The Times*, 11 Apr. 1848. For a sense of the attitude of *The Times* to the events of the 1840s and 1850s, see *History through 'The Times': A Collection of Leading Articles 1800–1937*, ed. Sir James Marchant (London, 1937).
27. 'The Revolutions in Europe', *Blackwood's Magazine*, 63 (May 1848), 652.
28. See Bernard Porter, op. cit., 139 ff. Porter points out, p. 148, that Parliament was not all-powerful. Popular feeling, weak party structures, and the unpredictable element of the jury system made it difficult for governments to appease friendly foreign powers and at the same time satisfy parliamentary and public opinion at home.
29. Max Schlesinger, *Wanderungen durch London*, 2 vols. (Berlin, 1852–3), translated and quoted by Frederick Hardman, 'Foreign Estimates of London', *Blackwood's Magazine*, 74 (Sept. 1853), 287.
30. *MECW*, xii. 345, 347.
31. Debate in the House of Lords, 4 Mar. 1853, *Hansard's Parliamentary Debates*, 3rd ser. cxxiv. 1054.
32. See Bernard Porter, op. cit., 22.
33. Johanna Kinkel, *Hans Ibeles in London. Ein Familienbild aus dem Flüchtlingsleben*, 2 vols. in one (Stuttgart, 1860), i. 23–4.
34. Weerth also took messages from Engels in Brussels to Harney in London in 1846; see Harney to Engels, 30 Mar. 1846, *MECW*, xxxviii. 533.
35. Ruge to Struve, Brighton, 11 Feb. 1851: 'Viele unserer Freunde sehnen sich nach dem *reinen Privatleben* zurück', Ruge MSS (Bundesarchiv, Aussenstelle Frankfurt-am-Main).
36. Prince Hermann von Pückler-Muskau, *Briefe eines Verstorbenen* (1831), trans. Sarah Austin in 1832 as *Tour in England. By a German Prince.* Dickens caricatured him as 'Count Smorltork' who is 'gathering materials for his great work on England', has been in England a fortnight, and scarcely speaks the language, *Pickwick Papers* (London, 1837), chap. xv.
37. See Freiligrath's enthusiastic letters about his translations in 1835, Wilhelm Buchner, *Ferdinand Freiligrath, ein Dichterleben in Briefen*, 2 vols. (Lahr, 1882), i. 148 ff.
38. Theodor Fontane, 'Erste Englische Reise, 25 Mai—10 Juni 1844', *Sämtliche Werke*, xvii. 457, 466–7.
39. Heine, 'Englische Fragmente' (1828), *Sämtliche Schriften*, ii. 538.
40. Liebknecht, 'Englische Skizzen' (1850–1), Haltern, op. cit., 77.
41. Georg Weerth, 'Skizzen aus dem sozialen und politischen Leben der Briten' (1843–7), *Sämtliche Werke*, ed. Bruno Kaiser, 5 vols. (Berlin, 1956–7), iii. 1 ff. Weerth wrote in conscious imitation of Dickens's *Sketches by 'Boz'* (1836). Engels, *The Condition of the Working Class in England*, *MECW*, iv. 328, 329.
42. Hettner to Fanny Lewald, 15 Oct. 1850, 'Aus Hermann Hettners Nachlass', ed. Ernst Glaser-Gerhard, *Euphorion*, 29 (1928), 449.
43. Fanny Lewald, *England und Schottland*, 2 vols. in one (Brunswick, 1851), i. 289–90.
44. Ibid. i. 221, 268; ii. 142–3, 206. There are several effusive letters from

Geraldine Jewsbury to Fanny Lewald in 1850–1 in the Lewald–Stahr Collection of manuscripts (Deutsche Staatsbibliothek Berlin).

45. Debate on the refugees, 5 Apr. 1852, *Hansard's Parliamentary Debates*, 3rd ser., cxx, 675.
46. Karl Heinrich Schaible, *Siebenunddreissig Jahre aus dem Leben eines Exilierten* (Stuttgart, 1895), 64.
47. Malwida von Meysenbug, *Memoiren einer Idealistin*, 2 vols. (Stuttgart, 1875, repr. 1922), i. 192 ff. See also the abridged English version, *Rebel in a Crinoline*, ed. Mildred Adams (London, 1937), 129. Malwida suspected one of her brothers, an arch-conservative Prussian civil servant, of being behind her expulsion from Berlin; see her letter to her mother, 29 May 1852, 'Briefe von Malwida von Meysenbug an ihre Mutter', ed. Gabriel Monod, *Deutsche Revue*, 31/1 (Jan.–Mar. 1906), 369.
48. Adolf Stahr to Hermann Hettner, 15 Aug. 1846, 'Aus dem Nachlass von Fanny Lewald und Adolf Stahr', ed. Rudolf Göhler, *Euphorion*, 31 (1930), 196. Fontane, 'Erste Englische Reise', *Sämtliche Werke*, xvii. 467.
49. See Nirad C. Chaudhuri, *Scholar Extraordinary: The Life of Professor Friedrich Max Müller* (London, 1974), 108; Theodor Goldstücker, *Literary Remains*, 2 vols. (London, 1879), i. viii.
50. Carl Schurz, *Lebenserinnerungen*, 2 vols. (Berlin, 1906–7), i. 381–2.
51. See Baron Bunsen to his son, 16 Mar. 1860, commenting on the publication of Varnhagen's diaries, *A Memoir of Baron Bunsen*, ed. Frances Baroness Bunsen, 2 vols. (London, 1868), ii. 541.
52. Lewes is reported in Varnhagen's diary for 2 Mar. 1855 as having made complaints about the coarse activities of the police, *Aus dem Nachlass Varnhagen's von Ense: Tagebücher*, ed. Ludmilla Assing, 15 vols. (Leipzig, 1861–70, and Berlin, 1905), xi. 461; *Memorials of Charlotte Williams-Wynn*, ed. her sister (London, 1877), 93–4.
53. Marx and Engels, 'Prussian Spies in London', letter published in *The Spectator*, 15 June 1850, *MECW*, x. 382, 381.
54. Fontane, article in the *Kreuzzeitung*, 27 Jan. 1857, *Sämtliche Werke*, xvii. 574.
55. *Hansard's Parliamentary Debates*, 3rd ser., cxx. 659.
56. An Austrian police agent's report of 1853 makes fun of the petty rifts between the German factions: 'the North German hates the South German, the man from the Palatinate does not like the Rhenian' and the whole picture is one of 'jealousy, disunity, and wretchedness': report, Badisches Generallandesarchiv, Karlsruhe (236/8757, p. 1). For Sanders's activities, see Bernard Porter, op. cit., 130 n., 151 ff.
57. See F. B. Smith, *Radical Artisan: W. J. Linton 1812–1897* (Manchester, 1973), 53 ff., for a detailed account of the Mazzini affair, in which Linton helped Mazzini discover and prove the letter-opening. For Carlyle's letter to *The Times*, see David Alec Wilson, *Life of Thomas Carlyle*, 6 vols. (London, 1923–34), iii. 264.
58. See Nicolaievsky and Maenchen-Helfen, op. cit., 235–6.
59. See Reginald Pound, op. cit., 229–30.
60. Dickens and W. H. Wills, 'The Metropolitan Protectives', *Household*

Words, 26 Apr. 1851; see Dickens, *Uncollected Writings*, i. 255; *Punch*, 20 (Jan.–June 1851), 193.

61. See Marx to Engels, 13 Feb. 1855, *MECW*, xxxix. 523.
62. Herzen, op. cit., iii. 1049.
63. *The Leader*, 2 (5 Apr. 1851), 318.
64. See Porter, op. cit., 146, 171–99. See also idem., 'The *Freiheit* Prosecutions 1881–1882', *The Historical Journal*, 23/4 (1980), 833–56, for a later case to be brought against a German refugee (Johann Most) in 1881. In this case the jury found the defendant guilty. See also Malwida von Meysenbug, 'Joseph Mazzini', *Gesammelte Werke*, ed. Berta Schleicher, 5 vols. (Stuttgart, 1922), iii. 487.
65. *MECW*, x. 511.
66. In the Haynau affair, Queen Victoria took the 'distinguished foreigner's' side against the 'ferocious mob', letter to Palmerston, 12 Oct. 1850, *Letters of Queen Victoria*, ii. 322. In October 1851 she actually commanded the wayward Palmerston not to receive Kossuth personally, ibid., ii. 394. She regretted 'the extravagant excitement respecting Garibaldi', letter to Earl Russell, 13 Apr. 1864, *Letters of Queen Victoria*, 2nd ser., ed. George Earle Buckle, 3 vols. (London, 1926–8), i. 169.
67. See Reginald Pound, op. cit., 260; letter of Queen Victoria to her daughter, the Crown Princess of Prussia, 5 Feb. 1867, *Your Dear Letter: Private Correspondence of Queen Victoria and the Crown Princess of Prussia 1865–1871*, ed. Roger Fulford (London, 1971), 120.
68. Liebknecht, 'Englische Skizzen' (1851), Haltern, op. cit., 75.
69. See *Letters of Queen Victoria*, 2nd ser. i. 245; *Punch*, 19 (July–Dec. 1850), 119; F. B. Smith, op. cit., 33.
70. Radical publishers like Richard Carlile, James Watson, and Henry Hetherington were regularly imprisoned for six months at a time in the 1820s, 1830s, and 1840s for infringing the law; see F. B. Smith, op. cit., 18. For details of the Stamp Act of 1820 see William Thomas, op. cit., 317. See Harney's correspondence with Marx and Engels in 1850, *The Harney Papers*, ed. F. G. Black and R. M. Black (Assen, 1969), 257 n.
71. *The Leader*, 2 (Jan. 1851), 60.
72. George Jacob Holyoake, *The History of the Last Trial by Jury for Atheism in England* (London, 1850), 5, 47, 50.
73. See John Saville, *Ernest Jones: Chartist*, 103–5. Even the judge at Jones's trial recognized that Jones's speech was full of ambiguities. And Jones himself was apparently in contact with Home Office officials before the 10 April demonstration, assuring them of his desire to avoid violence; see Henry Weisser, op. cit., 83–4, 268–9.
74. *Punch*, 31 (July–Dec. 1856), 199.
75. Jeremy Bentham, *Plan of Parliamentary Reform* (1817); see William Thomas, op. cit., 28–9.
76. Dickens, *Pickwick Papers*, chap. xl; Engels, 'The Condition of England', *Vorwärts!*, 16 Oct. 1844, *MECW*, iii. 506; F. B. Smith, op. cit., 29.
77. Marx to Engels, 4 Apr. 1854, *MECW*, xxxix. 429; 'The Great Men of the Exile', *MECW*, xi. 259; Dickens, 'A Parliamentary Sketch', *Sketches by 'Boz'* (London, 1836).

78. Marx, 'Corruption at Elections', *New York Daily Tribune*, 4 Sept. 1852, *MECW*, xi. 344.
79. See Schoyen, op. cit., 151; Engels to Marx, 18 Nov. 1868, *MEW*, xxxii. 207.
80. J. S. Mill to Mazzini, 15 Apr. 1858, *Collected Works*, xv. 553.
81. Heine, 'Englische Fragmente', *Sämtliche Schriften*, ii. 533–5.
82. Amely Bölte to Varnhagen von Ense, 13 July 1846, *Amely Böltes Briefe aus England an Varnhagen von Ense (1844—1858)*, ed. W. Fischer and A. Behrens (Düsseldorf, 1955), 39. Countess Hahn-Hahn was visiting England with her lover, Captain Bystram.
83. 'The Condition of England', *MECW*, iii. 445–6.
84. Engels, 'Letters from London', *Schweizerischer Republikaner*, 16 May 1843, ibid. 380; and 'The Condition of England', *Deutsch-Französische Jahrbücher* (1844), ibid. 446.
85. Lewes, prospectus for 'The Free Speaker', 4 Feb. 1850, MS Berg Collection (New York Public Library); letter to Robert Chambers, 8 Feb. 1850, ibid.
86. Edmund Larken, a clergyman involved in founding the paper, wrote to Thornton Hunt objecting to the title on the grounds that 'the name of Free *speaker* [is] likely to be confounded with *Free thinker*', 24 Dec. 1849, ibid. See also letters from Lewes in Manchester to Thornton Hunt, [Nov.] 1849, ibid.
87. See Amely Bölte's half-documentary short story, *Eine Deutsche Palette in London* (Berlin, 1853), 180, and Malwida von Meysenbug, *Memoiren einer Idealistin*, i. 278.
88. Johanna Kinkel to Kathinka Zitz, 31 May 1854, 'Briefe an Kathinka Zitz', 51; Malwida, *Memoiren einer Idealistin*, ii. 116.
89. Amely Bölte to Varnhagen von Ense, 7 Aug. 1850, *Amely Böltes Briefe aus England an Varnhagen von Ense*, 83.
90. See *Punch*, 'Good News for Governesses', 18 (Jan.–June 1850), 129; Malwida, *Memoiren einer Idealistin*, i. 338; Amely Bölte, *Erzählungen aus der Mappe einer Deutschen in London* (Leipzig, 1848), 65; Johanna Kinkel, *Hans Ibeles in London*, i. 296 ff; Theodor Fontane, *Ein Sommer in London* (1854), *Sämtliche Werke*, xvii. 177.
91. Amely Bölte to Varnhagen, 13 July 1846, *Amely Böltes Briefe aus England*, 38; Milnes to Varnhagen, 15 July 1846, *Briefe Richard Monckton Milnes' an Varnhagen von Ense*, ed. Walther Fischer (Heidelberg, 1922), 68.
92. Johanna Kinkel to Fanny Lewald, 28 Apr. 1854, *Zwölf Bilder nach dem Leben: Erinnerungen von Fanny Lewald* (Berlin, 1888), 17.
93. *Punch*, 33 (July–Dec. 1857), 103. See also Ann Blainey, *The Farthing Poet: A Biography of Richard Hengist Horne 1802–1884* (London, 1968), 214.
94. Malwida von Meysenbug to Johanna Kinkel, 23 May, 27 May, 29 July 1857, *Briefe an Johanna und Gottfried Kinkel 1849–1885*, ed. Stefania Rossi and Yoko Kikuchi (Bonn, 1982), 122 ff.
95. See Gordon S. Haight, *George Eliot: A Biography* (Oxford, 1968), 132, 145; George Eliot to Barbara Bodichon, 26 Dec. 1860, *The George Eliot Letters*, iii. 366.
96. See ibid., ii. 192 and n.; Haight, op. cit., 175. See also Johanna Kinkel to

Fanny Lewald, 25 May 1856, *Zwölf Bilder nach dem Leben*, 25. William Palmer was hanged in Stafford in June 1856.

97. See Anthony Heilbut, *Exiled in Paradise: German Refugee Artists and Intellectuals in America, from the 1930s to the Present* (New York, 1983), 45, 73.
98. See Bulwer Lytton's letters to Freiligrath in 1847, offering help and advice but saying there was little hope of a chair or a Civil Service post, in view of Freiligrath's politics, Lytton MSS (Hertford County Records Office). See also Freiligrath's correspondence with Longfellow in November 1847 about the possibility of a chair at Columbia, J. T. Hatfield, 'The Longfellow–Freiligrath Correspondence', *Publications of the Modern Language Association of America*, 48 (Dec. 1933), 1260, and *The Letters of Henry Wadsworth Longfellow*, ed. Andrew Hilen, in progress (Cambridge, Mass., 1966–), ii. 141–2.
99. Johanna Kinkel to Kathinka Zitz, 31 May 1854, 'Briefe an Kathinka Zitz', 51.

CHAPTER 2

1. Undated cutting from the *Daily Chronicle* in IISH (P16).
2. Engels to Marx, 10 Mar. 1853, *MECW*, xxxix. 283.
3. See Rosi Rudich, 'Wo wohnte Friedrich Engels in Manchester?' *Beiträge zur Marx-Engels Forschung*, 7 (Berlin, 1980), 69–81. Marx to Engels, 'Send me your private address', 17 Dec. 1858, *MECW*, xl. 363. For a psychoanalytical interpretation of Engels's life and writings in terms of his relationship with his domineering and pious father, see Steven Marcus, *Engels, Manchester and the Working Class* (New York, 1974).
4. See W. O. Henderson, *The Life of Friedrich Engels*, 2 vols. (London, 1976), i. 2 ff.
5. See David McLellan, op. cit., 130 ff; Engels to Marx, 17 Mar. 1845, *MECW*, xxxviii. 29.
6. Elisabeth Engels to Engels, [Oct.] 1848 and 5 Dec. 1848, ibid. 541, 545–6.
7. See *Reminiscences of Marx and Engels* (Foreign Languages Publishing House, Moscow, n.d.), 175, 192–3.
8. See Marx to Engels, 23 Feb. 1851, 1 Mar. 1851, and 4 Feb. 1852, *MECW*, xxxviii. 294, 311 and xxxix. 30.
9. For the influence of Owenite ideas, particularly Watts's, on Engels in 1843, see Harry Schmidtgall, *Friedrich Engels' Manchester-Aufenthalt 1842—1844* (Trier, 1981), and Gregory Claeys, 'Engels' *Outlines of a Critique of Political Economy* (1843) and the Origins of the Marxist Critique of Capitalism', *History of Political Economy*, 16 (1984), 207–32. See also idem., 'The Political Ideas of the Young Engels, 1842–1845: Owenism, Chartism, and the Question of Violent Revolution in the Transition from "Utopian" to "Scientific" Socialism', *History of Political Thought*, 6 (1985). I am indebted to Dr Claeys for sending me a copy of the latter article before its publication.
10. Harney to Engels, 30 Mar. 1846, *MECW*, xxxviii. 533.

11. Marx to Engels, 9 Apr. 1863, *MEW*, xxx. 343.
12. See Peter Cadogan, 'Harney and Engels', *International Review for Social History*, 10 (1965), 97; Eleanor to Jenny Marx, 2 Oct. 1882, *The Daughters of Karl Marx: Family Correspondence 1866–1898*, ed. Olga Meier, trans. Faith Evans (London, 1984), 157.
13. Engels, *The Condition of the Working Class in England*, *MECW*, iv. 512, 473–4.
14. Engels, 'The Condition of England. *Past and Present*', *MECW*, iii. 446.
15. See Steven Marcus, op. cit., 46. Marcus also quotes Dickens, Disraeli, and others on Manchester.
16. *MECW*, iv. 348, 329, 336.
17. Ibid. 566; *Alton Locke*, chap. xxviii (the chapter is entitled 'The Men who are Eaten').
18. Engels to Marx, 31 Dec. 1857, *MECW*, xl. 236. Copies of Engels's papers in relation to these clubs are in IISH (L42–3, M16, M17, L2152).
19. Engels to the Directorate of the Schiller Anstalt, 3 May 1861, *MEW*, xxx. 596.
20. Engels to Marx, 12 Dec. 1855, *MECW*, xxxix. 561.
21. See Engels to Marx, 23 Mar. 1854, ibid. 420; also 3 May 1854, ibid. 445.
22. See letters from Dronke to Engels in IISH (L1227–34).
23. See Marx to Engels, 29 or 30 Oct. 1848, *MECW*, xxxviii. 177–8.
24. Marx to Engels, 21 May 1869, *MEW*, xxxii. 320–1.
25. For 'Uncle Angels' see Jenny Marx to Engels, 2 Dec. 1850, *MECW*, xxxviii. 251; Ruge to Feuerbach, 15 May 1844, *Briefe und Tagebuchblätter*, i. 343.
26. See Lewes to the publisher Blackwood: 'When you see her, mind your care is to discountenance the idea of a Romance being the product of an Encyclopaedia', 14 Dec. 1861, *The George Eliot Letters*, iii. 474; Engels to Marx, 1 June 1853, *MECW*, xxxix. 329.
27. Engels to Marx, 3 Dec. 1851, *MECW*, xxxviii. 505; to the same, 27 Nov. 1851, ibid. 495.
28. See Henderson, op. cit., i. 79. See also Müller-Tellering's furious (and anti-Semitic) pamphlet, published at his own expense, *Vorgeschmack in die künftige deutsche Diktatur von Marx und Engels* (*Foretaste of the Future Dictatorship of Marx and Engels*, Cologne, 1850), in which he talks of Marx as the 'chief Rabbi' and the 'future Dalai Lama of Germany' and of Engels as Marx's 'remarkable protective angel', pp. 5, 7. See also 'W.B.', 'Eduard von Müller-Tellering, Verfasser des ersten anti-semitischen Pamphlets gegen Marx', *International Review for Social History*, 6 (1951), 178–97.
29. Engels to Marx, 22 Sept. 1859, *MECW*, xl. 490.
30. Engels to H. J. Lincoln, 30 Mar. 1854, *MECW*, xxxix. 424.
31. Engels to Marx, 3 Apr. 1854, ibid. 427, 428; Marx to Engels, 4 Apr. 1854, ibid. 429.
32. Engels to Marx, 20 Apr. 1854, ibid. 435.
33. See Fanny Lewald, *England und Schottland*, i. 217. Whole issues of the *Illustrated London News* in the autumn of 1852 dealt with Wellington's career and the astonishingly elaborate preparations for his funeral.
34. Engels to Marx, 11 Apr. 1851, *MECW*, xxxviii. 332. Heine had put the

same criticism more crudely in *Englische Fragmente* (1828): 'We see in him nothing but the victory of stupidity [Wellington] over genius [Napoleon]', *Sämtliche Schriften*, ii. 590.

35. Letters from H. M. Acton to Engels, 18, 19 June 1866 and 5 Jan. 1871, IISH (L1–2).
36. Queen Victoria to the Crown Princess of Prussia, 13 Sept. 1870, *Your Dear Letter*, 299.
37. Engels to Laura Lafargue, 16 Feb. 1884, *MEW*, xxxvi. 112.
38. Marx to Engels, 30 Apr. 1852, *MECW*, xxxix. 93.
39. Engels to Marx, 6 Oct. 1857, *MECW*, xl. 188.
40. Engels to Petr Lavrovich Lavrov, 20 Oct. 1885, *MEW*, xxxvi. 373.
41. See *A Young Revolutionary in 19th-Century England. Selected Writings of Georg Weerth*, ed. Ingrid and Peter Kuczynski (Berlin, 1971), 47, 226.
42. Engels to Laura Lafargue, 20 Jan. 1892, *MEW*, xxxviii. 302.
43. Engels, *Socialism: Utopian and Scientific* (London, 1892), in Marx and Engels, *Selected Works*, 2 vols. (London, 1951), ii. 91; Fontane, 'Thackeray und die schönwissenschaftlichen Politiker', *Kreuzzeitung*, 22 July 1857, *Sämtliche Werke*, xviii*a*. 741. Fontane quotes Thackeray himself on the probability of his free-thinking position having contributed to his failure to take the seat.
44. Jenny Marx to Johann Philipp Becker, *c.*29 Jan. 1866, *MEW*, xxxi. 586–7.
45. Engels, Preface to *The Condition of the Working Class in England* (London, 1892), in Marx and Engels, *Selected Works*, ii. 372, 378; W. R. Greg, 'English Socialism, and Communistic Associations', *Edinburgh Review*, 93 (Jan. 1851), 32; Thomas Frost, op. cit., 15.
46. Eleanor to Jenny Marx, 18 Oct. 1881, *The Daughters of Karl Marx*, 137; Henderson, op. cit., i. 203; Freiligrath to Carl Weerth, 27 Sept. 1857, *Freiligraths Briefwechsel mit Marx und Engels*, ii. 111.
47. Freiligrath to Engels, 14 July 1857, ibid., i. 93.
48. Weerth to his brother Wilhelm from Bradford, 12 Jan. 1845, *Sämtliche Werke*, v. 157.
49. Weerth to his mother, 19 July 1845, ibid. 172; Wilhelmine Weerth to Georg Weerth, 1 May 1847, *Zeitgenossen von Marx und Engels: Ausgewählte Briefe aus den Jahren 1844 bis 1852*, ed. Kurt Koszyk and Karl Obermann (Assen, 1975), 114.
50. Weerth, 'Die englische Mittelklasse', *Sämtliche Werke*, iii. 165; 'Eine Fabrikstadt', *Englische Reisen*, ed. Bruno Kaiser (Berlin, 1955), 11, 14. Kaiser's edition is illustrated, appropriately, with contemporary cartoons by Cruikshank and Leech from *Punch* and the *Comic Almanac*.
51. Weerth to Wilhelm Weerth, 24 Dec. 1844, *Sämtliche Werke*, v. 140, 141; *A Young Revolutionary in 19th-Century England*, 162.
52. Weerth's speech at the Free Trade Congress, reported by Engels, *Northern Star*, 9 Oct. 1847, *MECW*, vi. 284.
53. Weerth, 'Fragment eines Romans' (1846–7), *Sämtliche Werke*, ii. 256; Engels, *The Condition of the Working Class in England*, *MECW*, iv. 506; Weerth, *Sämtliche Werke*, ii. 229–30.
54. Weerth to Wilhelm Weerth, 12 Apr. 1845, ibid., v. 157.

55. P. M. Kemp-Ashraf, 'Georg Weerth in Bradford', *A Young Revolutionary in 19th-Century England*, 187.
56. Weerth, *Englische Reisen*, 39, 16; letter to his mother, 23 Jan. 1944, *Sämtliche Werke*, v. 117.
57. Dickens to Charles Knight, 17 Mar. 1854, *The Letters of Charles Dickens*, ed. Walter Dexter, 3 vols. (London, 1938), ii. 548; and 'The Great Baby', *Household Words*, 4 Aug. 1855, *Collected Papers of Charles Dickens*, 2 vols. (London, 1938), i. 610–11; *Punch*, 28 (Jan.–June 1855), 126; Marx, 'Anti-Church Movement', *Neue Oder-Zeitung*, 28 June 1855, *MECW*, xiv. 303; Marx to Engels, 29 June 1855, *MECW*, xxxix. 539.
58. See Florian Vassen, *Georg Weerth: Ein politischer Dichter des Vormärz und der Revolution von 1848/9* (Stuttgart, 1971), 19 ff.
59. See Weerth to his mother, 16 Sept. 1849, *Sämtliche Werke*, v. 329; letters of 2 June 1850 and 10 June 1851, ibid. 358, 412; Marx to Engels, 4 Feb. 1852, *MECW*, xxxix. 29.
60. Marx to Engels, 28 Sept. 1852, ibid. 198; to the same, 3 Dec. 1852, ibid. 255.
61. Weerth to Marx, 2 June 1850, *Sämtliche Werke*, v. 358. Marx used Weerth's account in his attack on Kinkel in 'The Great Men of the Exile', *MECW*, xi. 256.
62. See *A Young Revolutionary in 19th-Century England*, 226–7, 167, 168.
63. J. L. Joynes, *Songs of a Revolutionary Epoch* (London, 1888), preface.
64. Engels to Marx, 23–4 Nov. 1847, *MECW*, xxxviii. 150.
65. Freiligrath to Merckel, 29 Oct. 1833, Buchner, op. cit., i. 114; ibid. 150 n. 149; Freiligrath to Schwab, 1835, ibid. 148–9.
66. See W. O. Henderson, op. cit., i. 7.
67. See Buchner, op. cit., i. 288, 387; Walther Fischer, *Des Darmstädter Schriftstellers Johann Heinrich Künzel (1810—1873) Beziehungen zu England* (Giessen, 1939), 15; Freiligrath to Marx, 18 June 1852, *Freiligraths Briefwechsel mit Marx und Engels*, i. 51; Fischer, op. cit., 43.
68. Buchner, op. cit., i. 398.
69. Ibid. 400.
70. Freiligrath to Karl Buchner, 10 Feb. 1845, ibid., ii. 142.
71. See *Athenaeum*, no. 832 (7 Oct. 1843), 904, no. 865 (25 May 1844), 476; William Howitt, *The Rural and Domestic Life of Germany*, 477, and *German Experiences* (London, 1844), 114, 277–8; Howitt to Harney, 16 Aug. 1846, *The Harney Papers*, 24.
72. See Hermann Kellenbenz, 'German Immigrants in England', *Immigrants and Minorities in British Society*, ed. Colin Holmes (London, 1978), 63–80.
73. Freiligrath to Longfellow, 18 May and 3 Nov. 1847, Hatfield, op. cit., 1259, 1260.
74. Bulwer Lytton to Freiligrath, Jan. or Feb. 1847, and Freiligrath to Bulwer Lytton, 7 Feb. 1847, Lytton MSS (Hertford County Record Office).
75. Bulwer Lytton to Freiligrath, 20 May 1847, ibid. University College, founded in 1828, was originally known as the University of London. It was granted a charter in 1837 and was henceforth known as University College London, though many people, including Bulwer Lytton, still referred to it as the University of London.

76. See Fontane, *Journeys to England in Victoria's Early Days, 1844–1859*, trans. and ed. Dorothy Harrison (London, 1939), 64.
77. Bulwer Lytton to Freiligrath, 20 May 1847, Lytton MSS.
78. Bulwer Lytton to Freiligrath, 20 May 1847 and n.d., ibid.
79. See Freiligrath to Karl Heuberger, 17 Sept. 1846, Buchner, op. cit., ii. 187. Malwida von Meysenbug notes the new fashion for beards after the Crimean War in her memoirs, see *Rebel in a Crinoline*, 201; Freiligrath to Levin Schücking, 22 Apr. 1847, Buchner, op. cit., ii. 194–5.
80. Amely Bölte to Varnhagen von Ense, 8 Feb. 1847, *Amely Böltes Briefe an Varnhagen von Ense*, 42.
81. See her letters to Varnhagen, half self-reprimanding and half self-excusing, about the affair, ibid. 51 ff. Fontane noted the universal dislike of Bunsen as an 'upstart' in his diary in 1856, *Journeys to England*, 121.
82. See Buchner, op. cit., ii. 186, 195.
83. See ibid., 209–11; *Freiligraths Briefwechsel mit Marx und Engels*, i. xl. For the history of the *Neue Rheinische Zeitung* in Cologne, see McLellan, op. cit., 197 ff.
84. *Freiligraths Briefwechsel mit Marx und Engels*, i. lvii–lviii; Freiligrath to Wolff, 22 Oct. 1849, *Zeitgenossen von Marx und Engels*, 270, 271. See also *Freiligraths Briefwechsel mit Marx und Engels*, i. lxi–lxii.
85. Ibid., i. lxii.
86. Amely Bölte to Varnhagen, 31 Dec. 1849, *Briefe an Varnhagen von Ense*, 73.
87. Freiligrath to Longfellow, 19 June 1851, Hatfield, op. cit., 1270.
88. *The Leader*, 2 (15 Feb. 1851), 144, and 2 (3 May 1851), 411. There is a possibility—a remote one—that Freiligrath was a spy for the authorities. The grounds for suspicion are the fortunate flight to London when arrests were imminent and the fact that it was Freiligrath who introduced Marx to Hermann Ebner, the spy to whom Marx entrusted details of German exile activities in London. But, then, there have even been suggestions that Marx himself was a spy for the Austrian police. It is unlikely in both cases. See Rudolf Neck, 'Dokumente über die Londoner Emigration von Karl Marx', *Mitteilungen des Österreichischen Staatsarchivs*, 9 (Vienna, 1956), 263–76; and Ernst Hanisch, 'Karl Marx und die Berichte der österreichischen Geheimpolizei', *Schriften aus dem Karl-Marx-Haus* (Trier, 1976).
89. See Buchner, op. cit., ii. 241–2.
90. Ruge to Freiligrath, 4 July 1851, *Freiligraths Briefwechsel mit Marx und Engels*, ii. 28, 29.
91. Herzen, *My Past and Thoughts*, iii. 1155. Marx, Lessner, Dronke, Pieper, Eccarius, Liebknecht, and most of the poorer exiles lived in Soho. Kinkel, Frau von Bruiningk, Malwida von Meysenbug, and others lived in St John's Wood. See also Friedrich Althaus, 'Beiträge zur Geschichte der deutschen Colonie in England', *Unsere Zeit*, NS 9/2 (1873), 230–1.
92. Freiligrath to Marx, *c.*8 July 1851, *Freiligraths Briefwechsel mit Marx und Engels*, i. 21.
93. Ibid., ii. 75.
94. Freiligrath to Marx, *c.*12 Jan. 1852, ibid., i. 35. Heine parodied Freiligrath's declamatory and insistently rhyming style in *Atta Troll* (1846),

though he remarked in his Preface that he admired Freiligrath too, *Sämtliche Werke*, iv. 496.

95. Freiligrath to Marx, 26 Jan. 1850, *Freiligraths Briefwechsel mit Marx und Engels*, i. 14.
96. Freiligrath to Brockhaus, 9 July 1852, Buchner, op. cit., ii. 263; Freiligrath to Heinrich Koester, 26 Nov. 1859, *Freiligraths Briefwechsel mit Marx und Engels* i. lxxxv.
97. Marx to Engels, 26 Nov. 1859, *MECW*, xl. 543.
98. The annual reports of the German Hospital, which still exists in Dalston but is now a National Health Service hospital, note the professions of the patients. Sugar-bakers, furriers, tailors and skin-dressers are the largest groups which figure.
99. Freiligrath to Marx, *c.*29 Sept. 1852, *Freiligraths Briefwechsel mit Marx und Engels*, i. 60; Freiligrath to Marx, *c.*22 Mar. 1854, ibid. 71–2; Freiligrath to Marx, 2 July 1852, ibid. 52; Marx to Freiligrath, 26 Jan. 1852, *MECW*, xxxix. 23. Kinkel and Freiligrath are named as guests of the Lord Mayor in the *Kölnische Zeitung*, 18 July 1853, in the Kinkel Collection at Bonn University.
100. Marx to Engels, 11 Dec. 1858, *MECW*, xl. 359; Freiligrath to Ruge, 6 Jan. 1866, *Ruges Briefwechsel und Tagebuchblätter*, ii. 264 n.; Herzen to Malwida von Meysenbug, 18 Sept. 1857, Alexander Herzen, *Sobraniye Sochineniy*, 30 vols. (Moscow, 1954–65), xxvi. 121.
101. See Marx to Engels, 6 Dec. 1860, *MEW*, xxx. 123; Marx to Engels, 26 December 1860, ibid. 134; Marx to Engels, 7 July 1866, *MEW*, xxi. 233.
102. See Buchner, op. cit., ii. 245.
103. See *Freiligraths Briefwechsel mit Marx und Engels*, i. lxxv, lxxvii.
104. *Athenaeum*, no. 710 (5 June 1841), 445; no. 832 (7 Oct. 1843), 904, and no. 865 (25 May 1844), 476; no. 2240 (1 Oct. 1870), ii. 429. Kate Freiligrath also published translations of two poems by Freiligrath on the occasion of the Austro-Prussian War, ibid., no. 2019 (7 July 1866), ii. 7, and no. 2044 (29 Dec. 1866), ii. 878.
105. *Freiligraths Werke*, ed. Julius Schwering, 6 vols. in 2 (Berlin, Leipzig, Vienna, and Stuttgart, n.d.), ii. 41; William Howitt, *German Experiences*, 296.
106. Müller-Tellering, op. cit., 5.
107. Freiligrath to Longfellow, 2 Apr. 1857, Hatfield, op. cit., 1286.
108. *Freiligraths Werke*, v. 12, 13.
109. See *Athenaeum*, no. 1750 (11 May 1861), i. 633; no. 1751 (18 May 1861), i. 663; no. 1755 (15 June 1861), i. 797; no. 1766 (31 Aug. 1861), ii. 284. German critics in the later nineteenth century and beyond, not knowing of Freiligrath's discovery, blamed Coleridge for being too free. See, for example, Paul Machule, 'Coleridges *Wallenstein*-Übersetzung', *Englische Studien*, 31 (1902), 182–239.
110. *The Poems of Samuel Taylor Coleridge*, ed. Derwent and Sara Coleridge, with a biographical memoir by Ferdinand Freiligrath (Leipzig, 1860), xvii, xxii–xxiii. See also *Westminster Review*, NS 19 (Jan. 1861), 300.
111. Mary Howitt, *An Autobiography*, ii. 78 ff.

112. Althaus, 'Beiträge zur Geschichte der deutschen Colonie in England', 234.
113. Freiligrath to Karl Buchner, 2 Aug. 1857, Buchner, op. cit., ii. 316.
114. Johanna Kinkel to Auguste Heinrich, 20 June 1852, Adelheid von Asten-Kinkel, 'Johanna Kinkel in England', *Deutsche Revue*, 26 (Jan.–Mar. 1901), 75.
115. Marx to Engels, 7 July 1866, *MEW*, xxxi. 233; *Athenaeum*, no. 2019 (7 July 1866), ii. 17.
116. Freiligrath to August Boelling, 19 Aug. 1870, Buchner, op. cit., ii. 410; Marx to Engels, 2 Sept. 1870, *MEW*, xxxiii. 50.
117. See Marx to Engels, 8 Jan. 1868, *MEW*, xxxii. 10; Freiligrath to Marx, 6 Aug. 1863, *Freiligraths Briefwechsel mit Marx und Engels*, i. 168.
118. See Temple Orme, *University College School: Alphabetical and Chronological Register for 1831–1891* (London, n.d.).
119. According to information given to me by Pastor Albrecht Plag of the German Evangelical Church in Sydenham, Ida Freiligrath was buried there in 1899, her daughter Kate, widow of Edward Kroeker, in 1904, Bernhard Wiens, son of Freiligrath's other daughter Luise, in 1896, and Hermann Wiens in 1913.
120. Ruge to Prutz, 14 Jan. 1846, *Briefwechsel und Tagebuchblätter*, i. 411.

CHAPTER 3

1. See Nicolaievsky and Maenchen-Helfen, op. cit., 272–3.
2. Marx to Lafargue senior, 12 Nov. 1866, *MEW*, xxi. 536. Marx's father had owned a vineyard near Trier; see McLellan, op. cit., 8.
3. See, for example, Nicolaievsky and Maenchen-Helfen, op. cit., 403.
4. Marx to Engels, 11 Feb. 1851, *MECW*, xxxviii. 286.
5. Pieper to Engels, 27 Jan. 1851, ibid. 270–1; Engels to Marx, 29 Jan. 1851, ibid. 270.
6. Engels to Dronke, 9 July 1851, ibid. 380.
7. See, ibid. 612 n. 323, 697; Marx to Engels, 19 Nov. 1850, ibid. 241.
8. The census for 1851 shows that there were thirteen people in the house, in which Marx rented two rooms, and that the average number of inhabitants in each house in the area was fourteen; see Yvonne Kapp, *Eleanor Marx*, 2 vols. (London, 1972), i. 22–3. See also Marx to Engels, 13 Sept. 1854, *MECW*, xxxix. 481.
9. Marx to Ebner, 15–22 Aug. 1851, *MECW*, xxxviii. 432; Marx to Engels, 28 May 1851, ibid. 367. Only six numbers of *Kosmos*, edited by Ernst Haug, appeared before it failed, to Marx's satisfaction; see ibid. 696.
10. Marx to Weydemeyer, 27 June 1851, ibid. 377.
11. Engels, *The History of the Communist League* (1885), in Marx and Engels, *The Cologne Communist Trial*, 52; see Nicolaievsky and Maenchen-Helfen, op. cit., 115, 124–5; McLellan, op. cit., 155–7.
12. See Marx to Engels, 27 June 1851, *MECW*, xxxviii. 373, and Engels to Marx, 19 March 1851, ibid. 320; Engels, *History of the Communist League*, op. cit., 52.

13. *MECW*, xi. 305; Fontane, *Ein Sommer in London* (1854), *Sämtliche Werke*, xvii. 17.
14. See *MECW*, xxxviii. 612n. 328; Rodney Livingstone, introd. to *The Cologne Communist Trial*, 25.
15. For an account of Marx's wide reading and habit of literary allusion, see S. S. Prawer, *Karl Marx and World Literature* (Oxford, 1976).
16. Rodney Livingstone, op. cit., 24 ff.
17. See McLellan, op. cit., 311 ff., for an account of the complicated Vogt affair; Marx to the editor of the *Daily Telegraph*, 6 Feb. 1860, *MECW*, xvii. 14–15. See also two letters from the editor to Marx, 8 and 13 Feb. 1860, Marx–Engels Collection, IISH (D906–7).
18. See Marx to Engels, 15 Feb. 1854, *MECW*, xxxix. 413, and Marx to Lassalle, 1 June 1854, ibid. 455. See also Marx's anti-Palmerston articles and pamphlets, published under the title 'The Story of the Life of Lord Palmerston' in the *New York Daily Tribune* and Ernest Jones's *People's Paper* in 1853, reprinted as separate pamphlets in the same year by E. Tucker, and again in Urquhart's and Collet's *Free Press* from November 1855 to February 1856, Karl Marx, *Secret Diplomatic History of the Eighteenth Century*, ed. Lester Hutchinson (London, 1969).
19. C. D. Collet to Marx, 12 Feb. 1860, Marx–Engels Collection, IISH (D785).
20. Ernest Jones to Marx, 10 and 11 Feb. 1860, ibid. (D2497–8); 'Herr Vogt', *MECW*, xvii. 323.
21. *MECW*, xi. 641–2 n. 64; Jenny Marx to Cluss, 10 Mar. 1853, *MECW*, xxxix. 579–80. See also Edmund Wilson, *To the Finland Station* (London, 1940), 230.
22. See Nicolaievsky and Maenchen-Helfen, op. cit., 267–8.
23. Marx and Engels, 'Latter-Day Pamphlets', *Neue Rheinische Zeitung. Politisch-ökonomische Revue*, Apr. 1850, *MECW*, x. 300 ff.
24. See Prawer, op. cit., 131, for Marx's love of chiastic inversion.
25. J. G. Eccarius, *Eines Arbeiters Widerlegung der national-ökonomischen Lehren John Stuart Mill's* (Berlin, 1869), 73.
26. Immanuel Kant, Preface to the 2nd edn. of *Kritik der reinen Vernunft* (1787), *Werke*, ed. Wilhelm Weischedel, 6 vols. (Wiesbaden, 1956–64), ii. 255; Marx, postscript (1875) to *Revelations Concerning the Communist Trial in Cologne*, in Marx and Engels, *The Cologne Communist Trial*, 133.
27. See McLellan, op. cit., 102–3, and Nicolaievsky and Maenchen-Helfen, op. cit., 52. See also *MEW*, xxxi. 596–7, xxxii. 694–5; and Prawer, op. cit., 150.
28. Marx and Engels, 'Review', *Neue Rheinische Zeitung. Politisch-ökonomische Revue* (May–Oct. 1850), *MECW*, x. 512.
29. Marx, 'The Chartists', *New York Daily Tribune*, 25 Aug. 1852, and *The People's Paper*, 9 Oct. 1852, *MECW*, xi. 335–6.
30. See Pettie to Marx, 26 Dec. 1851, Marx–Engels Collection, IISH (D3642), and Engels to Marx, *c.*27 Oct. 1851, *MECW*, xxxviii. 488. See also Marx's complaint about Harney's 'inordinate admiration for official great men', 23 Feb. 1851, ibid. 295. For Jones's background see Saville, op. cit., 13.

31. Jenny Marx to Engels, 2 Dec. 1850, *MECW*, xxxviii. 251; Marx to Engels, 5 May 1851, ibid. 346, and Engels to Dronke, 9 July 1851, ibid. 380.
32. See ibid. 481 n.
33. Engels to Marx, 18 Mar. 1852, *MECW*, xxxix. 67–8.
34. Marx to Engels, 4 Nov. 1864; see *MECW*, xxxviii. 686 n. 360. See Jenny Marx 'A Short Sketch of an Eventful Life' (1865), *The Unknown Karl Marx*, ed. Robert Payne (London, 1972), 127, where she notes that Ernest Jones was 'paying us long and frequent visits' in the spring of 1852. For Marx's report of Jones's speech see *MECW*, xi. 338–9.
35. Marx to Engels, 2 Sept. 1852, *MECW*, xxxix. 176. See also Marx to Engels, 19 Nov. 1852, ibid. 247.
36. See Marx to Engels, 2 Dec. 1854, ibid. 502–3, and Marx to Engels, 2 and 13 Feb. 1855, ibid. 521, 522–3. For Marx's speech see *MECW*, xiv. 655–6. See also Marx to Engels, 21 Sept. 1858, *MECW*, xl. 342.
37. See Saville, op. cit., 73 ff.
38. Marx to Engels, 15 July 1858, *MECW*, xl. 329, and Jenny Marx to Engels, 13 Aug. 1859, ibid. 572–3. See also Marx to Engels, 15 July 1858, ibid. 331.
39. See McLellan, op. cit., 259, and *MECW*, xxxviii. 295, xl. 209.
40. Marx to Engels, 24 Jan. 1863, *MEW*, xxx. 315; Marx to Engels, 30 Nov. 1868, *MEW*, xxxii. 217.
41. Jenny Marx to Mrs Liebknecht, Apr. 1866, Yvonne Kapp, op. cit., i. 69, and to the same, Oct. 1866, ibid. 75; Engels to Marx, 16 Dec. 1867, *MEW*, xxi. 411.
42. See Jenny Marx's rather obscure criticism of Mary as 'Lady Macbeth', to Marx, 24 Mar. 1846, *MECW*, xxxviii. 530–1, and Marx to Jenny after Lizzie's death, 17 Sept. 1878, *MEW*, xxxiv. 344.
43. Marx to Engels, 8 Jan. 1863, Raddatz (ed.), op. cit., 104–5.
44. See McLellan, op. cit., 355; Hanisch, op. cit., 17.
45. Marx to Engels, 10 Mar. 1853, *MECW*, xxxix. 289–90; Marx to Engels, 8 Oct. 1853, ibid. 386; Marx to Weydemeyer, 20 Feb. 1852, ibid. 41.
46. See McLellan, op. cit., 223; Dronke to Weydemeyer, 1 Oct. 1849, *Zeitgenossen von Marx und Engels*, 268.
47. Engels to Dronke, 9 July 1851, *MECW*, xxxviii. 383; Marx to Engels, 13 Oct. 1851, ibid. 474.
48. Engels to Weydemeyer, 12 Apr. 1853, *MECW*, xxxix. 305; Marx to Engels, 22 Dec. 1856, *MECW*, xl. 88; and Dronke to Engels from Liverpool, 13 Nov. 1877, Marx–Engels Collection, IISH (L1241).
49. See *Freiligraths Briefwechsel mit Marx und Engels*, ii. 20.
50. Marx to Freiligrath, 11 Jan. 1850, *MECW*, xxxviii. 225.
51. See Marx, *Herr Vogt*, *MECW*, xvii. 84–6, and Marx to Cluss, 25 Mar. 1853, *MECW*, xxxix. 299.
52. Marx to Engels, 13 Sept. 1851, *MECW*, xxxviii. 457; Marx to Weydemeyer, 28 May 1852, *MECW*, xxxix. 115. See *MEW*, xxix. 250 ff., for Engels visiting Schramm in January 1858 and helping him financially until his death.
53. See Marx to Engels, 24 Feb. 1851, *MECW*, xxxviii. 297–8.

54. Marx to Engels, 2 Sept. 1852, *MECW*, xxxix. 175, and Engels to Marx, 23 Sept. 1852, ibid. 190.
55. See Jones to Marx, 29 July 1851, Marx–Engels Collection, IISH (D2483); Engels to Marx, 2 Feb. 1852, *MECW*, xxxix. 29.
56. See Marx to Engels, 3 May 1851, *MECW*, xxxviii. 343; Marx to Engels, 25 Jan. 1854, *MECW*, xxxix. 411.
57. Pieper to 'Charles Williams' (Marx), 1 Dec. 1851, Marx–Engels Collection, IISH (D3670).
58. See Engels to Marx, 9 June 1853, *MECW*, xxxix. 342; Cluss to Weydemeyer, 12 Dec. 1853, ibid. 587; Marx to Engels, 29 Mar. 1854, ibid. 421.
59. Marx to Engels, 27 July 1854, ibid. 472. Pieper was in the German Hospital in September 1853, in October 1858, and again in February 1859, each time with syphilis; see *MECW*, xxxix. 368, xl. 350, 384. For details of the commonness of syphilis see Annual Reports of the German Hospital for 1852 and 1856, also [Maureen Neumann], undated Ph.D. thesis in the possession of the German Hospital, 'An Account of the German Hospital in London from 1845 to 1948', 36.
60. Marx to Engels, 17 and 25 Oct. 1854, *MECW*, xxxix. 490, 491; Marx to Engels, 10 Nov. 1854, ibid. 498.
61. Pieper to Marx, 22 Feb. 1857, Marx–Engels Collection, IISH (D3680).
62. Marx to Engels, 10 Apr. 1856, *MECW*, xl. 32–3.
63. Engels to August Bebel, 26 Sept. 1892, *MEW*, xxxviii. 476.
64. See Engels's biographical sketch of Wolff, written in 1876 for Liebknecht's periodical, *Die Neue Welt*, and reprinted as an introduction to Wolff's *Gesammelte Schriften*, ed. Franz Mehring (Berlin, 1909), 30. See also Walter Schmidt, *Wilhelm Wolff: Kampfgefährte und Freund von Marx und Engels, 1846–1864* (Berlin, 1979), 314.
65. See Wolff Collection, IISH (folder 1).
66. Engels to Wolff, 1 May 1851, *MECW*, xxxviii. 339, 340.
67. See, for example, *Illustrated London News*, 18 (5 Apr. 1851), 265, for a report of the debate in the House of Commons on the possibility of disturbances during the Exhibition by refugees; William Howitt, 'A Pilgrimage to the Great Exhibition from Abroad', *Household Words*, 3 (28 June 1851), 324.
68. Engels to Marx, 8 May 1851, *MECW*, xxxviii. 348–9, and 15 May 1851, ibid. 354; Marx to Engels, 16 May 1851, ibid. 355.
69. See Wolff to Reichhelm, 3 Aug. 1851, *Zeitgenossen von Marx und Engels*, 416; Johanna Kinkel to Kathinka Zitz, 18 Mar. and 25 Sept. 1851, 'Briefe an Kathinka Zitz', 34, 41.
70. See Marx to Cluss, 17 Apr. 1853, *MECW*, xxxix. 313; Jane Carlyle to John Carlyle, Sept. 1853, *New Letters and Memorials of Jane Welsh Carlyle*, ed. Alexander Carlyle, 2 vols. (London, 1903), ii. 68.
71. See Schmidt, op. cit., 288 ff; Marx to Engels, 21 May 1853, *MECW*, xxxix. 324; Schmidt, op. cit., 286.
72. Ibid. 291.
73. Marx to Engels, 7 Sept. 1853, *MECW*, xxxix. 364–5.

74. Marx to Engels, 10 Jan. 1857, *MECW*, xl. 91; Engels to Marx, 20 May 1857, ibid. 131, and 3 Aug. 1859, ibid. 479.
75. See Marx to Engels, *c.*12 and 14 Dec. 1853, *MECW*, xxxix. 402, 403.
76. See Engels to Jenny Marx, 5 Nov. 1859 and to Marx, 17 Nov. 1859, *MECW*, xl. 517–18, 530–1.
77. In 1855; Freiligrath replied that he could hardly take 'five tender children' to the tropics; Freiligrath to Wolff, 30 Mar. 1855, Wolff Collection, IISH (folder 5).
78. Marx to Jenny Marx, 13 May 1864, *MEW*, xxx. 659.
79. For example, Marx wrote to Engels, 8 Aug. 1858, 'Lupus will be interested to hear that little Jenny has received THE FIRST GENERAL PRIZE IN THE FIRST CLASS (which also includes the *English* prize), and little Laura the second. They are the youngest in the class. Jenny also got the prize for French', *MECW*, xl. 337. See also Schmidt, op. cit., 290.
80. Dronke to Weydemeyer, 1 Oct. 1849, *Zeitgenossen von Marx und Engels*, 268; Dronke to Weydemeyer, 7 Aug. 1851, ibid. 417; Eugene Oswald, *Reminiscences of a Busy Life* (London, 1911), 234.
81. Engels to Marx, 18 Mar. 1852, *MECW*, xxxix. 66, 67; Engels to Marx, 10 June and 20 July 1854, ibid. 461, 468.
82. Imandt to Marx, 12 July 1857, *Freiligraths Briefwechsel mit Marx und Engels*, ii. 110.
83. Dronke sent money to Marx from Liverpool in December 1861: see Marx–Engels Collection, IISH (D1060 ff.); and again in March 1863: see *MEW*, xxx. 334. He asked Engels to stand surety for him on an insurance policy; see Dronke to Engels, 13 Oct. 1876, Marx–Engels Collection, IISH (L1227).
84. Dronke to Marx, 25 and 30 Jan. 1882, Marx–Engels Collection, IISH (D1078–9).
85. Carl Schurz was sent to Switzerland in 1851 to find guarantors. See Hermann Rösch-Sondermann, *Gottfried Kinkel als Ästhetiker, Politiker und Dichter* (Bonn, 1982), 306 and n. For Imandt's 'spying' see Marx to Engels, 19 Aug. 1852, *MECW*, xxxix. 161.
86. Alexander Herzen, *My Past and Thoughts*, iii. 1145.
87. Imandt to Marx, 12 July 1857, and Freiligrath to Engels, 14 July 1857, *Freiligraths Briefwechsel mit Marx und Engels*, ii. 109, i. 93.
88. *The Cologne Communist Trial*, 101–3; see Marx to Engels, 17 July 1855, *MECW*, xxxix. 543, and McLellan, op. cit., 263.
89. Marx to Engels, 1 Sept. 1855, *MECW*, xxxix. 545–6; Imandt to Engels, n.d., Marx–Engels Collection, IISH (L2494) and to Marx, 25 Sept. 1855, ibid. (D2406); Imandt to Marx, 6 Feb. 1856, ibid. (D2410); Marx to Engels, 24 May 1859, *MECW*, xl. 449.
90. Carl Imandt to Marx, 1 Mar. 1858, Marx–Engels Collection, IISH (D2402).
91. Imandt to Marx, 18 Feb. 1870, ibid. (D2444).
92. Liebknecht to Engels, Feb. or Mar. 1865, *Briefwechsel mit Marx und Engels*, 46; Engels to Marx, 11 Mar. 1865, *MEW*, xxxi. 96.
93. See Haltern, op. cit., 46.

94. Ibid. 9–10; Liebknecht, 'Reminiscences of Marx', Karl Marx, *Selected Works* (1942), i. 104.
95. Ibid., i. 108 (Dante's line *Segui il tuo corso, e lascia dir le genti*, 'Follow your own course, and let people talk', was adopted by Marx as his 'motto' in the Preface to *Capital*); ibid., i. 109.
96. Liebknecht to Engels, 19 Jan. 1853, *Briefwechsel mit Marx und Engels*, 26.
97. Marx to Engels, 10 Oct. 1854, *MECW*, xxxix. 485–6; Liebknecht to Cotta, 26 June 1856, Haltern, op. cit., 54.
98. Liebknecht, 'Die Industrieausstellung', *Morgenblatt für gebildete Leser*, 3 and 5 Mar. 1851, Haltern, op. cit., 82, 83.
99. See Haltern, op. cit., 28–49; Liebknecht, 'Die Trades Unions', *Die Neue Zeit* (1883), Haltern, op. cit., 49.
100. See Haltern, op. cit., 35; Liebknecht, 'Friedrich Engels' (1895), ibid. 43.
101. Liebknecht, 'Reminiscences of Marx', op. cit., i. 122–4.
102. See Marx to Engels, 4 Nov. 1864, *MEW*, xxxi. 10 ff. See also McLellan, op. cit., 360 ff., and Collins and Abramsky, op. cit., 42–3.
103. See Yvonne Kapp, op. cit., i. 65.
104. See Collins and Abramsky, op. cit., 52, and McLellan, op. cit., 366 and n.
105. Marx to Liebknecht, 4 May 1866, Liebknecht, *Briefwechsel mit Marx und Engels*, 73–5.
106. See Dorothy Thompson, 'Letters from Ernest Jones to Karl Marx 1865–1868', *Bulletin of the Society for the Study of Labour History*, 4 (Spring 1962), 11–12.
107. Marx to Engels, 9 and 13 May, 1865, *MEW*, xxxi, 116, 120; Jones to Marx, 7 Feb. 1865, 'Letters from Ernest Jones to Karl Marx', op. cit., 13; Marx to Engels, 23 Nov. 1868, *MEW*, xxxii. 211.
108. Marx to Engels, 28 Jan. 1869, ibid. 250; Engels to Marx, 29 Jan. 1869, ibid. 252–3.
109. Marx to Engels, 7 July 1866, *MEW*, xxxi. 234.
110. Marx to Engels, 10 Dec. 1864, ibid. 39; to the same, 19 Aug. 1865, ibid. 145.
111. Beesly to Marx, 24 Sept. 1867, Marx–Engels Collection, IISH (D245). Extracts from some of Beesly's letters to Marx have been published by Royden Harrison, 'E. S. Beesly and Karl Marx', *International Review for Social History*, 4 (1959), 22–58, and by Collins and Abramsky, op. cit., 184.
112. See Marx to Engels, 27 June 1867, *MEW*, xxxi. 316; McLellan, op. cit., 353.
113. See Collins and Abramsky, op. cit., 179.
114. Marx to Ludwig Kugelmann, 13 Dec. 1870, *MEW*, xxxiii. 163.
115. Beesly to Marx, 14 Sept. 1870, Collins and Abramsky, op. cit., 184; Beesly to Marx, 15 Sept. 1870, Marx–Engels Collection, IISH (D248), and his article on the International, *Fortnightly Review*, 8 (Nov. 1870), 529–30.
116. Beesly to Marx, 13 June 1871, Marx–Engels Collection, IISH (D258); Marx to Beesly, 12 June 1871, *MEW*, xxxiii. 228; Marx to Kugelmann, 13 Dec. 1870, ibid. 162.
117. Beesly in *Christian Socialist*, Mar. 1884; also to Eleanor Marx, 24 Mar. 1883, Royden Harrison, op. cit., 32.

118. Beesly to Marx, 5 Feb. 1872, Marx–Engels Collection, IISH (D271). The Collection contains several invitations to Marx to have dinner with the Beeslys at this time. See, for example, Beesly to Marx, 10 Apr. 1874 and 14 Apr. 1881, ibid. (D276 and D280). For Most's trial for incitement to assassination, see Bernard Porter, 'The *Freiheit* Prosecutions, 1881–1882', *The Historical Journal*, 23/4 (1980), 833–56.
119. Beesly, 'The Social Future of the Working Class', *Fortnightly Review*, 5 (Mar. 1869), 344–63.
120. Marx to Engels, 2 Apr. 1858, *MECW*, xl. 296–7; Allsop to Marx, 28 June 1871, Marx–Engels Collection, IISH (D7). For Allsop's part in the Orsini affair, see Bernard Porter, *The Refugee Question in Mid-Victorian Politics*, 192 ff.
121. See Engels to Marx, 23 Aug. 1871, *MEW*, xxxiii. 70, and Marx to Engels, 8 Sept. 1871, ibid. 73.
122. Allsop to Marx, 24 Aug. and 8 Sept. 1871, Marx–Engels Collection, IISH (D11, D13).
123. Allsop to Marx, 8 Sept. 1871, ibid. (D13), and 30 Oct. 1871, ibid. (D22).
124. See Herzen, *My Past and Thoughts*, iii. 1076. There are some enthusiastic letters from Allsop to Owen in 1848 in the Co-operative Union archives in Manchester.
125. Allsop to Marx, 21 Dec. 1873, Marx–Engels Collection, IISH (D30).
126. Darwin to Marx, 1 Oct. 1873, ibid. (D1013); Spencer to Marx, 21 Oct. 1873, ibid. (D4166).
127. Reviews of *Capital* in 1887, ibid. (P15).
128. *Capital*, i. 612, 274.
129. Ibid. 570–1; J. S. Mill, 'Bentham', *London and Westminster Review*, 29 (Aug. 1838), 467–506; *Capital*, i. 594, 572, 215.
130. Ibid. 507.
131. Engels to Marx, 22 May 1868, *MEW*, xxxii. 89. 'W–G–W' stands for 'Ware–Geld–Ware' ('Commodity–Money–Commodity'), one of the algebraic forms Marx employs to discuss the relations between money, value, and commodity in the opening chapter of *Capital.*
132. Marx, Afterword to the second German edition of *Capital* (1873), i. 29.
133. For example, 'A use-value, or useful article, therefore, has value only because human labour in the abstract has been embodied or materialised in it. How, then, is the magnitude of this value to be measured? Plainly, by the quantity of the value-creating substance, the labour, contained in it', *Capital*, i. 46.
134. Harney to Engels, 11 Apr. 1876, *The Harney Papers*, 271.
135. Ernest Belfort Bax, 'Leaders of Modern Thought. XXIII. Karl Marx', *Modern Thought*, 3 (1 Dec. 1881), 349–54.
136. Marx to Sorge, 15 Dec. 1881, *MEW*, xxxv. 247–8; John Rae, 'The Socialism of Karl Marx and the Young Hegelians', *Contemporary Review*, 40 (July–Dec. 1881), 585–607.
137. Harriet Law, 'Dr. Karl Marx', *Secular Chronicle*, 10 (7 July 1878), 1–3. This article includes a portrait of Marx, probably the first to be printed in Britain. (I am indebted to Professor Chimen Abramsky for this suggestion.) See also William Morris, 'How I Became a Socialist', *Justice*, 16 June

1894, repr. in *Political Writings of William Morris*, ed. A. L. Morton (London, 1973). For an account of some early criticisms of Marx's work, see E. J. Hobsbawm, 'Dr. Marx and the Victorian Critics', *Labouring Men: Studies in the History of Labour* (London, 1964, repr. 1974), 239 ff.

138. Marx to Sorge, 15 Dec. 1881, *MEW*, xxxv. 248.
139. Ruge to Steinthal, 25 Jan. 1869, *MEW*, xxxii. 696; Marx to Kugelmann, 11 Feb. 1869, ibid. 589.

CHAPTER 4

1. Friedrich Althaus, 'Beiträge zur Geschichte der deutschen Colonie in England', 235.
2. See Gustav Struve and Gustav Rasch, *Zwölf Streiter der Revolution*, 89. Jones's poem is quoted in an obituary by Alfred H. Miles in 1869 in an unnamed newspaper, Marx–Engels Collection, IISH (P7).
3. See Herzen, *My Past and Thoughts*, iii. 1156, and Bakunin's 'Confession' to Tsar Nicholas I, July–Aug. 1851, Jacques Duclos, *Bakounine et Marx* (Paris, 1974), 347.
4. See Heinrich Bettziech ('Beta'), 'Der Verbannte von Brighton', *Gartenlaube*, 24 (1863), 380–2.
5. Ibid. 382. Ruge's widow, Agnes, wrote her memoir of their life in Brighton some time after Ruge's death in 1880. This memoir is in the possession of Herr Arnold Ruge, Ruge's great-grandson, who kindly sent me a copy of it.
6. Marx to Weydemeyer, 23 Jan. 1852, *MECW*, xxxix. 14–15.
7. Ronge to Kinkel, 17 Mar. 1851, Kinkel Collection, UB Bonn (S2673); Agnes Ruge's memoir in Herr Ruge's possession.
8. One near-destitute refugee, Solger, appealed for help in getting a job, addressing Kinkel as 'the head of the emigration', 18 Sept. 1852, Kinkel Collection, UB Bonn (S2674).
9. Marx to Weydemeyer, 11 Sept. 1851, *MECW*, xxxviii. 455.
10. See *Red Republican* (7 Sept. 1850), 95, and *The Leader*, 1 (12 Oct. 1850), 679.
11. See Ruge, *Briefwechsel und Tagebuchblätter*, ii. 118.
12. Marx and Engels, *Neue Rheinische Zeitung. Politisch-ökonomische Revue* (Nov. 1850), *MECW*, x. 532; Herzen to Mazzini (in French), 13 Sept. 1850, *Sobraniye Sochineniy*, xxiv. 139.
13. Marx to Ebner, 15–22 Aug. 1851, *MECW*, xxxviii. 426; *The Leader*, 1 (23 Nov., 21 and 28 Dec. 1850), 825, 921, 944.
14. 'An die Deutschen', signed by Ruge, Struve, Haug, Ronge, and Kinkel, 13 Mar. 1851, Kinkel Collection, UB Bonn.
15. See *The Leader*, 2 (15 Mar. 1851), 243; Engels to Marx, 19 Mar. 1851, *MECW*, xxxviii. 319.
16. See Johanna Kinkel to Kathinka Zitz, 18 July 1851, 'Briefe an Kathinka Zitz', 36–7.
17. See Marx to Engels, 28 May 1851, *MECW*, xxxviii. 367–8; Marx to Ebner, 15–22 Aug. 1851, ibid. 427.

18. Strauss, *Reminiscences of an Old Bohemian*, ii. 134–5; Marx to Weydemeyer, 20 Feb. 1852, *MECW*, xxxix. 42.
19. See *The Leader*, 3 (13 Nov. 1852), 1082. See also Ingrid Donner and Birgit Matthies, 'Jenny Marx über das Robert-Blum-Meeting am 9. November 1852 in London', *Beiträge zur Marx-Engels Forschung*, 4 (Berlin, 1978), 74–5.
20. Ruge to Holyoake, [1853], Holyoake Collection, Co-operative Union, Manchester (619); Ruge to Linton, 16 Aug., 9 Oct. 1854, Smith, *Radical Artisan*, 118.
21. Ruge, *New Germany* (London, 1854), preface, 96.
22. Ruge to Johann Rösing, 18 Aug. 1853, *Briefwechsel und Tagebuchblätter*, ii. 135; Herzen, *My Past and Thoughts*, iii. 1157.
23. Ruge to Holyoake, 24 Feb. 1854, Holyoake Collection (642); to the same, 27 Mar. 1854, ibid. (651).
24. Ruge to Holyoake, [1854], ibid. (652, 653, 654).
25. Ruge to Austin Holyoake, 19 Sept. 1854, ibid. (691).
26. Ruge to Holyoake, [1854], ibid. (693); Frau Ruge's manuscript memoir.
27. See Heine's comments in 1844, *Sämtliche Schriften*, iv. 1001, 1017. See also Marx, 'The Great Men of the Exile', *MECW*, xi. 265, 266, 267, 274; statement by Marx and Engels refuting Ruge's attacks on them, 27 Jan. 1851, *MECW*, x. 536.
28. Ruge to Varnhagen, 18 Mar. 1857, manuscript in the Varnhagen Collection, Jagiellonian Library, Cracow; Ruge to Struve, 30 July 1864, manuscript in Federal Archives in Frankfurt.
29. See Ruge to his son Richard, 11 Mar. 1878, *Briefwechsel und Tagebuchblätter*, ii. 410; to the same, 18 July 1870, ibid. 352; Marx to Engels, 8 Aug. 1870, *MEW*, xxxiii. 33.
30. See *Briefwechsel und Tagebuchblätter*, ii. 360, 365–6. Ruge was ashamed of having translated 'this crazy stuff'. For the translation from Buckle see Mill to Ruge, 7 Feb. 1867, *Collected Works of John Stuart Mill*, xvi. 1233; for Althaus on Ruge see Althaus, 'Beiträge zur Geschichte der deutschen Colonie in England', 236.
31. Marx to Engels, 8 Aug. 1870, *MEW*, xxxiii. 31; McLellan, op. cit., 416.
32. Jenny Marx to Bertha Markheim, 28 Jan. 1863, Bert Andréas, *Briefe und Dokumente der Familie Marx aus den Jahren 1862—1873* (Hanover, 1962), 178–9.
33. Mr K. E. Ruge of North London very kindly responded to my letter enquiring whether he was a descendant of Ruge's. He and his family offered me hospitality, as well as putting me in touch with the German branch of the family.
34. Friedrich Althaus, 'Erinnerungen an Gottfried Kinkel', *Nord und Süd*, 24 (Feb. 1883), 229, 238.
35. See Adolph Strodtmann, *Gottfried Kinkel. Wahrheit ohne Dichtung*, 2 vols. in one (Hamburg, 1850–1), 83 ff. See also Alfred R. De Jonge, *Gottfried Kinkel as Political and Social Thinker* (New York, 1926), 15 ff.
36. Engels to Jenny Marx, 25 July 1849, *MECW*, xxxviii. 203.
37. Stahr wrote on Kinkel in the *National Zeitung* in May 1850, and Bettina von Arnim reported to Varnhagen on her correspondence with the King of

Prussia; see *Aus dem Nachlass Varnhagen's von Ense: Tagebücher*, vi. 260–1, vii. 161.

38. *The Leader*, 1 (2 Nov. 1850), 747–8. The article is unsigned but Kinkel's own copy in the Kinkel Collection at the University of Bonn has Fanny Lewald's name at the bottom of the article. *The Leader* had also carried a report of Kinkel's trial in May 1850 and a note in July on the probability of his being moved from one prison to another, 1 (11 May, 13 July), 149, 367.
39. R. H. Horne, 'Gottfried Kinkel', *Household Words*, 32 (2 Nov. 1850), 124.
40. 'The Great Men of the Exile', *MECW*, xi. 254–5.
41. Marx and Engels, 'Gottfried Kinkel', *Neue Rheinische Zeitung. Politisch-ökonomische Revue*, 4 (1850), *MECW*, x. 345.
42. 'The Great Men of the Exile', *MECW*, xi. 257, 253. I attribute 'The Great Men of the Exile' primarily to Marx, though he collaborated on it with Engels, who seems to have been willing to change his account of Kinkel's war in the interests of polemics.
43. See Varnhagen's diary for 9 Nov. 1850, *Aus dem Nachlass*, vii. 404–5; *Illustrated London News*, 17 (30 Nov. 1850), 417; *The Leader*, 1 (16 Nov. 1850), 813.
44. Schurz to Johanna Kinkel, 1 Dec. 1850, *Lebenserinnerungen*, iii. 74; *Punch*, 27 (July 1854), 19.
45. See Stahr to Kinkel, 16 Mar. 1851, *Zeitgenossen von Marx und Engels*, 405; Johanna Kinkel to Fanny Lewald, 2 May 1851, *Zwölf Bilder nach dem Leben*, 9.
46. See Mary Howitt, *Autobiography*, ii. 78. There are letters from several of these Englishmen to Kinkel in the Kinkel Collection in Bonn, and his diaries, also in Bonn, record his meetings with some of them. There is an undated letter from Johanna Kinkel to Harriet Grote, thanking her for some concert tickets, in the smaller Kinkel Collection in the Stadtarchiv, Bonn. For the Grotes and Mendelssohn, see M. L. Clarke, *George Grote: A Biography* (London, 1962), 81.
47. Johanna Kinkel to Fanny Lewald, 2 May 1851, *Zwölf Bilder nach dem Leben*, 10.
48. There are several rather gushing letters from Geraldine Jewsbury to Fanny Lewald during the latter's visit to Britain in 1850 in the Stahr–Lewald Collection, Deutsche Staatsbibliothek, East Berlin. Jane Carlyle wrote in July 1850 of Geraldine's having 'sworn eternal friendship with Fanny Lewald the German Authoress who is also lionizing in London at present', *I too am here, Selected Letters*, ed. Alan and Mary McQueen Simpson (Cambridge, 1977), 231.
49. Engels to Marx, 10 and 31 Oct. 1852, *MECW*, xxxix. 209, 233.
50. See *Blackwood's Magazine* 67 (Aug. 1850), 174–5.
51. Grote to Kinkel, 15 Sept. 1852, Kinkel Collection, UB Bonn (S2661).
52. See Report by Senate Committee, 4 Nov. 1852, MS University College London (College Collection AM/63); and University of London Council Minutes, vol. iv (1843–53), report of 6 Nov. 1852 (University College London Records Office).

53. Ruge to Kinkel, 31 Jan. 1851, Kinkel Collection, UB Bonn (S2674); Willich to Kinkel, 21 Feb. 1851, ibid. (S2675).
54. Esser to Kinkel, 26 Aug. 1851, ibid. (S2674); Solger to Kinkel, 18 Sept. 1852, ibid. (S2674); Johanna Kinkel to Therese Pulszky, 1851, Varnhagen Collection, Jagiellonian Library, Cracow.
55. In the London German paper *Hermann*, 22 Mar. 1862; see De Jonge, op. cit., 136–7.
56. *The Leader*, 2 (15 Feb. 1851), 146.
57. Marx, 'The Great Men of the Exile', *MECW*, xi. 256; *Kinkels Verteidigungsrede vor den Kölner Assisen* (Berlin, 1850); see also *Freiligraths Briefwechsel mit Marx und Engels*, ii. 26.
58. Kinkel 'was received with great enthusiasm', *The Leader*, 2 (15 Mar. 1851), 243. Amalie Struve's account in the *New Yorker Staatszeitung*, 12 Apr. 1851, describes Kinkel's speech as 'the high point of the celebration'.
59. See Schurz to Kinkel, 20 Jan. 1851, *Briefe von Carl Schurz an Gottfried Kinkel*, ed. Eberhard Kessel (Heidelberg, 1965), 54–5.
60. The lectures were announced in *The Leader*, 2 (26 Apr. 1851), 393, and Marx told Engels about them, 3 May 1851, *MECW*, xxxviii. 342.
61. Friedrich Althaus, 'Erinnerungen an Gottfried Kinkel', *Nord und Süd*, 25 (Apr. 1883), 67. For Kinkel's problems with the money see letters from Blind to Kinkel in UB Bonn (S2660); a letter from Blind to Struve, complaining of Kinkel's refusal, 8 Jan. [1861], and an exasperated letter from Kinkel to Struve, 21 Nov. 1857, both in the Federal Archives in Frankfurt. Kinkel did let Blind have £100 in May 1858; see Kinkel to Blind, 4 May 1858, Blind Papers, British Library Add. MS 40124, f. 43. See also *Briefe von Carl Schurz an Gottfried Kinkel*, 41, and Rösch-Sondermann, op. cit., 309–10.
62. See Kinkel's diary, UB Bonn (S2680*b*).
63. *Manchester Examiner and Times*, 10 Nov. 1852, in the University Library, Bonn; *Stirling Journal and Advertiser*, 26 Dec. 1856, ibid.
64. Althaus, 'Erinnerungen an Gottfried Kinkel', *Nord und Süd*, 25 (Apr. 1883), 71; 'Briefe von Malwida von Meysenbug an ihre Mutter', ed. Gabriel Monod, *Deutsche Revue*, 33/1 (Jan.–June 1908), 209.
65. Herzen to Karl Vogt, 5 and 11 Apr. 1853, *Sobraniye Sochineniy*, xxv. 41, 49; Marx to Cluss, 17 Apr. 1853, *MECW*, xxxix. 313–14.
66. Kinkel's notes for his Edinburgh lectures, Kinkel Collection, UB Bonn (S2705), and diary for 1853 and 1854, ibid. (S2680*b*).
67. Fontane took Bucher to task for this, as we have seen, *Sämtliche Werke*, xvii. 579–80.
68. Kinkel, 'Schülerbuch Jahrgang 1853/54', Kinkel Collection, UB Bonn (S2706); Johanna Kinkel to Fanny Lewald, 25 May 1856, *Zwölf Bilder nach dem Leben*, 21; Kinkel's account book for 1855, Kinkel Collection, UB Bonn (S2680*a*).
69. See Adelheid von Asten-Kinkel, 'Johanna Kinkel in England', *Deutsche Revue*, 26 (Jan.–Mar. 1901), 77.
70. Herzen, *My Past and Thoughts*, iii. 1158–9.
71. See Kinkel Collection, UB Bonn (S2705); Johanna Kinkel to Fanny Lewald, 16 Jan. 1854, *Zwölf Bilder nach dem Leben*, 16.

72. *My Past and Thoughts*, iii. 1158.
73. See Wolfgang Herrmann, *Gottfried Semper im Exil, Paris, London 1849—1855* (Basle, 1978), 74; Kinkel to Semper, 29 Sept. 1855, and Semper to Kinkel, 6 Oct. 1855, Wolfgang Beyrodt, *Gottfried Kinkel als Kunsthistoriker* (Bonn, 1979), 350–3.
74. See Friedrich Althaus, 'Beiträge zur Geschichte der deutschen Colonie in England', 244–5.
75. See Kinkel's diary, 18 Nov. 1855 and 5 Jan. 1856, Kinkel Collection, UB Bonn (S2680*b*); Temple Orme, op. cit., 31, 123, 171, and Freiligrath to Marx, 6 Aug. 1863, *Freiligraths Briefwechsel mit Marx und Engels*, i. 168; and Martin Bollert, *Ferdinand Freiligrath und Gottfried Kinkel* (Bromberg, 1916), 29.
76. Fontane, 'The Camberwell Germans and Gottfried Kinkel', 5 Dec. 1857, *Journeys to England in Victoria's Early Days*, 203, 204.
77. See Kinkel's diary, 31 Mar. 1860, Kinkel Collection, UB Bonn (S2680*b*).
78. Kinkel, *Hermann*, 3 Sept. 1859, ibid. (S2708).
79. *Marylebone Mercury*, 3 July 1858, ibid. (S2707). Marx told Engels about the MacDonald case on 9 June 1861, *MEW*, xxx. 175.
80. Kinkel's draft speech, 27 Sept. 1866, Kinkel Collection, UB Bonn (S2689); Mill, *On Liberty* (1859), chap. i (Introduction), chap. iii ('Of Individuality').
81. Althaus, 'Beiträge zur Geschichte der deutschen Colonie in England', 240; C. W. Siemens, *Fest-Rede zur Kinkel-Abschiedsfeier* (London, 1866), 7, 8 (copy in University of Bonn); for the guest list see Kinkel Collection, ibid. (S2708).
82. Kinkel to Jebens, 31 Oct. 1866, Rösch-Sondermann, op. cit., 319.
83. Marx to Ebner, 15–22 Aug. 1851, *MECW*, xxxviii. 430.
84. Herzen to Malwida von Meysenbug, 18 Sept. and 4 Oct. 1857, and to Vogt, 6 Apr. 1859, *Sobraniye Sochineniy*, xxvi. 121, 125, 249.
85. K. H. Schaible, *Siebenunddreissig Jahre aus dem Leben eines Exilierten*, 65.
86. See Blind to Gustav Struve, 6 Jan. 1857, manuscript in Federal Archives, Frankfurt. Blind probably got his job with the *Morning Advertiser* through his friend Julius Faucher, a prominent free trade advocate and friend of Richard Cobden.
87. See Marx to Engels, 9 Apr. 1863, *MEW*, xxx. 341–2, and 1 May 1865, *MEW*, xxxi. 110.
88. See Althaus, 'Beiträge zur Geschichte der deutschen Colonie in England', 242; see also Struve and Rasch, op. cit., 137, and Blind's letters about Russia to Dr David Soskice in 1905, Stow Hill Papers, House of Lords Record Office (BL 1/1–6).
89. See Porter, *The Refugee Question in Mid-Victorian Politics*, 207.
90. Blind, 'Appeal to the Russian Army', sent to David Soskice, editor of *Free Russia*, 22 Feb. 1905, Stow Hill Papers, House of Lords (BL 1/2*a*).
91. See the notice from the Paris police, ordering Blind to leave Paris within twenty-four hours and France as soon as possible, 13 June 1849, and Blind's letter from prison to the French Foreign Minister, saying he has done nothing against French law and asking to be released, 19 June 1849,

Blind Papers, BL Add. MS 40124, ff. 2, 5. He came to England with Marx at the end of August, McLellan, op. cit., 226.

92. Struve and Rasch, op. cit., 130–1.
93. See letter from Marx to Freiligrath, 5 Sept. 1849, *MECW*, xxxviii. 216. For the relationship between Marx and Blind around 1850 see Gustav Meyer, 'Letters of Karl Marx to Karl Blind', *International Review for Social History*, 4 (1939), 153–9; 'Walter' (Blind) to Marx, 12 Oct. and 1 November 1849, Marx–Engels Collection, IISH (D339, 340); Marx to Blind, 17 July 1850, *MECW*, xxxviii. 239–40, and Marx to Engels, 13 Oct. 1851, ibid. 474.
94. Marx to Liebknecht, 29 July 1870, *MEW*, xxxiii. 127; Ruge to Freiligrath, 9 July 1862, *Briefwechsel und Tagebuchblätter*, ii. 221. Agnes Ruge mentions Blind's hostility to Ruge in her memoir, MS Herr Arnold Ruge.
95. See Blind to Harney, 12 Dec. 1852 and 14 May 1863, *The Harney Papers*, 14, 98.
96. See Mrs Stansfeld to Mrs Blind from Eastbourne, 3 Sept. 1861, Blind Papers, BL Add. MS 40124, f. 215; Swinburne to Blind, [Mar. 1867], ibid., 40125, f. 1; Louis Blanc to Blind, 16 Oct. 1859, ibid., 40124, ff. 95, 97, and 23 and 24 Apr. 1858, ibid., ff. 39, 41.
97. Blind to Struve, 6 Jan. 1857, manuscript in Federal Archives, Frankfurt; Kinkel to Struve, 21 Nov. 1857, ibid.
98. Marx to Freiligrath, 29 Feb. 1860, *MEW*, xxx. 492–4.
99. See Prawer, op. cit., 100, 400, for Schiller's idealism being 'annexed', in Marx's opinion, by German philistines.
100. Pauer's children were baptized in the 1850s in the German Evangelical Church at Camberwell, as the Register of Births, now kept in the German Evangelical Church in Sydenham, shows.
101. See Marx to Engels, 3 Nov. 1859, *MECW*, xl. 511–13; Freiligrath to Marx, 14 Oct. and 28 Nov. 1859, *Freiligraths Briefwechsel mit Marx und Engels*, i. 118–9, 123–4. A copy of the advertisement for the festival is in the Kinkel Collection in the University of Bonn. See Blanc to Blind, 4 Nov. 1859, Blind Papers, BL Add. MS 40124, f. 100.
102. *Athenaeum*, no. 1902 (9 Apr. 1864), 511; Marx to Engels, 19 Apr. 1864, *MEW*, xxx. 390.
103. See the prospectus, in Marx–Engels Collection, IISH (P7); Garibaldi to Blind, 10 Apr. 1865, Blind Papers, BL Add. MS 40124, f. 308.
104. Crown Princess of Prussia to Queen Victoria, 9 May 1866, *Your Dear Letter*, 73; Caroline Stansfeld to Mrs Blind, 10/11 May 1866, Blind Papers, BL Add. MS 40124, f. 355; Marx to Engels, 10 May 1866, *MEW*, xxxi. 215.
105. See Althaus, 'Beiträge zur Geschichte der deutschen Colonie in England', 273.
106. See letter from the Honorary Secretary to Blind, 31 Jan. 1870, Blind Papers, BL Add. MS 40125, f. 67; Morley to Blind, 13 Dec. 1870, ibid., f. 97; *Fortnightly Review*, 9 (Jan.–June 1871), 53–66.
107. See letters to Blind from Max Müller, 1895–6, and from Joseph Chamberlain, Sept. 1893, Blind Papers, BL Add. MS 40126, ff. 14–43. See also Blind's self-defence against attacks by Lothar Bucher, 'Auch eine

Erinnerung an Lothar Bucher', *Deutsche Revue*, 19 (Apr.–June 1894), 196–9.

108. Ruge to Struve, 16 Nov. 1865, manuscript in Federal Archives, Frankfurt.
109. Bauer in 1850, see Marx to Bauer, 5 Feb. 1850, *MECW*, xxxviii. 226–7; and Freund in 1854–5, see Marx to Engels, 30 Nov. 1854, *MECW*, xxxix. 500.
110. See Jürgen Püschel, *Die Geschichte des German Hospital in London (1845 bis 1948)* (Münster, 1980), 22 ff., 14–15. Not all the German workers in the East End were new arrivals. Many worked as sugar-bakers, a trade which had been run by Germans from Hamburg for at least a century; see R. Campbell, *The London Tradesman* (London, 1747, repr. 1969), 272–3, and Thomas Fock, 'Über Londoner Zuckersiedereien und deutsche Arbeitskräfte', *Zuckerindustrie*, (1985), 233–5.
111. See Strauss, op. cit., ii. 19; Malwida von Meysenbug to Johanna Kinkel, May–June 1857, *Briefe an Johanna und Gottfried Kinkel 1849–1885*, 125. Mr Nigel Althaus, great-grandson of Friedrich Althaus, who lives in London, kindly gave me information about Julius.
112. See Reginald Pound, op. cit., 93, 184.
113. See Marx to Engels, 19 Aug. 1852, *MECW*, xxxix. 162. The cartoons are in the Kinkel Collection at the University of Bonn. See also Marx to Cluss, 17 Apr. 1853, *MECW*, xxxix. 313.
114. Rudolf Lehmann, *An Artist's Reminiscences* (London, 1894), 133, 155, 156, 185, 188, 197, 231, 235.
115. See *Illustrated London News*, 15 (15 Sept. 1849), 177, on the need for better sanitation and a stop to burials inside London.
116. See Wolfgang Herrmann, op. cit., 32, 56, 70, 74; *Illustrated London News*, 21 (6, 20, and 27 Nov. 1852), 383, 431, 439, 473 ff.
117. See Ernest Newman, *The Life of Richard Wagner*, 4 vols. (London, 1933, repr. 1976), ii. 459; *Briefe von Carl Schurz an Gottfried Kinkel*, 89.
118. See Newman, op. cit., ii. 448, 454; Berlioz, *Memoirs*, trans. David Cairns (London, 1970, repr. 1981), 305. For flattery of music critics see Newman, op. cit., ii. 461, 467, 473. For German criticism of English musical taste see Fontane, *Journeys to England in Victoria's Early Days*, 32, Weerth, *Englische Reisen*, 32, and Newman, op.cit., ii. 454.
119. *Punch*. 28 (Jan.–June 1855), 114, 127.
120. *Punch*, 15 (July–Dec. 1848), 129.
121. Newman, op. cit., ii. 463, 475, 460–1; Malwida to Johanna Kinkel, 15 May 1855, *Briefe an Johanna und Gottfried Kinkel*, 106; Althaus to von Bandel, 17 Mar. 1855, manuscript in Stadtarchiv und Landesgeschichtliche Bibliothek, Bielefeld.
122. Newman, op. cit., ii. 456–7.
123. Charles Hallé to his parents, 27 Apr. 1848, *Life and Letters*, 229.
124. Berlioz, *Memoirs*, 33–4; Hallé, *Life and Letters*, 102.
125. Ibid. 102, 109, 146.
126. Agnes Ruge's unpublished memoir of her life in Brighton, written in the 1880s, in the possession of Herr Arnold Ruge.
127. Friedrich Althaus, 'Beiträge zur Geschichte der deutschen Colonie in England', 547, 548.

128. See Malwida von Meysenbug, *Briefe an Johanna und Gottfried Kinkel*, 43 n; Ingrid Donner and Birgit Matthies, op. cit., 74, 76.
129. Ibid. 77; Marx to Engels, 19 Oct. 1851, *MECW*, xxxviii. 483; Johanna Kinkel to Kathinka Zitz, 18 Mar. 1851 and 22 Dec. 1854, 'Briefe an Kathinka Zitz', 34, 55; Amalie Struve to Frau von Chézy (in Strasbourg), 24 Mar. 1851, Varnhagen Collection, Jagiellonian Library, Cracow.
130. See Malwida von Meysenbug, *Briefe an Johanna und Gottfried Kinkel*, 38 ff. For Friedrich Fröbel see Baroness B. von Marenholz-Bülow, *Reminiscences of Freidrich Froebel*, trans. Mrs Horace Mann, with a sketch of the life of Fröbel by Emily Shirreff (Boston, Mass., 1877). See also Carl Froebel, *Explanation of the Kindergarten* (London, 1875), 8, 38, 53.
131. Johannes and Bertha Ronge, *A Practical Guide to the English Kinder Garten* (London, 1855), v, ix, 7, 55.
132. Baroness von Marenholz-Bülow, op. cit., 198; Ronge to Kinkel, 24 Jan. 1859, Kinkel Collection, UB Bonn (S2673).
133. See 'Heinrich Beta' (Bettziech), 'Der Verbannte von Brighton', *Gartenlaube*, 24 (1863), 380; J. Rieger, 'Theodor Fontane und die Deutschen in England', *Der Londoner Bote*, 37 (Jan. 1951), 4, and 'Der erste englische Kindergarten', ibid. 46 (Oct. 1952), 148. *Der Londoner Bote* is the parish magazine of the German Evangelical Churches at Sydenham and St George's, Whitehcapel. I am grateful to Pastor Albrecht Plag of Sydenham for allowing me to consult his copies of the magazine. For the attendance of Kinkel's children see Ronge to Kinkel, 9 Mar. [no year], Kinkel Collection, UB Bonn (S2673).
134. Ronge to Holyoake, 22 Jan. 1855, Holyoake Collection, Co-operative Union, Manchester (729); F. W. Newman to Holyoake, 11 Apr. 1855, ibid. (756).
135. Ronge to Kinkel, undated, Kinkel Collection, UB Bonn (S2673); to the same, 1 Nov. 1865 and 23 Jan. 1866, ibid. (S2673).
136. See *Report and Calendar* for 1885 of the Froebel Society for the Promotion of the Kindergarten System (London, 1885). See also North London Collegiate School for Girls, *Our Magazine* (Nov. 1885), 124. I am grateful to Mrs Townley, Archivist at the school, for allowing me to consult its records.
137. See Registers of North London Collegiate School from 1871. Ella Oswald became a civil servant, and during the Second World War she became a communist. I am indebted for this last piece of information to Professor Chimen Abramsky.
138. *Our Magazine* (July and Nov. 1884), 110, 171.
139. Eugene Oswald, *Reminiscences of a Busy Life*, 231, 238, 247, 250, 257–8, 351. For Marx's opinion of Oswald see Marx to Engels, 1 Aug. 1870, *MEW*, xxx. 21; also Collins and Abramsky, op. cit., 180. See also several letters from Oswald to Marx, July–Aug. 1870, Marx–Engels Collection, IISH (D3578 ff.).
140. Oswald, op. cit., 274, 299, 309. See also Temple Orme, op. cit., 19.
141. Oswald, op. cit., 336, 359 ff., 439, 628; Eduard Bernstein, *My Years of Exile: Reminiscences of a Socialist*, trans. Bernard Miall (London, 1921), 200.

142. Oswald, *Thomas Carlyle. Ein Lebensbild, und Goldkörner aus seinen Werken* (1881); Fontane's review of it, *Sämtliche Werke*, xxi/2, 333–8. The National Library of Scotland has a letter from Oswald to Carlyle in 1872, in which Oswald sends a copy of his work on early German courtesy books, published by the Early English Texts Society in 1869 (9 Nov. 1872, MS 1770, f. 188).
143. Oswald, *Reminiscences*, 439, 556; Harrison to Oswald, 17 Apr. 1900, Oswald Collection, IISH.
144. Ramsay MacDonald, 20 July 1908, ibid.
145. Oswald, *Reminiscences*, 186–7, 471.
146. Rasch and Struve, op. cit., 161, 162 ff.; Althaus, 'Beiträge zur Geschichte der deutschen Colonie in England', 243; and Jenny Marx on the Robert Blum banquet in 1852, Ingrid Donner and Birgit Matthies, op. cit., 76.
147. Johanna Kinkel to Fanny Lewald, 28 Apr. 1854, *Zwölf Bilder nach dem Leben*, 18; Althaus to Kinkel, 20 Oct. 1861, Kinkel Collection, UB Bonn (S2660).
148. Althaus, 'Beiträge zur Geschichte der deutschen Colonie in England'. 229.
149. Ibid. 241.
150. Althaus's great-grandson, Mr Nigel Althaus, kindly allowed me to consult Althaus's manuscript lectures at University College in the 1880s and 1890s, which are in a bound volume in his possession.
151. Althaus, *Englische Charakterbilder*, 2 vols. in one (Berlin, 1869), i. ix; Carlyle to Althaus, 7 Jan. 1870, manuscript in the possession of Mr Nigel Althaus.
152. Althaus, 'Erinnerungen an Thomas Carlyle', *Unsere Zeit*, 1/1 (1881), 824.
153. Carlyle's annotated copy of Althaus's essay is in the National Library of Scotland, and has been published in *Two Reminiscences of Thomas Carlyle*, ed. John Clubbe (Durham, N. Carolina, 1974). For Carlyle's comment, see 26.
154. Althaus, 'Thomas Carlyle', ibid. 82, 83, 97, 99–100.
155. Ibid. 100; Carlyle to Althaus, 12 July 1866, manuscript in Mr Nigel Althaus's possession.
156. *Two Reminiscences of Thomas Carlyle*, 23.
157. Althaus to Carlyle, 1 Sept. 1874, manuscript in National Library of Scotland (MS 666, ff. 226–7).
158. See Miriam Rothschild, *Dear Lord Rothschild* (London, 1983), 59 ff; T. F. Althaus, *Recollections of Mark Pattison* (London, 1885), 5.

CHAPTER 5

1. Malwida von Meysenbug, *Rebel in a Crinoline*, 131, 170; Johanna Kinkel to Fanny Lewald, 25 Nov. 1851, *Zwölf Bilder nach dem Leben*, 12.
2. Johanna Kinkel to Fanny Lewald, 25 Oct. 1852, manuscript in Deutsche Staatsbibliothek, East Berlin.
3. Johanna Kinkel to Kathinka Zitz, 31 May 1854, 'Briefe an Kathinka Zitz', 51.
4. Johanna Kinkel, *Hans Ibeles in London*, ii. 129.

5. Marx to Engels, 11 Dec. 1858, *MECW*, xl. 359–60; *Hans Ibeles in London*, i. 169.
6. Johanna Kinkel to Laura von Henning, 25 May 1851, 'Briefe von Johanna Kinkel', ed. Marie Goslich, *Preussische Jahrbücher*, 97 (July–Sept. 1899), 432; Johanna Kinkel to Fanny Lewald, 16 Jan. 1854, *Zwölf Bilder nach dem Leben*, 16; and letter of 20 June 1853, 'Briefe an Kathinka Zitz', 47.
7. See Johanna Kinkel to Emilie von Henning, 24 July 1851, 'Briefe von Johanna Kinkel', 433.
8. See Marianne Bröcker, 'Johanna Kinkels schriftstellerische und musikpädagogische Tätigkeit', *Bonner Geschichtsblätter*, 29 (1977), 45.
9. Johanna, 'Briefe aus London' and 'Musikalisches aus London', Kinkel Collection, UB Bonn (S2389, S2391); *Hans Ibeles in London*, ii. 69–70, i. 296.
10. Johanna Kinkel, 'Briefe aus London', Kinkel Collection, UB Bonn (S2389).
11. *Life and Letters of Sir Charles Hallé*, 110; Johanna Kinkel to Auguste Heinrich, 15 Jan. 1852, Adelheid von Asten-Kinkel, 'Johanna Kinkel in England', *Deutsche Revue*, 26 (Jan–Mar. 1901), 73–4.
12. See Marianne Bröcker, op. cit., 41.
13. Johanna Kinkel to Fanny Lewald, 4 Oct. 1857, *Zwölf Bilder nach dem Leben*, 29–30.
14. Johanna Kinkel to Fanny Lewald, 16 Jan. and 28 Apr. 1854, ibid. 16, 19; Johanna Kinkel to Auguste Heinrich, 5 May 1854, Adelheid von Asten-Kinkel, op. cit., 178.
15. See Temple Orme, op. cit., 31, 171; Ferencz Pulszky, *Meine Zeit, mein Leben*, 4 vols. in 3 (Leipzig, 1880–2), iii. 202–3.
16. Johanna Kinkel to Fanny Lewald, 16 Jan. 1854, *Zwölf Bilder nach dem Leben*, 16, and to Kathinka Zitz, 31 May 1854, 'Briefe an Kathinka Zitz', 52.
17. Johanna Kinkel junior to Kathinka Zitz, 13 Nov. 1861, ibid. 80–1.
18. *Hans Ibeles in London*, i. 277.
19. Mill, *On Liberty*, chap. ii ('Of the Liberty of Thought and Discussion'), and 'Introductory'.
20. Johanna Kinkel to Kathinka Zitz, 31 May 1854, 'Briefe an Kathinka Zitz', 51.
21. Agnes Ruge's memoir, in the possession of Herr Arnold Ruge.
22. See Marx to Engels, 26 June 1855, *MECW*, xxxix. 539, and Johanna Kinkel to Kathinka Zitz, 31 July 1855, 'Briefe an Kathinka Zitz', 55–6.
23. Johanna Kinkel, 'Erinnerungsblätter' (1849), ed. Ernst Schierenberg, *Deutsche Revue*, 19 (Apr.–June 1894), 95–7, 202.
24. Ibid. 201; Johanna Kinkel to Laura von Henning, 22 Sept. 1849, 'Briefe von Johanna Kinkel', 426.
25. Kinkel to Auguste Heinrich, 7 Dec. 1849, Friedrich Althaus, 'Erinnerungen an Gottfried Kinkel', 240.
26. Herzen, *My Past and Thoughts*, iii. 1159.
27. To Fanny Lewald, see *Zwölf Bilder nach dem Leben*, 6–7, and to Kathinka Zitz, 25 Dec. 1849, 'Briefe an Kathinka Zitz', 20.

28. Baroness Marie von Bruiningk to Johanna Kinkel, 19 Nov. 1849, Kinkel Collection, UB Bonn (S2671); *Rebel in a Crinoline*, 150.
29. Ibid. 150, 153; letters from Baron von Bruiningk to Kinkel, Mar.–Apr. 1852, Kinkel Collection, UB Bonn (S2671).
30. Marx to Engels, 22 May 1852, *MECW*, xxxix. 112; Jenny Marx, 'A Short Sketch of an Eventful Life', *The Unknown Karl Marx*, 124.
31. See Marx to Engels, 22–3 Mar. 1853, *MECW*, xxxix. 297; *Hans Ibeles in London*, i. 190 ff., 329 ff.
32. Johanna Kinkel to Kathinka Zitz, 30 July 1857, ibid. 59, and to Fanny Lewald, 25 May 1856, *Zwölf Bilder nach dem Leben*, 25.
33. Julius Rodenberg, *Alltagsleben in London* (Berlin, 1860), 37–8.
34. Kinkel's diary for 10 and 15 Nov. 1858, Kinkel collection, UB Bonn (S2680*b*); James John Garth Wilkinson to Kinkel, 19 Nov. 1858, ibid. (S2663).
35. Unsigned letter to Kinkel, June 1849, ibid. (S2664).
36. See Malwida von Meysenbug, *Briefe an Johanna und Gottfried Kinkel*, 121 ff., 154.
37. Jane Welsh Carlyle, *I too am here*, 234.
38. Johanna Kinkel to Kathinka Zitz, 31 July 1858, 'Briefe an Kathinka Zitz', 72, 73.
39. 23 July 1856, ibid. 57; *Punch*, 18 (Jan.–June 1850), 28.
40. Johanna Kinkel to Auguste Heinrich, 20 June 1852, Adelheid von Asten-Kinkel, op. cit., 75.
41. Althaus, 'Beiträge', 228; Johanna Kinkel to Auguste Heinrich, 22 Apr. 1851, Adelheid von Asten-Kinkel, op. cit., 72.
42. See Malwida von Meysenbug, *Briefe an Gottfried und Johanna Kinkel*, 7–8; Emil Reicke, *Malwida von Meysenbug* (Berlin, 1911), 5, 27; and *Rebel in a Crinoline*, 87.
43. See Reicke, op. cit., 32; Malwida to Johanna Kinkel, 19 Dec. 1849, *Briefe an Johanna und Gottfried Kinkel*, 29.
44. Malwida to Johanna, 16 Apr. 1850, ibid. 38; to the same, 6 May 1851, ibid. 73.
45. Malwida to her mother, 2, 10, 23, and 29 May 1852, 'Briefe von Malwida von Meysenbug an ihre Mutter', ed. Gabriel Monod, *Deutsche Revue*, 31/1 (Jan.–Mar. 1906), 365–7, 369.
46. *Rebel in a Crinoline*, 129–31, 132 ff.
47. Ibid. 133 ff.
48. Ibid. 135–6.
49. Ibid. 137.
50. *Punch*, 18 (Jan.–June 1850), 129; Eleanor Marx to Natalie Liebknecht, 23 Oct. 1874, Liebknecht, *Briefwechsel mit Marx und Engels*, 418–19.
51. See Lewes to Thornton Hunt, 23 Dec. 1849, MS Berg Collection; *Annual Report* of the German Hospital (1852), 30.
52. Malwida, *Rebel in a Crinoline*, 138.
53. Ibid. 139, 142. See also Malwida to Johanna Kinkel, 12 May and 28 Sept. 1857, *Briefe an Johanna und Gottfried Kinkel*, 119, 140; Malwida to Gottfried Kinkel, June 1859, ibid. 179, and to the same, 2 and 25 Oct. 1859, ibid. 185, 192.

54. *Rebel in a Crinoline*, 145, 169, 171.
55. E. H. Carr, *The Romantic Exiles*, 138–9, 164 ff.; Malwida, 'Briefe an ihre Mutter', *Deutsche Revue*, 33/1 (Jan.–June 1908), 209.
56. Malwida to her mother, [Nov. 1852], ibid. 52–3.
57. Malwida, 'Joseph Mazzini', *Gesammelte Werke*, iii. 487; *Rebel in a Crinoline*, 219 ff.
58. H. M. Hyndman, *Record of an Adventurous Life* (London, 1911), 50 ff.
59. *Rebel in a Crinoline*, 169, 235.
60. Report in an unnamed newspaper, quoted by Nicolaievsky and Maenchen-Helfen, op. cit., 217.
61. *Rebel in a Crinoline*, 238; Johanna Kinkel to Kathinka Zitz, 22 Dec. 1854, 'Briefe an Kathinka Zitz', 55; Johanna to Kinkel, 26 Jan. 1854, Kinkel Collection, UB Bonn (S2672).
62. Malwida to Gottfried Kinkel, 25 June 1858, *Briefe an Johanna und Gottfried Kinkel*, 147–8; Mazzini to Kinkel, [Nov. or Dec. 1858], Kinkel Collection, UB Bonn (S2662).
63. See *Briefe an Johanna und Gottfried Kinkel*, 121 ff.
64. Malwida to Kinkel, May 1859, ibid. 174–5. See also Louisa Garrett Anderson, *Elizabeth Garrett Anderson, 1836–1917* (London, 1939), 42–3, and E. Moberly Bell, *Storming the Citadel: The Rise of the Woman Doctor* (London, 1953), 44–5. Also Hester Burton, *Barbara Bodichon 1827–91* (London, 1949), 190.
65. See Malwida to Kinkel, July 1859, *Briefe an Johanna und Gottfried Kinkel*, 184; Reicke, op. cit., 69 ff.
66. *Briefe an Johanna und Gottfried Kinkel*, 250 ff.
67. For example, George Eliot went to Broadstairs in July 1852, whence she wrote her agonized love letters to the unresponsive Herbert Spencer, *The George Eliot Letters*, viii. 50 ff.
68. *Rebel in a Crinoline*, 132.
69. Amely Bölte to Varnhagen von Ense, 23 Mar. 1850, *Briefe aus England an Varnhagen von Ense*, 77.
70. Jane Carlyle to her husband, 28 July 1843, *New Letters and Memorials of Jane Welsh Carlyle*, i. 127. Amely had a recommendation to the Carlyles from Dr Hitzig in Berlin, manuscript in National Library of Scotland (MS 2883, f. 98).
71. Amely Bölte, *Briefe aus England an Varnhagen von Ense*, 1.
72. Amely Bölte to Varnhagen, 7 Aug. 1850, ibid. 83.
73. Jane Carlyle to her husband, 14 Aug. 1843, *Letters and Memorials of Jane Welsh Carlyle*, ed. J. A. Froude, 3 vols. (London, 1883), i. 235. Carlyle's comment is printed in a footnote by Froude, ibid. 234. See also Geraldine Jewsbury to Amely Bölte, [1846], manuscript in Varnhagen von Ense Collection, Jagiellonian Library, Cracow.
74. Amely Bölte to Varnhagen, 7 Aug. 1850 and 2 Apr. 1851, *Briefe an Varnhagen von Ense*, 82, 89; 23 Jan. 1848, ibid. 53; 21 Mar. 1848, ibid. 59; 7 Aug. 1850, ibid. 82.
75. 11 June 1851, ibid. 90.
76. J. A. Froude to Amely Bölte, 27 May [1882], Manfred Eimer, 'Briefe

an Amely Bölte aus Carlyles Freundeskreis', *Englische Studien*, 49 (1915–16), 269–71.

77. Charlotte Williams-Wynn to Ludmilla Assing, 23 June 1860, Walther Fischer, 'Thomas und Jane Carlyle im Spiegel der Briefe Amely Böltes an Varnhagen von Ense (1844–1853)', *Englische Studien*, 64 (1929), 424–5.
78. Amely Bölte to Varnhagen, 27 Feb. 1848, *Briefe an Varnhagen von Ense*, 58.
79. 7 Feb. 1848, ibid. 55. Back in Germany in the 1850s, she wrote to Carlyle asking if she could translate the autobiography she heard he was writing, and gossiping about Lewes's marriage and his liaison with George Eliot, undated letter in National Library of Scotland (MS 1773, f. 192). See also Jane Carlyle to her husband, 3 July 1849, *New Letters and Memorials*, i. 255; Jane Carlyle to Jeannie Welsh, 27 Feb. 1849, *I too am here*, 138; Jane Carlyle to her husband, 14 July 1846, *New Letters and Memorials*, i. 194.
80. Amely Bölte to Varnhagen, 13 July 1846, *Briefe an Varnhagen von Ense*, 39; ibid. 23; Amely Bölte to Varnhagen, 7 May 1848 and 19 Jan. 1850, ibid. 61, 75.
81. Amely Bölte, 'Die Frau des Missionärs', *Erzählungen aus der Mappe einer Deutschen in London* (Leipzig, 1848), 65–6; *Louise oder die Deutsche in England* (Bautzen, 1846), 23–4; *Eine deutsche Palette in London* (Berlin, 1853).
82. Jane Carlyle to John Sterling, 16 Aug. 1843, *New Letters and Memorials*, i. 129.
83. Amely Bölte to Varnhagen, 15 Sept. 1847, *Briefe an Varnhagen von Ense*, 47; Jane Carlyle to John Welsh, 13 Dec. 1847, *I too am here*, 71.
84. See Anthony Heilbut, *Exiled in Paradise*, 45.
85. Amalie Struve, *Erinnerungen aus den badischen Freiheitskämpfen* (Hamburg, 1850), 157–8; Amalie Struve to Bettina von Arnim, 16 Feb. 1850, manuscript in Varnhagen Collection, Jagiellonian Library. See also Amalie's complaining letters to Frau von Chézy in Strasbourg, in the same collection.
86. See Schurz to Kinkel, 15 Mar. 1851, *Briefe an Gottfried Kinkel*, 66, and Marx, 'The Great Men of the Exile', *MECW*, xi. 261 ff.
87. See James Pope-Hennessy, op. cit., 225; Marx and Engels, 'To the Editor of *The Times*', 27 May 1850, *MECW*, x. 352.
88. Amalie Struve to Frau von Chézy, from Whitehouse, near York, 2 Aug. 1850, Varnhagen Collection, Jagiellonian Library.
89. To the same, 10 Apr. 1851, ibid.
90. Johanna Kinkel to Kathinka Zitz, 18 Mar. 1851, 'Briefe an Kathinka Zitz', 34; Marx to Engels, 15 Apr. 1851, *MECW*, xxxviii. 334.
91. See *The Forty-Eighters*, ed. A. E. Zucker (New York, 1950), 143, 346.
92. 'The Great Men of the Exile', *MECW*, xi. 261–2.
93. What follows, unless otherwise stated, is taken from Agnes Ruge's manuscript memoir, a copy of which was sent to me by Herr Arnold Ruge. The copy covers twenty-five typed A4 pages.
94. Herzen, *My Past and Thoughts*, iii. 1156.
95. See *Wilhelm Liebknecht, sein Leben und Wirken*, ed. Kurt Eisner (Berlin, 1900), 28, and Liebknecht, 'Marx und die Kinder', Friedrich Engels *et al.*, *Karl Marx* (Basle, 1946), 90.

96. Jenny Marx, 'A Short Sketch of an Eventful Life', in *The Unknown Karl Marx*, 119ff. Unless otherwise stated, what follows is taken from this memoir, first published in German in *Mohr und General. Erinnerungen an Marx und Engels* (Berlin, 1965).
97. Jenny Marx to Weydemeyer, 20 May 1850, *MECW*, xxxviii. 556–7.
98. Marx to Paul Lafargue, 13 Aug. 1866, *MEW*, xxi. 518–19.
99. See Yvonne Kapp, *Eleanor Marx*, i. 32, 36.

CHAPTER 6

1. Jenny Marx to Engels, beginning of Apr. 1861, *MEW*, xxx. 689.
2. Freiligrath to Marx, 28 Nov. and 5 Dec. 1860, *Briefwechsel mit Marx und Engels*, i. 150–3.
3. See Porter, *The Refugee Question*, 20–1.
4. Herzen, *My Past and Thoughts*, iii. 1180–1.
5. Amely Bölte to Varnhagen, 25 June 1847, *Briefe an Varnhagen von Ense*, 45–6; Jane Carlyle to Jeannie Welsh, 22 Aug. 1844, *I too am here*, 77–8.
6. Jane Carlyle to Dr Carlyle, Sept. 1853, *New Letters and Memorials*, ii. 68.
7. Herzen, *My Past and Thoughts*, iii. 1192.
8. Johanna Kinkel to Kinkel, 2 and 5 Feb. 1854, Kinkel Collection, UB Bonn (S2672).
9. Reiff to Marx and to Engels, undated, *Freiligraths Briefwechsel mit Marx und Engels*, ii. 165.
10. Engels to Marx, 11 Mar. 1857, *MECW*, xl. 104; Selmnitz to Engels, 9 Mar. 1857, *Freiligraths Briefwechsel mit Marx und Engels*, ii. 103.
11. Marx to Engels, 13 Oct. 1851, *MECW*, xxxviii. 475, and 22 Nov. 1854, *MECW*, xxxix. 498.
12. Engels to Marx, 20 Sept. 1852, ibid. 186–7.
13. Freiligrath to Marx, 10 Feb. 1858, *Briefwechsel mit Marx und Engels*, i. 97.
14. See H. Gustav Klaus, *The Literature of Labour: Two Hundred Years of Working-Class Writing* (Brighton, 1985). See also David Vincent, *Bread, Knowledge and Freedom: A Study of Nineteenth-Century Working-Class Autobiography* (London, 1981) and John Burnett, ed., *Destiny Obscure: Autobiographies of Childhood, Education and Family from the 1820s to the 1920s* (London, 1982), both of which show that, though there was more working-class autobiographical writing during the period than has been thought, much of it remained unpublished. Moreover, it was only the exceptional working man who could find, or make, the time to write.
15. See Nicolaievsky and Maenchen-Helfen, op. cit., 120.
16. Marx to Engels, 3 July 1852, *MECW*, xxxix. 126.
17. Marx to Engels, 25 Aug. and 24 Nov. 1851, *MECW*, xxxviii. 442, 492.
18. Details of Schapper's life are mainly taken from an unpublished thesis, A. W. Fehling, 'Karl Schapper und die Anfänge der Arbeiterbewegung bis zur Revolution von 1848' (Rostock, 1922). For a brief account of Schapper in London, see Henry Weisser, *British Working-Class Movements and Europe, 1815–48* (Manchester, 1975) 125ff. See also Alexander Brandenburg, 'Der kommunistische Arbeiterbildungsverein in London', *International Review for Social History*, 24 (1979), 341–70.

19. Marx to Engels, 28 Apr. 1870, *MEW*, xxxii. 485.
20. Friedrich Lessner, 'Vor 1848 und nachher. Erinnerungen eines alten Kommunisten', *Deutsche Worte*, 18 (1898), 104; Engels, 'History of the Communist League' (1885), *The Cologne Communist Trial*, 47.
21. Lessner, op. cit., 156.
22. Ibid. 110.
23. See Eccarius to Marx, 20 Feb. 1850, Marx–Engels Collection, IISH (D1133).
24. Marx and Engels, editorial comment on Eccarius's article, *MECW*, x. 485; Eccarius, preface to *Eines Arbeiters Widerlegung der national-ökonomischen Lehren John Stuart Mill's*, iii.
25. Eccarius, 'Der Kampf des grossen und des kleinen Kapitals, oder die Schneiderei in London', first published in *Neue Rheinische Zeitung. Politisch-ökonomische Revue* (1850), reprinted as a pamphlet (Leipzig, 1876), 17.
26. Eccarius, *Eines Arbeiters Widerlegung der national-ökonomischen Lehren John Stuart Mill's*, 73–6, 47–8, 14, 38.
27. Marx to Weydemeyer, 30 Jan. 1852, *MECW*, xxxix. 26.
28. Engels to Marx, 10 Feb. 1859, *MECW*, xl. 386; Eccarius to Marx, 8 Feb. 1859, Marx–Engels Collection, IISH (D1134); Marx to Engels, 22 Mar. 1859, *MECW*, xl. 406.
29. See Marx to Engels, 9 Nov. 1862, *MEW*, xxx. 296; Eccarius to Marx, 15 Nov. 1862, Marx–Engels Collection, IISH (D1137).
30. Marx, *Capital*, i. 667.
31. Eccarius to Marx, undated but probably 1862, Marx–Engels Collection, IISH (D1136); to Wilhelm Wolff, 2 Nov. 1863, Wolff Collection, ibid. (folder 2).
32. Eccarius to Wolff, 27 June 1863, ibid; to the same, 2 Nov. 1863, ibid.
33. Eccarius to Marx, 5 Sept. 1866 and 31 Aug. 1868, Marx–Engels Collection, IISH (D1145, D1151).
34. See Engels to Marx, 11 Sept. 1867, *MEW*, xxxi. 344.
35. Marx to Engels, 16 and 19 Sept. 1868, *MEW*, xxxii. 150, 155, 743.
36. To the same, 24 June 1865, *MEW*, xxi. 126.
37. To the same, 16 Sept. 1868, *MEW*, xxxii. 150–1. See also Engels to Hermann Jung, 10 May 1871, *MEW*, xxxiii. 224.
38. For the full story of the possibility of Eccarius being a spy, see Collins and Abramsky, op. cit., 305 ff. The authors decide that there is insufficient evidence to conclude that he was.
39. Eccarius to Marx, 8 Nov. 1869, Marx–Engels Collection, IISH (D1163).
40. See Paul Lafargue to Marx, Apr. 1867, *The Daughters of Karl Marx*, 21; to the same, 16 Oct. 1867 and Jan. 1868, Marx–Engels Collection, IISH (D1149, D1150); Eccarius to Engels, 16 Dec. 1870, ibid. (L1323).
41. See Engels to Liebknecht, 27–8 May 1872, *MEW*, xxxiii. 472 ff.
42. Eccarius to Marx, 2 May 1872, Marx–Engels Collection, IISH (D1177); Marx to Eccarius, 3 May 1872, *MEW*, xxxiii. 454.
43. Eccarius's certificate of naturalization, Oct. 1872 (Public Record Office); Engels to George Shipton, 15 Aug. 1881, *MEW*, xxxv. 212.

44. Engels to Schlüter, 7 Dec. 1885, *MEW*, xxxvi. 408; *The Cologne Communist Trial*, 47 n.; Engels to Sorge, 8 June 1889, *MEW*, xxxvii. 231.
45. See Collins and Abramsky, op. cit., 52, 302–3; also Henry Pelling, *A History of British Trade Unionism* (London, 1963, repr. 1975), 116–7.
46. A. W. Humphrey, *Robert Applegarth: Trade Unionist, Educationist, Reformer* (London, 1913), 96, 119.
47. Manuscript in Marx–Engels Collection, IISH (E74).
48. Lessner's wife died at Christmas 1868; see 'Vor 1848 und nachher', 202. See also Eleanor Marx to her sister Jenny, 2 June 1869, *The Daughters of Karl Marx*, 50, and letters from Lessner to Engels, 1870–2, Marx–Engels Collection, IISH (L3341 ff.).
49. See codicil of 26 July 1895 to Engels's will, *MEW*, xxxix. 509.
50. Foreword to Lessner, *Sixty Years in the Social-Democratic Movement* (London, 1907). As the translation, by Thalmeyer, is sometimes inaccurate, I have quoted mostly from the German original in my own translation, while occasionally referring to Thalmeyer's version.
51. Lessner, 'Vor 1848 und nachher', 99.
52. Marx, article in *Vorwärts!*, 10 Aug. 1844, *MECW*, iii. 201.
53. Lessner, *Sixty Years in the Social-Democratic Movement*, 7.
54. Lessner, 'Vor 1848 und nachher', 109.
55. Ibid. 148; Peter Gerhard Röser to Marx, 2 Nov. 1850, and Freiligrath to Marx, 25 July 1852, *Freiligraths Briefwechsel mit Marx und Engels*, ii. 69, i. 54.
56. Lessner, 'Vor 1848 und nachher', 153.
57. Ibid. 154.
58. See Engels to Karl Kautsky, 20 Mar. 1893, *MEW*, xxxix. 55; Lessner, 'Vor 1848 und nachher', 155 ff.
59. Manuscript letters in Marx–Engels Collection, IISH (D3024–36).
60. Lessner, 'Vor 1848 und nachher', 214; Yvonne Kapp, op. cit., ii. 66, 527.
61. Engels to F. Walter, 21 Dec. 1888, *MEW*, xxxvii. 126.
62. Lessner, 'Vor 1848 und nachher', 98.
63. Yvonne Kapp, op. cit., ii. 599, 702.
64. See A. W. Humphrey, op. cit., 119, for Jung's death. For a reference to Lessner's funeral speech, and for the accounts of his activities during the last ten years of his life, see Friedrich Lessner, *Ich brachte das „Kommunistische Manifest" zum Drucker*, ed. Ursula Herrmann and Gerhard Winkler (Berlin, 1975), 339 ff.
65. Lessner, *Sixty Years in the Social-Democratic Movement*, 66–7.

Select Bibliography

ALTHAUS, FRIEDRICH, 'Beiträge zur Geschichte der deutschen Colonie in England', *Unsere Zeit*, NS 9, parts 1 and 2 (1873).

—— *Englische Charakterbilder*, 2 vols. in one (Berlin, 1869).

—— 'Erinnerungen an Gottfried Kinkel', *Nord und Süd*, 24 and 25 (Feb. and Apr. 1883).

—— 'Erinnerungen an Thomas Carlyle', *Unsere Zeit*, 1/1 (1881).

ALTHAUS, THEODORE FREDERICK, *Recollections of Mark Pattison* (London, 1885).

ANDERSON, LOUISA GARRETT, *Elizabeth Garrett Anderson, 1836–1917* (London, 1939).

ANDRÉAS, BERT, *Briefe und Dokumente der Familie Marx aus den Jahren 1862—1873* (Hanover, 1962).

—— 'Marx' Verhaftung und Ausweisung Brüssel Februar/März 1848', *Schriften aus dem Karl-Marx-Haus* (Trier, 1978).

Archiv für die Geschichte des Sozialismus, 10 (Leipzig, 1922).

ASHTON, ROSEMARY, *The German Idea: Four English Writers and the Reception of German Thought 1800–1860* (Cambridge, 1980).

ASTEN-KINKEL, ADELHEID VON, 'Johanna Kinkel in England', *Deutsche Revue*, 26 (Jan.–Mar. 1901).

'W.B.', 'Eduard von Müller-Tellering, Verfasser des ersten anti-semitischen Pamphlets gegen Marx', *International Review for Social History*, 6 (1951).

BAKUNIN, MIKHAIL, *Michael Bakunins Beichte aus der Peter-Pauls-Festung an Zar Nikolaus I*, trans. and ed. Kurt Kersten (Berlin, 1926).

BARKER, THEO, and DRAKE, MICHAEL (eds.), *Population and Society in Britain 1850–1980* (London, 1982).

BAX, ERNEST BELFORT, 'Leaders of Modern Thought. XXIII. Karl Marx', *Modern Thought*, 3 (Dec. 1881).

BEESLY, EDWARD, 'The Social Future of the Working Class', *Fortnightly Review*, 5 (Mar. 1869).

BELL, E. MOBERLY, *Storming the Citadel: The Rise of the Woman Doctor* (London, 1953).

BENSON, A. C., and VISCOUNT ESHER (eds.), *The Letters of Queen Victoria*, 3 vols. (London, 1907).

BENTWICH, NORMAN, *The Rescue and Achievement of Refugee Scholars: The Story of Displaced Scholars and Scientists 1933–1952* (The Hague, 1953).

BERLIN, ISAIAH, *Karl Marx: His Life and Environment* (London, 1939, repr. 1963).

BERLIOZ, HECTOR, *Memoirs*, trans. David Cairns (London, 1970, repr. 1981).

BERNSTEIN, EDUARD, *My Years of Exile: Reminiscences of a Socialist*, trans. Bernard Miall (London, 1921).

'BETA, HEINRICH' [Bettziech], 'Der Verbannte von Brighton', *Gartenlaube*, 24 (1863).

BEYRODT, WOLFGANG, *Gottfried Kinkel als Kunsthistoriker* (Bonn, 1979).

BLAINEY, ANN, *The Farthing Poet: A Biography of Richard Hengist Horne 1802–1884* (London, 1968).

BLIND, KARL, 'Auch eine Erinnerung an Lothar Bucher', *Deutsche Revue*, 19 (Apr.–June 1894).

—— *Zur Geschichte der Republikanischen Partei in England* (Berlin, 1873).

BLIND, MATHILDE, *George Eliot* (London, 1883).

—— *Poetical Works*, ed. Arthur Symons, with a memoir by Richard Garnett (London, 1900).

BLUM, OSCAR, 'Zur Psychologie der Emigration', *Archiv für die Geschichte des Sozialismus und der Arbeiterbewegung*, 17 (1916).

BÖLTE, AMELY, *Briefe aus England an Varnhagen von Ense* (1844–1858), ed. W. Fischer and A. Behrens (Düsseldorf, 1955).

—— *Eine deutsche Palette in London* (Berlin, 1853).

—— *Erzählungen aus der Mappe einer Deutschen in London* (Leipzig, 1848).

—— *Louise oder die Deutsche in England* (Bautzen, 1846).

BOLLERT, MARTIN, *Ferdinand Freiligrath und Gottfried Kinkel* (Bromberg, 1916).

BORN, STEPHAN, *Erinnerungen eines Achtundvierzigers* (Leipzig, 1898).

BRANDENBURG, ALEXANDER, 'Der kommunistische Arbeiterbildungsverein in London', *International Review for Social History*, 24 (1979).

BRÖCKER, MARIANNE, 'Johanna Kinkels schriftstellerische und musikpädagogische Tätigkeit', *Bonner Geschichtsblätter*, 29 (1977).

BUCHNER, WILHELM, *Ferdinand Freiligrath, ein Dichterleben in Briefen*, 2 vols. (Lahr, 1882).

BUCKLE, GEORGE EARLE (ed.), *Letters of Queen Victoria*, 2nd ser., 3 vols. (London, 1926–8).

BUNSEN, FRANCES BARONESS (ed.), *A Memoir of Baron Bunsen*, 2 vols. (London, 1868).

BURNETT, JOHN (ed.), *Destiny Obscure: Autobiographies of Childhood, Education and Family from the 1820s to the 1920s* (London, 1982).

BURTON, HESTER, *Barbara Bodichon 1827–91* (London, 1949).

CADOGAN, PETER, 'Harney and Engels', *International Review for Social History*, 10 (1965).

CARLYLE, JANE WELSH, *I too am here, Selected Letters*, ed. Alan and Mary McQueen Simpson (Cambridge, 1977).

—— *Letters and Memorials*, ed. J. A. Froude, 3 vols. (London, 1883).

—— *New Letters and Memorials*, ed. Alexander Carlyle, 2 vols. (London, 1903).

CARLYLE, THOMAS, *Past and Present* (London, 1843).

CARR, E. H., *The Romantic Exiles* (London, 1933).

CHAUDHURI, NIRAD C., *Scholar Extraordinary: The Life of Professor Friedrich Max Müller* (London, 1974).

CLAEYS, GREGORY, 'Engels' *Outlines of a Critique of Political Economy* (1843) and the Origins of the Marxist Critique of Capitalism', *History of Political Economy*, 16 (1984).

—— 'The Political Ideas of the Young Engels, 1842–1845: Owenism, Chartism, and the Question of Violent Revolution in the Transition from "Utopian" to "Scientific" Socialism', *History of Political Thought*, 6 (1985).

CLARKE, M. L., *George Grote: A Biography* (London, 1962).

CLUBBE, JOHN (ed.), *Two Reminiscences of Thomas Carlyle* (Durham, N. Carolina, 1974).
COLERIDGE, SAMUEL TAYLOR, *Poems*, ed. Derwent and Sara Coleridge, with a biographical memoir by Ferdinand Freiligrath (Leipzig, 1860).
COLLINS, H., and ABRAMSKY, C., *Karl Marx and the British Labour Movement* (London, 1965).
DE JONGE, ALFRED R., *Gottfried Kinkel as Political and Social Thinker* (New York, 1926).
DICKENS, CHARLES, *Collected Papers*, 2 vols. (London, 1938).
—— *Letters*, ed. Walter Dexter, 3 vols. (London, 1938).
—— *Letters*, ed. G. Storey and K. J. Fielding, in progress (Oxford, 1965–).
—— *Pickwick Papers* (London, 1837).
—— *Sketches by 'Boz'*, (London, 1836).
—— *Uncollected Writings: Household Words 1850–9*, ed. Harry Stone, 2 vols. (London, 1969).
DISRAELI, BENJAMIN, *Coningsby* (London, 1844).
DONNER, INGRID, and MATTHIES, BIRGIT, 'Jenny Marx über das Robert-Blum-Meeting am 9. November 1852 in London', *Beiträge zur Marx-Engels Forschung*, 4 (1978).
DUCLOS, JACQUES, *Bakounine et Marx* (Paris, 1974).
EASTON, LLOYD D., *Hegel's First American Followers* (Cleveland, Ohio, 1966).
ECCARIUS, JOHANN GEORG, *Eines Arbeiters Widerlegung der national-ökonomischen Lehren John Stuart Mill's* (Berlin, 1869).
—— *Der Kampf des grossen und des kleinen Kapitals, oder die Schneiderei in London* (Leipzig, 1876).
EIMER, MANFRED, 'Briefe an Amely Bölte aus Carlyles Freundeskreis', *Englische Studien*, 49 (1915–16).
EISNER, KURT (ed.), *Wilhelm Liebknecht, sein Leben und Wirken* (Berlin, 1900).
ELIOT, GEORGE, *Letters*, ed. Gordon S. Haight, 9 vols. (New Haven, 1954–5 and 1978).
ENGELS, FRIEDRICH, *et al.*, *Karl Marx* (Basle, 1946).
FEHLING, A. W., 'Karl Schapper und die Anfänge der Arbeiterbewegung bis zur Revolution von 1848', unpublished doctoral thesis (Rostock, 1922).
FISCHER, WALTHER, *Des Darmstädter Schriftstellers Johann Heinrich Künzel (1810–1873) Beziehungen zu England* (Giessen, 1939).
—— 'Thomas und Jane Carlyle im Spiegel der Briefe Amely Böltes an Varnhagen von Ense (1844—1853)', *Englische Studien*, 64 (1929).
FOCK, THOMAS, 'Über Londoner Zuckersiedereien und deutsche Arbeitskräfte', *Zuckerindustrie*, 3 (1985).
FONTANE, THEODOR, *Journeys to England in Victoria's Early Days, 1844–1859*, trans. and ed. Dorothy Harrison (London, 1939).
—— *Sämtliche Werke*, ed. Edgar Gross *et al.*, 24 vols. (Munich, 1959–75).
FREILIGRATH, FERDINAND, *Briefwechsel mit Marx und Engels*, ed. Manfred Häckel, 2 vols. (Berlin, 1976).
—— *Werke*, ed. Julius Schwering, 6 vols. in 2 (Berlin, Leipzig, Vienna, and Stuttgart, n.d.).
FROEBEL, CARL, *Explanation of the Kindergarten* (London, 1875).
FROST, THOMAS, *Forty Years' Recollections: Literary and Political* (London, 1880).

FULFORD, ROGER (ed.), *Your Dear Letter: Private Correspondence of Queen Victoria and the Crown Princess of Prussia 1865–1871* (London, 1971).

GLASER-GERHARD, ERNST (ed.), 'Aus Hermann Hettners Nachlass', *Euphorion*, 29 (1928).

GÖHLER, RUDOLF (ed.), 'Aus dem Nachlass von Fanny Lewald und Adolf Stahr', *Euphorion*, 31 (1930).

GOLDSTÜCKER, THEODOR, *Literary Remains*, 2 vols. (London, 1879).

GOODWAY, DAVID, *London Chartism 1838–1848* (Cambridge, 1982).

GOSLICH, MARIE (ed.), 'Briefe von Johanna Kinkel', *Preussische Jahrbücher*, 97 (July–Sept. 1899).

GREG, W. R., 'English Socialism, and Communistic Associations', *Edinburgh Review*, 93 (Jan. 1851).

GRITZNER, M. C., *Flüchtlingsleben* (Zurich, 1867).

HAIGHT, GORDON S., *George Eliot: A Biography* (Oxford, 1968).

HALLÉ, SIR CHARLES, *Life and Letters*, ed. C. E. Hallé and Marie Hallé (London, 1896).

HALTERN, UTZ, *Liebknecht und England. Zur Publizistik Wilhelm Liebknechts während seines Londoner Exils (1850–1862)* (Trier, 1977).

HANISCH, ERNST, 'Karl Marx und die Berichte der österreichischen Geheimpolizei', *Schriften aus dem Karl-Marx-Haus* (Trier, 1976).

Hansard's Parliamentary Debates, 3rd ser.

HARNEY, GEORGE JULIAN, *The Harney Papers*, ed. F. G. Black and R. M. Black (Assen, 1969).

HARRISON, ROYDEN, 'E. S. Beesly and Karl Marx', *International Review for Social History*, 4 (1959).

HARTMANN, MORITZ, *Briefe*, selected and ed. Rudolf Wolkan (Vienna, 1921).

HATFIELD, J. T., 'The Longfellow–Freiligrath Correspondence', *Publications of the Modern Language Association of America*, 48 (Dec. 1933).

HEILBUT, ANTHONY, *Exiled in Paradise: German Refugee Artists and Intellectuals in America, from the 1930s to the Present* (New York, 1983).

HEINE, HEINRICH, *Sämtliche Schriften*, ed. Klaus Briegleb, 6 vols. in 7 (Munich, 1968–76).

HENDERSON, W. O., *The Life of Friedrich Engels*, 2 vols. (London, 1976).

HERRMANN, WOLFGANG, *Gottfried Semper im Exil, Paris, London 1849—1855* (Basle, 1978).

HERZEN, ALEXANDER, *My Past and Thoughts*, trans. Constance Garnett, rev. Humphrey Higgins, 4 vols. (London, 1968).

—— *Sobraniye Sochineniy*, 30 vols. (Moscow, 1954–65).

HIRSCHFELD, GERHARD (ed.), *Exil in Grossbritannien: zur Emigration aus dem nationalsozialistischen Deutschland* (Stuttgart, 1983).

HOBSBAWM, E. J., 'Dr. Marx and the Victorian Critics', *Labouring Men: Studies in the History of Labour* (London, 1964).

HOLMES, COLIN (ed.), *Immigrants and Minorities in British Society* (London, 1978).

HOLYOAKE, GEORGE JACOB, *The History of the Last Trial by Jury for Atheism in England* (London, 1850).

—— *Sixty Years of an Agitator's Life* (London, 1893).

HOWITT, MARY, *An Autobiography*, ed. Margaret Howitt, 2 vols. (London, 1889).

HOWITT, WILLIAM, *German Experiences* (London, 1844).
—— *The Rural and Domestic Life of Germany* (London, 1842).
HUMPHREY, A. W., *Robert Applegarth: Trade Unionist, Educationist, Reformer* (London, 1913).
HYNDMAN, H. M., *Record of an Adventurous Life* (London, 1911).
JOYNES, J. L., *Songs of a Revolutionary Epoch* (London, 1888).
KANT, IMMANUEL, *Werke*, ed. Wilhelm Weischedel, 6 vols. (Wiesbaden, 1956–64).
KAPP, YVONNE, *Eleanor Marx*, 2 vols. (London, 1972).
KESSEL, EBERHARD (ed.), *Briefe von Carl Schurz an Gottfried Kinkel* (Heidelberg, 1965).
KINGSLEY, CHARLES, *Alton Locke, Tailor and Poet* (London, 1850, repr. 1983).
KINKEL, JOHANNA, 'Erinnerungsblätter', ed. Ernst Schierenberg, *Deutsche Revue*, 19 (Apr.–June 1894).
—— *Hans Ibeles in London. Ein Familienbild aus dem Flüchtlingsleben*, 2 vols. in one (Stuttgart, 1860).
KLAUS, H. GUSTAV, *The Literature of Labour: Two Hundred Years of Working-Class Writing* (Brighton, 1985).
KOSZYK, KURT, and OBERMANN, KARL (eds.), *Zeitgenossen von Marx und Engels: Ausgewählte Briefe aus den Jahren 1844 bis 1852* (Assen, 1975).
LAW, HARRIET, 'Dr. Karl Marx', *Secular Chronicle*, 10 (July 1878).
LEHMANN, RUDOLF, *An Artist's Reminiscences* (London, 1894).
LEIGH SMITH, BARBARA, 'Johanna Kinkel', *The Englishwoman's Journal*, 2 (Jan. 1859).
LEPPLA, RUPPRECHT (ed.), 'Johanna und Gottfried Kinkels Briefe an Kathinka Zitz', *Bonner Geschichtsblätter*, 12 (1958).
LESSNER, FRIEDRICH, *Ich brachte das „Kommunistische Manifest" zum Drucker*, ed. Ursula Herrmann and Gerhard Winkler (Berlin, 1975).
—— *Sixty Years in the Social-Democratic Movement*, trans. Thalmeyer (London, 1907).
—— 'Vor 1848 und nachher. Erinnerungen eines alten Kommunisten', *Deutsche Worte*, 18 (1898).
LEWALD, FANNY, *England und Schottland*, 2 vols. in one (Brunswick, 1851).
—— *Zwölf Bilder nach dem Leben: Erinnerungen* (Berlin, 1888).
LEWES, G. H., *Biographical History of Philosophy*, 4 vols. (London, 1845–6).
LIEBKNECHT, WILHELM, *Briefwechsel mit Karl Marx und Friedrich Engels*, ed. Georg Eckert (The Hague, 1963).
LONGFELLOW, HENRY WADSWORTH, *Letters*, ed. Andrew Hilen, in progress (Cambridge, Mass., 1966–).
MACAULAY, THOMAS BABINGTON, *The History of England*, 4th edn., 5 vols. (London, 1849–61).
MACHULE, PAUL, 'Coleridges *Wallenstein*-Übersetzung', *Englische Studien*, 31 (1902).
MCLELLAN, DAVID, *Karl Marx: His Life and Thought* (London, 1976).
MANN, GOLO, *The History of Germany since 1789* (Frankfurt, 1958; London, 1968, repr. 1974).
MARCHANT, SIR JAMES (ed.), *History through 'The Times': A Collection of Leading Articles 1800–1937* (London, 1937).

MARCUS, STEVEN, *Engels, Manchester and the Working Class* (New York, 1974).

MARENHOLZ-BÜLOW, BARONESS B. VON, *Reminiscences of Friedrich Froebel*, trans. Mrs Horace Mann (Boston, Mass., 1877).

MARX, KARL, *Capital: A Critique of Political Economy*, 3 vols. (London, 1954, repr. 1977).

—— *Early Texts*, ed. David McLellan (Oxford, 1971).

—— *Secret Diplomatic History of the Eighteenth Century*, ed. Lester Hutchinson (London, 1969).

—— *Selected Works*, ed. V. Adoratsky, 2 vols. (London, 1942).

—— *The Unknown Karl Marx*, ed. Robert Payne (London, 1972).

Marx-Engels-Werke, 39 vols. (Berlin, 1956–68).

Marx–Engels Collected Works, in progress (London, New York, Moscow, 1975–).

MARX, KARL, and ENGELS, FRIEDRICH, *The Cologne Communist Trial*, trans. and ed. Rodney Livingstone (London, 1971).

—— —— *The Marx–Engels Correspondence, the Personal Letters 1844–1877*, ed. F. J. Raddatz (London, 1981).

—— —— *Mohr und General. Erinnerungen an Marx und Engels* (Berlin, 1965).

—— —— *Reminiscences of Marx and Engels* (Moscow, n.d.).

—— —— *Marx and Engels through the Eyes of their Contemporaries* (Moscow, 1972).

—— —— *Selected Works*, 2 vols. (London, 1951).

MAYHEW, HENRY, *The Unknown Mayhew: Selections from the Morning Chronicle 1849–1850*, ed. E. P. Thompson and Eileen Yeo (London, 1971, repr. 1984).

MEIER, OLGA (ed.), *The Daughters of Karl Marx: Family Correspondence 1866–1898*, trans. Faith Evans (London, 1984).

MEYER, GUSTAV, 'Letters of Karl Marx to Karl Blind', *International Review for Social History*, 4 (1939).

MEYSENBUG, MALWIDA VON, *Briefe an Johanna und Gottfried Kinkel 1849–1885*, ed. Stefania Rossi and Yoko Kikuchi (Bonn, 1982).

—— *Gesammelte Werke*, ed. Berta Schleicher, 5 vols. (Stuttgart, 1922).

—— *Memoiren einer Idealistin*, 2 vols. (Stuttgart, 1875, repr. 1922).

—— *Rebel in a Crinoline*, ed. Mildred Adams (London, 1937).

MILL, JOHN STUART, *Collected Works*, ed. F. E. L. Priestley, 17 vols. (Toronto, 1963–72).

—— *Mill on Bentham and Coleridge*, ed. F. R. Leavis (London, 1950).

MILNES, RICHARD MONCKTON, *Briefe an Varnhagen von Ense*, ed. Walther Fischer (Heidelberg, 1922).

MONOD, GABRIEL (ed.), 'Briefe von Malwida von Meysenbug an ihre Mutter', *Deutsche Revue*, 31/1 (Jan.–Mar. 1906) and 33/1 (Jan.–June 1908).

MORRIS, WILLIAM, *Political Writings*, ed. A. L. Morton (London, 1973).

MÜLLER-TELLERING, EDUARD, *Vorgeschmack in die künftige deutsche Diktatur von Marx und Engels* (Cologne, 1850).

NECK, RUDOLF, 'Dokumente über die Londoner Emigration von Karl Marx', *Mitteilungen des Österreichischen Staatsarchivs*, 9 (1956).

[NEUMANN, MAUREEN], 'An Account of the German Hospital in London from 1845 to 1948', unpublished thesis (London, n.d.).

NEWMAN, ERNEST, *The Life of Richard Wagner*, 4 vols. (London, 1933, repr. 1976).

NICOLAIEVSKY, BORIS, and MAENCHEN-HELFEN, OTTO, *Karl Marx: Man and Fighter* (London, 1936, repr. 1983).

ORME, TEMPLE, *University College School: Alphabetical and Chronological Register for 1831–1891* (London, n.d.).

OSWALD, EUGENE, *Reminiscences of a Busy Life* (London, 1911).

—— *Thomas Carlyle. Ein Lebensbild, und Goldkörner aus seinen Werken* (Leipzig, 1881).

PELLING, HENRY, *A History of British Trade Unionism* (London, 1963, repr. 1975).

POPE-HENNESSY, JAMES, *Richard Monckton Milnes: The Years of Promise 1809–1851* (London, 1949).

PORTER, BERNARD, 'The *Freiheit* Prosecutions 1881–1882', *The Historical Journal*, 23/4 (1980).

—— *The Refugee Question in Mid-Victorian Politics* (Cambridge, 1979).

POUND, REGINALD, *Albert: A Biography of the Prince Consort* (London, 1973).

PRAWER, S. S., *Karl Marx and World Literature* (Oxford, 1976).

PÜSCHEL, JÜRGEN, *Die Geschichte des German Hospital in London (1845 bis 1948)* (Münster, 1980).

PULSZKY, FERENCZ, *Meine Zeit, mein Leben*, 4 vols. in 3 (Leipzig, 1880–2).

PULSZKY, THERESE, *Memoirs of a Hungarian Lady* (London, 1850).

RAE, JOHN, 'The Socialism of Karl Marx and the Young Hegelians', *Contemporary Review*, 40 (July–Dec. 1881).

REICKE, EMIL, *Malwida von Meysenbug* (Berlin, 1911).

RIEGER, J., 'Der erste englische Kindergarten', *Der Londoner Bote*, 46 (Oct. 1952).

—— 'Theodor Fontane und die Deutschen in England', *Der Londoner Bote*, 37 (Jan. 1951).

RODENBERG, JULIUS, *Alltagsleben in London. Ein Skizzenbuch* (Berlin, 1860).

RÖSCH-SONDERMANN, HERMANN, *Gottfried Kinkel als Ästhetiker, Politiker und Dichter* (Bonn, 1982).

RONGE, JOHANNES and BERTHA, *A Practical Guide to the English Kindergarten* (London, 1855).

ROTHSCHILD, MIRIAM, *Dear Lord Rothschild* (London, 1983).

RUDICH, ROSI, 'Wo wohnte Friedrich Engels in Manchester?', *Beiträge zur Marx-Engels Forschung*, 7 (Berlin, 1980).

RUGE, ARNOLD, *Briefwechsel und Tagebuchblätter aus den Jahren 1825–1880*, ed. Paul Nerrlich, 2 vols. in one (Berlin, 1886).

—— *New Germany, its Modern History, Literature, Philosophy, Religion, and Art* (London, 1854).

SAVILLE, JOHN, *Ernest Jones: Chartist* (London, 1952).

SCHAIBLE, KARL HEINRICH, *Exercises in the Art of Thinking* (London, 1860).

—— *Siebenunddreissig Jahre aus dem Leben eines Exilierten* (Stuttgart, 1895).

—— and ALTHAUS, THEODORE FREDERICK, *Seeing and Thinking: Elementary Lessons and Exercises Introductory to Grammar, Composition, and Logical Analysis* (London, 1883).

SCHLESINGER, MAX, *Wanderungen durch London*, 2 vols. (Berlin, 1852–3).

SCHMIDT, WALTER, *Wilhelm Wolff: Kampfgefährte und Freund von Marx und Engels, 1846–1864* (Berlin, 1979).

SCHMIDTGALL, HARRY, *Friedrich Engels' Manchester-Aufenthalt 1842—1844* (Trier, 1981).

SCHOYEN, A. R., *The Chartist Challenge: A Portrait of George Julian Harney* (London, 1958).

SCHURZ, CARL, *Lebenserinnerungen*, 2 vols. (Berlin, 1906–7).

SHADWELL, ARTHUR, 'The German Colony in London', *National Review*, 26 (Feb. 1896).

SHERMAN, A. J., *Island Refuge: Britain and Refugees from the Third Reich 1933–1939* (London, 1973).

SIEMENS, C. W., *Fest-Rede zur Kinkel-Abschiedsfeier* (London, 1866).

SMITH, F. B., *Radical Artisan: W. J. Linton 1812–1897* (Manchester, 1973).

STRAUSS, G. L. M., *Reminiscences of an Old Bohemian*, 2 vols. (London, 1882).

STRODTMANN, ADOLPH, *Gottfried Kinkel. Wahrheit ohne Dichtung*, 2 vols. in one (Hamburg, 1850–1).

STRUVE, AMALIE, *Erinnerungen aus den badischen Freiheitskämpfen* (Hamburg, 1850).

STRUVE, GUSTAV, and RASCH, GUSTAV, *Zwölf Streiter der Revolution* (Berlin, 1867).

THOMAS, WILLIAM, *The Philosophical Radicals* (Oxford, 1979).

THOMPSON, DOROTHY, 'Letters from Ernest Jones to Karl Marx 1865–1868', *Bulletin of the Society for the Study of Labour History*, 4 (Spring 1962).

THORNE, WILL, *My Life's Battles* (London, 1925).

TRESSELL, ROBERT, *The Ragged Trousered Philanthropists* (London, 1914, repr. with corrections, 1955).

VARNHAGEN VON ENSE, *Aus dem Nachlass: Tagebücher*, ed. Ludmilla Assing, 15 vols. (Leipzig, 1861–70, and Berlin, 1905).

VASSEN, FLORIAN, *Georg Weerth: Ein Politischer Dichter des Vormärz und der Revolution von 1848/9* (Stuttgart, 1971).

VINCENT, DAVID, *Bread, Knowledge and Freedom: A Study of Nineteenth-Century Working-Class Autobiography* (London, 1981).

WEERTH, GEORG, *Englische Reisen*, ed. Bruno Kaiser (Berlin, 1955).

—— *Sämtliche Werke*, ed. Bruno Kaiser, 5 vols. (Berlin, 1956–7).

—— *A Young Revolutionary in 19th-Century England. Selected Writings*, ed. Ingrid and Peter Kuczynski (Berlin, 1971).

WEISSER, HENRY, *April 10: Challenge and Response in England in 1848* (London, 1983).

—— *British Working-Class Movements and Europe, 1815–48* (Manchester, 1975).

WERMUTH and STIEBER, *Die Communisten-Verschwörungen des neunzehnten Jahrhunderts* (Berlin, 1853).

WILLIAMS-WYNN, CHARLOTTE, *Memorials*, ed. her sister (London, 1877).

WILSON, DAVID ALEC, *The Life of Thomas Carlyle*, 6 vols. (London, 1923–34).

WILSON, EDMUND, *To the Finland Station* (London, 1940).

WOLFF, WILHELM, *Gesammelte Schriften*, ed. Franz Mehring (Berlin, 1909).

ZADDACH, CARL, *Lothar Bucher bis zum Ende seines Londoner Exils (1817—1861)* (Heidelberg, 1915).

ZUCKER, A. E. (ed.), *The Forty-Eighters* (New York, 1950).

Index